SEMANTIC WEB AND EDUCATION

INTEGRATED SERIES IN INFORMATION SYSTEMS

Series Editors

Professor Ramesh Sharda
Oklahoma State University

Prof. Dr. Stefan Voß
Universität Hamburg

Other published titles in the series:

E-BUSINESS MANAGEMENT: *Integration of Web Technologies with Business Models*/ edited by Michael J. Shaw

VIRTUAL CORPORATE UNIVERSITIES: *A Matrix of Knowledge and Learning for the New Digital Dawn*/ Walter R.J. Baets & Gert Van der Linden

SCALABLE ENTERPRISE SYSTEMS: *An Introduction to Recent Advances*/ edited by Vittal Prabhu, Soundar Kumara, Manjunath Kamath

LEGAL PROGRAMMING*: Legal Compliance for RFID and Software Agent Ecosystems in Retail Processes and Beyond*/ Brian Subirana and Malcolm Bain

LOGICAL DATA MODELING: *What It Is and How To Do It*/ Alan Chmura and J. Mark Heumann

DESIGNING AND EVALUATING E-MANAGEMENT DECISION TOOLS: *The Integration of Decision and Negotiation Models into Internet-Multimedia Technologies*/ Giampiero E.G. Beroggi

INFORMATION AND MANAGEMENT SYSTEMS FOR PRODUCT CUSTOMIZATION/ Thorsten Blecker et al

MEDICAL INFORMATICS: *Knowledge Management and Data Mining in Biomedicine*/ Hsinchun Chen et al

KNOWLEDGE MANAGEMENT AND MANAGEMENT LEARNING: *Extending the Horizons of Knowledge-Based Management*/ edited by Walter Baets

INTELLIGENCE AND SECURITY INFORMATICS FOR INTERNATIONAL SECURITY: *Information Sharing and Data Mining*/ Hsinchun Chen

ENTERPRISE COLLABORATION: *On-Demand Information Exchange for Extended Enterprises*/ David Levermore & Cheng Hsu

SEMANTIC WEB AND EDUCATION

by

Vladan Devedžić

 Springer

Vladan Devedžić
University of Belgrade
Serbia and Montenegro

ISBN-10: 0-387-35417-4 (e-book)

ISBN-13: 978-1-4419-4201-2   ISBN-13: 978-0387-35417-0 (e-book)

Printed on acid-free paper.

© 2006 by Springer Science+Business Media, LLC
Softcover reprint of the hardcover 1st edition 2006
All rights reserved. This work may not be translated or copied in whole or in part without the written permission of the publisher (Springer Science + Business Media, LLC, 233 Spring Street, New York, NY 10013, USA), except for brief excerpts in connection with reviews or scholarly analysis. Use in connection with any form of information storage and retrieval, electronic adaptation, computer software, or by similar or dissimilar methodology now know or hereafter developed is forbidden.
The use in this publication of trade names, trademarks, service marks and similar terms, even if the are not identified as such, is not to be taken as an expression of opinion as to whether or not they are subject to proprietary rights.

9 8 7 6 5 4 3 2 1

springer.com

Dedication

To my family

Contents

Preface

Writing the preface for a book feels good, because once you find yourself in a situation to write the preface, it usually means that you have already written the rest of the book.

Writing this book was a real challenge. I would have probably never written it if there was not Stefan Voss from the University of Hamburg to propose me to write it - thanks Stefan! It may seem that it is not very difficult to describe the application of a relatively young technology, such as the Semantic Web, to the domain of education. It may seem that there is actually not much to write about that topic. But it just seems so. On the contrary, the greatest challenge in writing this book was the abundance of material and exciting ideas about how to apply Semantic Web technologies to education. I knew from the very beginning that I will have to select carefully from many theories, practices, evolving ideas and approaches, and important research efforts, in order to compose a coherent whole. Worse still, I also knew that I will have to leave out of the book many other results, initiatives, and ongoing projects that would certainly be worth describing under more relaxed constraints. Thus, the endeavor was exhausting.

The Semantic Web is about how to deploy artificial intelligence concepts and techniques on the Web, in order to harness the Web and make it more useful, more user-centered, and more responsive to human interaction. It is about how to represent knowledge on the Web, and how to make the Web process that knowledge and reason about it. It is about how to make the Web itself look and act more intelligently when it interacts with humans. The Web can look and act more intelligently only if it complies with the huge variety of its users by proactively and adaptively creating a correspondingly huge variety of behaviors, to meet the users' needs.

Essential elements of the Semantic Web are ontologies. Much of this book is about them, albeit in the context of education. They represent deep knowledge of various domains and topics, i.e. classes of objects, their relations, and concept hierarchies that exist in various domains. Ontologies enable machine understanding and machine processing of knowledge and meanings on the Semantic Web. Hence they are the cornerstone of the Semantic Web's intelligent interaction with the users.

However, to most end users ontologies appear just as elements of the Semantic Web infrastructure, and infrastructure is never impressive just by itself. What is impressive are usually the results, or even just the capabilities, enabled by the infrastructure.

And this is where the exciting part starts. Education is a very fertile soil for applying Web technologies anyway, and the Semantic Web opens a number of new doors and multiplies the prospects of Web-based education. Being always fascinated with education in general, and being a person who always wants to learn more, I believe the Semantic Web is the way to go if we want to improve Web-based education for the benefit of the learners. To this end, the Semantic Web-based education brings intriguing opportunities to combine advanced technologies of the Semantic Web with inspiring and imaginative theories and practices of learning and teaching. Moreover, Semantic Web-based education strongly supports interactions between learners, teachers, and authors of educational materials, thus facilitating development of online learning communities.

In 1990s, I joined the community of researchers interested in applying artificial intelligence to the domain of education, the AIED community. Nice people! Some of them are interested in psychological aspects of learning and teaching processes, whereas others focus more on learning technologies and artificial intelligence. Altogether, I found that community to be an extremely suitable milieu for me to learn more, do more research, and expand my professional interests. It is within that community that I developed my understanding of what Semantic Web-based education should look like.

Another group of people that I owe very much are the researchers of the GOOD OLD AI research group (http://goodoldai.org.yu). They are bright young people, full of creative ideas, brilliant minds, and dear friends of mine. I found exchanging ideas and socializing with them a great source of energy in writing this book. Special thanks goes to one of them, Jelena Jovanović, who carefully proof-read the manuscript and suggested a number of improvements that I incorporated in the book.

Of course, the most important group of people one can belong to is family. I must stress the extreme support and patience that my family has shown in supporting me to complete this book. Without their understanding, it would not be possible to stand all the efforts that have been involved. The encouragement that I had from my family and friends.

Apart from the support from family and friends, this book includes another three key elements. The first one was my decision and commitment to write it. Although I hesitated a bit in the beginning, I remember that it was last summer in Edinburgh that I definitely decided to write it. One day, I was admiring the view of the Edinburgh Castle from a nice café on Princess Street, and then in the evening I was sitting in a pub, watching a video of Green Day performing in an open-air concert. That day brought a lot of pleasure and positive energy, and after that I knew I will manage to write this book.

The second one is education. The fulfillment it brings can be very diverse. Sometimes it is so intense, like Wednesday market in Anjuna, or like seeing Patti Smith on stage. But it can also be subtle and iridescent, like Norah Jones' ballads. If I was asked to associate a color with education, I think I would suggest the color of sand at sunrise. Or the color of Al-Khazneh in Petra, seen through the crack of As-Siq.

The third element of this book is the Semantic Web and its ontologies. They fit so will with education, by building a strong platform for it, by bringing reflection, and by interweaving everything. The feeling they bring is like that of still water; or that of sitting on the top of a hill in Hampi; or like driving back from Fletcher Bay to Coromandel Town, on a dirt road, at dusk, slowly, gazing at the shadows of nearby islets, listening to Brian Eno's voice and music from the tape; or like Peter Gabriel, alone in a spotlight, playing piano and singing *Here Comes The Flood*. If I was to associate a color with ontologies, then it would definitely be deep blue. Ocean blue.

That's it. I am going to have a long rest now. Wake me up when September ends.

Vladan Devedžić
March-April 2006, Belgrade

Chapter 1

INTRODUCTION TO WEB-BASED EDUCATION

Informally, *Web-based education* (*WBE*) encompasses all aspects and processes of education that use World Wide Web as a communication medium and supporting technology. There are many other terms for WBE; some of them are *online education, virtual education, Internet-based education*, and *education via computer-mediated communication* (Paulsen, 2003).

Adapting from (Keegan, 1995) and (Paulsen, 2003), it can be said that WBE is characterized by:

- the separation of teachers and learners (which distinguishes it from face-to-face education);
- the influence of an educational organization (which distinguishes it from self-study and private tutoring);
- the use of Web technologies to present and/or distribute some educational content;
- the provision of two-way communication via the Internet, so that students may benefit from communication with each other, teachers, and staff.

Since 1990s, Web-based education has become a very important branch of educational technology. For learners, it provides access to information and knowledge sources that are practically unlimited, enabling a number of opportunities for personalized learning, tele-learning, distance-learning, and collaboration, with clear advantages of classroom independence and platform independence (Brusilovsky, 1999). On the other hand, teachers and authors of educational material can use numerous possibilities for Web-based course offering and teleteaching, availability of authoring tools for developing Web-based courseware, and cheap and efficient storage and distribution of course materials, hyperlinks to suggested readings, digital libraries, and other sources of references relevant for the course (Devedžić, 2003a, 2003b).

There is a number of important concepts related to Web-based education, such as e-Learning, distance education, and adaptive learning. The objective of this chapter is to introduce such concepts and the related technologies.

1.   E-LEARNING

Electronic learning or *E-Learning* is interactive learning in which the learning content is available online and provides automatic feedback to the student's learning activities (Paulsen, 2003). In fact, it is much like *computer-based training (CBT)* and *computer-aided instruction (CAI)*, but the point is that it requires Internet for access to learning material and for monitoring the student's activities. E-Learners usually can communicate with their tutors through the Internet. However, the focus is not on that communication; organization of and access to the learning content are more central to e-Learning.

Note the difference between WBE and e-Learning: learning is just one element of education, so WBE covers a much broader range of services than e-Learning. More precisely, e-Learning companies and other providers of e-Learning material usually focus on learning content, while different educational institutions interested in organizing WBE provide the whole range of educational services and support. Unfortunately, the terms e-Learning and WBE are often used as synonyms, which generates some confusion.

1.1   Alternative definitions

In this book, we adopt the aforementioned Paulsen's interpretation of the term e-Learning. Yet, for the sake of completeness it should be noted that there are definitions of e-Learning that include not only Internet as technological support for learning, but other media and resources as well. As an illustration, consider the definition that Eva Kaplan-Leiserson has included in her online e-learning glossary (2000):

> "E-learning covers a wide set of applications and processes, such as Web-based learning, computer-based learning, virtual classrooms, and digital collaboration. It includes the delivery of content via Internet, intranet/extranet (LAN/WAN), audio and videotape, satellite broadcast, interactive TV, and CD-ROM." (Kaplan-Leiserson, 2000)

The Web is full of definitions of e-Learning that provide even broader interpretation than Kaplan-Leiserson's. For example:

"[E-Learning:] Broad definition of the field of using technology to deliver learning and training programs. Typically used to describe media such as CD-ROM, Internet, Intranet, wireless and mobile learning. Some include knowledge management as a form of e-Learning." (e-Learning Guru, 2005)

Explaining the possible inclusion of knowledge management as a form of e-Learning is beyond the scope of this book. *Mobile learning* (often abbreviated to *m-learning*) is a subform of e-Learning that can take place anytime, anywhere with the help of a mobile computer device. The role of that device is two-fold:
- to present the learning content;
- to provide wireless two-way communication between teacher(s) and learner(s).

1.2 Objectives, perspectives, tools, and learning modes

The convergence of the Internet and learning in e-Learning qualifies e-Learning as Internet-enabled learning, in terms of using Internet technologies to create, foster, deliver, and facilitate learning, anytime and anywhere (Obringer, 2005). One of the objectives of e-Learning is the delivery of *individualized*, comprehensive, dynamic learning content in real time - people and organizations need to keep up with the rapid changes and advancements of knowledge related to different disciplines, as well as to keep ahead of the rapidly changing global economy. Another objective is to facilitate the development of *learning communities* - communities of knowledge, linking learners and practitioners with teachers and experts.

There are two major perspectives of e-Learning - technological and pedagogical. Many interpretations focus on the technology (i.e., on the "e"). Others take technology only as a means of content delivery, emphasizing the need for learner-centered approach; to them, e-Learning in its essence is learning. The pedagogical perspective is interested primarily in explaining how people learn, how do they acquire skills and information, how their skills develop through learning over time, what are their preferred learning styles, and so on - and, only then, how the electronic delivery can be adapted to the learner.

E-Learning usually comes through an interaction between a learner and a simulated electronic environment pertaining to the domain of interest to the learner. In the context of WBE, the environment is Internet-based; in other variants, it can be Intranet-based, as well as CD-ROM-based. In all cases, it brings up a rich learning experience through interactive use of text, images, audio, video, animations, and simulations. It can also include entire virtual environments. It can be practiced individually, or in the classroom. It is self-paced hands-on learning.

E-learning environments can offer a number of learning tools, in a wide range of interactivity and sophistication. At the lower end of the scale are *indexed explanations and guidance* for learner's questions. The learner typically types in a keyword or phrase (or selects a keyword from a list) to search an underlying database for explanation. The environment replies with an explanation, or perhaps with step-by-step instructions for performing specific tasks. These can be further augmented through additional forms of online support like links to reference materials, forums, chat rooms, discussion groups, online bulletin boards, e-mail, or live instant-messaging support. The tools like chat rooms, discussion groups, online bulletin boards, and e-mail support access to instructors, but they all essentially pertain to *asynchronous mode* of learning. The most sophisticated and the most interactive environments provide tools for *synchronous mode* of training and learning, with instructor(s) organizing and guiding learning/training sessions in real time. With such environments, the learners log in and can communicate directly with the instructor and with each other through the Internet. In addition to Internet Web sites, supporting tools include audio-and/or video-conferencing, Internet telephony, or even two-way live broadcasts to students in a classroom (Obringer, 2005). The sessions can be scheduled at regular times for weeks or even months, enabling the learners to walk through the entire course. Within a single session, there is a range for possible collaboration between the learners - from purely individual learning and minimum cooperation with the other learners, to tight collaboration through shared electronic whiteboards and different communication tools. The instructor can monitor the learners' progress in a variety of ways, both disruptive and interactive.

1.3   Pros and cons

Before moving on to further discuss e-Learning in more details, it is necessary to answer a simple question: Why should we care about e-Learning? In other words, what are the advantages of e-Learning over traditional, classroom-based, face-to-face learning?

Self-paced character of e-Learning is just one of the answers. Another one is that the costs of e-Learning are usually lower, once the course is put up - no physical resource allocation (location, time, and equipment). True, in synchronous learning additional costs are associated with the instructor managing the class, but altogether the costs should still be lower than in traditional courses. There is also some evidence that e-Learning progresses faster than traditional learning; this can be attributed to the fact that in e-Learning students can go much faster through the material they may be already familiar with. Furthermore, the material they consume is consistent - no slight differences caused by different instructors teaching the same material. Learning anytime and anywhere is attractive to people who have never been able to work it into their schedules prior to the development of e-learning. Another attractive feature is that online learning material can be kept up-to-date more easily than traditional one - the updated version is simply uploaded on a server and the students get access to improved material immediately. The material can make use of many didactic elements and tools, such as audio, video, related links, simulations, and so on, which can lead to increased retention and a stronger grasp on the subject. E-Learning is much easier to adapt to groups of students of different sizes and to corporate learning situations than traditional learning.

There is always some resistance to e-Learning by more traditionally oriented instructors and learners alike. Some instructors complain that organizing learning material for e-Learning requires much more work than in traditional settings, as well as that electronic communication with students is more time-consuming and less effective than face-to-face communication. Possibilities for "creative divergence" from the lecture topic and explanation of details and examples made up on the spot are still more numerous in traditional classrooms. Charisma of good teachers is lost in e-Learning, and so is socializing with peer learners.

A good alternative to "pure" e-Learning is *blended learning*, which is a combination of traditional classroom-based learning and e-Learning. In practice, it is worth considering an option of using blended learning to assure for initial acceptance of e-Learning. Moreover, and contrary to the loss of charismatic face-to-face teaching, in some cases experts who have problems articulating their knowledge and experience in the classroom provide excellent e-Learning courses.

1.4   Organizing e-Learning material

Back to learning content again, it is crucial to the success of e-Learning that instructors organize the learning material in a way suitable for interactive electronic delivery. The worst thing to do here is to copy traditionally written learning materials and simply paste them in the course for learners to display them on their screens. Contrary to that naïve practice, putting up an e-Learning course is a long process that requires maximum effort from the instructor and the support team. There are many hurdles along the way in that process, hence educational institutions offering online courses (e.g., universities) may have entire departments for helping instructors organize their e-Learning material. It is no wonder that even experienced instructors often need such a help - they may be teachers in domains like humanities and medicine, that focus on things other than computer-based delivery of knowledge.

There are a few simple rules to follow in organizing e-Learning material. All of them can be seen as learner-centered instances of more general rules of good pedagogy and human-computer interaction (HCI). First of all, it is important to clearly define the target audience (the learners and their skill levels) and the learning objectives (i.e., what the learners should be able to do once they go through the course). If the course delivery medium is the Web, organizing the learning material on the server side is only one part of the problem - it is also necessary to bear in mind the client's hardware and bandwidth to ensure for real time delivery. Next, it is a must to break the material into manageable modules (chunks) such as chapters and lessons, enabling the learners to grasp the overall structure of the material and map it to the course objectives, as well as to follow details in chapters and lessons more easily. There are authoring tools that support instructors in preparing their material that way. For example, Figure 1-1 shows how the instructors create chapters and lessons for an e-Learning course in the domain of radio communications and coding systems (Šimić and Devedžić, 2003), (Šimić et al., 2005). Each module should typically take a learner about 15-30 minutes to cover. Also, online learning material must be as easy as possible to navigate. Difficult navigation frustrates the learners and causes them to leave, which in the case of WBE is a matter of a mouse click. Indexing topics and terms across the course and interconnecting them with hyperlinks is usually the key to effective navigation. Last but not the least, animation and multimedia contents should add value and improve learning efficiency, recall, and retention, but not drive the learner away from the main objective(s). Overdone animation and multimedia can produce as much frustration as poor and clumsy navigation. Authoring tools normally support easy incorporation of animation and multimedia in e-Learning material by providing a set of easy-to-use controls.

Studies have shown that for e-Learning systems and applications to be effective, the presentation of information on the screen is important. The way the information organized on the screen, as well as different interactivity options (such as quizzes, hints, and multimedia to enhance all that) should clearly reflect frequently used structures and metaphors in the domain of interest. For example, Figure 1-2 shows a screenshot from Code Tutor, the actual system for learning radio communications and coding systems that uses the learning material mentioned in the context of Figure 1-1. In this case, the text and graphics presented on the screen (related to the domain concept "FSK transmission") can be augmented by a suitable audio clip and a spectral analysis diagram. They are the usual means of illustrating concepts in the domain of radio communication and coding. Still, it is left to the learner to activate them or to decide to go along without them.

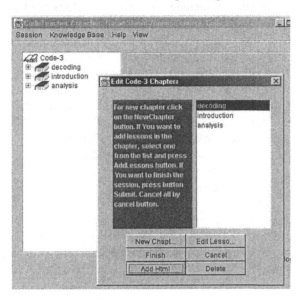

Figure 1-1. An example of creating material for an e-Learning course

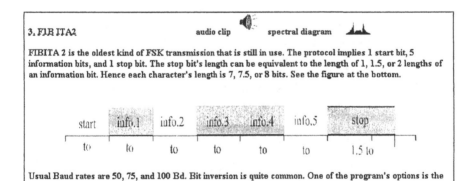

Figure 1-2. An illustration of how multimedia should be used discretely and at the learner's will

Using video in e-Learning applications can put the subject into its context of use, encourage active participation from trainees, and build on existing knowledge. Video clips can be followed by some questions (Obringer, 2005). Further augmentation includes combining portions of video clips with question answering in order to explore different scenarios. For example, a portion of a video can "formulate a problem" for a learner to work on, and can be ended with a couple of related questions. Based on the learner's answers, another video clip will be shown next, along with some explanations. Each further video clip corresponds to a different scenario, thus the learner can understand the consequences of making his/her choices when answering the set of questions put after the first clip was shown.

The same line of reasoning can be followed when deciding to incorporate animation and simulation in the material. A typical example is capturing a series of mouse moves and keystrokes to select a menu item or perform a certain action that an application enables, and using the capture as an animated example of interacting with the application. Likewise, the so-called *rollover* enables changing an image on the screen when the student moves the mouse over it (or over a "hot spot"), thus bringing his/her attention to another graphics of interest. Rollovers can be also effective when used to bring up a question to answer, or to open another line of exploring the material.

Finally, some further tips from HCI apply to e-Learning as well. For example, colors and fonts should be used with care. Contrast must be ensured between background and font colors, and complex coloring such as gradients may interfere with the system performance over the Internet. Of course, sacrificing quality and aesthetics is never a preferred option, so whenever possible good-quality graphics and multimedia are worth keeping (provided, of course, that they are used to reinforce learning, not just for the sake of using it). Too much text on the screen should be avoided, and feedback should be given to the student after each quiz he/she takes.

2.   DISTANCE EDUCATION

Nowadays, *distance education* and WBE are often used as synonyms. However, distance education is a more general concept of the two, and is certainly broader than and entails the concept of e-Learning. The term distance education is also often used interchangeably with *distance learning*; strictly speaking, distance learning is only one aspect and the desired outcome of distance education.

Distance education uses a wide spectrum of technologies to reach learners at a distance, not only the Web - written correspondence, text, graphics, audio- and videotape, CD-ROM, audio- and videoconferencing, interactive TV, and fax. Distance education or training courses can be delivered to remote locations in both synchronous and asynchronous mode, and do not exclude classroom-based learning and blended mode.

Distance education has long history. In the past, it was conducted mainly through written correspondence. Then from the Early XX century radio broadcast program was used in distance education extensively, and was gradually replaced by TV from 1950s onwards. Then came PC computers, the Internet, and other modern technologies.

This book adopts the following definition of distance education:

"Distance education is planned learning that normally occurs in a different place from teaching and as a result requires special techniques of course design, special instructional techniques, special methods of communication by electronic and other technology, as well as special organizational and administrative arrangements." (Moore and Kearsley, 1996)

2.1   Features

The most important features of distance education include:
- separation of teachers and learners (as in WBE) in time, location, or both;
- mediated information and instruction;
- organizational and planning activities (as in both e-Learning and WBE);
- the use of pedagogy and instructional design;
- the use of technology (e.g., telecommunications facilities) when live instruction should be conveyed at a distance in real time;
- a range of educational services (such as learning, communication, and assessment);
- different services to account for the administration of learners, teachers, and courses;
- delivery away from an academic institution, in an alternate location such as at work, at home or a learning or community center, yet in the form of a structured learning experience.

Distance education is a planned teaching/learning experience designed to encourage learner interaction and certification of learning. It may be accomplished on a point-to-point basis or on a point-to-multipoint basis. The forms of distance education include individual participation, teleseminars, teleconferences, Web conferences, electronic classrooms, and so on.

2.2   Pros and cons

Bonk and King (1998) list a number of advantages of distance education over traditional classroom-based education:
- students can do their work and "attend" class at their convenience;
- learning anytime and anywhere, which is specially convenient for adults with professional and social commitments;
- extensive curricula, often with international span;
- shy students sometimes open up;
- student disruptions and dominance are minimal;
- students can generate a huge amount of useful information through their postings; these can be used to enforce reflection and creative comments, hence teachers can support using the postings to extend interaction among students while driving them to focus on the content, as well as to initiate metacognitive activities and comments while pulling out interesting questions, themes, or questions for discussion;
- numerous opportunities for online advice and mentoring by experts, practitioners, and other professionals in the field;
- discussion can extend across the semester and create opportunities to share perspectives beyond a particular course or module.

Despite these obvious advantages of distance learning, there are also problems that have to be resolved (Valentine, 2005):
- the quality of distance instruction may be lower than that of face-to-face instruction - it is effective teachers who teach students, not the technology used;
- cost effectiveness of distance education is not always as high as promised - there are many elements in the cost of distance education that are often underestimated (e.g., the cost of converting the teaching material, the cost of extra equipment needed, and the like) and that, when taken into account more realistically, can make the cost of distance education quite comparable to that of classroom-based education;
- the technology may be expensive, and there is a possibility of not utilizing all of its potential (due to, e.g., the lack of training, the instructor's attitudes about using the technology, and hardware problems like malfunction of equipment (it can ruin the delivery and the entire course!));
- instructors' concerns must be taken into account (not all instructors' attitudes towards using technology are positive, and many instructors complain that distance education incurs much more work than face-to-face lecturing due to the fact that Internet-based communication may take considerably more time than live communication in class);

- students' concerns must be taken into account (for a variety of reasons, not all students are positive about distance education; for example, they may prefer live instruction and teachers using visual clues, or more intensive collaboration than that enabled by current technology, or they may show less tolerance for ambiguity, and so on).

3.   VIRTUAL CLASSROOMS

The terms *virtual classroom* and *Web classroom* are often used in the context of contemporary distance education and WBE to denote any means of live or pre-programmed Internet broadcast of information and/or a Web-based environment meant to support teaching and learning. When learners and teachers "meet" in the virtual classroom, they actually simultaneously access a particular URL that is dispensing information.

Such a computer-accessible, online learning environment can fulfill many of the learning facilitation roles of a physical classroom in much the same way a blackboard does for a real classroom. In fact, virtual classrooms are often modeled after the metaphor of a physical classroom. The interface of the supporting software may present a desk for each student, a teacher's desk, cupboards of resources, presentation board (virtual blackboard), module/assignment notebook, tools for chats and written communication among the teacher and the class or among the peer learners, access to online resources and tests, and even classroom posters (Rodriguez, 2000).

Note a difference between classrooms with physically present learners and virtual classrooms with remote interaction. In the former, Web technologies and other electronic devices and tools support teaching, learning, and communication *in addition* to live interaction among the students and the teacher(s). Such classrooms are also often called Web classrooms, but are in fact technology-enriched typical teacher-moderated classroom situations with physical presence of both the students and the teachers. In the latter case, physically remote students and teachers use appropriate software environments and Web technologies as *the* means to interact, both synchronously and asynchronously.

3.1   Architecture and modes of interaction

Architecturally, a Web classroom is usually a client-server learning environment designed as in Figure 1-3. Students and teachers work in a real or in a virtual classroom; in both cases, students can learn either individually or collaboratively. The Web technology connects the teacher(s) on the server and the student(s) on the client side.

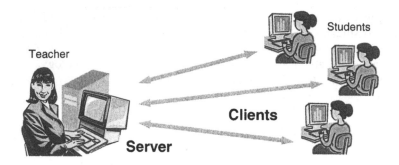

Figure 1-3. Client-server architecture of a virtual classroom

As a minimum, there are four modes of a student's interaction with a virtual classroom (Devedžić, 2005a):

- *authentication* - logging in for a new session;
- *learning* - selecting a material to learn from and browsing and reading the corresponding illustrated modules; in a typical case, some of the module pages are filled with text and graphics, and some of them also have supporting audio and video clips;
- *assessment* - answering questions the system asks after the learning of a module is completed;
- *validation* - the mode in which the system checks and updates the student model (see section 5 in this chapter for more details about student models) by estimating the student's knowledge about different topics from the material he/she was supposed to learn.

In addition to these four basic modes, virtual classrooms often support other means of interaction, such as referencing (e.g., browsing digital libraries from within the virtual classroom), collaboration (among peer learners, by using specific software tools integrated with the virtual classroom (see below)), and running simulations and online experiments.

The teacher(s) on the server side typically perform(s) the tasks such as authentication, starting the server, monitoring the students' sessions, editing and updating the learning material, and stopping the server, as well as complete class and course administration[1]. Of course, these tasks are rather diverse (system administration, authoring, teaching, and assessment), hence in practice they are done by several specialists. Some of the tasks are very different from those on the student side - for example, course administration, as well as editing and updating the learning and assessment material, which are allowed only to the teacher(s). A specific server-side module, also accessible only by the teacher, is used for monitoring the students' sessions.

---

[1] This may be done by using either an integrated or an external learning management system.

In some cases, the server can also arrange for personalization of the learning tasks it supports. In fact, from the learner's perspective the server supporting personalization appears as an intelligent tutor with both domain and pedagogical knowledge to conduct a learning session (again, see section 5 in this chapter for more details). It uses a presentation planner to select, prepare, and adapt the domain material to show to the student. It also gradually builds the student model during the session, in order to keep track of the student's actions and learning progress, detect and correct his/her errors and misconceptions, and possibly redirect the session accordingly.

3.2   Technology and software

There is a variety of Internet-enabled technologies that can be involved in virtual classrooms (Erickson and Siau, 2003), (Muehlenbrock and Hoppe, 2001), (Pinkwart, 2003):
- video conferencing;
- digital video (searching digital video libraries and live digital video transmission);
- Internet television (high definition TV transmission over the Internet);
- streaming media Web casts (playing multimedia contents as they are downloaded, without waiting for the entire download to complete);
- a range of different local student computers (desktop, notebooks, tablets, etc.), all locally networked and with access to the Internet;
- live board and other devices and accessories.

Likewise, depending on the domain and the pedagogical setting, different specific software components can be involved as well (Constantino-González et al., 2002), (Pinkwart, 2003):
- specific workspace tools for different domains, integrated with visual modeling languages and various construction kits (e.g., entity-relationship modeling elements for the domain of database design), to help the students learn more efficiently by solving problems in the domain of interest;
- different modeling and simulation tools, all with specific domain-related functionality and semantics; these can be defined externally, in the form of tool palettes (e.g., stochastic palette, system dynamics palette, Petri net palette,...) that encapsulate domain dependent semantics;
- general "discussion board";
- editing tool for taking and collecting individual notes;
- hooks to standard text processors, spreadsheet programs, and other frequently used applications;
- electronic worksheets that can be distributed and collected by the teacher;

- intelligent monitoring tools that can give both individual feedback and information for the teacher; the teacher can use such information to possibly enforce independent thinking and more active participation by some students;
- student tracking tools; for example, when a student finishes navigating a particular module, the system may record it so that the next time it will automatically bring the student to the next module or "learning space";
- collaborative learning support tools (such as shared and private workspace environments, tools for exchanging settings and data between learners and groups, chat rooms, and discussion forums);
- specific problem-creation tools for teachers to prepare initial problem descriptions for students to solve, using some corresponding visually orientated languages;
- specific help-creation tools for teachers to help the students when solving problems (by providing hints, using annotation elements and free hand input);
- electronic gradebook for teachers; students can also see their own grades and compare them to class averages;

More advanced and certainly technically more demanding virtual classrooms enable real-time, two-way, or multisite link between participating students using virtual reality software (Erickson and Siau, 2003), (Johnson et al., 2000). For example, in the approach called tele-immersion (Ott and Mayer-Patel, 2004), remote teachers and learners may appear to each other as virtual reality avatars (usually represented as cartoon-like figures) who can converse, demonstrate work in progress, lecture to a classroom, or even "get together" in a virtual laboratory to perform an online experiment. The technical, hardware, software, and telecommunications requirements here are extremely complex.

3.3   Problems, challenges, and open issues

Teaching in a Web classroom is definitely not just posting notes and readings. Individual instructors participating as teachers in virtual classrooms must completely rethink and reorganize and prepare their courses to be delivered via virtual classrooms. This includes preparing slides, course notes, handouts, etc. especially for virtual classrooms, as well as designing new types of assignments for remote students participating in virtual classrooms. Moreover, they need to devise interesting activities such as debates and role plays or games, and put all of their material in digital form on the Web regularly during the course.

All such activities mean hard work. In other words, technology for virtual classrooms is there, but it does not reduce the workload for instructors; it just changes its nature to an extent. In spite of technological differences, the goals and objectives of teaching in virtual classrooms remain the same as in traditional classrooms - increasing the learning outcomes, accommodating differences among the students in terms of their learning styles, goals, and capabilities, giving individual attention to students in need, and so forth. To achieve all this, instructors often need to give more feedback to students outside the class, to increase the course development time, and to continuously improve the learning material they prepare. Also, all activities and assignments must be pre-planned and uploaded. As a result, the workload for teachers often increases beyond the expected level.

Furthermore, appropriate logistics must be organized to support Web classes; for example, new students should be able to put course material orders, arrange for downloading large and restricted multimedia files, and get their accounts to participate in class conferences. This creates the need for a distance student support office and computer system support team. Even simple technical problems can easily lock out the students if the solution is not found quickly and effectively.

Another important open issue of Web classrooms is that of realistic evaluation of the student's activities and the environment itself. It is a good idea to have the students fill in some questionnaires periodically, to get an insight into how their attitudes and attributes change over time. Still, it is not enough. The monitoring tools mentioned in the previous section complement direct communication and feedback, and can indicate problems in using and acceptance of the Web classroom. For example, such tools may help the teacher(s) track the amount and type of the students' activities, the hours they spent in the virtual classroom, the number of logons, and the number and proportion of individual student contributions to the class activities. All these parameters indirectly indicate the students' motivation and possible problems in using the software tools involved. On the long run, internal assessment of student performance through comparison of grades for the same exams and assignments (as in traditional classes) can indicate problems with the class, the software support, and the communication between the teachers and the learners.

Success of a Web classroom depends also on the students' sense of being a part of it, just as with real classrooms. The students should feel the virtual classroom is *the* place for them to go not only to participate to learning activities, but also to find the resources they need. The classroom should be their starting point ("portal") in looking for the necessary resources such as different documents, multimedia objects, links, and problem-solution examples to practice with. A virtual classroom should be designed after the metaphor of a real classroom full of resources. Furthermore, the design of virtual classrooms must support the students in developing a sense of "going to the classroom" from their own locations to present intermediate results of their longer term projects, unconstrained by contact time of limited duration that often occurs in traditional settings. So, virtual classrooms should be the platforms for display of student projects as well, not only the course material.

An interesting question that still requires a lot of efforts and elaboration in spite of some initial developments is related to the possibility of building software "shells" for creating configurable Web classrooms. An early idea of Rodriguez (2000) along this line suggests development of a domain- and class-independent general Web-based environment that can be instantiated into a virtual classroom by tailoring it according to the teachers', students' and educational institutions' preferences.

4.   PREREQUISITES FOR ACCEPTANCE

End-users of WBE expect not only provision of effective, high-quality educational and training material, but also smooth integration of this material and training with advanced educational and technological frameworks and Web classrooms. They also want to integrate the material and educational services they get from WBE with their day-to-day operational environments and workflows within which they operate (e.g., industrial, government or academic settings). As a consequence, it is necessary to map the WBE technology to core educational workflows in order to achieve effective instruction through WBE.

That mapping is not easy; education workflows are often extremely complex, with many complicated dependencies. Most of educational workflows involve creation of, access to, teaching and/or manipulation of learning material and other resources, as well as interaction and communication between different categories of users of WBE systems (teachers, researchers, learners, advisors, and administrators).

On the other hand, learners (who are the most important end-users of WBE systems) demand high-quality WBE in terms of content, pedagogy, and technological framework.

4.1   Educational workflow issues

Education workflows provide the necessary abstractions that enable effective usage of computational resources, and development of robust, open problem-solving environments that marshal educational, computing and networking resources (Vouk et al., 1999).

WBE systems must support coexistence, interaction, and seamless integration of end-user's education workflows with his/her other workflows, such as legislative, scientific and business workflows. For example, many students from industry that work during the day may prefer to schedule their logs onto a WBE system at times that suite them, e.g., evenings or weekends. They cannot match their work-place processes with the traditional school, college or university teaching workflows. To account for problems like this one, WBE systems have to disaggregate the traditional synchronous teaching/learning cycle into a number of smaller, primarily asynchronous components with only minor synchronous interactions.

The complexity of educational workflows is the primary reason why many WBE systems remain in laboratories and never make their way to practical environments and use. Many unsuccessful systems suffer from inappropriate functionality and instruction models, poor evaluation of the system usability and users' interaction with it, and the lack of flexible, plug-in design for incorporating new functionalities easily to accommodate different learners' needs.

To better understand the workflows in educational processes and how WBE systems map to those workflows, it is necessary to clearly identify different (albeit non-exclusive) categories of people involved and their roles in the processes.

There are four major categories of users of WBE systems - students, instructors, authors, and system developers. In addition to them, other categories of users may be interested in WBE systems, such as parents of the students, employers of continuing and adult education students, educational administrators, and government officials.

System developers are responsible for development and maintenance of the WBE system framework. They must be knowledgeable in software and communications engineering, Web engineering, HCI and interface design, education, knowledge bases, and artificial intelligence. They develop authoring tools, Web-based platforms for end users, and system interfaces, and assist authors in courseware generation.

Authors are courseware developers. In most of cases, they are not computer and system experts, so the authoring tools and interfaces that system developers create for them must be easy-to-learn and easy-to-use; in other words, the authors should concentrate on the content development rather than struggle with the system intricacies (Vouk et al., 1999).

Instructors sample, select, customize, and combine learning materials, existing lessons, projects and courses, and develop new curricula, courses, and projects. They also deliver the course material and take care of teaching, assessment, grading, and reviewing student projects.

Students and *trainees* (i.e., *learners*) are the most important and most numerous users of WBE systems. The entire design of a WBE system and framework must be learner-centered, bearing in mind that they demand easy-to-use and intuitive interfaces, timely access to and updates of learning materials, reliable communications, teacher's support when needed, collaboration with peer learners in virtual classrooms, information about their grades and/or progress in the courses, and so on. Security issues are of prime concern to learners; it is mandatory for a successful WBE system to ensure for protecting the learners' work and projects from data losses and unauthorized access. Also, WBE systems must account for learners' diversity. This is especially true for the systems that target international adult learners interested in continuing education and lifelong learning. The learners' age differences and geographic distribution, different times they log on to "attend classes", their different profiles and backgrounds, as well as different cultures they come from and lifestyles they practice, make WBE system design, organization, and administration extremely complex. Instructors must support this diversity and simultaneously maintain high quality and integrity of the educational delivery.

Incorporating different education workflows in a WBE system for such a diverse user population requires careful elaboration of many possible scenarios that frequently occur in practice, and designing the system to support such scenarios. For example, consider the course delivery workflow. To support it, the system first needs information about the course syllabus, schedule, and learner profiles. Based on an analysis of the learners' backgrounds, qualifications, and preferred learning styles, the system can produce a suitable mapping between the learners' profiles and course topics. This mapping can be used as the basis for deciding about the teaching approaches and strategies to apply when teaching specific topics. The mapping should clearly indicate feedback points and an estimate of the process feedback rates, as well as requirements and points for assessment and material reinforcement information. In the end, all this information should be represented in terms of the system functionalities, taking into account available resources, teacher's and author's preferences, and so on. This final representation may include teaching alternatives to increase the system's adaptivity.

Education workflow information can be appropriately combined with the system's options for collaborative activities. Typical collaboration options include:

- collaboration among the learners - groupware that facilitates sharing of results, explanations, discussion among remote learners, etc.);
- collaboration among the authors - this often comes in the form of joint courseware development (each author contributes to the part of the course related to his/her domain of expertise); the authoring tools and the educational institution's access to repositories of learning material may reduce effort through reuse of existing material in new courseware, provided that consistent formats are enforced throughout the institution's courseware;

- collaboration among educational institutions through *virtual laboratories* - access to and sharing of special, expensive state-of-the-art facilities (e.g., remote electron-microscope labs and similar applications), online experiments, and simulations developed by different educational institutions and made accessible to other institutions or remote groups of learners.

4.2 Quality-of-service in WBE

In learner-centered WBE systems, quality-of-service (QoS) can be measured in terms of quality of the educational content, quality of the system's pedagogy, and quality of the technological framework (including educational paradigm support and networks) (Vouk et al., 1999).

Quality of educational content. Intuitively, learners will more frequently want to access good-quality educational material than poor one, and will have better understanding of the topics covered by high-quality material. In order to assure wide acceptance of educational material by different students, it is necessary to constantly evaluate the material and to insist on instructors' and authors' responsibility to constantly update the material according to the evaluation results.

Typical measures of quality of educational content in learner-oriented workflows include quality of lessons, appropriateness of the teaching/learning paradigm, quality of user-system interactions, semantic interoperability, and so on.

High-quality WBE systems also support rapid integration of new developments and research results in the fields they cover into their curricula. To achieve that, the instructors must keep up-to-date with the latest advances in rapidly changing fields and collaborate intensively with authors and system developers, so that they can update the courseware in a timely way. Research in rapidly changing domains (such as genetics and computing) is very intense, hence courseware updates must be frequent in spite of geographical, institutional, and other dispersion of researchers, all categories of WBE users, and educational institutions. The key to achieving such a high level of QoS is intensive network-based collaboration between researchers and the WBE instructors, authors, and students.

Quality of pedagogy. Good pedagogy of learner-centered teaching means adaptation to the learners' individual and group needs, learning goals, and preferred learning styles, in order to increase learning efficiency. To this end, a WBE system must have some means of measuring learning and providing adaptive feedback to the learner in terms of the pace and depth of the presented material. The adaptive feedback should result from the learner's observed interaction with the system and from the system's estimate of the knowledge transfer rate specific to the particular learner. The system typically observes the learner's interaction during tests, problem solving, question/answer sessions, and explanation requests/generation.

In addition, learner-centered WBE systems must support using different benchmarks and measurements for evaluation of teaching and learning effectiveness, as well as evaluation of educational paradigms, with respect to knowledge transfer, retention rates, assessment statistics, graduation rates, and other related metrics.

Quality of technological framework. True, content and pedagogy may be thought of as central to the learning efficiency, but the quality of the technology involved *does* matter. Attractive technology may be a driving force in the initial acceptance of a WBE system, and vice versa - poor technology and low performance of the system may frustrate the learners and drive them away.

Much of the metrics used to qualify the QoS of the technological framework applied in a WBE system are related to the network. Traditionally, they include the network bandwidth the system requires to operate at a certain level of performance, keystroke delays, end-to-end response delay, probability of loss of data, jitter, and throughput. These are objective measures. Other metrics involve subjective factors, e.g., the system's availability, reliability performance, scalability, and effectiveness, as perceived by the learners.

One of the frequently used approaches to adaptation of a WBE system to different network access conditions at learners' sites is to provide different representations of the same content and let the learners configure the system's presentation facilities to match their situation. The representations to consider range from simple text-based ones that sacrifice much of the richer HCI capabilities for the sake of quicker response times, to bandwith-greedy representations like rich animations and video.

It is crucial to the system's success to maintain direct communication lines for learners' feedback and error reporting, as well as to provide rapid and timely response to their feedback. Another important QoS issue here is centralized maintenance and system-wide synchronization of content and software. Master storage and version history of educational content should be a must.

Finally, there are a number of issues related to security and privacy. To name but a few, note that administration of remote assessment, electronic cheating and copying of homework and assignments, and letting only the right student know his/her grades without revealing that information to the others, must be considered in WBE with extreme care.

5. INTELLIGENCE AND ADAPTIVITY

Two effective ways of improving QoS of a WBE system are to introduce intelligence in the system and to make it adaptive to individual learner's needs and interactions. Introducing intelligence in WBE comes in the form of synergy between WBE and the more traditional field of intelligent tutoring systems. Achieving WBE system's adaptivity leads to an intersection of WBE with the field of adaptive hypermedia systems, and the result is called adaptive educational hypermedia systems.

5.1 Intelligent tutoring systems

Intelligent tutoring systems (*ITSs*), or *intelligent educational systems* (*IESs*), use methods and techniques of *artificial intelligence* (*AI*) to improve the processes of computer-based teaching and learning.

5.1.1 Architecture

Figure 1-4 shows traditional organization of an ITS, discussed extensively in (Wenger, 1987). *Domain* or *instructional content* of an ITS (specifying what to teach) is referred to as *Expert Module*, whereas different *teaching strategies* (specifying how to teach) from the *Pedagogical Module* drive the teaching/learning sessions. The purpose of the *Student Model* (or *Learner Model*) is modeling the student's mastery of the topics being taught, in order to dynamically adapt the process of instruction to the student. ITSs can support *individual learning*, where one human student learns from the artificial *tutor* (the three modules just mentioned) and all the communication goes through the *Interface Module*. Others support *collaborative learning*, by enabling multiple students to learn from the system as a group, interacting both with the system and among themselves. There can also be one or more *learning companions* in the system. These are artificial co-learners, programs that learn from the tutor (using machine learning techniques and simulated knowledge acquisition) the same topics as the student does, providing competition, assistance, and further motivation to the student. All ITSs use various *knowledge representation* and *reasoning* techniques from AI. *ITS shells* and *authoring tools* are integrated software environments that support development of the actual systems (Devedžić, 2003a; 2003b).

The Student Model is typically an *overlay model*, which means a vector of numerical values each one denoting the level of mastery of a single topic or concept from the domain model. Numerical values correspond to a certain scale, the highest value on the scale representing the expert level (complete mastery). The values get constantly updated as the student continues to learn from the system, to reflect the changes in his/her knowledge and learning. Alternatively, the Student Model can be organized as a set of *stereotypes*, each one defined as a fixed vector of numerical values. The system then categorizes each student into one from the predefined finite set of stereotypes (e.g., novice, advanced, expert, and so on).

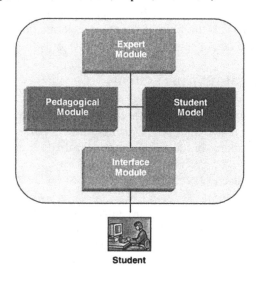

Student

Figure 1-4. Traditional ITS architecture

From the perspective of learner-centered design and increased learning efficiency as an ultimate goal of ITSs, it is important to stress tight relation between the Student Model component and the personalization of the learning process. The Student Model stores all the necessary parameters about the specific student, such as his/her learning goals, learning history, learning style and other preferences, current level of topic/course mastery, and the like. It enables personalization of learning-material presentation and adaptive, learner-centered individualization of the learning process.

5.1.2   Instructional design

An important component of ITS engineering is *instructional design*. Instructional design comprises applying a set of principles to achieve effective, efficient, and relevant instruction. It usually includes five phases: analysis, design, development, implementation, and evaluation. In the context of ITSs, instructional design encompasses the theory and practice of design, development, utilization, management and evaluation of processes and resources for learning, as well as building them into intelligent learning environments (Devedžić, 2003a; 2003b). Instructional design issues affect the design of all four major components of an ITS shown in Figure 1-4.

The ultimate goal of instructional design in ITSs is to achieve a desired level of the learner's performance. The performance should be measurable.

For a good starting point in looking for comprehensive theoretical sources of instructional design, see (Ryder, 2005). A good glossary of instructional design can be found at (ID Glossary, 2005).

5.1.3   Web-based ITSs

One of the recent trends in the field of ITSs is development of *Web-based ITSs*. Other trends include simulation-based learning, dialogue modeling for instruction, multimedia support for teaching and learning, open learning environments, and support for life-long learning. There is also a growing attention on educational technology and standardization issues, software engineering of educational applications, pedagogical agents, and virtual reality environments for education. All of these trends clearly overlap with more general WBE approaches and methodology.

Development of Web-based ITSs has started in Mid-1990s. First-wave Web-based ITS like ELM-ART (Brusilovsky et al., 1996) and PAT Online (Ritter, 1997), to name but a few, were followed by a number of other learning environments that used Web technology as means of delivering instruction. More recent Web-based ITSs address other important issues, such as integration with standalone, external, domain-service Web systems (Melis et al., 2001), using standards and practices from international standardization bodies in designing Web-based learning environments (Retalis and Avgeriou, 2002), and architectural design of systems for Web-based teaching and learning (Alpert et al., 1999), (Mitrović and Hausler, 2000). Rebai and de la Passardiere try to capture educational metadata for Web-based learning environments (Rebai and de la Passardiere, 2002).

5.2   Adaptive learning

It is not feasible in conventional WBE to create static learning material that can be read in any arbitrary sequence, because of many interdependences and prerequisite relationships between the course pages (De Bra, 2002). However, *adaptive hypermedia (AH)* methods and techniques make it possible to inform learners that certain links lead to material they are not ready for, to suggest visiting pages the learner should consult, or automatically provide additional explanations at the pages the learner visits, in order to scaffold his/her progress. *Adaptive educational hypermedia systems* (*AEHSs*) apply different forms of learner models to adapt the content and the links of hypermedia course pages to the learner (Brusilovsky, 1999), (Henze and Nejdl, 2003).

AEHSs support *adaptive learning*, using technology to constantly measure the learner's knowledge and progress in order to adapt learning content delivery, presentation, feedback, assessment, or environment to the learner's needs, pace, preferences, and goals. Such systems make predictions of what the learner needs to attain his/her goals, respond to such needs, allocate resources, implement change, and thus improve personalization of the learning process. The system can be designed to use predictive strategies prior to instruction delivery and learning sessions, during the instruction (based on the learner's interaction), or both.

5.2.1   Adaptive hypermedia

AH systems merge hypermedia with user modeling technology and can be applied in a variety of application areas; however, one dominating area is education (De Bra, 2002).

AH enables overcoming the problem of presenting the same content to different users in the same way, regardless of their different interests, needs, and backgrounds. The AH approach is to maintain a user model for each specific user and to adapt its interaction with the user in different ways according to that model.

AH provides two general categories of adaptation:

- *content adaptation* (Wu et al., 1998), or *adaptive presentation* (Brusilovsky, 1999) - presenting the content in different ways, according to the domain model (concepts, their relationships, prerequisite information, etc.) *and* information from the user model;
- *link adaptation* (Wu et al., 1998), or *adaptive navigation* (Brusilovsky, 1998) - the system modifies the availability and/or appearance of every link that appears on a Web page, in order to show the user whether the link leads to interesting new information, to new information the user is not ready for, or to a page that provides no new knowledge (De Bra, 2002).

There are several techniques for content adaptation. The system may provide explanations using *conditional text* - different segments of text-based explanations are turned on and off and presented to the user as needed, based on whether his/her user model meets some condition(s) or not. Some systems use a variant of conditional text called *stretchtext* - allowing the user access to the portions of explanation estimated to be either beyond his current comprehension or irrelevant/unimportant. The same idea can be applied not only in explanation generation, but also in ordinary presentation of material - the system simply maintains *different versions of pages* it presents to the users (or just *different versions of information fragments* within the pages), and selects the version to show according to the user model. A simple variant can be hiding advanced content from a novice user, or showing suitable additional content to more advanced users. A more sophisticated variant of different fragment presentation includes deciding also on the order of presenting them.

Two most popular forms of adaptive navigation support are link annotation and link hiding. *Link annotation* refers to providing additional information about the page the link leads to, in the form of suitable visual clues such as color, additional text, additional symbol (e.g., bullet or icon), different shape of accompanying symbol (e.g., different bullet style), and blinking, all reflecting current information from the user model. For example, blue-colored links may be used to denote pages for novices, and red-colored ones may lead to pages for advanced users. *Link hiding* makes some links inaccessible or invisible to the user if the system estimates from the user model that such links take him/her to irrelevant information. In addition, an AH system may use *direct guidance* to make the user go exactly to the page the system deems the right one for the next step, or some *global guidance* such as showing the user a list of links for further steps sorted according to some criteria related to the information from the user model. In a more sophisticated variant called *map adaptation* (Wu et al., 1998), the hierarchical structure of links leading to different information is presented to the user in a form more suitable for navigation, such as a table, a tree, or a graphical map.

5.2.2   Adaptive educational hypermedia systems

AEHSs apply AH techniques to WBE systems. The users are now learners, and the adaptation comes at three levels (DeBra et al., 2004):

- *connectivity* - parts of the learning content are interlinked in a number of ways, allowing the learners to navigate it in numerous ways; the AEHS presents different links with different visual indicators of suitability and relevance for the learner, according to his/her learner model;
- *content* - the system shows additional information to the student to compensate for his/her lack of sufficient knowledge (as indicated in the student model), or it hides unnecessary information from the student if it concludes from the student model that the student already knows it and would not benefit from seeing it again;
- *culture* - AEHSs take into account different backgrounds, motivation, preferences, and styles of different learners and adapt the educational tasks to them according to differences in such information.

Adapting from (Brusilovsky, 1999), (De Bra, 2002), (De Bra et al., 2004a; 2004b), and (Wu et al., 1998), one can identify four major components of AEHSs, Figure 1-5[2]. *Domain Model* defines domain concepts and structure and roughly corresponds to the *Expert Module* in the traditional ITS architecture, Figure 1-4. *Student Model* represents the student's characteristics, most importantly his/her levels of knowledge of domain concepts. As with traditional ITS, the Student Model is typically an overlay model or a stereotype model. *Pedagogical Model* defines rules of access to parts of the Domain Model, according to the information from the Student Model. Many pedagogical rules follow directly from the structure of the domain, but many also come from the system's instructional design.

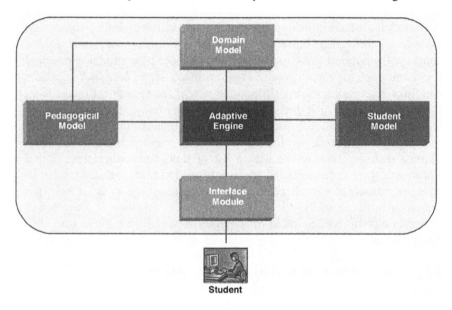

Figure 1-5. Simplified generic architecture of AEHSs

The distinctive feature of each AEHS is its *Adaptive Engine*. In reality, it is usually not just an engine, but an entire software environment for creating and adapting domain concepts and links. During the system operation, the adaptation mechanism itself uses information from the other modules to select, annotate, and present content to the user adaptively.

Obviously, AEHSs rely heavily on student modeling. Research and development of student models is one of the most important topics in adaptive WBE.

---

[2] The figure is shown in a simplified form for the sake of functional clarity; in reality, additional components exist to reflect the distributed nature of AEHSs.

6. SUMMARY

WBE is an important and fast growing segment of educational technology. It largely overlaps with the field of e-Learning, but it must be noted that learning represents only one aspect of education. WBE covers many other educational services, such as teaching, authoring, assessment, collaboration, and so on. Nowadays, most of distance education is implemented as WBE and use of virtual classrooms.

There is a lot of technological issues involved there, but it must be never forgotten that the ultimate goal of WBE is increasing the learning opportunities and efficiency, not the technology itself. In learner-centered design of WBE, educational workflows determine desired functionalities of WBE systems and quality of service provided to the learners is crucial to success or failure of any such a system.

Two important ways of increasing the quality of service of WBE systems and thus the likelihood of their success are to make them intelligent and adaptive. Intelligent tutoring systems already have a long tradition and recently often make a synergy with WBE. Adaptive educational hypermedia systems use many different techniques to adapt content delivery to individual learners according to their learning characteristics, preferences, styles, and goals.

However, there are several problems with WBE that both teachers and learners face (Devedžić, 2003a). Educational material on the Web is still highly unstructured, heterogeneous, and distributed as everything else on the Web, and current learning and authoring tools offer limited support for accessing and processing such material. The main burden of organizing and linking the learning contents on the Web, as well as extracting and interpreting them, is on the human user.

Next-generation WBE applications should exhibit more theory- and content-oriented intelligence and adaptivity, pay more attention to interoperability, reusability, and knowledge sharing issues, and look more closely to general trends in Web development. New fields of research and development, such as Semantic Web and Web intelligence, provide means for representing, organizing, and interconnecting knowledge of human educators in a machine-understandable and machine-processable form, as well as for creating intelligent Web-based services for teachers and learners. The following chapters discuss extensively how to use the results and technology of these other fields to make WBE more effective and more appealing to learners, teachers, and authors alike. Specifically, the chapters that follow introduce Semantic Web technologies and explain common prerequisites for creating *intelligent* WBE systems and applications. They also describe the kinds of intelligent WBE services that such systems should support and how to ensure for such support. They attempt to answer many practical questions of both engineering and instructional importance. For example, how can a search engine from the sea of educational Web pages select automatically those of most value to the authors, teachers, and learners in pursuing their educational goals?

Chapter 2

INTRODUCTION TO THE SEMANTIC WEB

Semantic Web is the new-generation Web that tries to represent information such that it can be used by machines not just for display purposes, but for automation, integration, and reuse across applications (Boley et al., 2001). It is one of the hottest research and development (R&D) topics in recent years in the AI community, as well as in the Internet community - Semantic Web is an important activity of the World Wide Web Consortium, W3C (W3C SW Activity, 2005).

Semantic Web is about making the Web more understandable by machines (Heflin and Hendler, 2001). It is also about building an appropriate infrastructure for intelligent agents to run around the Web performing complex actions for their users (Hendler, 2001). In order to do that, agents must retrieve and manipulate pertinent information, which requires seamless agent integration with the Web and taking full advantage of the existing infrastructure (such as message sending, security, authentication, directory services, and application service frameworks) (Scott Cost et al., 2002). Furthermore, Semantic Web is about explicitly declaring the knowledge embedded in many Web-based applications, integrating information in an intelligent way, providing semantic-based access to the Internet, and extracting information from texts (Gómez-Pérez and Corcho, 2002). Ultimately, Semantic Web is about how to implement reliable, large-scale interoperation of Web services, to make such services computer interpretable - to create a Web of machine-understandable and interoperable services that intelligent agents can discover, execute, and compose automatically (McIlraith et al., 2001).[3]

1.   FROM THE WEB OF INFORMATION TO THE WEB OF KNOWLEDGE[4]

Why do we need all that? Isn't the Web an immense, practically unlimited source of information and knowledge that everyone can use?

The problem is that the Web is huge, but not smart enough to easily integrate all of those numerous pieces of information from the Web that a user really needs. Such integration at a high, user-oriented level is desirable in nearly all uses of the Web. Today, most of the Web information is represented in natural-language; however, our computers cannot understand and interpret its meaning. Humans themselves can process only a tiny fraction of information available on the Web, and would benefit enormously if they could turn to machines for help in processing and analyzing the Web contents (Fridman-Noy et al., 2001). Unfortunately, the Web was built for human consumption, not for machine consumption - although everything on the Web is *machine-readable*, it is not *machine-understandable* (Lassila, 1998). We need the Semantic Web to express information in a precise, machine-interpretable form, ready for software agents to process, share, and reuse it, as well as to understand what the terms describing the data mean. That would enable Web-based applications to interoperate both on the syntactic and the semantic level.

Note that it is Tim Berners-Lee himself who pushes the idea of the Semantic Web forward. The father of the Web first envisioned a Semantic Web that provides automated information access based on machine-processable semantics of data and heuristics that use this semantics (Berners-Lee et al., 1999), (Berners-Lee et al., 2001). The explicit representation of the semantics of data, accompanied with domain theories (that is, ontologies; see the next section), will enable a Web that provides a qualitatively new level of service - for example, intelligent search engines, information brokers, and information filters (Decker et al., 2000), (Fensel and Musen, 2001). Ontologies and intelligent services enable transformation of the

---

[3] Paragraph reprinted (with minor citation formatting adjustments) from International Journal of Artificial Intelligence in Education (IJAIED), Vol.14, Vladan Devedžić, Education and The Semantic Web, Pages No. 39-65, Copyright (2004), with permission from IOS Press.

[4] Reprinted (with minor citation formatting adjustments) from International Journal of Artificial Intelligence in Education (IJAIED), Vol.14, Vladan Devedžić, Education and The Semantic Web, Pages No. 39-65, Copyright (2004), with permission from IOS Press.

today's Web of information and data into the Web of knowledge - the Semantic Web.

People from W3C already develop new technologies for Web-friendly data description. Moreover, AI people have already developed some useful applications and tools for the Semantic Web (Fridman-Noy et al., 2001), (Scott Cost et al., 2002).

There is a number of important issues related to the Semantic Web. Roughly speaking, they belong to four categories: ontologies, languages for the Semantic Web, semantic markup of pages on the Semantic Web, and services that the Semantic Web is supposed to provide.

2. ONTOLOGIES

The word *ontology* comes from the Greek *ontos*, for being, and *logos*, for word. In philosophy, it refers to the subject of existence, i.e. to the study of being as such. More precisely, it is the study of the *categories* of things that exist or may exist in some domain (Sowa, 2000). A domain ontology explains the types of things in that domain.

Informally, ontology of a certain domain is about terminology (domain vocabulary), all essential concepts in the domain, their classification, their taxonomy, their relations (including all important hierarchies and constraints), and about domain axioms. More formally, to someone who wants to discuss about topics in a domain D using a language L, ontology provides a catalog of the types of things assumed to exist in D; the types in the ontology are represented in terms of the concepts, relations, and predicates of L.

Both formally and informally, ontology is an extremely important part of knowledge of any domain. Moreover, ontology is the fundamental part of knowledge and all other knowledge should rely on it and refer to it. Many branches of science and technology realize this fact and have recently started their efforts in developing ontologies to represent their domains. These efforts are largely facilitated by existing formal languages for representing ontologies and software tools that support their development (see sections 2.2 and 3 in this chapter). For a more comprehensive coverage of the field of ontologies, see (Staab and Studer, 2004).

2.1 Basic Concepts

In AI, the term ontology has largely come to mean one of two related things (Chandrasekaran, et al., 1999):

- a representation vocabulary, often specialized to some domain or subject matter;
- a body of knowledge describing some domain, using a representation vocabulary.

In both cases, there is always an associated underlying data structure that represents the ontology.

2.1.1   Definitions

There are many definitions of the concept of ontology in AI and in computing in general. The most widely cited one is:

"Ontology is a specification of a conceptualization." (Gruber, 1993)

This definition is certainly the most concise one and requires some further clarification. *Conceptualization* means an abstract, simplified view of the world. If a knowledge base of an intelligent system should represent the world for some purpose, then it must be committed to some conceptualization, explicitly or implicitly. That is, the body of any formally represented knowledge is based on a certain conceptualization. Every conceptualization is based on the concepts, objects, and other entities that are assumed to exist in some area of interest and the relationships that hold among them. This also clarifies the meaning of the term "world" - in practice, the "world" actually refers to some phenomenon in the world, or to some topic (or topics), or to some subject area.

The other part of the above definition - *specification* - means a formal and declarative representation. In a data structure representing an ontology, the type of concepts used and the constraints on their use are stated declaratively, explicitly, and using a certain formal language. Formal representation implies that ontology should be *machine-readable.* However, ontology is not "active"; it cannot be run as a program. It declaratively represents some knowledge to be used by different programs.

"Ontology is a set of knowledge terms, including the vocabulary, the semantic interconnections, and some simple rules of inference and logic for some particular topic." (Hendler, 2001)

The important parts in Hendler's definition are the *semantic interconnections* and *inference and logic.* The former is to say that ontology specifies the meaning of relations among the concepts used. Also, it may be interpreted as a suggestion that ontologies themselves are interconnected as well; for example, the ontologies of hand and arm may be built to be logically, semantically, and formally interconnected. The latter part means that ontologies enable some forms of reasoning. For example, the ontology of musician may specify categories of musicians by the instruments they play. Using this categorization, it would be possible for an intelligent system to infer that, for example, a *pianist* is a *musician*.

Swartout and Tate (2001) offer an informal and metaphoric but extremely useful definition for understanding of ontology essentials:

"Ontology is the basic structure or armature around which a knowledge base can be built." (Swartout and Tate, 2001)

Figure 2-1 illustrates this idea. Like armature in the concrete, an ontology should provide a firm and stable "knowledge skeleton" to which all other knowledge should stick. Ontology represents the fundamental knowledge about a topic of interest; it is possible for much of other knowledge about the same topic to grow around the ontology, referring to it, yet representing a whole in itself.

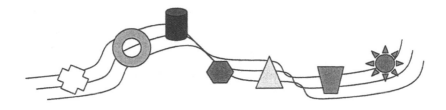

Figure 2-1. Illustraion of Swartout and Tate's definition of ontologies

Kalfoglou (2001) stresses yet another important issue related to ontologies:

"An ontology is an explicit representation of a shared understanding of the important concepts in some domain of interest." (Kalfoglou, 2001)

The word *shared* here indicates that an ontology captures some *consensual* knowledge. It is not supposed to represent the subjective knowledge of some individual, but the knowledge accepted by a group or a community. All individual knowledge is subjective; ontology implements an explicit cognitive structure that helps present objectivity as an agreement about subjectivity. Hence ontology conveys a shared understanding of a domain that is agreed between a number of individuals or agents. Such an agreement facilitates accurate and effective communication of meaning. This, in turn, opens the possibility for knowledge sharing and reuse, which enables semantic interoperability between intelligent agents and applications.

2.1.2   What do ontologies look like?

The answer to the above question depends on the level of abstraction. When implemented in a computer, they typically look like XML-based files. Alternatively, they can be represented in a computer using a logic language, such as KIF (Genesereth and Fikes, 1992). Since ontologies are always about some concepts and their relations, they can be represented graphically using a visual language. Graphical tools for building ontologies always support conversion from graphical format to XML and other text-based formats (see section 2.2.1).

Humans can express ontologies as sets of declarative statements in a natural language. However, natural language statements are difficult to process in a computer. Recall also from definitions that representing ontologies in a computer requires a formal language.

As an example of representing ontologies at different levels of abstraction, consider again the concept of a musician. For the sake of simplicity, assume that the concepts used to describe the essential knowledge of the notion of a musician are *musician, instrument,* some products of his/her work - *albums* the musician has recorded and music *events* (e.g., concerts) to which he/she has participated - and devoted *admirers* (fans) who keep his/her artist fame growing. Also, assume that all the variety and multitude of relations that can be considered among these concepts is reduced to just a couple of the most essential ones, such as the facts that each musician *plays* some instrument, that when giving concerts he/she *plays at* that concert, that the admirers come to *attend* such events, and that the musician also *records* music albums. We deliberately avoid in this simple example numerous kind-of and part-of relations to other concepts associated with musicians and their work.

These natural language statements represent the conceptualization of the Musician ontology. At a high level of abstraction, that ontology can be informally diagrammed as the semantic network shown in Figure 2-2.

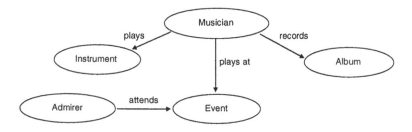

Figure 2-2. Musician ontology visualized as a semantic network

Obviously, the representation in Figure 2-2 suffers from many deficiencies. It is not a formal specification, i.e. it is not expressed in any formal language. It does not show any details, such as properties of the concepts shown or some characteristics of the relations between them. For example, musicians have their names, and albums have their titles, durations, and years when they are recorded. Likewise, nothing in that semantic network shows explicitly that the musician is the *author* of the album he/she records (note that recording engineers in music studios can be also said to record albums, but they are usually not the authors). Still, the semantic network in Figure 2-2 does show some of the initial ideas about the Musician ontology.

For more details and for a formal graphical representation, consider the UML[5] model Figure 2-3. It represents the same world as the semantic network from Figure 2-2, but allows for specifying properties of all the concepts used, as well as the roles of concepts in their relations unambiguously. Another important detail in this representation is an explicit specification of the cardinalities of all concepts.

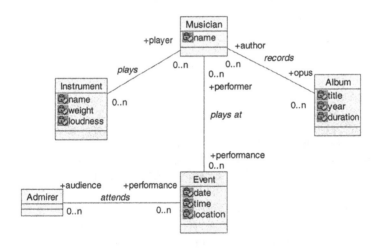

Figure 2-3. UML model of the Musician ontology

Figure 2-4 shows a part of the Musician ontology in an equivalent XML-based format. The OWL language (Smith et al., 2004) used in that representation is described in more details in section 3. It is not necessary to go into all the details of this representation, since in practice it is always generated automatically by a graphical ontology editor (see section 2.2.1).

---

[5] Unified Modeling Language (Fowler and Scott, 1999; OMG, 2003).

However, note that it is exactly *that* representation of ontologies that is nowadays most widely used at the implementation level.

```
<owl:Class rdf:ID="Event"/>
<owl:Class rdf:ID="Album"/>
<owl:Class rdf:ID="Instrument"/>
<owl:Class rdf:ID="Musician"/>
<owl:Class rdf:ID="Admirer"/>
<owl:ObjectProperty rdf:ID="author">
        <owl:inverseOf>
                <owl:ObjectProperty rdf:ID="opus"/>
        </owl:inverseOf>
        <rdfs:domain rdf:resource="#Album"/>
        <rdfs:range rdf:resource="#Musician"/>
</owl:ObjectProperty>
<owl:ObjectProperty rdf:ID="player">
        <rdfs:range rdf:resource="#Musician"/>
        <rdfs:domain rdf:resource="#Instrument"/>
</owl:ObjectProperty>
...
<owl: DatatypeProperty rdf:ID="loudness">
        <rdf:type
rdf:resource="http://www.w3.org/2002/07/owl#FunctionalProperty"/>
        <rdfs:domain rdf:resource="#Instrument"/>
                ...
</owl: DatatypeProperty>
...
```

Figure 2-4. Musician ontology represented in OWL (excerpt)

2.1.3   Why ontologies?

Ontology provides a number of useful features to intelligent systems, as well as to knowledge representation in general and to the knowledge engineering process. This subsection summarizes the most important ones, starting from (Chandrasekaran, et al., 1999), (Gruber, 1993), (Guarino, 1995), (McGuinness, 2002), and (Schreiber et al., 1994).

Vocabulary. Ontology provides the *vocabulary* (or names) for referring to the *terms* in that subject area. It is different from human-oriented vocabularies such as glossaries and thesauri (that rely on natural languages and are subject to different interpretations by different people) in that it provides *logical statements* that describe what the terms are, how they are related to each other, how they can or cannot be related to each other. An ontology also specifies *rules* for combining the terms and their relations to define extensions to the vocabulary. As Chandrasekaran et al. (1999) note carefully, it is not the vocabulary as such that qualifies as an ontology, but the conceptualizations that the terms in the vocabulary are intended to capture. Ontology specifies the terms with *unambiguous meanings*, with semantics independent of reader and context. Translating the terms in an ontology from one language to another does not change the ontology conceptually. Thus an ontology provides the vocabulary *and* a machine-processable *common understanding* of the topics the terms denote. The *meanings* of the terms from an ontology can be communicated between users and applications.

Taxonomy. Taxonomy (or *concept hierarchy*) is a hierarchical categorization or classification of entities within the corresponding domain. Each ontology provides a taxonomy in a machine-readable and machine-processable form. However, an ontology is more than the corresponding taxonomy - it is a full specification of a domain. An important taxonomical feature of ontologies is strict subclassing - *subclass-of* relations in an ontology are formally specified, include formal instance relationships, and ensure for consistency in deductive uses of the ontology.

Content theory. Since ontologies identify classes of objects, their relations, and concept hierarchies that exist in some domain, they are quintessentially *content theories* (Chandrasekaran, et al., 1999). Ontologies not only identify those classes, relations, and taxonomies - they specify them in an elaborate way, using specific *ontology representation languages* (see sections 2.2.1 and 3). Classes are specified using frame-based representation principles, i.e. their properties, property values, and possible value restrictions (restrictions on what can fill a property) are specified as well.

Well-structured and elaborated ontologies enable different kinds of *consistency checking* from applications (e.g., type and value checking with ontologies that include class properties and restrictions). They also enable and/or enhance *interoperability* among different applications. For example, we may want to expand the Musician ontology from Figures 2-2 thru 2-4 to include the concept of *street musician* to denote a musician who entertains people in the streets. One way to do it is to define the *performsIn* property in the Musician class and include in the ontology the definition that a street musician is a Musician whose *performsIn* property has the value "Street". This definition may be used to expand the term "StreetMusician" in an application that does not understand that term, but does understand the terms "Musician", "performsAt", and "Street". If that application is asked by another application if a person with certain name is a street musician, it will "understand" the question and may be able to answer by querying a database of musicians to see if it contains an entry with the appropriate values of *name* and *performsAt* fields.

Knowledge sharing and reuse. The major purpose of ontologies is not to serve as vocabularies and taxonomies; they are primarily aimed at *knowledge sharing* and *knowledge reuse* among applications. The point is that each ontology provides a description of the concepts and relationships that can exist in its domain and that can be shared and reused among different intelligent agents and applications (recall that the description looks like a formal specification of a program, as in Figures 2-3 and 2-4). Moreover, working agents and applications should be able to communicate such ontological knowledge. Shared ontologies let us build specific knowledge bases that describe specific situations and yet clearly rely on the same underlying knowledge structure and organization.

There are numerous ways of facilitating knowledge sharing and reuse through ontologies; subsequent chapters of this book cover a number of such ways in the domain of education. Here is another hypothetical example of achieving knowledge sharing and reuse by means of ontologies. Suppose that someone has conducted a thorough ontological analysis of the topic of musicians, and has developed a much more elaborated Musician ontology than that shown in Figures 2-2 thru 2-4. The ontology would include domain-specific terms like *musician* and *musical event*, some general terms such as *profession*, *location*, and *attendance*, as well as terms that describe behavior, such as *playing* and *recording*. The ontology captures the intrinsic conceptual structure of the domain (Chandrasekaran, et al., 1999), and can be used as the basis for developing a rich domain-specific knowledge representation language for building knowledge bases in that domain. The language would provide syntax for encoding knowledge about musicians in terms of the vocabulary, concepts, and relations in the ontology. Anyone who wants to build a knowledge base related to musicians may use that content-rich knowledge representation language and thus eliminate performing the time-consuming knowledge analysis task again - the language will already have a large number of terms that embody the complex content theory of the domain. That way the Musician ontology would be shared among different developers, and reused as the "armature" knowledge in a number of knowledge bases and applications.

Make no mistake, though - in practice, knowledge sharing and reuse is still not easy even if an ontology is readily available for a given purpose. To name but a few reasons, note that there are different languages for representing ontologies, and knowledge base development tools may not support the one used to develop the ontology. There are also competing approaches and working groups, creating different technologies, traditions, and cultures. There may be different ontologies developed to describe the same topic or domain. Selecting one of them may not satisfy all the requirements the knowledge engineer must support. Combining them is anything but easy because subtle differences between them require a lot of manual adjustments, and the resulting ontology may still be inadequate. On top of all that, there is the problem of knowledge maintenance, since all parts of knowledge (including the ontological knowledge) evolve over time.

2.1.4   Key application areas

There are many potential applications of ontologies, but Fikes (1998) offered a high-level list of key application areas: collaboration, interoperation, education, and modeling.

Collaboration. Different people may have different views of the same problem area when working on a team project. To them, ontologies provide a unifying knowledge skeleton as a common and shared reference for further development and participation. Perhaps even more importantly, ontologies play the same role in collaboration between intelligent agents in terms of agent-to-agent communication. Knowledge exchange among different agents is much more feasible when the agents are aware of the ontologies the other agents use as world models.

Interoperation. Ontologies enable information integration from different and disparate sources. End users typically don't show much interest in how they get the information; they are much more interested in getting the information they need, and getting all of it. Distributed applications may need to access different knowledge sources in order to get all the information available, and those different sources may supply information in different formats and at different levels of detail. However, if all the sources recognize the same ontology, data conversion and information integration is easier to do automatically and in a more natural way.

Education. Ontologies are also a good publication medium and source of reference. Since they presumably always result from a wide consensus about the underlying structure of the domain they represent, they can provide reliable and objective information to those who want to learn more about the domain. Simultaneously, domain experts can use ontologies to share their understanding of the domain conceptualization and structure.

Modeling. In modeling intelligent, knowledge-based applications, ontologies represent important reusable building blocks that many specific applications should include as pre-developed knowledge modules. For example, the Musician ontology defines the knowledge that can be used as is in both a recommender system that suggests the users what new musical CD to buy, as well as in a Web-based intelligent educational system that learners may want to use to find out more about famous instrumentalists of the twentieth century.

Fikes' classification can be seen from a more pragmatic perspective as well. In fact, many consider e-commerce to be *the* application domain for ontologies. Ontologies can enable machine-based communication between buyers and sellers, can help in customer profiling tasks, can support vertical integration of markets, and can describe reuse between different marketplaces. In e-commerce, ontologies can be applied in terms of all four categories (roles) that Fikes suggested.

Another extremely demanding general application area provides very fertile soil for applying ontologies - search engines. Ontologies can support structured, comparative, and customized search (McGuinness, 2002). Concepts and taxonomies from ontologies can be used to find pages with syntactically different but semantically similar content, simultaneously eliminating many irrelevant hits.

2.1.5   Examples

A number of useful ontologies developed so far can be found in (and reused from) ontology libraries available on the Web, such as (DAML Ontology Library, 2005), (OWL Ontology Library, 2005), and (Protege Ontologies Library, 2005). As browsing of such libraries shows, the spectrum of domains in which some ontologies have been developed is really wide. The following are but a two examples that show the variety of ontologies and their potential uses. More examples are shown in section 3 of theis chapter; many other examples, related to the domain of education, are discussed in subsequent chapters.

Example 1 - The Gene Ontology project (http://www.geneontology.org/). The project provides a controlled vocabulary to describe gene and gene product attributes in any organism. The ontology has three organizing principles: molecular function, biological process and cellular component. A gene product has one or more molecular functions. Also, a gene product is used in one or more biological processes, and might be associated with one or more cellular components. The ontology is frequently updated and is available for download in various formats.

Example 2 - The Object-Oriented Software Design Ontology (ODOL). The main objective of The Web of Patterns project (http://www-ist.massey.ac.nz/wop/) is to create an ontology to describe the design of object-oriented software. Software design patterns (Gamma et al., 1994) and the related topics should be represented using the concepts developed in the ontology. The aim is to provide a flexible framework that can be used by the software engineering community to share knowledge about software design. The ODOL-based descriptions of patterns are OWL documents that can be imported by popular ontology development editors like Protégé (see section 2.2.1) for a more detailed description of Protégé).

2.2   Ontological engineering

To develop a really useful ontology requires a lot of engineering effort, discipline, and rigor. *Ontological engineering* denotes a set of design principles, development processes and activities, supporting technologies, as well as systematic methodologies that facilitate ontology development and use throughout its life cycle - design, implementation, evaluation, validation, maintenance, deployment, mapping, integration, sharing, and reuse.

Ontological engineering provides design rationale for development of knowledge bases and enables knowledge systematization of the world of interest and accumulation of knowledge (Mizoguchi and Kitamura, 2001). Being content theories, ontologies clarify the structure of domain knowledge. Knowledge engineering of an intelligent system should always include ontological engineering, which implies using specific development tools and methodologies. Developing an ontology requires an effective *ontological analysis* of the domain whose content the ontology should represent. Ontological analysis reveals the domain knowledge concepts, their taxonomies, and the underlying organization. Without it, no knowledge representation for that domain can be well-founded. Through ontological analysis, the entire process of knowledge engineering gets a strong modeling flavor. The resulting knowledge base does not merely transfer the knowledge extracted from a human expert. It also models the behavior of an intelligent agent that can solve problems in the domain (Gaines, 1991), (Gruber, 1993), (Guarino, 1995), (Schreiber et al., 1994).

2.2.1   Ontology development tools

Standard toolset of an ontology engineer includes ontology representation languages and graphical ontology development environments. More recently, ontology learning tools have also started to appear in order to partially automate the development process and help in ontology evolution, updating, and maintenance. Other tools are also required in the context of developing ontologies for deployment on the Semantic Web (see sections 5 and 6 in this chapter).

Ontology representation languages. There are a number of ontology representation languages around. Some of them were developed in the beginning of the 1990s within the AI community. Others appeared in late 1990s and later, resulting from efforts of AI specialists and W3C. Roughly speaking, early ontology representation languages belong to the pre-XML era, whereas the later ones are XML-based. Also, most of the later ones were developed to support ontology representation on the Semantic Web, hence they are also called *Semantic Web languages*. Other common names for them are *Web-based ontology languages* and *ontology markup languages* (Corcho et al., 2003).

Describing different ontology representation languages is beyond the scope of this book. For such descriptions and examples of early ontology representation languages see (Genesereth and Fikes, 1992), (Gruber, 1992), (MacGregor, 1991). Some of the widely used Web-based ontology languages are briefly covered in section 3. Recently, the trend is to represent ontologies in OWL (Smith et al., 2004).

Ontology development environments. No matter what ontology representation language is used, there is usually a graphical *ontology editor* to aid the developer organize the overall conceptual structure of the ontology, add concepts, properties, relations, and constraints, and possibly reconcile syntactic, logical, and semantic inconsistencies among the ontology elements. In addition to ontology editors, there are also other tools that help manage different versions of ontologies, convert them into other formats and languages, map and link between ontologies from heterogeneous sources, compare them, reconcile and validate them, as well as merge them. Still other tools can help acquire, organize, and visualize the domain knowledge before and during the building of a formal ontology (Denny, 2002).

Graphical *ontology development environments* integrate an ontology editor with other tools and usually support multiple ontology representation languages. They are aimed at providing support for the entire ontology development process and for the subsequent ontology usage (Corcho et al., 2003).

Currently, the leading ontology development editor and environment is *Protégé*, developed at Stanford University (Protégé, 2005). It facilitates defining ontology concepts (classes), properties, taxonomies, and various restrictions, as well as class instances (the actual data in the knowledge base). Furthermore, its uniform GUI, Figure 2-5, also has a tab for creation of a knowledge-acquisition tool for collecting knowledge in a knowledge base conforming to the ontology. Customizable forms determine how instance information is presented and entered. The knowledge base can then be used with a problem-solving method to perform different inference tasks.

Protégé supports several ontology representation languages, including OWL. Some forms of reasoning over the ontologies developed with Protégé are also facilitated; for example, since OWL is based on description logics, inferences such as satisfiability and subsumption tests are automatically enabled. Also, Protégé's plug-in based extensible architecture allows for integration with a number of other tools, applications, knowledge bases, and storage formats.

Other environments. Although Protégé is currently the most widely used ontology development environment, there are literally dozens of other tools and environments. A relatively recent comparative survey by Denny (2004) discovered the fact that there is a lot of room for improvement in all such environments. For example, a number of users suggested an enhancement in the form of a higher-level abstraction of ontology language constructs to allow for more intuitive and more powerful knowledge modeling expressions. Many users also demand friendlier visual/spatial navigation among concept trees/graphs and linking relations, more options for using reasoning facilities to help explore, compose and check ontologies, more features for aligning ontologies with one another, and tools that would help integrate them with other data resources like enterprise databases. Desirable improvements also include support for natural language processing and collaborative development.

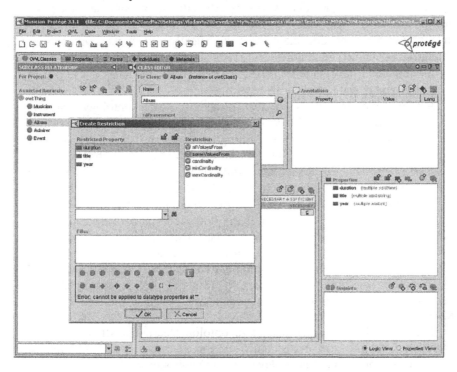

Figure 2-5. A screen from Protégé

The overall sentiment expressed by users of different ontology development environments clearly reflected the need for facilitating the use of such tools by domain experts rather than by ontologists. Likewise, there is a strong need for integration of ontology development environments with existing domain and core ontologies and libraries, as well as with standard vocabularies. Another, more contemporary focus is emerging as well - ontology development in concert with enterprise application integration and development trends.

Ontology learning tools. Ontology development is hard work. Even with the most advanced ontology development languages, environments, and methodologies, the major problem in ontological engineering still remains in the area of knowledge acquisition and maintenance - collection of domain concepts and relations, achieving consensus on them among the domain experts and other interested parties, and frequent updates due to the dynamics of the domain knowledge structure and its unpredictable changes over time.

That fact has created the idea of *ontology learning* with the objective to partially automate the processes of ontology development and maintenance by developing tools and frameworks to help extract, annotate, and integrate new information with the old one in the ontology. Typical sources of information are Web documents that sufficiently reflect the dynamics of changes in most domains. A typical prerequisite for enabling (semi)automated information extraction from Web documents is the use of natural language and text processing technologies.

An example of efforts in this direction is the ontology learning framework proposed by Maedche and Staab (2001). They have also developed a supporting ontology learning environment called Text-To-Onto workbench. The framework and the tool are based on an architecture that combines knowledge acquisition with machine learning from Web documents. The framework recognizes the fact that traditional machine learning techniques rely on data from structured knowledge bases or databases, hence are not applicable to documents and other sources of information on the Web, which are at best partially structured or semi-structured. Instead, the framework relies on natural language processing, data mining, and text mining technologies. The specific techniques it applies are ontology learning from free text, dictionaries, and legacy ontologies, reverse engineering of ontologies from database schemata, and learning from XML documents.

There are also other approaches to ontology learning. All of them are promising, but are still pretty much in the research phase and are not integrated in common ontology development environments like Protégé.

2.2.2   Ontology development methodology

Ontology development methodology comprises a set of established principles, processes, practices, methods, and activities used to design, construct, evaluate, and deploy ontologies. Several such methodologies have been reported in the literature. From surveys like those in (Corcho et al., 2003) and (Staab and Studer, 2004), it follows that:

• most ontology development methodologies that have been proposed focus on *building* ontologies;
• some other methodologies also include methods for *merging, re-engineering, maintaining,* and *evolving* ontologies;
• yet other methodologies build on general software development processes and practices and apply them to ontology development.

There is such a thing as the best methodology, because there is no single "correct" way to model a domain. Also, ontology development is necessarily an iterative process.

Among the methodologies from the first of the above three categories, some are fairly general and merely suggest steps to follow in the ontology development process. An example is the simple methodology proposed by Fridman-Noy and McGuinness (2001). Other advise specific ontology development processes (like the one proposed by Van der Vet and Mars (1998) for bottom-up construction of ontologies).

An example of more comprehensive methodologies is the *Methontology framework* (Fernández-López et al., 1999). Methontology's starting point is that ontological engineering requires definition and standardization of the entire ontology life cycle - from requirements specification to maintenance - as well as methodologies and techniques that drive ontology development through the life cycle. So, the Methontology framework includes:

- identification of the ontology development process;
- a life cycle based on evolving prototypes;
- the methodology itself, which specifies the steps for performing each activity, the techniques used, the products of each activity, and an ontology evaluation procedure.

Examples of the third category of ontology development methodologies and processes - those that rely on general software engineering principles - can be found in (Devedžić, 1999), (Devedžić, 2002), and (Gašević et al., 2006). These ontology development methodologies heavily rely on the principles of object-oriented software analysis and design. The rationale is as follows. Ontologies represent concepts, their properties, property values, events and their causes and effects, processes, and time (Chandrasekaran et al., 1999). Also, ontologies always comprise some hierarchy, and most ontologies represent and support generalization, inheritance, aggregation (part-of), and instantiation relationships among their concepts. Almost all of these issues are relevant in any object-oriented analysis and design of a problem domain. Moreover, the processes that ontological engineers use in ontology development (see above) almost coincide with established processes of object-oriented analysis and design (e.g., see Larman, 2001). In both cases, it is important to assemble the domain vocabulary in the beginning, often starting from the domain's generic nouns, verbs, and adjectives. The result of object-oriented analysis is actually a draft of the domain ontology relevant to the application. True, software analysts don't call that result ontology. Object-oriented analysis stresses different aspects than ontological analysis does, but parallels are obvious.

2.3   Applications

Ontologies become a major conceptual backbone for a broad spectrum of applications (Staab and Studer, 2004). There is an increasing awareness among researchers and developers that ontologies are not just for knowledge-based systems, but for all software systems - all software needs models of the world, hence can make use of ontologies at design time (Chandrasekaran et al., 1999). Major application fields for ontologies nowadays include knowledge management, e-Learning, e-Commerce, integration of Web resources, intranet documents, and databases, as well as cooperation of Web services and enterprise applications, natural language processing, intelligent information retrieval (especially from the Internet), virtual organizations, and simulation and modeling. The following examples from a broad spectrum of ontology application scenarios are but a few typical illustrations. However, they have been carefully selected to also serve as an introduction to Semantic Web-based education, which this book is about - there is a notable importance of the ideas underlying these examples for educational applications on the Semantic Web.

Magpie (Domingue et al., 2004). Magpie is a tool that supports semantic interpretation of Web pages, thus enabling intelligent Web browsing. It automatically associates an ontology-based semantic layer to Web resources, which enables invoking relevant services within a standard Web browser. In other words, ontologies make possible to associate meaning to information on a Web page and then, on the basis of the identified meaning, to offer the user appropriate functionalities. In fact, Magpie offers complementary knowledge sources relevant to a Web resource, thus facilitating quick access to the underlying background knowledge and making sense out of content and contextual information on the Web pages the user may be unfamiliar with.

Magpie works as a plug-in to standard Web browsers and appears as an additional toolbar in the browser. It relies on the availability of ontologies that represent different domains of discourse. The user can select an ontology for Magpie to work with, and the buttons that will appear in the Magpie toolbar will correspond to the concepts in the ontology. He/She can then use the Magpie toolbar to toggle highlighting for specific concepts of his/her interest for the browsing session. The underlying selected ontology must be populated with instances, possibly automatically mined from relevant Web pages. The browser showing a Web page will then highlight information related to the types of entities from the ontology that the user has selected in the Magpie toolbar. For example, if the selected ontology is the Musician ontology, and the highlighted concepts in the Magpie toolbar are Instrument and Album, in the home page of, say, a rock 'n' roll star shown in the browser the words like "guitar" and "keyboards" will be highlighted, and so will be the titles of the star's albums.

Magpie detects patterns in the browsing session by tracking interesting items in the browsing log with the aid of the ontology-based filter. When a pattern is detected, Magpie activates an appropriate context-dependent trigger service. In the case of the Musician ontology and Web pages related to musicians and their activities, Magpie may use one panel to show the names of the musicians it semantically recognized from the Web pages in the browsing log, and another panel to show the titles of all of the albums related to them one way or another. Moreover, in yet another panel it may show musicians and albums not explicitly mentioned on the pages accessed in that session, but coming from the populated ontology. This explicitly reveals to the user the information semantically related to the context of the browsing session. Right-clicking any of the highlighted concepts on the page shown, the user can access from a pop-up menu any of the context-dependent (ontology-dependent) semantic services. In the case of musicians, these might be their concerts and tours, colleagues, managers, and so forth.

Briefing Associate (Tallis et al., 2002). Knowledge sharing and reuse through automatic exchange of Web documents among applications and agents is possible only if the documents contain ontologically encoded information, often called semantic markup or semantic annotation, that software agents and tools can accurately and reliably interpret. Current annotation technology is covered in more detail in section 5, but it suffices for this overview of Briefing Associate to note that annotation is usually performed manually (using annotation tools), which is a tedious and error prone process. Briefing Associate deploys ontological knowledge to encode document annotation automatically as authors produce documents.

The approach used in Briefing Associate can be simply described as extending a commercial, frequently used document editor with ontology-based additional tools that targeted category of authors will be highly motivated to use. Whenever such an author applies any of the additional tools, an appropriate annotation gets automatically created and inserted into the document. Thus annotation comes at virtually no extra cost, as a byproduct of activities the author would perform anyway. The prerequisites include the existence of domain ontologies that authors creating documents could rely on, and easy creation of specific widgets to represent the ontology-based additional editing tools.

To this end, Briefing Associate is implemented as an extension of Microsoft's PowerPoint in much the same way Magpie extends standard Web browsers (see above) - it appears in PowerPoint's native GUI as a toolbar for adding graphics that represent a particular ontology's classes and properties. The graphical symbols on the toolbar come from a special-purpose tool that lets graphic designers create such symbols to visually annotate ontologies. In a hypothetical example, the Musician ontology might be visualized with that tool and different graphical symbols might be created to represent musical events, instruments, and the other concepts from the ontology. These symbols would then be inserted in the toolbar to represent the domain ontology (Musician) in PowerPoint.

To the domain author, the native PowerPoint GUI is still there, and the editing process continues normally, and the resulting slide show looks as if the ontology was not used in the presentation editing. However, using any graphical symbol from the additional toolbar in the presentation document results in inserting a transparent annotation into the slides, which is saved with the document. PowerPoint installations not extended with Briefing Associate ignore such transparent annotation. However, the point is that the annotation can be used by Briefing Associate internally to produce different metadata (such as document title, author, reference to the ontology used, etc.). Furthermore, additional XML-based documents that can be published on the Web for other agents and applications to locate the main document more easily, and to automatically interpret its contents in terms of the concepts from the ontology.

Quickstep and *Foxtrot* (Middleton et al., 2004). Quickstep and Foxtrot are ontology-based recommender systems that recommend online academic research papers. Although they both focus on a relatively small target group of Web users, the principles built in these two systems can be translated to other target groups as well.

In general, recommender systems unobtrusively watch user behavior and recommend new items that correlate with a user's profile. A typical example of such recommendation can be found on Amazon.com, where the users get suggestions on what books, CDs, and other items to buy, according to their observed shopping behavior and a previously created set of user profiles. Recommender systems usually create user profiles based on user ratings of specific items and item contents, which in many cases may be insufficient and can lead to inconsistent recommendations.

Quickstep and Foxtrot rely on ontology-based user profiling. They use a research paper topic ontology to represent user interests in ontological terms. True, some of the fine-grained information held in the raw examples of interest gets lost that way. However, the ontology allows inference to assist user profiling through is-a relationships in the topic classification. Moreover, communication with other external ontologies is enabled, and so is visualization of user profiles in terms of the topic ontology. Both systems provide a set of labeled example papers for each concept in the ontology to assist creation of initial user profiles. The users themselves can add papers of their interests to such sets in order to fine-tune their profiles and to reflect their changing needs. Through profile visualization, the users can better understand what the recommenders "think" about their interests and adjust the profiles interactively.

3. SEMANTIC WEB LANGUAGES

In literature, the terms Web-based ontology languages and Semantic Web languages are used interchangeably. However, W3C is more specific on what Semantic Web languages are:

"The Semantic Web Activity develops specifications for technologies that are ready for large scale deployment, and identifies infrastructure components through open source advanced development. The principal technologies of the Semantic Web fit into a set of layered specifications. The current components are the Resource Description Framework (RDF) Core Model, the RDF Schema language and the Web Ontology language (OWL). Building on these core components is a standardized query language, SPARQL (pronounced "sparkle"), enabling the 'joining' of decentralized collections of RDF data. These languages all build on the foundation of URIs, XML, and XML namespaces." (W3C SW Activity, 2005)

The above statement is a rough textual equivalent of Tim Berners-Lee's vision of Web development, aptly nicknamed *Semantic Web layer-cake*, Figure 2-6 (Berners-Lee et al., 1999), (Berners-Lee et al., 2001). Note that higher-level languages in the Semantic Web layer-cake use the syntax and semantics of the lower levels.

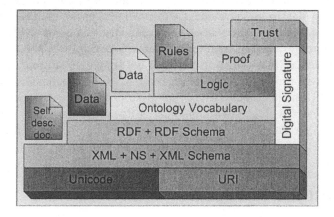

Figure 2-6. Tim Berners-Lee's Semantic Web layer-cake

3.1   XML and XML Schema

It is important for Semantic Web developers to agree on the data's syntax and semantics before hard-coding them into their applications, since changes to syntax and semantics necessitate expensive application modifications (Wuwongse et al., 2002). That's why all Semantic Web languages use XML syntax; in fact, XML is a metalanguage for representing other Semantic Web languages. For example, XML Schema defines a class of XML documents using the XML syntax. RDF provides a framework for representing metadata about Web resources, and can be expressed in XML as well. RDF Schema, OWL, and other ontology languages also use the XML syntax.

Generally, *XML (eXtensible Markup Language)* enables specification and markup of computer-readable documents (Klein, 2001), (XML, 2004). It looks very much like HTML in that special sequences of characters - tags - are used to mark up the document content, and that XML data is stored as ordinary text. Unlike HTML, XML can be used to represent documents of arbitrary structure, and there is no fixed tag vocabulary.

Each *XML Schema* provides the necessary framework for creating a category of XML documents (XML Schema, 2005). The schema describes the various tags, elements, and attributes of an XML document of that specific category, the valid document structure, constraints, and custom data types (these are based on built-in types, such as integer, string, etc.). XML Schema language also provides some limited support for specifying the number of occurrences of child elements, default values, choice groups, etc. The encoding syntax of XML Schema language is XML. To disambiguate between possibly identical tags defined by different parties and used in the same schema definition, XML Schema documents use *namespaces* that are declared using the *xmlns* attribute. Different namespaces in XML Shema documents (as well as other documents encoded using an XML-based language) are represented by prefixes such as *rdfs:* and *owl:* in Figure 2-4.

Note, however, that XML itself does not imply a specific machine interpretation of the data. The information in XML documents is only encoded in an unambiguous syntax, but its use and the semantics is not specified. In other words, XML aims only at document structure, not at its common machine interpretation. It provides only a data format for structured documents, without specifying a vocabulary. To represent knowledge and semantics, more expressive XML-based languages are necessary.

3.2   RDF and RDF Schema

Resource Description Framework (RDF) is a language that provides a model for representing data about "things on the Web" (resources) in terms of *object-attribute-value triplets* (*O-A-V triplets*) and semantic networks, well-known knowledge representation techniques from AI. A resource description in RDF is a list of *statements* (triplets), each expressed in terms of a Web *resource* (object), one of its *properties* (attributes), and the property *value* (Manola and Miller, 2004). The value can be a literal (text), or another resource. Each RDF description can be also represented as a directed labeled graph (semantic network), parts of which are equivalent to RDF statements. Figure 2-7 shows several such triplets and the corresponding graph. They can be represented in RDF encoding (which also uses XML syntax) as in Figure 2-8.

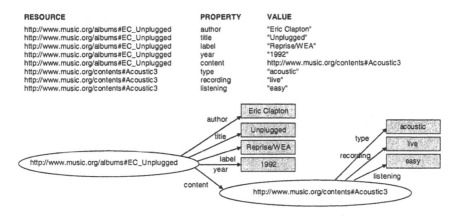

RESOURCE	PROPERTY	VALUE
http://www.music.org/albums#EC_Unplugged	author	"Eric Clapton"
http://www.music.org/albums#EC_Unplugged	title	"Unplugged"
http://www.music.org/albums#EC_Unplugged	label	"Reprise/WEA"
http://www.music.org/albums#EC_Unplugged	year	"1992"
http://www.music.org/albums#EC_Unplugged	content	http://www.music.org/contents#Acoustic3
http://www.music.org/contents#Acoustic3	type	"acoustic"
http://www.music.org/contents#Acoustic3	recording	"live"
http://www.music.org/contents#Acoustic3	listening	"easy"

Figure 2-7. Examples of RDF resources, properties, and values, and the corresponding graph

```
<Album rdf:ID="EC_Unplugged"
       xmlns:rdf="http://www.w3.org/1999/02/22-rdf-syntax-ns#"
       xmlns="http://www.music.org/albums#"
       xml:base="http://www.music.org/albums">
  <author>Eric Clapton</author>
  <title>Unplugged</title>
  <label>Reprise/WEA</label>
  <year>1992</year>
  <content>
    <Content rdf:ID="Acoustic3"
             xmlns="http://www.music.org/contents#">
      <type>acoustic</type>
      <listening>easy</listening>
      <recording>live</recording>
    </Content>
  </content>
</Album>
```

Figure 2-8. RDF encoding of the resources from Figure 2-7

RDF model itself provides only a domain-neutral mechanism to describe individual resources. It neither defines (a priori) the semantics of any application domain, nor makes assumptions about a particular domain. Defining domain-specific features and their semantics, i.e. ontologies, requires additional facilities. RDF itself is used to describe instances of ontologies, whereas RDF Schema encodes ontologies.

RDF Schema (or RDFS) provides an XML-based vocabulary to specify classes and their relationships, to define properties and associate them with classes, and to enable creating taxonomies (Brickley and Guha, 2004). To do all that, RDFS uses frame-based modeling primitives from AI, such as *Class*, *subClassOf*, *Property*, and *subPropertyOf*. The *Resource* concept is in the root of all hierarchies and taxonomies. Figure 2-9 shows an example of RDFS encoding.

```
<rdf:RDF        xmlns:rdf="http://www.w3.org/1999/02/22-rdf-syntax-ns#"
                xmlns:rdfs="http://www.w3.org/2000/01/rdf-schema#"
                xml:base="http://www.music.org/albums">

   <rdfs:Class rdf:ID="Album">
      <rdfs:subClassOf rdf:resource="http://www.w3.org/2000/01/rdf-schema#Resource"/>
   </rdfs:Class>

   <rdfs:Class rdf:ID="Content">
      <rdfs:subClassOf rdf:resource="http://www.w3.org/2000/01/rdf-schema#Resource"/>
   </rdfs:Class>

   ...

   <rdf:Property rdf:ID="author">
      <rdfs:domain rdf:resource="#Album"/>
      <rdfs:range rdf:resource="#Musician"/>
   </rdf:Property>

   ...

   <rdf:Property rdf:ID="year">
      <rdfs:domain rdf:resource="#Album"/>
      <rdfs:range rdf:resource="http://www.w3.org/2000/01/rdf-schema#Literal"/>
   </rdf:Property>

   ...

</rdf:RDF>
```

Figure 2-9. RDFS encoding of albums (excerpt)

There is an important departure in RDFS from the classic frame-based paradigm: properties are defined separately from classes. An implication is that anyone, anywhere, anytime can create a property and state that it is usable with a class, or with multiple classes. Each property is typically described by *rdfs:domain* and *rdfs:range*, which restrict the possible combinations of properties and classes. For example, in Figure 2-9 the domain of the *year* property is restricted to the *Album* class, which means that the property is used only with that class. On the other hand, a property may be defined to feature multiple classes. As in the classic case, in class hierarchies classes inherit properties from their ancestors.

RDF and RDF Schema (or RDF(S), for short) provide a standard model to describe facts about Web resources, but modelers often need still richer and more expressive primitives to specify formal semantics of Web resources. RDFS is quite simple compared to full-fledged knowledge representation languages. For example, one cannot state in RDFS that "this class is equivalent to this second class", and cannot specify cardinality constraints.

3.3 OWL

OWL (Smith et al., 2004) is a direct successor of *DAML+OIL* (Horrocks and van Harmelen, 2002), (Scott Cost et al., 2002), which in turn is a Semantic Web language resulted from merging two other Web ontology languages, *DAML* (more precisely, *DAML-ONT* (Hendler and McGuinness, 2000)), and OIL (Fensel et al., 2001), both of which were heavily influenced by RDF(S), Figure 2-10.

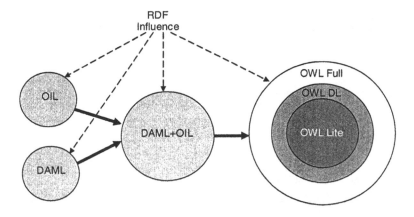

Figure 2-10. Genesis of OWL

Like its predecessors, OWL vocabulary includes a set of XML elements and attributes, with well-defined meanings. They are used to describe domain terms and their relationships in an ontology. In fact, OWL vocabulary is built on top of RDF(S) vocabulary. Things like *Class* and *subClassOf* exist in OWL as well, and so do many more as DAML+OIL heritage. For example, OWL (just like DAML+OIL) divides the universe into two disjoint parts - the *datatype domain* (the values that belong to XML Schema datatypes), and *object domain* (individual objects considered to be instances of classes described within OWL or RDF). Likewise, there are generally two sorts of OWL properties - those that relate objects to other objects (specified with *owl:ObjectProperty*), and those that relate objects to datatype values (specified with *owl:DatatypeProperty*). The syntax for classes and properties is similar to that of DAML+OIL (Horrocks and van Harmelen, 2002), Figure 2-11; instances of classes and properties are written in RDF(S) syntax, Figure 2-9.

```
<?xml version="1.0"?>
<rdf:RDF
   xmlns="http://www.music.org/musicians.owl#"
   xmlns:rdf="http://www.w3.org/1999/02/22-rdf-syntax-ns#"
   xmlns:xsd="http://www.w3.org/2001/XMLSchema#"
   xmlns:rdfs="http://www.w3.org/2000/01/rdf-schema#"
   xmlns:owl="http://www.w3.org/2002/07/owl#"
 xml:base="http://www.music.org/musicians.owl">
 <owl:Ontology rdf:about="Musician"/>
 <owl:Class rdf:ID="Musician"/>
 <owl:Class rdf:ID="musician_Class_13">
   <rdfs:subClassOf rdf:resource="#Musician"/>
 </owl:Class>
 <owl:Class rdf:ID="Instrument"/>
 <owl:Class rdf:ID="Album">
   <rdfs:subClassOf rdf:resource="http://www.w3.org/2002/07/owl#Thing"/>
   <rdfs:subClassOf>
    <owl:Restriction>
     <owl:onProperty rdf:resource="#title"/>
     <owl:cardinality rdf:datatype="http://www.w3.org/2001/XMLSchema#int">1</owl:cardinality>
    </owl:Restriction>
   </rdfs:subClassOf>
   <rdfs:subClassOf>
    <owl:Restriction>
     <owl:onProperty rdf:resource="#year"/>
     <owl:cardinality rdf:datatype="http://www.w3.org/2001/XMLSchema#int">1</owl:cardinality>
    </owl:Restriction>
   </rdfs:subClassOf>
 </owl:Class>
 <owl:ObjectProperty rdf:ID="author">
   <owl:equivalentProperty rdf:resource="#artist"/>
   <rdfs:domain rdf:resource="#Album"/>
   <rdfs:range rdf:resource="#Musician"/>
 </owl:ObjectProperty>
 <owl:ObjectProperty rdf:about="#artist">
   <rdfs:range rdf:resource="#Musician"/>
   <rdfs:domain rdf:resource="#Album"/>
 </owl:ObjectProperty>
 ...
```

Figure 2-11. An excerpt of the Musician ontology developed in Protégé

Nowadays, OWL is *the* language for representing ontologies and a universal Semantic Web language that can enable machines to read and interpret data and draw inferences from it. In addition to providing rules and definitions similar to RDF(S), OWL also enables specifying further constraints and relationships among resources, including cardinality, domain and range restrictions, and union, disjunction, inverse, and transitive rules.

A great feature of OWL vocabulary is its extreme richness for describing relations among classes, properties, and individuals. For example, we can specify in OWL that a property is, e.g., *Symmetric*, *InverseOf* another one, *equivalentProperty* of another one, and *Transitive*; that a certain property has some specific *cardinality*, or *minCardinality*, or *maxCardinality*; we can also state that a class is defined to be an *intersectionOf* or a *unionOf* some other classes, and that it is a *complementOf* another class; similarly, a class instance can be the *sameIndividualAs* another instance, or it can be required to be *differentFrom* a certain other instance; and so on. For example, using the *equivalentProperty* relation in Figure 2-11 the object properties *author* and *artist* are specified to be equivalent. Thus if an instance of Album specifies its *artist*, and an application "knowing" that an album must have its *author* consults the ontology to "understand" what the instance is about, it will infer that the *artist* specified in the instance is actually the *author* of the album. A nice consequence is that reasoning can be performed in spite of such terminological differences.

Another important DAML+OIL heritage is OWL's layered structure, also indicated in Figure 2-10. In fact, OWL is not a closed language; it is rather a combination of three increasingly expressive sublanguages building on top of each other, designed to suit different communities of implementers and users. *OWL Lite* is supposed to support building simple classification hierarchies and simple constraints. To this end, specifying some constrains in OWL Lite is rather restricted; for example, the only cardinality values permitted in OWL Lite are 0 or 1. *OWL DL* reflects the description logics foundation of its predecessor, DAML+OIL. OWL DL provides the maximum expressiveness, but also guarantees that all conclusions computable and will finish in finite time. It includes all OWL language constructs, although it imposes certain restrictions for using them. *OWL Full* supports users who want maximum expressiveness and the syntactic freedom of RDF, but does not guarantee computational completeness and decidability. OWL Full can be viewed as an extension of RDF, while OWL Lite and OWL DL can be viewed as extensions of a restricted view of RDF (see (Smith et al., 2004) for details).

3.4   SPARQL

Unlike OWL and RDF(S), SPARQL is not intended for ontology and resource representation, but for querying Web data; precisely, it is a query language for RDF (W3C SPARQL, 2005).

To understand SPARQL, the view of RDF resources as semantic networks (set of triplets, Figure 2-7) helps. SPARQL can be used to:
- extract information from RDF graphs in the form of URIs, bNodes, plain and typed literals;
- extract RDF subgraphs;
- construct new RDF graphs based on information in the queried graphs.

Conceptually, SPARQL queries match graph patterns against the target graph of the query. The patterns are like RDF graphs, but may contain named variables in place of some of the nodes (resources) or links/predicates (i.e., properties). The simplest graph pattern is like a single RDF triplet (resource-property-value triplet, or O-A-V triplet). For example, consider two RDF triplets in Figure 2-12. Clearly, they both match the simple triplet pattern shown in Figure 2-13. A *binding* is a mapping from a variable in a query to terms. Each triplet from Figure 2-12 is a *pattern solution* (a set of correct bindings) for the pattern in Figure 2-13. *Query results* in SPARQL are sets of *pattern solutions*. The results of the query represented by the pattern in Figure 2-13 are the following pattern solutions:

album	**author**
http://www.music.org/albums#EC_Unplugged	Eric Clapton
http://www.music.org/albums#PG_UP	Peter Gabriel

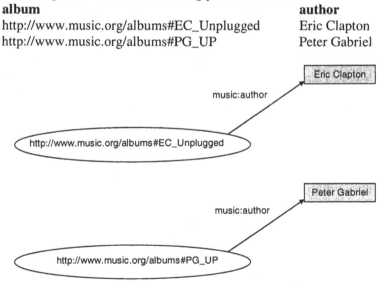

Figure 2-12. Simple RDF triplets

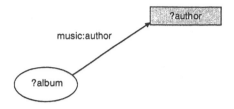

Figure 2-13. A simple RDF triplet pattern

Simple graph patterns can be combined using various operators into more complicated graph patterns. For example, the graph in Figure 2-14 matches the more complex pattern shown in Figure 2-15, and the pattern solution is:

album http://www.music.org/albums#EC_Unplugged
ccontent http://www.music.org/contents#Acoustic3
recording live

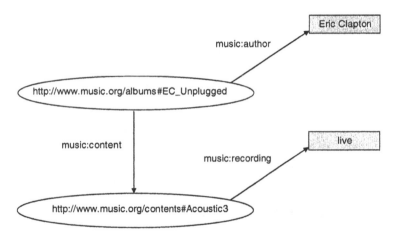

Figure 2-14. A more complex RDF graph

Syntactically, SPARQL queries are of the form presented in Figure 2-16. Obviously, the syntax closely resembles that of database query languages such as SQL. The SELECT clause contains variables, beginning with "?" or "$". The WHERE clause contains a pattern. Prefixes are used as an abbreviation mechanism for URIs/namespaces and apply to the whole query.

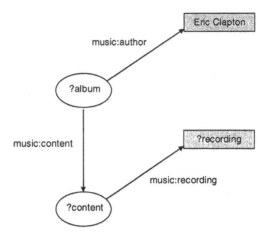

Figure 2-15. A more complex SPARQL pattern

```
SELECT      ?author
WHERE       { <http://www.music.org/albums#EC_Unplugged> <http://www.music.org/elements/auhor> ?author }

PREFIX      music: <http://www.music.org/elements/>
SELECT      ?author
WHERE       { <http://www.music.org/albums#EC_Unplugged> music:author ?author }

PREFIX      music: <http://www.music.org/elements/>
PREFIX      : <http://www.music.org/albums>
SELECT      $author
WHERE       { :EC_Unplugged  music:author  $author }
```

Figure 2-16. Examples of SPARQL queries

4.   THE ROLE OF ONTOLOGIES

Another direct answer to the question "Why ontologies?" posed in section 2.1.3 is: Because they are essential building blocks in the infrastructure of the Semantic Web. Semantic-level interoperation among Web applications is possible only if semantics of Web data is explicitly represented on the Web as well, in the form of machine-understandable domain and content theories - ontologies. Through automatic use and machine interpretation of ontologies, computers themselves can offer enhanced support and automation in accessing and processing Web information. This is qualitatively different from the established practices of using the Web in terms of extracting and interpreting information - instead of putting the main burden on the user, Semantic Web should do much of that job itself (Fensel and Musen, 2001).

Ontologies enable access to a huge network of machine-understandable and machine-processable human knowledge, Figure 2-17, encoded in XML-based formats. Once the essential knowledge of a certain domain is put on the Web in the form of interconnecting ontologies, it creates a solid basis for further development of intelligent applications in the domain because it alleviates the problem of knowledge acquisition.

More specifically, ontologies play multiple roles in the architecture of the Semantic Web (see Figure 2-6):

- they enable Web-based knowledge processing, sharing, and reuse between applications, by sharing of common concepts and specialization of concepts and vocabulary for reuse across multiple applications;
- they establish further levels of interoperability (semantic interoperability) on the Web in terms of mappings between terms within the data, which requires content analysis;
- they add a further representation and inference layer on top of the Web's current layers, Figure 2-6;
- they enable intelligent services (information brokers, search agents, information filters, intelligent information integration, knowledge management,... - see section 6 for details).

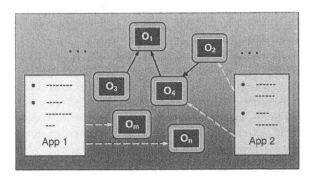

Figure 2-17. Interconnecting ontologies and applications on the Semantic Web

Note, however, that prerequisites for all of the above roles include not only an initial effort of interested communities in creating ontologies, but also considerable discipline in annotating relevant applications and Web resources to make them aware of and interconnected with ontologies (see the next section). Also, supporting tools are needed for those millions of developers of Web pages and applications who weave their domain knowledge into the Web daily. Using knowledge representation techniques in such tools becomes increasingly important. Last but not the least, an all-encompassing framework for developing the network of ontologies and interconnecting them across domains is also highly desirable. Efforts are underway to provide such a framework in the form of a *standard upper ontology* (SUO WG, 2005). Such an ontology should formulate a comprehensive set of formal definitions of upper-level, general-purpose terms to act as a foundation for more specific domain ontologies. For example, standard upper ontology is supposed to define and formally represent concepts like *thing, entity, object, relation, time, quantity, abstraction, collection*, and the like.

5.   SEMANTIC MARKUP

Ontologies merely serve to standardize and provide interpretations for Web content. To make content machine-understandable, Web resources must contain *semantic markup*, or *semantic annotation* - descriptions which use the terminology that one or more ontologies define (Heflin and Hendler, 2001). Such ontologically annotated Web resources enable reasoning about their contents and advanced query-answering services. They also support ontology creation and maintenance, and help map between different ontologies.

Through the process of semantic markup of Web resources, information is added to the resources without changing the originals. The added information may serve human users in much the same way highlighted text does in paper-based documents, or, more importantly, may enhance semantic analysis and processing of Web resources by computers. For example, semantic annotations may help intelligent agents discover Web resources more easily, or they may indicate that contents of different resources are semantically similar. Also, adequate metadata about semantic markup of a resource might help search engines locate the right information.

There are several levels of sophistication in annotating Web resources and make applications using the markup. The simplest approach is to use annotation tools to mark up downloaded Web pages manually and save the annotations together with the pages locally. Typically, such annotations come in the form of highlighted text, new elements inserted in the document, and hyperlinks. However, Web servers normally do not allow uploading annotated Web resources back. A more sophisticated approach is to save the markup in a separate document (locally, or on a remote server) and load it in browser along with the document. The next step up in sophistication is provided by collaborative Wiki sites that let their users insert and share their comments and other annotations along with the Web pages.

None of the above cases has to be supported by explicitly represented ontologies. As a consequence, such approaches are aimed mainly to support human users. On the other hand, if ontologies are used to drive the markup creation, then machine consumers can make use of annotations as well. Ontology-based annotation tools enable linking unstructured and semistructured information sources with ontologies.

There are numerous approaches to ontology-based markup (Handschuh and Staab, 2003a). As an illustration, consider how semantic markup is done according to the CREAM framework (Handschuh and Staab, 2002; 2003b). The framework is suitable for both annotation of existing Web pages and content annotation while authoring a Web page. The key concept in the CREAM framework is *relational metadata*, i.e. metadata that instantiate interrelated definitions of classes in a domain ontology. More precisely, for different instantiations of classes and properties in an ontology there may exist several semantic relationships; relational metadata are annotations that contain relationship instances. The annotations are represented as XML serialization of RDF triplets and are attached to HTML pages as in the hypothetical and simplified example shown in Figure 2-18. Assume a Web page at the hypothetical URL http://www.guitar.org/legendaryrecordings contains information about the *Unplugged* album by Eric Clapton, whose homepage is at http://www.ericclapton.com/. Assume also that the Musician ontology sketched in Figure 2-2 is implemented in OWL and used to annotate the two Web pages. Furthermore, let two namespaces be defined as:

xmlns:musician="http://www.music.org/musicians#"
xmlns:album="http://www.music.org/albums#"

Obviously, the markup attached to the Web pages uses the terminology defined in the ontology. The *musician:records* part of the markup attached to the musician's homepage points to the Web page of the album, thus making a semantic connection between the two pages. The annotation itself may be created using a user-friendly graphical tool such as Ont-O-Mat, which is a specific implementation of the CREAM framework that Handschuh and Staab used (2002; 2003b). In Ont-O-Mat, the author can design a new Web page or can load and display an existing one to be annotated. In either case, while editing the Web page the author can also load an ontology to be used for markup and display its term hierarchies and concept/attribute descriptions graphically. By selecting parts of the contents of the Web page being edited and connecting them with the terms in the ontology by simple mouse clicks and drag-and-drop operations, the author can produce the markup almost for free - not much additional effort is needed to insert the annotations with such a graphical tool. When in the end the author saves the Web page, the markup is saved as well.

The CREAM framework has evolved over the years (Handschuh et al., 2003a, 2003b) to enable querying semantically a Web site about the resources it publishes. The resources are typically kept in a database on a server, and the site developer may annotate the database model (i.e., the entities and their relationships) and publish such annotations in RDF. The annotations will describe the structure of all the tables involved in query to the site, thus acting as an API that hides the intricacies of the database access on the server side. A suitable place for publishing the annotations is the header part of the site's main Web page. A client may want to use a specific ontology to put semantic queries to the server. To do that, the client must first create rules for mapping between the terms in his/her ontology and the terms used in the database model on the server side and published there as a set of RDF annotations. The tool called OntoEdit can be used to create and publish the mapping rules. The user (or the third party) can then load both the ontology and the mapping rules to query the database, e.g. through a Web-service API.

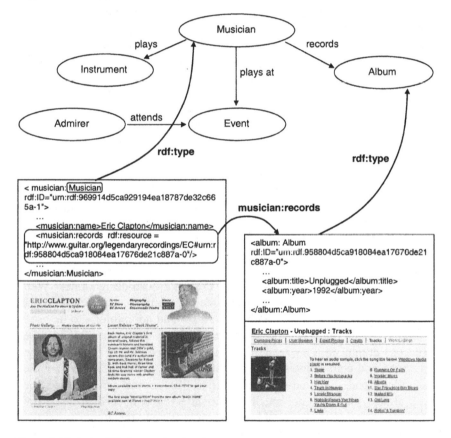

Figure 2-18. A simplified example of applying semantic annotation principles of the CREAM framework, after the idea from (Handschuh and Staab, 2002); the namespaces and URIs shown are hypothetical

It follows from the above example and from (Heflin and Hendler, 2001) and (Hendler, 2001) that for annotation of Web pages with ontological information to be effective:

- non-experts in ontological engineering must be able to do it, starting from existing ontologies, transparently, through normal computer use;
- most Web page developers need not even know that ontologies exist, and can still do (almost) free markup;
- ontology-aware authoring tools should support both authoring and annotation processes by enabling underlying ontologies to drive the creation of Web pages;
- the contents of the pages being designed and developed should be presented, modified, and mixed consistently, using ontologies linked to libraries of terms, and interlinked in order to reuse or change terms;
- tool developers should enable accessing libraries of ontologies from the tools they develop, in order to support appropriate markup of pages in a wide range of domains.

6. SEMANTIC WEB SERVICES

Roughly speaking, *Web services* are activities allowing both end users and, under appropriate circumstances, software agents to invoke them directly (Preece and Decker, 2002). In the traditional Web model, users follow hypertext links manually. In the Web services model, they invoke tasks that facilitate some useful activity (e.g., meaningful content-based discovery of some resources, fusion of similar contents from multiple sites, or commercial activities such as course advertising and registration for distance learning (Devedžić, 2004a)).

Technically, Web services are autonomous, platform-independent computational elements that can be described, published, discovered, orchestrated, and programmed using XML artifacts for the purpose of developing massively distributed interoperable applications. Platform-neutral and self-describing nature of Web services and particularly their ability to automate collaboration between Web applications, make them more than just software components. In the *service-oriented architecture* (Vinoski, 2002), Figure 2-19, Web services advertise themselves in the registry, allowing client applications to query the registry for service details and interact with the service using those details.

Service-oriented architecture from Figure 2-19 in Web application development can greatly enhance the traditional development process, since the client-side system can be built based on Web services even if these services are not yet available or they are not known by the developers. This due to the fact that each Web service is described through a service description language, dynamically discovered by applications that need to use it, and invoked through the communication protocol defined in its interface (Vinoski, 2002). The central component in Figure 2-19 - the service directory - is dynamically organized, but highly structured (e.g., as a tree, or as a table/database) information pool pertaining to different services. The underlying assumption is that at each point in time the directory lists those services that are ready to be invoked by the user; those are supposed to advertise their readiness and availability to the directory. Hence an agent can find out about the available services by looking up the directory. Then it can decide whether to automatically invoke a suitable service on the user's behalf, or merely to suggest the user to interact with the service directly.

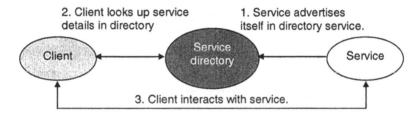

Figure 2-19. Service-oriented architecture

There is a lot of supporting technology for developing, publishing, and using Web services, such as WSDL (Web Services Description Language), WSFL (Web Services Flow Language), UDDI (Universal Description, Discovery, and Integration), and SOAP (Simple Object Access Protocol). See (Preece and Decker, 2002) for starting points on the use of these technologies.

Note, however, that on the Semantic Web the idea is to employ *intelligent* Web services to go beyond XML/RDF infrastructure of Web pages, i.e. to explore Web services that intelligent systems technology can make possible. Intelligent Web services may turn the Web into a collection of different resources, each with a well-defined interface for invoking its services (Vinoski, 2002). In other words, intelligent Web services deploy intelligent systems techniques to perform useful, reusable tasks for Web users. This view of Web services implies that properties, capabilities, interfaces, and effects of Web services must be encoded in an unambiguous, machine-understandable form, and properly marked-up to make the services computer-interpretable, use-apparent, and agent-ready (McIlraith et al., 2001). Such requirements, in turn, imply the need for ontologies of Web services, as machine-readable descriptions of services (as to how they run), including the consequences of using the services. Each such an ontology should explicitly represent the service logic and the invocation of the service. Web service ontologies bring intelligence to Web services as they enable integration of agents and ontologies in some exciting ways. For example, an agent performing keyword-based Web search may invoke services such as controlled vocabularies that enable fuzzy-terms-based search and inexact matches; if the requested keyword is not in the dictionary, the service can come up with an immediate more general concept suggested in the ontology.

The difference between conventional and intelligent Web services is best understood through the pragmatics of their use. In the conventional case, the user has to discover the desired service first (using a search engine). In most of cases, the next step involves a lot of reading on the discovered Web page. Alternatively, the user may execute the service to see whether it satisfies his/her request; this, in turn, means filling the forms of the service manually and composing manually the sequence of services required to complete a complex task.

On the other hand, intelligent Web services enable automatic service discovery, using pre-provided semantic markup of Web pages and ontology-enhanced search engines. Intelligent agents can execute such services on behalf of their users automatically, since the semantic markup of services provides declarative API that tells the agents what input is necessary for automatic invocation, what information will be returned, and how to execute and potentially interact with the service automatically. Automatic service composition and interoperation is also provided, since semantic markup of services provides all the necessary information to select, compose, and respond to services. The markup is encoded and stored at the service sites, and appropriate software tools manipulate the markup together with specifications of the service's objectives.

Obviously, the real power of intelligent Web services results not from their individual use, but from combining them in a variety of ways (Preece and Decker, 2002). This creates the need for standard models of interaction among the services (McIlraith et al., 2001). Such models should be implemented as declarative, machine-processable descriptions of how to combine intelligent Web services to achieve more sophisticated tasks. The descriptions can be encoded in Web Service composition languages such as WSFL or OWL-S (see below), and contain the knowledge of how to perform sophisticated real-life tasks that the services perform (Preece and Decker, 2002). The point is that implementing these composition descriptions on the Web makes them downloadable, understandable, and executable for everyone, not only humans but also automated agents.

Recently, the idea of intelligent Web services has slightly evolved into the concept of *Semantic Web services* (Payne and Lassila, 2004) as the augmentation of Web Service descriptions through Semantic Web annotations to facilitate higher-level automation of service discovery, composition, invocation, and monitoring in an open, unregulated, and often chaotic environment (that is, the Web). The objective of Semantic Web services is to provide ubiquitous infrastructure for deploying intelligent multiagent systems on the Web.

Semantic Web community has already developed *OWL-S*, an OWL-based ontology of Web services and a core set of markup language constructs for describing the properties and capabilities of Web services in unambiguous, computer-intepretable form (OWL-S, 2005). OWL-S comes with supporting tools and agent technology to enable automation of services on the Semantic Web, including automated Web service discovery, execution, interoperation, composition and execution monitoring.

Conceptually, the top level of the OWL-S ontology looks as in Figure 2-20 (Martin et al., 2004). The *ServiceProfile* describes what the service does. It specifies the service's input and output types, preconditions, and effects. The *ServiceModel* describes how the service works, i.e. its process model; each service is either an *AtomicProcess* that executes directly, or a *CompositeProcess*, i.e. a composition that combines subprocesses, Figure 2-21. The *ServiceGrounding* contains the details of how an agent can access the service. The grounding specifies a communications protocol, parameters to use in the protocol, and serialization techniques to be employed for the communication. Such a rich description of services greatly supports automation of their discovery and composition.

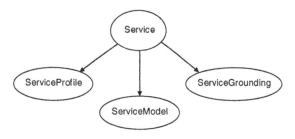

Figure 2-20. Top level of the service ontology (after (Martin et al., 2004))

OWL-S service descriptions are structured as OWL documents, so developers can build them using all of the OWL's domain modeling features, as well as concepts from other ontologies (Sirin et al., 2004). Also, some aspects of deriving OWL-S descriptions directly from WSDL descriptions can be partially automated.

```
<owl:Class rdf:ID="CompositeProcess">
  <rdfs:subClassOf rdf:resource="#Process"/>
  <owl:disjointWith rdf:resource="#AtomicProcess"/>
  <owl:disjointWith rdf:resource="#SimpleProcess"/>
  <rdfs:comment>
    A CompositeProcess must have exactly 1 composedOf property.
  </rdfs:comment>
  <owl:intersectionOf rdf:parseType="Collection">
    <owl:Class rdf:about="#Process"/>
    <owl:Restriction>
      <owl:onProperty rdf:resource="#composedOf"/>
      <owl:cardinality rdf:datatype="&xsd;#nonNegativeInteger">
        1</owl:cardinality>
    </owl:Restriction>
  </owl:intersectionOf>
</owl:Class>
```

Figure 2-21. An excerpt from the OWL-S ontology defined in (Martin et al., 2004)

The tricky part in building Semantic Web service descriptions using OWL-S is combining different services from different providers - these services might assume different ontologies (Payne and Lassila, 2004). Thus mapping of concepts between different ontologies and composition of new concepts from multiple ontologies is necessary. One way around this problem is to have agents and service requesters translate the service descriptions into a familiar ontology to formulate valid requests. This translation can be done by employing a set of "bridging axioms". Sirin et al. (2004) have proposed an alternative approach - generating service compositions that satisfy user requirements through an interactive metaphor. This approach assumes knowledge-based indexing and retrieval of services by agent brokers and humans alike, as well automated reasoning about the services, but is essentially semi-automated since the user is involved in the service composition as well. Still, the supporting tool that Sirin et al. have developed uses contextual information to locate semantically interoperable services that it can present to the user at each stage of the composition framework. Built on top of OWL-S, the tool enables semantic discovery and filtering to determine a meaningful set of candidate services based on advertised Semantic Web Service descriptions. The user's involvement here is reduced to a necessary minimum - it is the user who has the final word about selecting a particular service (for the next step in composition) from the set of candidate services. The next step in automation might be creating an intelligent agent to do it on behalf of the user. However, due to a huge variety of possible services, the respective domain ontologies and their representations, as well as composition variations, such an agent (or even a multiagent system) may not be easy to build.

7.   OPEN ISSUES

While Semantic Web is certainly getting momentum, it is important to realize some still unresolved problems and factors that hold back its more rapid development. Critics of the Semantic Web frequently complain that there is no a "killer app" for the Semantic Web yet, which they interpret as a sign of a poorly grounded field and a poorly envisioned future development.

In spite of the fast growing representational and technological support, development of ontologies is still hard work. Tools like Protégé are easy to use, but still - someone always has to transfer human knowledge about a topic or a subject domain into ontological representation. Given the fact that a domain ontology is supposed to represent essential domain concepts and their relationships, it always takes a good deal of human expert involvement in knowledge acquisition activities. Building and representing ontologies in computers is not that much a technical matter as it is a matter of obtaining and organizing high-quality human knowledge about the domain of interest. True, partial automation of that process is possible by applying machine learning techniques, but such approaches are still largely under development.

Moreover, domain knowledge is seldom static - it evolves over time, much of once relevant information may easily become obsolete, and new important information may be discovered after the ontology is built and represented on the Web explicitly. That raises an important issue of knowledge maintenance.

Automation is a key issue in many aspects of the Semantic Web, including annotation/markup. In practice, much of the semantic markup of Web resources was done more or less manually. It is not only time consuming and error prone - it is tedious. Moreover, any markup is good only as long as the resource remains unchanged; what if the resource is modified and the markup is no longer valid? Note that creating semantic markup is one of the key factors in the success of the Semantic Web, but certainly not the ultimate goal. It is therefore necessary to enable easy annotation and automate the process as much as possible, as well as to achieve effortless markup update in the ever changing environment of the Web. Automated annotation is a hot topic, and there are several approaches.

Some also argue that the success of the Semantic Web largely depends on integration of Semantic Web technology with commercial software products. A good example to this end is Briefing Associate (Tallis et al., 2002), discussed in section 2.3. Its integration with MS PowerPoint, a really widespread tool for creating presentations, indicates ways to a mass annotation of certain categories of documents without having the authors care about it. Efforts are underway to enable such "semantic markup as side effect" for different categories of Web resources, as well as to provide multiple annotations of the same resource to facilitate its reuse by multiple applications.

As Preece and Decker carefully note (2002), there is a trade-off between the functionality of Semantic Web services and the cost of developing the underlying markups and computational processes. The greater the functionality, the greater the cost. A more detailed study of the real users' needs may indicate the way to reduce this trade-off. This issue is closely related to another one - the trust the users will put to automated Semantic Web services. As Semantic Web services become more common, the users will want to know about their quality before they delegate their hands-on browsing to hands-off "black box" services. This creates the need for introducing a set of objective and subjective metrics for quality of Semantic Web services, such as how well the service has "understood" the user's needs, how good it was in fulfilling those needs, and how accurate and complete was the result.

8. SUMMARY

Semantic Web is a hot R&D topic in both AI and Internet research communities. It aims at transforming the Web that we know into a new one, much more suitable for machine processing and much more responsive to the users' real needs. Ontologies are the key concept in the development of this next-generation Web. They represent domain and content theories in machine-understandable form and enable Web-based knowledge processing, sharing, and reuse between applications.

Semantic Web services represent an important step toward the full-blown vision of the Semantic Web, in terms of utilizing, managing, and creating semantic markup (Payne and Lassila, 2004). Note that Semantic Web services nicely complement ontologies - services tackle behavioral issues of the Semantic Web (e.g., interactions between intelligent agents), whereas ontologies implement the Semantic Web's original objective to create representational and logical frameworks for increasing automation in processing Web-based information and improving the interoperability of Web-based applications.

9. END NOTES

Much of the material presented in this chapter originally appeared in another Springer monograph, *Model Driven Architecture and Ontology Development* (Gašević et al., 2006), co-authored by Vladan Devedžić.

Chapter 3

THE SETTING FOR SEMANTIC WEB-BASED EDUCATION

Putting WBE in the context of the Semantic Web immediately creates the idea of new generation WBE, or *Semantic WBE (SWBE)*. Since the Semantic Web itself offers numerous improvements over the traditional Web usage and applications, it is expected that SWBE will make profound effects on all aspects and processes of education that rely on Web technologies.

There are prerequisites for that, though. The Semantic Web must first become as ubiquitous as the Web is today. It is a process, not a one-time event. In parallel to that, more and more educational content on the Web must be made Semantic Web ready, which implies development of myriads of ontologies, annotation of educational content with such ontologies, development of special educational Semantic Web services, as well as wide proliferation of different Semantic Web languages, tools, and supporting technologies.

As a consequence, SWBE is not yet a pervasive reality. At the moment, it is rather a futuristic vision grounded in current developments in Internet technologies and the Semantic Web in general. However, initial developments are already there, and many results are impressive. The driving force for further development of SWBE is not the technology; it is the strong motivation to fulfill the learners' growing needs in more comfortable ways, enabled by the technology.

Anderson and Whitelock (2004) call that vision and the multitude of supporting efforts and developments *The Educational Semantic Web*. As they carefully note, this vision (as any other vision) has both a number of enthusiastic proponents and concerned skeptics. In order for further efforts and a wider acceptance to prevail over the skepticism of critics, it is necessary for end-user applications to become simple enough to support seamless integration of activities controlled and created by ordinary students, teachers, and authors (i.e., non-specialists in computing and Web technologies), exciting learning experiences, useful teaching practices, and highly creative authoring tasks.

This chapter explains the setting for SWBE relying on existing technologies and technological trends, and starting from the needs and perspectives of the major categories of actors in WBE, as outlined in Chapter 1, section 4.1. The chapter also briefly overviews current efforts and developments in the field of SWBE.

1.   THE ACTORS AND THE SUPPORT[6]

Figure 3-1 shows a likely setting for teaching, learning, collaboration, assessment, and other educational activities on the Semantic Web (Devedžić, 2003b; 2004a). This setting is a generalization of the virtual classroom architecture from Figure 1-3. Educational material may be distributed among different *educational servers* - specific Web applications running on physical servers and responsible for management and administration of, as well as access to the material. Learners, teachers, and authors access the educational material from the client side. *Educational content* is any educational material pedagogically organized and structured in such a way that interested learners can use to get introduced to a knowledge domain, deepen their understanding of that domain, and practice the related problem-solving skills.

Intelligent *pedagogical agents* provide the necessary infrastructure for knowledge, content, and information flow between the clients and the servers. They are autonomous software entities that support human learning by interacting with students/learners, teachers, and authors, and by collaborating with other similar agents, in the context of interactive learning environments (Johnson et al., 2000). On behalf of the learners, pedagogical agents access educational content on the servers by using high-level educational services. An *educational service* is a Web service designed specifically to support a learning, a teaching, or an authoring goal (see section 4 for details).

---

[6] Portions of this section reprinted (with minor adjustments) from International Journal of Artificial Intelligence in Education (IJAIED), Vol.14, Vladan Devedžić, Education and The Semantic Web, Pages No. 39-65, Copyright (2004), with permission from IOS Press. Other portions reprinted (with minor citation formatting adjustments), with permission, from Devedžić, V., 2003, Key issues in next-generation Web-based education, IEEE Transactions on Systems, Man, and Cybernetics, Part C - Applications and Reviews 33(3):339-349. © 2003 IEEE.

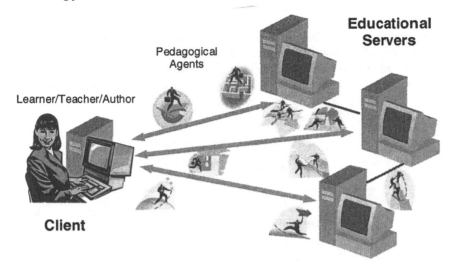

Educational
Servers

Pedagogical
Agents

Learner/Teacher/Author

Client

Figure 3-1. The setting for SWBE: the major actors and the technology[7]

1.1   Key issues

Figure 3-2 sums up important concepts and issues of SWBE. They are covered in detail in the following sections and in several other chapters, but their brief specification is as follows:

- Authors prepare educational content in the form of multimedia learning objects, examples, questions, exercises, simulations, and the like. The content is usually structured into coherent learning units, such as lessons, chapters, or tests, based on some underlying pedagogical objectives and goals.
- Ontologies represent essential knowledge (both domain and pedagogical) by defining terminology, concepts, relations, concept hierarchies, and constraints. They enable sharing and reuse of educational content and interoperability of different educational applications. Ideally, all content should be properly annotated using the concepts and terminology that ontologies define. Ontologies also enable registration, discovery, invocation, composition, and monitoring of intelligent educational services on the Semantic Web.
- Pedagogical agents help very much in locating, browsing, selecting, arranging, integrating, and otherwise using educational content from

---

[7] Figure reprinted (with minor adjustments), with permission, from Devedžić, V., 2003, Key issues in next-generation Web-based education, IEEE Transactions on Systems, Man, and Cybernetics, Part C - Applications and Reviews 33(3):339-349. © 2003 IEEE.

different educational servers. They can support both collaborative and individualized learning, as well as the students' cognitive processes.

- Learners are always interested in personalized learning experiences, since all people have their own learning approaches, styles, goals, preferences, and pace. SWBE should accommodate seamless adaptation of educational systems and applications to the learners' individual characteristics.

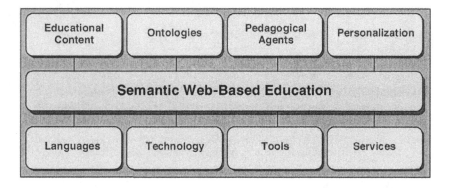

Figure 3-2. Important issues in SWBE[8]

- Different natural, visual, and representational languages are used to encode and present information contained in the learning material. Also, different formal languages may be used when developing educational content, and when representing ontologies and educational services. Different agent communication languages may characterize interaction among pedagogical agents.
- Although technology is not the ultimate goal of SWBE, it is certainly a key enabler. The trends and the reality of the current technological support must not be ignored when building a SWBE application. Section 3.2 of Chapter 1 lists a number of useful technologies related to WBE, and section 4.2 of the same chapter stresses the importance of high-quality technological framework for wide acceptance of all kinds of Web-based educational applications.
- Learning, teaching, and authoring tools for SWBE often come as rich Web-based software applications such as integrated learning environments, learning management systems, integrated authoring tools, and the like. However, there exist numerous other software tools of different size that authors often use to prepare educational content. It is

[8] Figure reprinted (with minor adjustments), with permission, from Devedžić, V., 2003, Key issues in next-generation Web-based education, IEEE Transactions on Systems, Man, and Cybernetics, Part C - Applications and Reviews 33(3):339-349. © 2003 IEEE.

important for integrated tools to support appropriate import/export operations and format conversions that enable using such external tools.

- Semantic Web services are used to offer teachers, learners, and authors service-oriented access to educational content in (a) specific domain(s) of interest. They are typically associated with educational servers, and can support a number of different educational activities.

1.2   The learner's view

There are different categories of learners in SWBE in terms of age, individual capabilities, cultural backgrounds, and occupational characteristics. Some of them are school kids; others are college and university students. Still other learners are actually trainees, taking SWBE courses to improve their on-the-job efficiency. Researchers, some government officials, and administration personnel can be also seen as occasional learners when browsing different educational content for their own purposes.

Despite of their different motivations and workloads, all of them are clearly interested in exciting and rich learning experience and high-level QoS. Their experience and learning efficiency will certainly largely depend on the educational content, which preferably must be attractive, up-to-date, easy-to-reach, easy-to-follow, and stimulating. Since all learners are different, their individual learning characteristics must be supported by personalization of different kinds (such as taking their knowledge levels into account, applying different AH principles and techniques, providing tailored hints, explanations, and learning paths through the curriculum, and so on). Since the learners' interaction with the system includes occasional uploads and downloads of assignments and projects, the system must ensure for secure access and maximum privacy to that end. Each learner also wants to see his/her results and progress achieved up to a certain point in time, his/her marks, rankings, and statistics.

Learners may want to progress through the learning material individually, interacting only with the SWBE environment. They may also want to learn collaboratively with other people, taking advantage of group learning experience, interaction with peer learners, and compare their own solutions to problems with those achieved by the group.

SWBE environments should enable learners to register for courses when the underlying learning management an administration requires so, and should also provide for unrestricted access to some educational content from different open libraries and repositories.

In all types of the learners' interaction with a SWBE environment, ease of access and learner-centered content filtering are a must. Ontologies are there to ensure for personalization and semantic search and integration of content from different repositories, but the learners need not necessarily be aware of the extent to which the ontologies are involved. What they want is getting the right material when needed, composed on their terminals dynamically and in a way that is intuitively clear and easy to comprehend. The fact that different formats, languages, and vocabularies may have been used for representing and storing the course material should be transparent to the learners as end-users of SWBE. Likewise, the learners need not necessarily know the details of the teaching strategies the system applies (albeit he/she should be able to select a preferable one), the peculiarities of the assessment procedures, and all elements of the learner models.

1.3   The teacher's (instructor's) view

SWBE should provide support for each teacher to select and combine learning materials and put up a course easily. Domain ontologies should be available to support this process, and to help the teachers annotate, filter, and structure the educational material from multiple sources.

The teacher may want to enforce a certain instructional strategy through his/her instructional design, thus the SWBE environment must enable selection and customization of teaching strategies as well. There must be a way of editing and adapting the strategy later as well, hence each strategy should be saved and documented for later use. That's where ontologies are also useful - they may provide means for developing machine understandable representations of teaching strategies and instructional designs to be shared and reused (at least in parts) by different teachers. Various Semantic Web services provide further support for monitoring, assessment, and evaluation activities.

Teachers also monitor the students' progress and problem solving, conduct assessments and tests, and perform grading, so for teachers a SWBE environment has to enable flexible access to students' models. Preferably, the student models should be represented according to a standardized scheme.

An important role of a SWBE environment from the teacher's perspective is support for intervention while monitoring the class (although the monitoring itself should be automated as much as possible). For example, the teacher may decide to direct the students to an interesting learning content when he/she notices such an action may be desirable. At that moment, there may be no enough time or capacity for the teacher to remember all candidate content and provide a timely advice or explanation to the class. Instead, the environment should enable the teacher to get a list of candidate materials and resources in a couple of mouse clicks. When filtered by Semantic Web techniques, the list will show right away the semantically relevant resources, and will omit the unimportant ones. The same logic of such semantic content retrieval applies to the teacher's tasks like setting up assignments, conducting online experiments, and evaluating the student's projects.

1.4   The author's view

In SWBE, the authoring process comprises three groups of authoring activities (Aroyo and Dicheva, 2004a): authoring of educational content, authoring of instructional process, and authoring of adaptation and personalization.

Content authoring includes creation and annotation of learning material, as well as creation of links (conceptual and functional) between different parts of the learning material and other learning resources. Content authors perform two kinds of activities:

- domain-related authoring activities - constructing the domain ontology, defining the terminology, describing the domain concepts, relations, taxonomies, and constraints;
- resource-related authoring activities - building a collection of educational resources by inserting new resource into an appropriate resource library or repository, editing and updating existing resources in the repository, and removing obsolete resources from the repository.

Note a clear separation between authoring ontological contents (domain model) and resources; the domain ontology may be instantiated by different resources, thus enabling adaptation and personalization of the content presentation. Also, authors can benefit enormously from using Semantic Web services to automatically discover existing resources on the Web and possibly filter them and include them in the collection. In other words, a product of content authoring may be also a semantic aggregation of relevant learning resources physically scattered across the Web.

Authoring of instructional process is the set of activities where teachers play a major role; it is typically related to course construction and design, i.e. to defining the course objectives, goals, topics, structure, sequencing, and activities (all of these should be carefully mapped to the concepts from the domain ontology).

Authoring of adaptation and personalization is actually authoring of learner models and applying different adaptation strategies and techniques to ensure for efficient tailoring of the learning content to the individual learners and personalized curriculum and task sequencing. This group of authoring activities also requires active participation of instructors, since it is them who have to specify the relevant attributes of the learner models the system should use.

1.5   The system developer's view

It is not easy to develop a SWBE system to get a wide acceptance. There are many issues involved, such as technological, architectural, software engineering, usability, pedagogical, and maintenance issues - all that in the context of the still evolving Semantic Web and many ontologies still lacking. However, it is possible to formulate a few basic principles for system developers to follow as necessary preconditions for success of a SWBE application.

First of all, it is imperative for each SWBE system developer to assume that most of end users - learners, teachers, and authors - will not be computer specialists. This fact must be reflected in the design of SWBE tools - they must be highly intuitive and easy to use by non-specialists. The interaction of end users with ontologies when necessary must be absolutely natural and must create no doubts about their meanings. It is a good idea to design the system with ontologies acting from under the surface, making the end users easily understand and/or adopt the domain and pedagogical mindsets reflected in the ontologies.

Second, the tools must be easy to customize to different domains. The best way to do it is to enable domain specialists to create ontologies to represent domain processes and workflows and integrate them with authoring and instructional tools. This level of modularity allows for easier maintenance as the domain processes and workflows evolve.

Third, system developers must provide a variety of pedagogical and didactic tools in order to accommodate a variety of instructional approaches. True, not all authors and teachers will want to use the all the pedagogical tools provided, but certainly different domains may require different toolsets.

Next, SWBE systems' design should reflect the idea of open learning architectures - it should be easy to integrate the system with other Web-based environments and applications, different Web directories and services, repositories of learning resources, and external tools.

Finally, enabling porting of the system software to different technology gradually becomes a very important issue. For example, desktop-based learning applications should be easy to port to different mobile and wireless technologies in order to support ubiquitous learning needs.

2. EDUCATIONAL CONTENT

SWBE assumes that educational content on the Web is represented in terms of clearly defined, manageable units (chunks; items) of information designed with educational intent, nowadays often called *learning objects*. Such learning objects may come in a variety of forms, and may serve diverse educational purposes (Duval and Hodgins, 2003). The educational content of learning objects can be pedagogically described using semantically rich *educational modeling languages* (Koper and Manderveld, 2004).

2.1 The concept of learning objects

Learning objects (LOs) can be thought of as educational resources that can be employed in technology-supported learning (McGreal, 2004). They are self-contained units of instruction, i.e. items or pieces of learning material that people can learn from a learning activity or from a lesson.

Some authors consider LOs to be such educational items of any size and in a range of media. Others make a strict distinction between LOs and learning resources, stipulating that a learning resource can be an individual LO, but also a collection of LOs, or (an) educational service(s) of interest to a person or organization (e.g., see (Barker et al., 2003)).

Regardless of the possible conceptual difference between LOs and learning resources, the following points are important for understanding the notion of LOs properly:

- In practice, LOs come in a number of digital *forms*[9]: electronic texts, multimedia content, images, animations, video clips, simulations, lectures, presentations, educational games, Web sites, digital movies, Java applets, on-line tutorials, courses, presentations, tests, quizzes, project outlines, study guides, case studies, exercises, glossaries, and in any other form that can be used for a learning resource. Some people also include here any instructional content, instructional software, and software tools.
- The central idea of LOs is not their form, but their *reusability* - LOs enable and facilitate reuse of educational content online. They can be combined with other LOs for different learning purposes. For example, an image showing the Earth may be reused in different lessons and courses in the domains such as geography, astronomy, and media sciences. LO reusability is important for several reasons. First, it takes a

---

[9] A widely quoted definition says that LO is any entity, *digital or non-digital*, that can be used, re-used, or referenced during technology-supported learning (IEEE LOM, 2002). However, most of the e-Learning and SWBE literature and efforts are focused on digital LOs only.

lot of time and effort to develop high-quality educational content. Second, different educational organizations and institutions may teach the same topics; in such a case, it is highly likely that they will develop rather similar educational content. Third, reusing existing high-quality material may gradually lead to partial unification of educational approaches of different organizations, which contributes to the increase of the students' common backgrounds and of their mobility across educational institutions. Fourth, reusing some LOs across different organizations may over time reduce the human resources and the costs needed to develop learning resources by simply sharing the costs among the interested parties (Mohan and Brooks, 2003). Fifth, LOs can be reused not only by different educational organizations, but in training as well.

- In order to reuse a LO in different contexts, it is necessary to create descriptions of the LO content (which calls for specific data formats). Fortunately, there already exist internationally accepted *specifications* and *standards* make LOs interoperable and reusable by different applications and in diverse learning environments. Such standards and specifications define *metadata* that describe LOs, which facilitates searching and makes LOs accessible. Different LO metadata are used for different purposes (i.e., to describe LOs from different perspectives), and there are many metadata defined in the specifications.

- Reusing LOs in practice means first getting them from somewhere. *Learning object repositories* (*LORs*) store collections of different LOs and their metadata and make them searchable, accessible, and reusable to potential users.

- Another implication of LO reuse is their *composition*. A simple LO can be reused (as is, or after some modifications appropriate for the case) with other LOs to create a more complex LO, which in turn can itself be reused. Obviously, there are LOs of different *granularity*. For example, one can reuse simple information objects such as text and images to create a reusable LO such as a slide. Slides can be reused in composing different topical units, and these are combined to create presentations. A teacher/author can create a lesson from different presentations and other components (LOs), such as simulations and exercises. Several lessons make a module, and they in turn make a course. These different granularities of LOs and different levels of their complexity lead to a conceptual hierarchy. The point is that at all levels of this hierarchy the user can ideally select from "various pieces in stock", possibly reusing pieces that may have been previously used in thousands of courses, from which he/she can assemble different and yet well-designed multimedia LOs. WBE courses should therefore be designed as a collection of LOs rather than as whole, inseparable, long courses (McGreal, 2004).

There are ongoing debates on what counts as a LO and what does not. Note, for example, that a simple information object may, but need not necessarily be designed with a formal, expressed learning purpose. In case it is, the object becomes useful to learners; however, learners cannot always tell whether such an object is useful to them or not. That's where instructional design comes into the play - it changes information or knowledge objects to LOs and enables putting the LOs into specific learning contexts intentionally.

In the rest of this book, it is assumed that LOs are any reusable digital items with explicit educational purpose(s) and of any granularity, which can be assembled into different units, lessons, courses and other pieces of instruction.

2.2 Educational modeling languages

How exactly does instructional design change information and knowledge objects into LOs?

A short answer is: by adding some pedagogy. Consider again the composition of a complex LO (or *unit of learning*), e.g. a course, from simpler LOs represented in different forms. A WBE course is more than a mechanically collected set of LOs. The composition process must use instructional design to structure reusable LOs into a coherent whole and integrate them with learning activities and services, such as communication facilities, search facilities, monitoring facilities, etc. (Koper and Manderveld, 2004). An instructional design can be based on explicitly identified pedagogical models and theories, but in practice always depends also on the instructors' personal experience and subjective views on rules of good teaching and learning.

Educational modeling languages (EMLs) contribute to SWBE by providing semantic notation to support the reuse of pedagogy built into LOs. They complement the LOs' aspect of syntactic specification, associated metamodels and metadata, and interoperability across WBE applications, by implementing pedagogical models and frameworks for analysis, design, and implementation of LOs. More specifically, EMLs support the reuse of pedagogical entities like learning designs, learning objectives, learning activities, etc. By definition, EML specifies a semantic information model and binding (typically an XML Schema or an RDF Schema binding), describing the content and process within a unit of learning from a pedagogical perspective in order to support reuse and interoperability (Rawlings et al., 2002).

General requirements for the notation of an EML include (Koper and Manderveld, 2004):

- formalisation - enabling formal descriptions of simple LOs and more complex units of learning, in order to enable automatic processing;
- explicit typing - expressing the meaning of different smaller-scale LOs within the context of larger ones explicitly, i.e. the capability of describing a semantic structure of the content or functionality of the typed LOs in addition to a reference possibility;
- completeness - the capability of describing all the typed LOs that compose a more complex one, the relationships between them, and the activities and the workflows of the end users;
- reproducibility - specifying complex units of learning so that their repeated execution is possible;
- sustainability - separating the standards underlying the notation from the technique used to interpret the notation of LOs, in order to become resistant to technical changes and conversion problems;
- compatibility - fitting in with available standards and specifications (see Chapter 5, covering standardization efforts, for details on such available standards and specifications);
- interoperability and reusability - making it possible to identify and isolate useful LOs, eliminate context-dependent contents from them, exchange them among applications, and reuse them in other contexts;
- medium and setting neutrality - using the same notation in different publication formats (Web, paper, e-books, mobile, etc.) and also in different settings (WBE, blended learning, hybrid learning, and so on);
- life cycle - making it possible to create, modify, store, and distribute complex LOs (such as online courses) and all of their component LOs.

In addition to these general requirements, each EML should also support the following specific instructional design requirements:

- enabling the use and adaptation of different theories and models of learning and instruction;
- defining the conditions and constraints under which different LOs can be aggregated into valid complex LOs and units of learning;
- making distinction between different educational roles, especially learner and staff roles;
- expressing the meaning of different LOs within a unit of learning using a pedagogical vocabulary from the educational domain;
- enabling diverse assessment procedures and tools (e.g., multiple-choice testing, performance testing, portfolio assessment, etc.), and defining formal criteria for a student to meet in order to complete a unit of learning;
- describing LOs and units of learning in such a way that they can be controlled (if necessary) by the end users and adapted to their preferences, background, learning goals, and other personal characteristics;

- defining properties in a learner dossier, in order to build portfolios, and support monitoring facilities and student tracking;
- mapping the pedagogical terminology used in EML to the users' own terminology.

A number of different EMLs have been proposed and developed so far. Rawlings et al. have surveyed (2002) early ones, such as the OUN EML developed at the Open University of The Netherlands (OUN EML, 2000) and PALO (Rodríguez-Artacho and Verdejo Maíllo, 2004). The purpose of their survey was to find a good candidate EML for standardization. The EMLs included in the survey had a clearly specified information model and binding aimed at the semantic modeling of units of learning and LOs and semantic description of teaching-learning environments. Later on, the IMS Consortium has adopted the OUN EML as the basis for their Learning Design Specification (IMS LD, 2003) (see Chapter 5 for details). Examples of more recent EMLs are MelaPass (Morimoto et al., 2004), and the PPP pattern-based language proposed by Rodríguez et al. (2004).

As an illustration of an EML-based encoding of instructional design of a LO, consider the OUN EML example shown in Figure 3-3. The important concepts represented include educational roles (such as the Learner role), various learning objectives, different learning and supporting activities, the outcomes they produce, the methods they use, the environment they use (LOs and services), and so forth. There is a detailed specification of the OUN EML information model (Koper, 2001), (Koper and Manderveld, 2004). The specification is made using Unified Modeling Language (UML). OUN EML XML binding is publicly available (OUN EML, 2000).

Once an EML document like that from Figure 3-3 is developed, it can be published in LORs, on educational servers, or at learning portals. It can be also imported into workflow management systems and learning management systems. In this last case, the learner's study progress and preferences are stored in his/her dossier.

3.   EDUCATIONAL SERVERS[10]

Figure 3-4 shows a general model of educational servers for SWBE (see also Figure 3-1 again). From the learners' perspective, the server appears to act as a powerful extension of the intelligent tutor built into the *learning tools* the learner uses. For the purpose of this discussion, assume that the learning tools include different Web-based ITSs, AEHSs, and similar intelligent learning environments. In combination, the educational server and the intelligent tutor possess enough *domain* and *pedagogical* knowledge to conduct a learning session (Devedžić, 2003b; 2004a). The two kinds of knowledge are represented as pieces of educational content, such as LOs, as well as EML descriptions of instructional design and the tutor's heuristics. In fact, it is a generalization of the knowledge model of an ITS (the Expert Module and the Pedagogical Module represented in Figure 1-4).

---

[10] Portions of this section reprinted (with minor adjustments) from International Journal of Artificial Intelligence in Education (IJAIED), Vol.14, Vladan Devedžić, Education and The Semantic Web, Pages No. 39-65, Copyright (2004), with permission from IOS Press. Other portions reprinted (with minor citation formatting adjustments), with permission, from Devedžić, V., 2003, Key issues in next-generation Web-based education, IEEE Transactions on Systems, Man, and Cybernetics, Part C - Applications and Reviews 33(3):339-349. © 2003 IEEE.

```
<Unit-of-learning Type="Course">
    <Metadata><Title>Semantic Web</Title></Metadata>
    <Roles><Learner Id="Student"/>
            <Property Id="Show example"><String/></Property>
            </Learner>
    </Roles>
    <Learning-objectives>
        <Learning-objective>
            <Objective-description>Introduction to the Semantic Web technologies<\Objective-description>
            <Objective-type><Insight/></Objective-type>
        </Learning-objective>
    </Learning-objectives>
    <Content>
        <Activity Id="Preparation">
            . . .
        </Activity>
        <Activity Id= "Assignment 3">
            <Environment>
                <Knowledge-object Id="SWLC">
                    <Metadata><Title>Semantic Web layer-cake</Title></Metadata>
                    <Source>
                        <P>Schematic representation of the Semantic Web layer-cake </P>
                    </Source>
                </Knowledge-object>
            </Environment>
            <What><P>Read about the Semantic Web layer-cake</P></What>
            <Completed><User-choice/></Completed>
        </Activity>
        <Activity Id= "Assignment 4">
            . . .
            <Completed><User-choice/></Completed>
        </Activity>
    </Content>
    <Method>
        <Play>
            <Role-ref Id-ref="Student"/><Activity-ref Id-ref="Preparation"/>
            . . .
            <Role-ref Id-ref="Student"/><Activity-ref Id-ref="Assignment 3"/>
            <Role-ref Id-ref="Student"/><Activity-ref Id-ref="Assignment 4"/>
            . . .
        </Play>
        <Conditions>
            . . .
        </Conditions>
    </Method>
</Unit-of-learning>
```

Figure 3-3. An EML encoding (excerpt, adapted from (Koper and Manderveld, 2004))

An educational server is also supposed to possess enough intelligence to arrange for *personalization* of the learning tasks it supports. The server may include a *presentation planner* to help the intelligent tutor select, prepare, and adapt the domain material to show to the learner. The tutor gradually builds the *learner model (student model)* during the session, in order to keep track of the student's actions and learning progress, detect and correct his/her errors and misconceptions, and possibly redirect the session accordingly. In the end of the session, the learner model is saved. It is then used along with other information and knowledge to initialize the next session with the same learner.

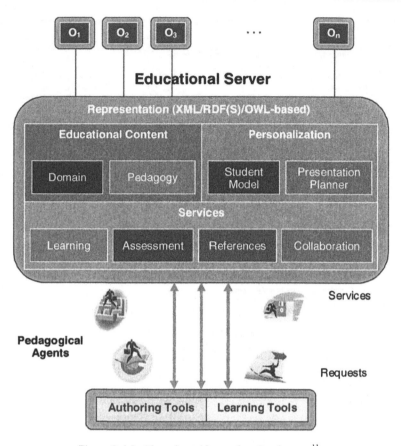

Figure 3-4. Inside and outside an educational server[11]

From the instructor's (teacher's) perspective, an educational server enables ontology-based access to and browsing of constantly updated collection of LOs of different granularities, as well as access to resources related to selection and customization of teaching strategies. The server also provides different class monitoring and intervention options to support virtual classrooms, as well as direct access to students' models both during and after the learning session. The server itself may provide the tools to support teachers in their activities, or they may use client-side tools to connect to the educational server and use the resources it provides.

From the author's perspective, educational servers extend authoring tools. Through authoring tools, domain authors access different ontologies (see the

[11] Figure reprinted (with minor adjustments), with permission, from Devedžić, V., 2003, Key issues in next-generation Web-based education, IEEE Transactions on Systems, Man, and Cybernetics, Part C - Applications and Reviews 33(3):339-349. © 2003 IEEE.

O_i boxes in Figure 3-4) stored in ontology libraries managed by educational servers. The authors can develop their own ontologies and publish them in the libraries. They can also reuse and extend ontologies from the libraries for their own authoring purposes. Furthermore, authors can create, store, update, and delete LOs, instructional designs, courses, and the like, all accessible through the server. Likewise, they can access student models stored on educational servers and use them to create more advanced models, with different adaptation and personalization options enabled by AH techniques.

Note that Figure 3-4 does not imply any specific physical distribution of educational resources. From the perspective of all categories of end users (learners, teachers, and authors), the resources should appear as if they were located on a single server. In other words, each educational server should support seamless integration of resources it provides itself with resources provided by other similar educational servers. It is the task of system developers to make educational servers support this important option for SWBE by deploying the latest Semantic Web engineering technologies.

Once again, Figure 3-4 represents a generalized *model* of an educational server. A number of variations may be used in practical implementations. For example, as an alternative to having a full range of intelligent tutoring functionalities implemented in a WBE learning environment on the client side, the educational server may provide at least some of them by means of intelligent Web services (see the next section).

At a first glance, the model from Figure 3-4 may appear as a mere vision of some faraway future development (Aroyo and Dicheva, 2004a). However, the model can be easily mapped (instantiated) to different other models and architectures proposed in the literature. For example, a correspondence can be drawn between the educational server model as presented here and the AHA! architecture proposed by De Bra et al. (2004b) and the IRS-II/UPML model of Motta et al. (2003). There is also a good deal of overlap between the model from Figure 3-4 and the models underlying popular LORs (such as ARIADNE (ARIADNE, 2004) and MERLOT (MERLOT, 2005)) and their accompanying tools. Chapter 4 analyzes these other models and architectures in detail.

The remaining building blocks of the educational server model from Figure 3-4 are described in the next three sections.

4. EDUCATIONAL WEB SERVICES

An educational server provides a number of educational Web services that implement different functionalities of interest to learners, teachers, authors, and the tools/applications they use. Technically, educational Web services are modular and reusable educational software components wrapped inside a Web service interface. For example, such services may provide access to, or metadata about, LOs and LORs. They may also provide the student's registration and enrollment for a course. Other services may offer guidance for project preparation and development, some functions of an intelligent tutor, and different personalization options. Semantic Web search services may help teachers and authors find course-related material elsewhere on the Web and automatically create the "Related links" LO for a course.

One can also name numerous other examples of useful functionalities that educational Web services may implement. In all such cases, services increase reusability and interoperability of the functionalities they implement.

The model shown in Figure 3-4 assumes that an educational server organizes its services in groups according to the categories of functionalities it offers and the educational goals the end users may have.

The categories of services shown in Figure 3-4 are just *some* of the many possible categories; there is no widely accepted consensus on which categories exactly should be considered and how precisely to organize the hierarchy of categories and subcategories. For example, Brusilovsky and Miller (2001) suggest four top-level categories: presentation (delivery of learning material), activity (involving the students in doing something), communication (between teachers and students, and between the students in a group), and administration (e.g., student registration, payments, grading, course administration). Others (e.g., see (Chen, 2003)) differentiate between five top-level categories: content services (managing educational content), collaboration/communication services, people/personalization services, course management services (syllabus, evaluation, grading, etc), and administrative services (supporting general administrative tasks such as registration, reporting, etc.).

The four sample categories of educational services shown in Fig. 3-4 are detailed to an extent in Table 3-1. The Learning category is rather general and encompasses all services that support the learning process directly. It could certainly be divided into a number of subcategories (like reading, interactive activities, problem solving), but the point is that all (sub)categories of services have their distinct educational purpose, properties, and effects. It is exactly these features that must be properly marked-up to make each educational service ready-to-use by pedagogical agents (see also section 6).

Table 3-1. A possible partial classification of educational Web services and some examples

Service category	Learning	Assessment	References	Collaboration
Services	Presentation,	On-line tests,	Browsing,	Group

Service category	Learning	Assessment	References	Collaboration
	exercise, practice, online experiment, further reading	performance tracking, grading	search, libraries, repositories, portals	formation and matching, class monitoring

Recall from Chapter 2, section 6, that Web services need to be properly described in service directiories in order to allow for automatic discovery and invocation. An important implication of this fact for SWBE system developers is that when building educational servers and services they must provide detailed descriptions of services and ensure that the descriptions get published in service directories. End users of SWBE systems need not worry much about how to find the services they need, whether they are up-to-date or not, and what to supply in order to use the services - all of it should just appear when they start their activities.

Automatic service invocation requires detailed description of both the service interface and the service implementation. When a service requestor (such as a pedagogical agent) retrieves a service using various lookup mechanisms, it uses the service description to generate a SOAP message to invoke the service. This implies that the requestor must know how to build SOAP messages, send them over the Web, and possibly receive and parse similar messages the service may send back in return.

5. PEDAGOGICAL AGENTS[12]

"The Educational Semantic Web is based on three fundamental affordances. The first is the capacity for effective information storage and retrieval. *The second is the capacity for nonhuman autonomous agents to augment the learning and information retrieval and processing power of human beings.* The third affordance is the capacity of the Internet to support, extend and expand communications capabilities of humans in multiple formats across the bounds of time and space." (Anderson and Whitelock, 2004)

Pedagogical agents are a kind of intelligent software agents, hence they are autonomous software entities, capable of performing specific tasks. They can communicate among themselves, using specific agent communication languages. They are also often capable of intelligent reasoning about their

---

[12] Portions of this section reprinted (with minor adjustments) from International Journal of Artificial Intelligence in Education (IJAIED), Vol.14, Vladan Devedžić, Education and The Semantic Web, Pages No. 39-65, Copyright (2004), with permission from IOS Press.

environments, as well as of showing a good deal of initiative in performing their tasks on behalf of their users.

Figure 3-4 clearly shows that pedagogical agents represent a necessary part of the SWBE infrastructure. Their role is to reduce the learners' workload in finding and accessing the LOs they need, in using different learning services, and in communicating and collaborating when solving problems during the learning sessions. They also help teachers and instructors prepare the lessons and courses, deploy different teaching strategies, and monitor the learners' work and progress. Pedagogical agents also assist authors by automatically suggesting high-quality design alternatives when authoring different LOs, integrating portions of collaboratively authored contents, and ensuring that all the necessary format conversions are applied when storing the resulting learning material happen without the need for the authors to intervene. Pedagogical agents automatically perform a lot of search on behalf of all end users of educational servers.

The point is that pedagogical agents typically do all that acting behind the scenes of the learners'/teachers'/authors' activities. The end users of SWBE systems simply do not have to care much about infrastructural tasks and activities - seamlessly, using educational Web servers and services, pedagogical agents intelligently perform such tasks and activities themselves.

Obviously the interaction and interoperation between pedagogical agents and educational services on the Semantic Web is the central issue here. As an illustration how such an interaction and interoperation happen in practice, consider the following hypothetical scenario. A learner wants to apply for a course in computer literacy, but is not quite sure which one to take. She might want to take such a course from The European Computer Driving Licence® provider, or ECDL (ECDL, 2004), Fig. 3-5. ECDL is European-wide qualification which enables people to take courses in a range of certification programs in the domain of computer technology and use and demonstrate their knowledge and skills. Suppose, however, that the user does not know about the existence of ECDL.

Provided that the learner has access to an agent-supported learning environment ready to interact with the Semantic Web, she might want to use her personal agent to arrange for the course for her. Knowing the learner's profile and goals, the agent will try to discover the most suitable courses in computer literacy automatically. The success will depend, of course, also on existing ontological support and on whether the relevant services are suitably marked-up. Assuming that such pre-conditions are met (which may not yet be the case in reality), the agent will use Web service directories, ontology-enhanced search engines, and pre-provided semantic markup of the services'

Web pages and will find the services eventually. In doing so, it may well collaborate and interoperate with other pedagogical agents (see Fig. 3-4).

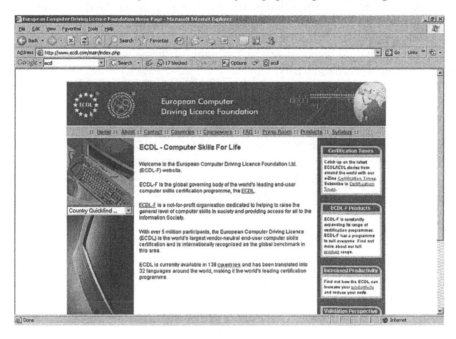

Figure 3-5. ECDL home page

The agent will then reason about the service(s) discovered and may decide that ECDL is appropriate for its owner. Before showing the ECDL courses and tests to the learner, the agent will use ECDL's semantic description as a declarative API that specifies what input is necessary to execute the service; what information will be returned; and how to actually invoke - and potentially interact with - the service automatically. That may involve automatic service composition and interoperation, in terms of creating a procedure that first registers the user to ECDL (supplying the user's personal data and filling the registration form automatically on behalf of the learner), then collecting the learner's authentication data generated by the registration service (for possible future (re)use), then selecting the suitable course and test level for the learner (see Fig. 3-6), and finally invoking the service for that level and displaying the course information to the learner. Alternatively, the learner may have instructed the agent just to find and display relevant information first, without registering automatically. The agent may reason that the procedure to execute is "access-the-programs; select-the-knowledge-area; find-sample-courses; select-sample-courses-for-the-knowledge-area". The result may be a sequence of two pages displayed to the learner, Figures 3-6 and 3-7. Again, semantic description of services at their site (a hypothetical ECDL educational server) and at a service directory provides the necessary information for the pedagogical agent(s) to select, compose, and respond to services without much of the learner's intervention. For example, each of the four certification program levels in Fig. 3-6 may be a service that should be annotated accordingly for the pedagogical agents to access and interpret them easily.

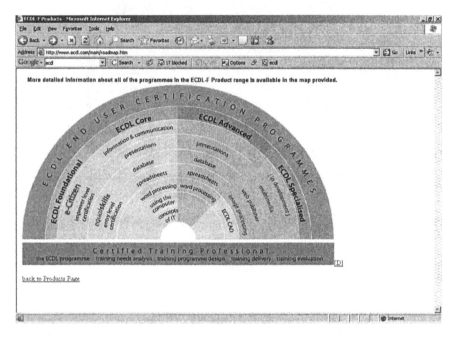

Figure 3-6. ECDL sample tests by knowledge areas

Although possibly not implemented at the moment, the above example gives a flavor of what kind of services the learner may expect from SWBE. It is difficult to say at the moment how long it might take before such a scenario becomes widely available, but initial practical developments in that direction have already started. Section 7 introduces such developments, and several remaining chapters of the book discuss examples.

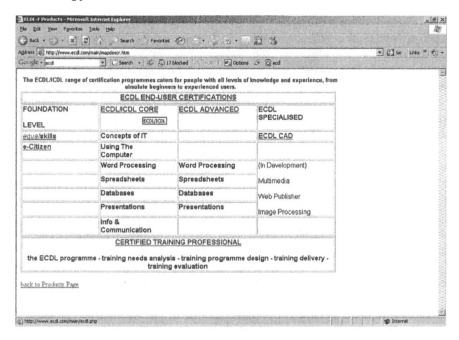

Figure 3-7. ECDL sample test in *Basic concepts of IT*

6. EDUCATIONAL ONTOLOGIES

If we stick to the armature metaphor of Swartout and Tate (2001) when describing the role and importance of ontologies to the Semantic Web in general (see Chapter 2, section 2.1.1), then educational ontologies are the armature of SWBE. What learners, teachers, and authors really need from SWBE are intelligent, high-level educational services like intelligent search services, filters of LOs and other educational resources, automatic and intelligent LO integration, intelligent integration of educational services, and knowledge management. The users can delegate such tasks to pedagogical agents, but the tasks are viable only if a number of educational ontologies populate the Web. They would enable semantic interoperation between the agents and the applications on the Semantic Web, i.e. semantic mappings between terms within the data, which requires content analysis.

6.1 An example scenario

In order to clarify the roles of educational ontologies, consider another hypothetical example, adapted from (Devedžić, V., 2004b).

A learner is interested in deepening his/her knowledge of Greek mythology. His/her personal agent realizes the learner's goal either by being told explicitly, or by observing the learner's interactions with educational servers, LOs, LORs, and other Web resources. The agent can compare the learner's interactions to his/her previous activities it knows about. Presumably, the learner's personal agent knows enough about the learner's goals or can access such information elsewhere, e.g. in a relevant database of learners. The agent then contacts educational servers it knows about. Alternatively, it can contact other similar pedagogical agents it is aware of, such as a facilitator agent that may help the learner's agent find another educational server.

When contacting an educational server modeled after the scheme depicted in Figure 3-4, the agent first queries learning services in order to identify the ontology of Greek mythology and return it to the learner. The learner may browse the ontology and refine his/her search to the concept of *god*. The agent then invokes different learning and reference services from the educational server in order to build for the learner an initial selection of suitable and available LOs in the form of a dynamically generated multimedia HTML page. All contents on that page are marked-up with ontological information coming from the server side.

The learner may proceed by selecting *Titans* on that initial page, which triggers the agent to interact with the educational services that acquire, integrate, and arrange the corresponding LOs and other learning material from heterogeneous sources, build the initial learner model, and select and invoke suitable tutoring services on the server side to begin the learning session. The learner's agent monitors the session and intelligently assists the learner in all administration and communication with the server. It also takes care of the changes in the learner's focus and dynamically checks the availability of educational services, thus making the underlying technical complexity of the session fully transparent to the learner. The learner can concentrate on his/her learning goals.

Thus educational ontologies are there to help meaningfully annotate the LOs, educational services, educational Web pages, and other learning resources. They are there to enable pedagogical agents do their jobs on behalf of the learners, teachers, and authors. Furthermore, they are there to make intelligent, semantic search for LOs and educational services more effective. They also define the knowledge structures that all analysis, interpretation, and other automatic processing rely on.

6.2   Categories of educational ontologies

Generally, an educational ontology is any ontology that can be used to support SWBE. However, it often helps to have a more systematic view. From the work of Aroyo and Dicheva (2004a; 2004b), Bourdeau and Mizoguchi (2002), Chen et al. (1998), Ikeda et al. (1997), and Mizoguchi (2001), several general categories of ontologies important in SWBE can be identified.

Domain ontologies. SWBE is not viable without domain ontologies describing essential concepts, relations, and theories of many domains of interest. Of course, domain ontologies are not necessary only for educational purposes, but for all Semantic Web applications. Still, they are included here because the ultimate goal of learner-centered educational design is the learner's proficiency in various domains. In SWBE systems, instructors and authors should represent their domain knowledge starting from domain ontologies.

Task ontology. In any application domain, including education, task ontology complements the domain ontology in that it represents semantic features of the problem solving. The concepts and relations included in a task ontology pertain to the problem types, structures, parts, activities, and steps one should follow in problem-solving processes. For example, a task ontology in educational applications may include concepts like *problem, scenario, question, answer, guidance, hint, exercise, explanation, simulation,* and the like. Task ontologies in SWBE formalize the tasks and activities of the major actors in the process (learners, teachers, authors); thus, there are *instructional design ontologies (learning design ontologies), training ontologies, authoring task ontologies,* and so forth.

Teaching strategy ontology. This ontology provides instructors and authors with the facility to model teaching experiences, by specifying the knowledge and principles underlying pedagogical actions and behaviors. For example, teaching strategy ontology may specify sequences of corrective actions to take when the learner makes an error, or it may specify behaviors to encourage the learner to explore alternative solutions. Teaching strategies are partially domain-dependent and learner-dependent.

Learner model ontology. Designers and developers of SWBE systems use concepts from learner model ontology to build learner models. This ontology and the corresponding learner models are essential for the system's adaptive behavior. Depending on the domain, task, and the system's functionality, learner model ontology may include concepts to represent the learner's performance (such as their current level of knowledge, the pace with which they progress through the learning material, the need to repeat portions of the material, and the like), and also their cognitive traits (e.g., working memory capacity, motivation, and inductive reasoning capabilities).

Interface ontology. The purpose of this ontology is to specify a SWBE system's adaptive behaviors and techniques at the user interface level. Thus interface ontology makes the modeling of the system's adaptivity to different learners more explicit.

Communication ontology. Different SWBE systems, pedagogical agents, educational servers, and educational services communicate with each other by exchanging messages. Communication ontology defines the semantics of message content languages, i.e. the vocabulary of terms used in the messages at both message and content levels.

Educational service ontology. One specific kind of ontology, certainly related to the communication ontology, is necessary to enable interoperation of high-level educational Web services - ontology of the services themselves (Devedžić, 2004a). Educational service ontology should be based on OWL-S (see Figure 2-20) and must provide means of creating machine-readable descriptions of services (as to how they run), the consequences of using the service (e.g., the fee), and an explicit representation of the service logic (e.g., automatic invocation of another service) (McIlraith et al., 2001; Preece & Decker, 2002). Educational Web services have their properties, capabilities, interfaces, and effects, all of which must be encoded in an unambiguous, machine-understandable form, to enable pedagogical agents to recognize the services and invoke them automatically. For example, a pedagogical agent coming to a digital library to retrieve a specific bibliographical item on behalf of its user must be able to determine (Devedžić, 2004a):

• how to find the library's Web page;
• how to invoke the search facility;
• what arguments to pass;
• what kind of results to expect (e.g., just the abstract or the full text, the text formats available);
• what are the conditions of retrieving the reference (e.g., cost, subscription, special offer).

The agent will then reason about these issues and, provided that there are no collisions with its internal logic, will automatically invoke the service eventually. Note that this is completely different from the current situation, in which the user must first discover the digital library manually, using a search engine, then read the discovered Web page, and also fill in the forms of the service manually.

7.   CURRENT EFFORTS

The SWBE community is growing. As a result of a recent initiative, much of the community's efforts are represented on and are accessible through an ontology-driven Web portal called *Ontologies for Education*, or *O4E* (O4E, 2005). The portal provides a single place on the Web where researchers, students, and practitioners can find information about available research projects and successful practices in the field of SWBE (Dicheva et al., 2005).

The term "ontology-driven" means that an underlying ontology of O4E (the field largely overlapping with SWBE) is essentially visualized in a number of ways on the portal. The ontology itself is downloadable and is being constantly updated. The taxonomy of SWBE concepts that constitute the ontology is represented as a glossary, Figure 3-8. Clicking on a concept in the taxonomy further reveals its "position" in the ontology by relating it to other concepts and instances, Figures 3-9 and 3-10. The portal also has links to important projects and SWBE tools for practitioners, as well as abundant information for researchers (publications, conferences, people, other related portals, mailing lists, etc.).

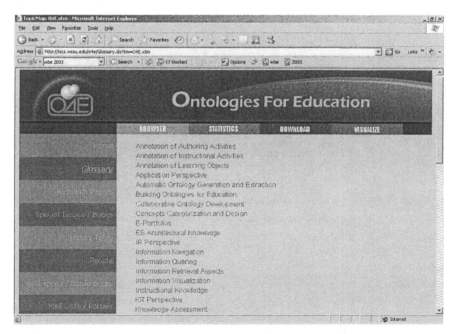

Figure 3-8. First-level concepts in the O4E (SWBE) taxonomy

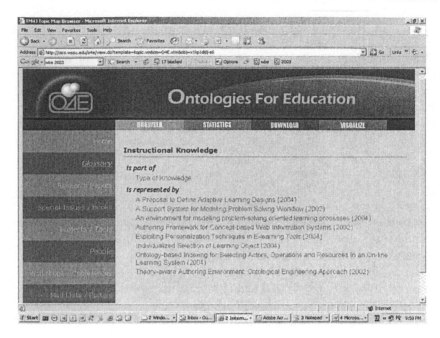

Figure 3-9. An example of relations among concepts in the O4E (SWBE) ontology

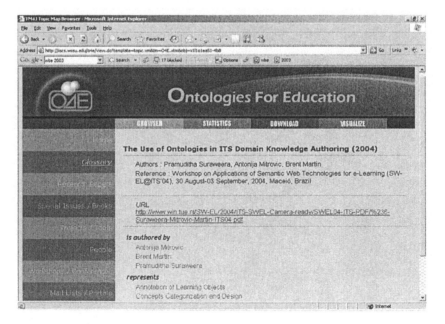

Figure 3-10. An example of a resource representing concepts in the O4E (SWBE) ontology

Apart from the O4E portal, notable efforts are related to standardization of SWBE issues (covered in detail in Chapter 5), personalization, learner modeling, and adaptivity of SWBE systems and applications (Chapter 6), and ontological engineering of SWBE (Chapter 7). Issues related to learning management systems, collaborative learning, and learning communities on the Semantic Web recently also receive increasing attention of researchers and practitioners.

8.   SUMMARY

Semantic Web-based education is currently getting momentum, and the interest of the e-Learning community for SWBE is rising. There is a good chance for SWBE to progress at the same pace as the Semantic Web itself, since much of the technology needed is already there.

Key concepts and issues of SWBE include:

- educational content, represented as learning objects of different granularity, stored in different digital libraries, learning object repositories, and on different educational servers;
- educational servers, as specific Web applications running on physical servers and enabling storing, retrieving, updating LOs, as well as different educational services;
- educational Web services, as Semantic Web services that support learning, teaching, and authoring processes;
- personalization and adaptivity of educational processes, based on learner modeling;
- educational ontologies of different kinds (domain, pedagogical, communication, task-related, and so forth), used for annotation of learning resources, educational Web services, and interoperation between the services and applications;
- intelligent pedagogical agents that reduce the manual efforts of end users by performing intelligent search and retrieval of LOs, locating, invocation, and composition of educational Web services, and otherwise acting on behalf of the end users;
- Semantic Web technology and standardization efforts, as well as related standardization initiatives related to WBE.

Chapter 4

ARCHITECTURAL ISSUES

One of the first issues that SWBE application developers should consider is the application architecture. More specifically, important issues of interest here include:

- architectural reference model - as with any other software system, the architecture of a SWBE system usually follows some general principles, guidelines, and application logic that reflect core workflows of educational tasks and processes;
- learning object structure and organization - all SWBE systems include authoring, representing, storing, updating, combining, integrating, delivering, interchanging, and otherwise manipulating LOs, hence precise characterization of LOs and decisions on LOR organization are a must;
- previous experience - experience from architectural design of more traditional e-Learning systems, virtual classrooms, Web-based ITSs, and AEHSs;
- ontology-related processing - since different kinds of educational ontologies are of primary importance in SWBE, they are usually given special attention in the system's architectural design, especially in the context of educational servers;
- current trends and technologies - grounding the system architecture in current overall software engineering and Web engineering approaches, trends, and standards, as well as in well-proven AI technologies;
- open learning environments - designing the system architecture for easy interoperation with different other SWBE systems, educational servers, learning portals, LORs, and other Web-based learning resources, as well as for supporting development of learning communities.

1.   ARCHITECTURAL REFERENCE MODEL

Architectural reference model for SWBE provides a conceptual framework for practical architectural design of SWBE systems. Figure 4-1 shows such an architectural reference model used/assumed in this book when discussing other topics. The model builds upon the work of Koper (2001). Relations (Associations) between the architectural components shown in Figure 4-1 use the standard UML notation (Fowler and Scott, 1999) to increase the overall readability of the architecture. For example, the association between *Design* and *Development* components is a generalization relation, whereas the dashed arrow lines represent the using (dependency) relationships.

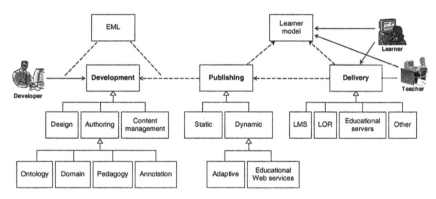

Figure 4-1. High-level architectural reference model for SWBE

The architectural reference model from Figure 4-1 can be interpreted as follows. Developers work with development environments (various authoring, design, and content management environments) and create/update educational content, typically in the form of LOs of different granularity. Authoring requires domain authoring, ontology authoring/development, and pedagogy authoring (learning/instructional design). Also, the resulting LOs must be properly annotated to facilitate search, location, and filtering. Developers use EMLs to encode pedagogical descriptions of LOs and units of learning. Content management tools are used to structure the LOs and units of learning that the authors create.

Publishing ensures that the material the developers create gets available to the learners. Note that the line between publishing and delivery is not very strict - publishing enables delivery of learning material over the Web, hence the publishing and delivery are, in fact, tightly coupled. Publishing may be organized in a *static* (*non-adaptive*) way, to support delivery of learning material in the form of static HTML pages, e-books, or CDs (the *Other* category of delivery). However, the "normal" SWBE delivery comes through educational servers, LORs, and learning management systems (LMSs). Thus SWBE publishing components usually interpret EML encoding and the learner model to provide personalization and adaptivity of the learning process. This *dynamic* publishing may also include publishing educational Web services that support different uses of LOs and more complex units of learning.

Note that Figure 4-1 complements Figure 3-4 to an extent; the architectural reference model from Figure 4-1 stresses the functional categorization of the components and tools included in the reference architecture, whereas the educational server model shown in Figure 3-4 rather provides a knowledge/information viewpoint. Both figures implicitly support the idea of open learning architectures as well; ontology-supported publishing and delivery of the learning content enables interoperability of different SWBE systems and reuse of LOs.

2. LEARNING OBJECTS

Much of the architectural reference model shown in Figure 4-1 is related (directly or indirectly) to the development, publishing, and delivery of LOs. Today, much of the LOs have a common high-level structure and are stored in LORs.

2.1 Learning object size and structure

In Chapter 3, section 2, it was already mentioned that there is still no clear terminological consensus about LOs of different granularities. To some authors, the fundamental idea that a LO can exist on its own and can be reused in different learning materials implicitly suggests that in practice LOs are mostly objects smaller than courses and that different courses can reuse LOs (Koper, 2001). So, a LO on the Web may be pragmatically thought of as some specific chunk of educational content and its associated metadata, a chunk representing things like an assessment, an exercise, an instructional content, and so forth, but not really things like a course, a module, and a study program. One of the arguments for such an attitude is that courses and modules are much more difficult to reuse than LOs of smaller granularity. An opposing argument is that a learning experience is actually achieved through more complex units of learning, providing learning events for learners and satisfying one or more interrelated educational objectives. Such *units of learning*, or *units of study*, include "coarse grained LOs" such as lessons, courses, workshops, and so on. An important point here is that a unit of study cannot be broken down to smaller pieces without loosing its semantic and pragmatic meaning and identity in terms of satisfying some learning objectives effectively.

Others support the view that LOs can be of any granularity and hence can include lessons, courses, and study programs. Their major argument is that, from the architectural point of view, components of a SWBE system manipulate LOs structured as in Figure 4-2. The figure implies nothing about the LOs complexity and granularity, and only conforms to the LO definition from IEEE, mentioned in Chapter 3, section 2.1 (IEEE, 2002). *Learning object content (LO content)* may be simple attributes (such as text and graphics), as well as other LOs (in case of composite LOs). A *learning object method (LO method)* is a description of the LO's behavior (operations). For example, an audio clip intended to be used as a LO includes such a method. A LO is described and referred to by the *learning object metadata (LO metadata)* - things like the LO title, author(s), language, keywords, and the like.

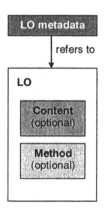

Figure 4-2. Common high-level structure of learning objects (after (Koper, 2001))

This book assumes that a LO can be of any granularity, but makes a clear distinction between smaller granularity LOs and units of learning (units of study, complex LOs) wherever that distinction is important.

If a LO is a composite LO (of any granularity), then a number of parameters of its internal structure affect the LO's reusability:
- the number of elements - the number of individual elements (such as video clips, images, or other LOs) composing the LO;
- the types of the composing elements;
- reusable LO components - the LO components that can be accessed and reused individually (i.e., taken out of the LO) to create new learning contents;

- the ways the LO can be combined with other LOs;
- interdependency between the LO's elements and components.

2.2   Learning objects and instructional design

For a unit of learning such as a course and a module, it may be more suitable to think of its contents and method as of an EML description of the associated learning design. The description may refer to and/or specify (Koper and Manderveld, 2004):
- the physical entities representing the composing LOs (files or services);
- the end user's role (learner, teacher);
- the activity he/she performs (learning, support activities) and the LOs and services involved;
- different prerequisites, conditions, and triggers designed to meet the desired learning objectives.

In addition to explicating the underlying learning (instructional) design theory used when developing a LO, authors should address another two issues as well if the goal is to increase the learning efficiency (Wiley, 2000):
- LO taxonomy - each LO typically has its place in a hierarchical categorization or in a clustering of LOs within the corresponding domain, based on the domain ontology; in other words, each concept from the domain ontology has, in general, its "associated" LOs (the LOs that describe the concept);
- prescriptive linking material - by specifying the learning goal that can be achieved when using the LO, the author can link the instructional design theory supporting the LO to the LO's taxonomy.

It is also of interest for a specific LO to estimate the extent to which the LO is domain specific. Some LOs can be reused only within a single domain; others can be used across a number of domains. For example, a LO representing timeline can be used in teaching history, physics, geology, astronomy, and even literature.

2.3   Learning object metadata

LO metadata fulfill many roles. One of them is the role of an indexing system that allows instructors and authors to easily find educational content that matches their instructional needs. Physically, the metadata are often separated from the LO itself; for example, a LOR can store just metadata and links to LOs physically stored elsewhere on the Web. When a user queries a LOR, an educational server, or an educational Web service for some content, in most cases he/she formulates the search criteria in terms of LO metadata. Likewise, when an author creates a new LO and wants to register it with a

LOR, he/she must provide the metadata for the LO in order to facilitate future queries to the LOR.

Metadata include a listing of commonly defined fields for each LO (McGreal, 2004). In practice, there is a good deal of consensus on what these fields should be - there are international standards that specify the fields and enable international interoperability. When creating a LO, authors use these fields to specify the associated metadata. The standards and specifications are generally extensible - in addition to the fields they specify, it is typically possible to add other fields.

The principal metadata standard for LOs is the Learning Object Metadata (LOM) standard, defined by the IEEE Learning Technology Standards Committee, or LTSC (IEEE LOM, 2002). It defines fields for describing LOs in terms of their general properties (e.g., fields like *title*, *language*, and *keyword*), technical requirements and characteristics (fields like *format*, *type*, and *duration*), pedagogical characteristics (e.g., *interactivity type*, *intended end user role*, *context*, *difficulty*, etc.), and so forth. The LOM standard is covered in detail in Chapter 5.

Standards like IEEE LOM specify a number of fields; institutions, systems, and applications normally insist only on a subset of mandatory fields and support a larger listing of optional fields. An *application profile* is a simplified and interpreted version of a standard or specification that is created to serve the needs of a particular community of users or implementers (Friesen and McGreal, 2002).

It is of particular interest to SWBE applications to work with XML-based representations of LO metadata. LTSC has developed the *XML LOM binding* standard (LTSC, 2005) that defines an XML Schema representation of the metadata fields specified in the LOM standard. In other words, the XML LOM binding standard defines the structure and constraints on the contents of XML documents that can be used to represent LO metadata instances compliant with the LOM standard. It is a mapping between the LOM standard metadata and XML Schema language that allows for creation of LOM instances in XML (i.e., serialization of LOM instances to XML) and for validation of LOM XML instances.

Likewise, *RDF LOM binding* defines a set of RDF constructs that facilitate introduction of educational metadata into the Semantic Web by enabling the exchange of LOM instances between conforming systems that implement the LOM standard (Nilsson, 2002). Both RDF LOM binding and XML LOM binding are discussed more extensively in Chapter 5.

Note that LO metadata are not necessarily static and do not necessarily contain just indisputable factual information about a LO, such as its title, author, and identifier (Nilsson et al., 2002). Much of the other kinds of metadata, such as the type and granularity of the LO, its pedagogical purpose, learning objectives, etc., are in practice not authoritative, objective information consisting of facts that do not change and can thus be produced just once. On the contrary, such metadata evolve over time; rather than being just factual data about the LO, they are subjective interpretations about the LO. For example, metadata related to the intended use of a LO are largely context-dependent and are typically not known precisely at the LO creation time (e.g., recall again the example from Chapter 3, section 2.1, of reusing an image of the Earth in courses related to different domains). Since RDF is designed as a framework for expressing metadata about resources on the Web, authors may use it to represent metadata about LOs. As a consequence, and because standards like LOM are extensible in terms of adding new fields, different kinds and layers of context-specific metadata can always be added by different authors when the need arises. This further implies the fact that metadata about a specific LO need not necessarily be contained in a single document - an application may use just a subset (or a single layer) of all metadata available for the LO. Defining really useful subset of LO metadata for the purpose is always a matter of consensus between instructors, domain specialists, and other interested parties, so it is essential that a number of people participate to this process of dynamic evolution of metadata.

This introduces LO metadata roles other than the LO indexing (Nilsson et al., 2002). Because of the distributed nature of LO metadata layers, an important role of LO metadata is to provide extensible and expandable descriptions of learning content, allowing the uses outside the domain foreseen by the content author. Also, metadata can fulfill the LO certification role - teachers, authors, and institutions may use LO metadata to certify some LOs as high-quality learning resources that are well suited for specific learning tasks. Another essential role of metadata is that of annotating LOs on the Semantic Web. Extending standard set of metadata by concepts and terms defined in external ontologies enables building metadata descriptions of LOs that along the usual information convey the meaning of LOs as well. Other useful roles of LO metadata include version management, personalization, and storing results from learning process monitoring and tracking.

2.4   Learning object repositories

LOs are not scattered all over the Web just like that; they are organized in *learning object repositories* (*LORs*) that store both LOs and their metadata[13]. In practice, most LORs store LOs compliant to the LOM standard.

---

[13] More precisely, LORs *appear* to store both LOs and their metadata; it means that LORs actually *present* combinations of LOs and their metadata to the outside world, while the

The purpose of LORs is to allow the users structured access to the LOs, i.e. the possibility to search, discover, retrieve, browse, and exchange the LOs.

"A LOR typically supports simple and advanced queries, as well as browsing through the material by subject or discipline. In a simple query, keywords given by the user are matched against the text in a number (or all) of the metadata elements. An advanced query allows a user to specify values for specific metadata elements (e.g. 'easy' or 'medium' for 'Difficulty level'), and sometimes also to rely on logical combinations of search criteria. Browsing typically allows the end user to descend in a tree of disciplines and sub-disciplines to get an impression of the objects available in different domains." (Neven and Duval, 2002)

There are three typical architectures of LORs (Mohan and Greer, 2003):

- *Global, client/server LORs.* These LORs maintain links to LOs stored elsewhere on the Web. Typical examples of such LORs are ARIADNE (ARIADNE, 2004) and MERLOT (MERLOT, 2005). They are essentially catalogs of LOs at different levels of granularity (from simple images and videos, to coarse-grain units of study such as courses and even curricula). A LO found at one of these LORs can be reused by, for example, providing a link to the LO in the course material being developed. Another way is to use educational Web services; it comprises wrapping queries to LORs into SOAP messages, interpreting them by the LOR's query engines, and returning the results in the form of LO metadata using SOAP. These LORs can be centralized on a single physical server, or distributed among multiple servers. The server(s) may store the LOs themselves, or they can maintain only the links to the LOs distributed all over the Internet. In the latter case, the metadata and/or the LOs can be replicated on different servers to facilitate search, or different servers cooperate in handling a search request (as in federated search, see below).
- *LORs based on brokerage services.* Brokerage services support exchange of LOs between producers and consumers (users). The LOs are catalogued in the LOR using metadata. The user enters search parameters for the LOs he/she is interested in, and the LOR informs him/her when these LOs become available. Brokerage services ensure for payment and protecting intellectual property rights (copyright) for LOs when necessary. For example, a brokerage service may require the user to agree on the offer terms associated with a LO before it can be accessed.

LOs and their metadata can be stored physically together or separately (Neven & Duval, 2002).

EducaNext, powered by the Universal Brokering Platform, is an example (EducaNext, 2005).

- *LORs based on peer-to-peer (P2P) networking.* Section 4 covers P2P architectures for LORs in detail. In brief, the point is that each peer in the network can act as a client (analogous to the Napster client software) and communicate with other peers using a specifically designed P2P protocol. Simultaneously, each peer site stores some LOs and can discover LOs stored by the other peers. The peers can exchange LOs and their metadata with other members of the network. The best known example to date is Edutella, a P2P networking infrastructure for LORs based on RDF (Nejdl et al., 2002).

LOs in different LORs can be related to topics in diverse domains, or can be more focused (both thematically and in terms of target users). For example, ARIADNE and MERLOT cover all subjects. On the other hand, there are LORs that cover only the domains of science, mathematics, engineering and technology, such as SMETE (SMETE, 2005). LearnAlberta (LearnAlberta, 2005) covers only kindergarten to grade 12 (K-12) education.

Today's LORs typically do not support IEEE LOM standard entirely, but define their own LOM application profiles. Some LORs support only simple keyword-based search, whereas others also enable search and browsing of LOs by discipline, resource type, or different metadata fields. Many LORs allow free access to the LOs they store; others (like LearnAlberta) implement some forms of restricted access in order to protect intellectual property rights.

LORs also largely differ in terms of the functionalities they support for end users. Some LORs support personalized interaction. For example, SMETE maintains user profiles as the basis for creating personalized workspaces. It also tracks the user's interaction with the LOs in order to recommend other LOs that may be of interest to the user, and identifies users with similar interests.

In addition to effective search engines, LORs should also support their users by effective navigation/orientation/browsing tools. These include:

- tools that process metadata files to provide LO preview;
- tools for sorting and categorizing LOs in more then one level;
- tools for contributing new LOs; these are of special interest to authors and teachers, as well as for building learning communities (see Chapter 10 for discussion of learning communities in the context of the Semantic Web).

An important issue related to LORs is how to interconnect them. For example, if a LOR cannot provide results for a query, can it forward the query to other LORs covering the same or related domains? If so, what metadata or LOM application profiles support the other LORs? Is there a need for query conversion, and also for LO format conversion if another

LOR can supply some LOs after processing the query? Is there a need to clear copyright issues when exchanging the LOs among different LORs?

There are several efforts and initiatives related to the above questions. One of the objectives of the LORNET project (LORNET, 2005) is to ensure that a LO created in a learning context can be reused or reconfigured for another environment. LO metadata are used for "digital packaging" of the LO to catalogue it for local and global identification (i.e., within a single LOR or across a network of LORs), enabling different users to search, find, exchange LOs with one another across LORs and transport them to other contexts. Full-scale automation of these activities requires processing metadata contents as semantically rich ontologies, through the use of educational Semantic Web services. Note that the processing is inherently complex, because of the fact that LOs can embody both educational contents and learning activities, as when using an EML to encode the LOs' pedagogy. On the other hand, educational content enriched by EML descriptions of learning activities is more elaborate and provides more diverse options for publishing and accessing the LO by educational Semantic Web services (see the architectural reference model in Figure 4-1).

Based on the similar driving forces as LORNET, the Celebrate project implements a federation of different learning management systems (LMS), content management systems (CMS), and independent LORs that can search through one another's repositories and share LOs amongst the partners (Van Assche and Massart, 2004). The federation is open, i.e. it can grow (add new members) without any additional administration burden placed on the existing partners. In a way, the Celebrate federation architecture is a combination of brokerage and ideas from P2P networking. There is a service broker and a number of clients, Figure 4-3. The clients can act as LO providers (LORs offering content to the federation), as consumers (only consuming content and services from the federation), or both at the same time. The service broker receives queries and requests from clients, validates them in terms of checking if they are well formed and if they have required access rights, and forwards them to the appropriate clients using Java Messaging Service (JMS) and SOAP protocol as the basic communication technologies. The clients process the requests and send the results back to the broker that forwards them to the requesters.

Both individual LORs and interconnected multiple LORs are encompassed by the general scheme of the conceptual model of educational servers, Figure 3-4, as well as by the architectural reference model shown in Figure 4-1. They store LOs' content and pedagogy in a highly structured way that provides easy search, retrieval, browsing and exchange, and enables educational services to manipulate them automatically. The metadata they store can make use of terms from external educational ontologies, thus supporting semantic annotation of LOs and facilitating semantic search and retrieval. LO metadata are an important element of adaptive dynamic publishing of LOs (Figure 4-1). In addition, semantic integration of multiple LORs that support different metadata profiles can be achieved by exploiting technologies such as educational Semantic Web services, pedagogical agents, P2P networking, and intelligent brokerage.

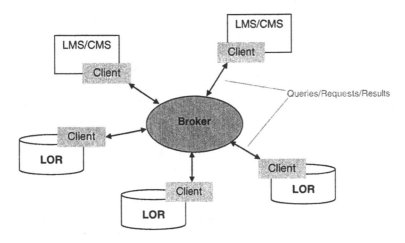

Figure 4-3. Federated LORs (after (Van Assche and Massart, 2004))

3. ARCHITECTURES OF WEB-BASED ITSs

Traditional Web-based ITSs do not include ontologies and Semantic Web languages, but still represent a useful source of architecture-relevant information for SWBE systems.

There is apparently a great variety in architectural details of traditional Web-based ITSs. Still, much of these systems are essentially client/server systems. True, client/server architectures are certainly not the only ones used in SWBE systems, but experiences and lessons learned with Web-based ITSs are prerequisites for development and deployment of improved architectures for SWBE systems.

It is possible to categorize Web-based ITS architectures into a relatively small number of architectural styles, based on the criterion of where the tutorial behavior resides - on the client side, on the server side, or both. Some of these styles are (Alpert et al., 1999), (Mitrović and Hausler, 2000):

- replicated architecture (or Java-only solution) - all the tutorial behavior resides on the client side; the entire ITS program is downloaded from the Web into the learner's Web browser as Java Web applet and all interaction between the program and the student happen locally;

- centralized architecture (or HTML-CGI[14] architecture) - all tutorial functionality resides on the server side (in a CGI program) but the learner interacts with it using a standard Web browser; essentially, the learner fills in HTML-based Web forms, and the information he/she enters is transferred to the server; the CGI program gets the information and replies with new HTML pages;
- distributed client/server architecture - some of the tutorial functionality resides on the server side, and some other on the client side; typically, for increasing the performance and responsiveness of the graphical part of a Web-based ITS' GUI, a downloadable Java applet implements all the interaction between the learner and the system and possibly some teaching functions, whereas the rest of the tutorial functionality is implemented as an application server and resides on the server side.

As an illustration, Figure 4-4 compares the traditional standalone ITS architecture with the third option from above. An example Web-based ITS that uses the architecture from Figure 4-4b is AlgeBrain, the system that teaches elementary high school algebra (Alpert et al., 1999). Another well-known system that also uses a variant of the distributed architecture is SQLT-Web, for teaching SQL language in the domain of databases (Mitrović and Hausler, 2000). Its UI Proxy / Communication module includes a session manager that records all learner actions and the corresponding feedback in a log file.

Various (and often contradicting) forces may drive architectural decisions in favor of one style or another. For example, replicated architectures are fast, since all processing happens on the client side. However, a significant limitation is that the student model is stored locally, which implies that the student must always use the system from the same machine if he/she wants to benefit from the latest version of the student model stored. A variant used in some Web-based ITSs with replicated architecture copies the student model to the server at the end of the session for more persistent storage. It may be acceptable in most of cases, but the downside is the reliance on network connections - if a network error occurs before the end of the session, the student model will not be updated on the server.

Replicated and distributed architectures imply downloading the software in order to start using the system or to get the software updates. Some students may find it frustrating (Mitrović and Hausler, 2000). Centralized architectures eliminate such problems, store all student models on the server (distributed architectures do the same), and enable using the system from any machine. However, the system may run at reduced speed because of intensive communication between the client and the server. Distributed

---

[14] CGI stands for Common Gateway Interface.

architectures may improve this by delegating some of the tutoring functionality to the client side, but it may also increase the system development effort.

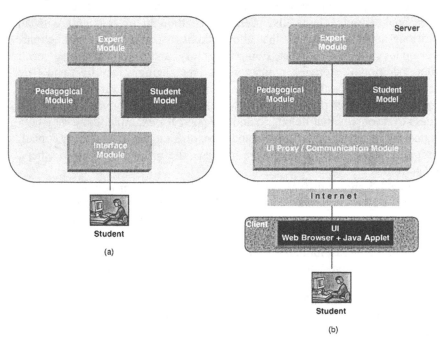

Figure 4-4. Comparing (a) traditional ITS architecture with (b) a Web-based ITS architecture

4. P2P NETWORKING

The concept of P2P networking is not a new computing concept. P2P computing model comprises direct exchange and sharing of files and resources between the node computers of a computer network. It can be applied to many domains, including education. P2P architectures are of interest to SWBE in terms of networking LORs, educational servers, learning management systems, and content management systems.

4.1 P2P computing essentials

P2P computing is the sharing of computer resources and services by direct exchange (Barkai, 2000). It provides an alternative to and complements the traditional client/server architecture. The P2P computing model can actually coexist with the client/server model. P2P computing architectures use the existing network, servers, and clients infrastructure.

Each participating computer in a P2P network is a *peer*, acting simultaneously as a client, as a server, and as a router within the context of a given application. Technically, peers can be thought of as clients with an additional layer of software that allows them to perform server functions. Peer nodes contribute content, storage, memory, and CPU, and provide each other additional storage, computations, messaging, security, and file distribution functionalities. A peer can initiate requests, and it can respond to requests from other peers in the network. Requests are typically related to access to resources that belong to another peer; for example, there may be a request for information on content and files, or for a file to be read or copied, computations to be performed, or a message file to be passed on to others, and so forth.

Figure 4-5 shows differences between the client/server computing model and the P2P computing model, and how the two models can be superimposed and coexist with each other. In the client/server model, all communication and resource exchange between the clients goes through the server. In the P2P model, peers communicate and exchange resources directly. There may be a server as well, and occasionally peers can communicate with it. The central server can perform some of the functions required by the application. For example, the application may require the users to first connect to a control server, where the directory of all available resources is stored (as in Napster). However, there are "pure" P2P architectures without a server at all (Kant et al., 2002).

Interesting features of P2P networks and architectures include (Barkai, 2000; Kant et al., 2002; Mohan and Greer, 2003; Nilsson et al., 2002):

- the network is dynamic; peers enter and leave the network frequently;
- the computing environment becomes decentralized; much of the computing is performed on the periphery of the net (see Figure 4-5b);
- resources are used more efficiently; in the client/server architecture, there is much of unused bandwidth, storage, and processing power at the edge of the network;
- reliability is increased; the users do not depend much on central servers, there is no single point of failure, and the peers are geographically distributed and may be replicated;
- data and control and load balance requests are distributed across the net;

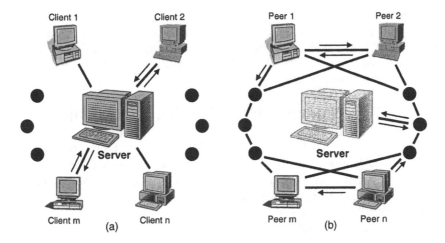

Figure 4-5. Client/server computing model (a) vs. P2P computing model

- the users have a higher degree of autonomy and control over the services they utilize;
- the users can organize themselves into online communities that can efficiently and securely communicate, fulfill requests, share resources, and collaborate; users can come and go, or be active or not; they can bypass centralized control, which greatly increases their feeling of autonomy;
- application types possible with P2P networking are different, but all of them are featured by sharing of resources with some form of collaboration;
- scalability is increased; consumers also donate resources, and aggregated resources grow naturally with their utilization;
- administration is easy; it is localized at individual nodes, which are autonomous (no centralized administrative authority);
- remote maintenance is enabled, since the P2P infrastructure allows direct access and shared space;

When a P2P network is used within an enterprise of any kind, it may be able to replace some costly data center functions with distributed services between clients (Barkai, 2000). Storage, for data retrieval and backup, can be placed on clients.

The killer apps of P2P networks were Napster and Gnutella. Napster was an MP3 music file sharing application, and Gnutella was a file sharing network used primarily to exchange music, films and software. There is no central server in Gnutella; client programs connect to the network and share files directly. Search queries are passed from one node to another in round-robin fashion.

After Napster and Gnutella, P2P computing has achieved considerable attraction with mainstream computer users and members of the PC industry (Barkai, 2000). Today, P2P application domains range from different kinds of e-Business, thru collaborative development, thru gaming, to virus detection and warning, and, yes - to education.

4.2   P2P architectures for exchanging learning objects

P2P networking enables addressing the following issues related to exchanging LOs among different learning applications, LORs, educational servers, and learning/content management systems (Barkai, 2000; Kant et al., 2002; Mohan and Greer, 2003; Nilsson et al., 2002):

- interoperability between heterogeneous LORs and other systems - each LOR and each external system/application may have its own set of basic services and plug-ins, and may rely on its own set of LO metadata; P2P networking may help by providing a common set of services (like a middleware and application interfaces) that provide the functionalities needed by all peers in the network, above the idiosyncrasies of metadata sets and protocols used by individual peers;
- increasing the provider's control over the LOs - if a LO is stored in a central LOR, its provider may loose the sense of ownership; on the other hand, in a typical P2P learning scenario LO providers and consumers are the same entities (such as university departments) interested in controlling the LOs they provide for use within the network and simultaneously gaining access not only to a local repository, but to a whole network;
- placing LOs closer to the learners for increased performance and reliability - in situations like online training with large video clips, the overall effects and flexibility may be improved if multiple peers offer storage for such large-size LOs;

All of these issues were in the focus of the Edutella project (Nejdl et al., 2002). Edutella uses a metadata infrastructure based on RDF for querying, replicating, exchanging, and otherwise manipulating LOs, assuming that each peer provides metadata describing the LOs and units of learning it manages. The metadata may follow the IEEE LOM standard, or another specification - the peers are supposed to say so through the services they provide, so that other peers will know. Thus Edutella can integrate heterogeneous peers (using different repositories, query languages and functionalities), as well as different metadata schemas.

An essential assumption underlying Edutella is that all resources maintained in the network can be described in RDF. All functionality in an Edutella-based network is mediated through RDF statements and queries on them. Each Edutella-based network provides learners, teachers, and LO authors with a transparent access to distributed LOs, LORs, and other kinds of clients/peers which all can be used to access these resources. Each peer is required to support a set of basic services (see below). In addition, each peer may offer other advanced services.

The easiest way to understand the Edutella infrastructure is to follow an example explaining one of its services. The most important service in a P2P network of LORs and learning applications is the query service. Figure 4-6 shows how a query is processed in an Edutella-based network. If a peer application needs to search the network for a LO, it normally uses its own query language to specify the query. An *Edutella wrapper* translates the query into the *Edutella query exchange format* and sends it to the network.

Figure 4-6. Edutella query exchange architecture (after (Nejdl et al., 2002))

The network is based on the JXTA framework for P2P applications (JXTA, 2005). The framework specifies a set of open protocols that allow any connected device on the network to communicate and collaborate in a P2P manner.

Once on the network, the query is expressed in an RDF/XML form based on the *Edutella Common Data Model* (*ECDM*). In fact, the Edutella wrapper also translates the application's local data model into ECDM. LORs, as well as other peers providing educational content and services in the network, also have their own Edutella wrappers. Having received the query, a LOR's wrapper translates it into the LOR's native query format and executes it. The query results are then wrapped back to the Edutella query exchange format and ECDM, and sent to the requester through the JXTA-based primitives.

In addition to the query service for standardized query and retrieval of RDF metadata, other services that Edutella peers are required to support include (Nejdl et al., 2002):
- replication service - providing data persistence / availability and workload balancing while maintaining data integrity and consistency;
- mapping service - translating between different metadata vocabularies to enable interoperability between different peers[15];

---

[15] Note that for a single LO there may be many metadata instances, created by different users at different peers. Moreover, subjective metadata like translations, extensions, comments on the metadata of others, etc. can be added by anyone and stored locally. Supportive tools

- mediation service - defining views that join data from different metadata sources and reconcile conflicting and overlapping information;
- annotation service - annotating materials stored on any peer within the Edutella Network.

Edutella services fit nicely into the JXTA layered framework of services and protocols. JXTA provides Java binding at three layers - core, services, and applications - for creating P2P applications:

- JXTA Core protocols and services include peer discovery, peer groups, peer pipes, and peer monitors;
- JXTA Services are related to things like indexing, file sharing, and searching; Edutella services, Edutella query exchange format, and ECDM are specified using common JXTA services;
- JXTA Applications layer allows for creating different peer functionalities on a P2P network; Edutella peers (LORs, annotation tools, and the like) are developed to live on the JXTA Applications layer, using the functionality provided by the Edutella services and possibly other JXTA services.

Nilsson et al. (2002) list a number of SWBE- relevant issues that P2P architectures support:

- distributed educational material and distributed search;
- combinations of metadata schemas (for example, personal information and content descriptions) being searched in combination;
- distributed annotation of any LO by anyone;
- machine-understandable semantics of ontology-based metadata;
- human-understandable semantics of metadata (contexts, persons, classifications).
- interoperability between tools; any tool can use P2P technology;
- personalization of tools, queries and interfaces, affecting the experience in several ways;
- competency declarations and discovery for personal contacts.

5.   ADAPTIVE LEARNING SYSTEMS

There is a number of proposals to use Semantic Web technologies and infrastructure to support AEHSs (e.g., see (Aroyo and Dicheva, 2004a; De Bra et al., 2004a; 2004b; Henze and Herrlich, 2004; Karampiperis and Sampson, 2004; Motta et al., 2003)). Designing powerful AEHS frameworks

---

need to be able to combine existing metadata sets with newly added ones. Graphically oriented metadata editors are needed for ontology-based, conceptual and classification metadata, and text-oriented ones can support metadata like title, author, keywords, and similar properties (Nilsson et al., 2002).

and architectures to provide adaptive navigation and adaptive courseware generation by merging different approaches and techniques from AH and the Semantic Web is recognized as one of the most challenging issues in the field of AEHSs.

A simple way to develop a good understanding of what exactly are the improvements that the Semantic Web can bring to AEHSs is to compare two AEHS architectures - one that does not use the Semantic Web infrastructure (Semantic Web languages, ontologies, and Semantic Web services), and another one that does. A well-known example of AEHS architectures is the *AHA! architecture* (De Bra et al., 2004a; 2004b)[16]; originally, AHA! was not based on the Semantic Web technologies. On the other hand, the IRS-II/UPML framework/architecture[17] introduced by Motta et al. (2003) deploys Semantic Web services and ontologies to enhance adaptation capabilities of AEHSs.

AHA! is essentially a centralized architecture, Figure 4-7. The core of the architecture includes the *domain model* (DM), the *learner model* (LM), and the *adaptation model* (AM), all of them stored on a central server. Authors typically create DM/AM using different authoring tools, and the system administrator configures the server and manages the users' accounts. AHA!'s *adaptation engine* uses Java servlets that serve pages from the local file system or from external http servers. The servlets interact with the combined DM/AM and with the LM.

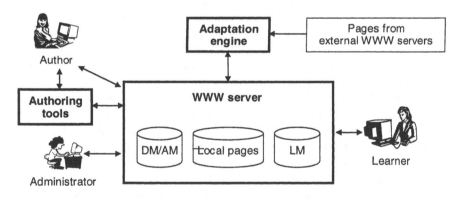

Figure 4-7. The AHA! system architecture (after (Bra et al., 2004b))

---

[16] In fact, AHA! is developed as a general-purpose AH system architecture; however, its most successful applications include some adaptive *learning* systems, hence it described here from that perspective only.

[17] IRS-II stands for Internet Reasoning Service, and UPML for Unified Problem-solving Method description Language.

An underlying assumption of the AHA! architecture is that each Web page that an adaptive WBE system can show to a learner corresponds to a concept in the DM, as well as in the LM (which uses the overlay model). By clicking on a link, the learner requests a Web page. The page may be suitable for his/her level and prerequisite knowledge or not; the system uses its adaptation engine, the AM rules, and the relevant LM values to check for suitability of the requested page for the learner. The system also uses the AM rules to update the LM. For example, AM rules may specify that the values of some parameters in the LM related to the requested concept may be increased when the learner requests a specific page and it turns out that the page is suitable for her/his knowledge level. The adaptation engine uses different adaptation techniques, covered in Chapter 1, section 5.2.1, to make the learning content presentation suit the learner's needs and current knowledge the best way possible. For example, it may decide to use some link annotation/hiding, or to show additional explanation automatically. In certain cases the type of adaptation used in the content presentation may cause additional LM updates as well.

The AHA! architecture has several drawbacks (in addition to those mentioned in section 3 for all intelligent WBE systems based on a centralized architecture):

- its DM/AM combination blurs both the domain representation and the adaptation representation; the semantics of the application domain is at least partially hidden inside the adaptation rules;
- it is not well suited for collaboration between different AEHSs; it is difficult to export the semantics of the DM/AM combination to applications that deal with concepts and relationships in another way, and is equally difficult to import external semantic information (e.g., an ontology), into an AHA! application;
- its centralized architecture stores all LMs on a central server; as a consequence, LMs cannot be accessed by external applications
- it is difficult to combine the LMs of a single learner recorded by different AEHSs; the LM representing a learner's knowledge gained through an online course cannot be used automatically to initialize the LM for the same learner at another AHA!-based AEHS.

IRS-II/UPML architecture, Figure 4-8, deploys ontologies and Semantic Web services to mitigate the above problems. In this architecture, the *adaptation model* is explicitly separated from the *domain model*, and another component is introduced as well - the *application model*. The application model contains a generic description of the user's tasks, captured by the *Role-Goals-Tasks* model. In fact, the application model explicates the instructional design of the AEHS based on this architecture. By making instructional design decisions explicit and separated from the adaptation model, IRS-II/UPML makes sharing and exchanging different functionalities between systems easier. The application model drives the adaptation - the adaptation follows the instructional directions specified explicitly by the application model.

In this highly modular architecture, three (out of four) central components - the application model, the adaptation model, and the learner model - are driven by Semantic Web services and can communicate with each other and with external systems and applications in terms of service invocations. The *bridges* specify the mappings between different model services within the architecture. Note that different ontologies define and unify the system's terminology and properties and describe the knowledge of each system service, as well as the services' pragmatics (invocation, composition, and monitoring). The services described this way provide a common ground for knowledge sharing, exploitation, and interoperability.

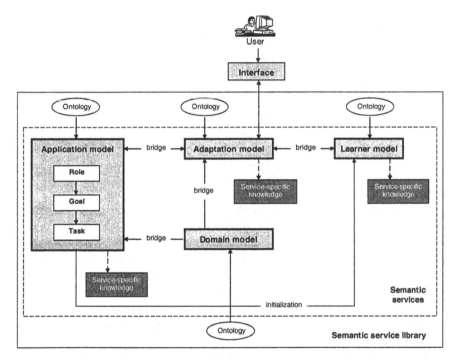

Figure 4-8. An architecture for ontology-supported adaptive WBE systems based on the IRS-II/UPML framework (after (Motta et al., 2003; De Bra et al., 2004b))

Accessing the learners' models by means of Web services introduces additional flexibility and collaboration opportunities. It is not necessary for a system to know anything in advance about a new learner if it can access his/her learner model (stored at another server) by invoking another system's appropriate learner model service. The system can then simply interpret the learner model initiated and updated by another application; the interpretation may i only the learner model parameters the system is interested in. From the learner's perspective, this learner model sharing between applications increases his/her mobility across different learning environments.

The IRS-II/UPML architecture nicely instantiates the architectural reference model shown in Figure 4-1. Many of its characteristics can be also traced in the educational server model shown in Figure 3-4. Note also that the pedagogical agents shown explicitly in Figure 3-4 can be also deployed in the context of IRS-II/UPML architecture to invoke different services.

A final but important remark on the application model of the IRS-II/UPML architecture - it largely parallels the notion of task ontology, mentioned in Chapter 3, section 6.2, and further elaborated in Chapter 7.

6.   ONTOLOGY PROCESSOR

Mitrović and Devedžić have introduced (2004) the notion of *ontology processor* as a distinct module in the architecture of a Web-based ITS that helps turning an ordinary Web-based ITS into a SWBE application. Figure 4-9 illustrates how an ontology processor extends the architecture of KERMIT, a Web-based tutor that teaches conceptual database design using the Entity-Relationship (ER) model (Suraweera and Mitrović, 2002). The original system - everything in Figure 4-9 except the dashed-line box - uses constraint-based modeling paradigm to model the domain and the learner's knowledge. The things in the dashed-line box are the extension.

It is beyond the scope of this book to describe the theory of constraint-based modeling and KERMIT in detail - see (Ohlsson, 1994) and (Suraweera and Mitrović, 2002) for thorough explanations. In brief, KERMIT contains a set of problems and the ideal solutions to them, but has no problem solver. KERMIT's pedagogical module determines the timing and the content of pedagogical actions, and the learner modeler analyses the learners' answers and generates the learner models. In order to check the correctness of a learner's solution, KERMIT compares it to the correct solution, using the domain knowledge represented in the form of more than 90 constraints.

The idea of extending KERMIT's architecture by introducing an ontology processor came from some observations and heuristics related to the practice of learning in general. If a learner is happy with an intelligent tutor he/she is using and with the learning material he/she can access, it is likely that he/she will want to learn more. If the knowledge domain is complex enough, chances are also that the developers of a successful intelligent tutor may want to extend or upgrade their tutor, as well as to build other tutors to cover other parts of the knowledge domain. Moreover, two or more different teams may develop different tutors that partially overlap in expertise. Therefore, the need for automatic knowledge sharing, reuse, and exchange among several different tutors in the same complex domain is highly likely to arise.

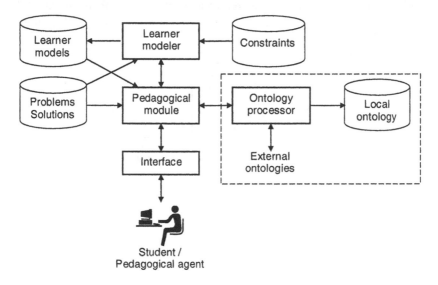

Figure 4-9. Ontology-based extension of KERMIT's architecture

Ontology processor, Figures 4-9 and 4-10, performs all ontology-related knowledge processing in the system, thus helping the traditional components (student modeler and pedagogical module) to handle knowledge of a complex domain and interoperability issues more effectively. It uses a *local ontology*, describing the domain of that specific tutor, and *external ontologies*, describing more general concepts.

The pedagogical module can request a service from the ontology processor either as a part of its internal processing, or in order to interpret a request for a certain educational service and provide it. There is a difference between a service provided by the ontology processor and an educational Semantic Web service - the latter is accessible externally, through the tutor's Web page or through a service directory. The *request interpreter* of the ontology processor, Figure 4-10, parses the request and its parameters (e.g., a request can carry an external URL). A possible result of the parsing process is a decomposition of the request into a sequence of simpler tasks to be carried out by the *request processor*. Certain requests may refer to the local ontology only; others may require accessing an external ontology. In either case, as a result of processing the ontology the request processor may output a set of items (such as a sequence or a tree of domain concepts, an indicator of a relevant part of the local ontology, or the URL of an external ontology). The *service composer* takes such items and rearranges them into an output form suitable for the pedagogical module. This activity may involve adaptivity, heuristics, and various constraint processing. For example, the request processor may return a set of concepts from an external ontology, and the service composer may need to relate them to the input parameters (Mitrović and Devedžić, 2004).

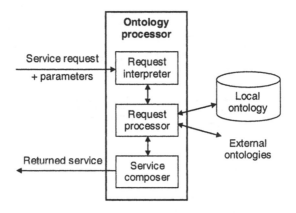

Figure 4-10. Ontology processor

The following scenario illustrates the role of the ontology processor in KERMIT. Suppose that a distant learner's agent consults KERMIT's Web page about the possibility for the learner to find out examples of binary relationships in conceptual database modeling. The agent invokes the "Examples" Web service on the KERMIT's site and passes the term "binary relationship" and the URL of the corresponding ontology. The "Examples" service invokes the pedagogical module, which in turn may decide to invoke the ontology processor (see "Service request" in Figure 4-10). The ontology processor could perform an ordinary text-based search in the KERMIT's knowledge and databases. However, the returned information based on such a trivial search may not be fully relevant. Hence the ontology processor performs semantic search instead. It parses the remote ontology represented at the site identified by the URL supplied by the learner's agent and passed on by the pedagogical module. As a result, the ontology processor finds out the relevant hierarchy of concepts: binary relationship - regular relationship - relationship type - ER construct. The ontology processor then tries to identify these concepts (or similar ones) in KERMIT's local ontology of ER model, as well as in the (external) more general ontology of data models. In case of success, the ontology processor provides the learner's agent with the exact pointers to the parts of KERMIT's knowledge focusing on examples of binary relationships.

7. ADOPTING SOFTWARE ENGINEERING TRENDS[18]

In order to design and develop a reliable, robust, well-architectured, and easy-to-extend application or tool in any field, it is important to conform with sound principles and rules of software engineering. SWBE systems are no exception to that rule. It is especially important for SWBE authoring tools to be designed closely following software engineering (SE) practices.

Keeping an eye on current SE developments and trends can help design SWBE tools to remain stable over a longer period of time. For example, a general trend in software engineering is the use of tailored versions of UML to alleviate design of the system specifics. In practice, this usually means defining *UML stereotypes* and *profiles* to facilitate modeling of a specific domain, such as SWBE. Essentially, this means introducing new kinds of UML modeling elements by extending the basic ones, and adding them to the modeler's tools repertoire (see (Đurić et al., 2006) for further explanation of such UML mechanisms).

Another emerging software engineering trend, with intensive support from Object Management Group (OMG)[19], is application development based on *Model-Driven Architecture* (*MDA*) (Miller and Mukerji, 2003).

7.1   Model-Driven Architecture

MDA is a generally applicable idea, but is simultaneously of specific interest to AI developers since it has much in common with ontology modeling and development. Essentially, MDA defines three levels of abstraction in system modeling. *Computation Independent Model* (*CIM*) corresponds to the system's domain model and is similar to the domain ontology. It does not show details of the system structure. *Platform Independent Model* (*PIM*) is computationally dependent, but not aware of specific computer platform details. In other words, PIM shows how a technology-neutral virtual machine runs the system. *Platform Specific Model* (*PSM*) introduces platform-specific issues and implementation details. The

---

[18] Portions of this section reprinted (with minor adjustments), with permission, from Đurić, D., Devedžić, V., Gašević, D., 2006, Adopting software engineering trends in AI, *IEEE Intelligent Systems* **21** (forthcoming). © 2006 IEEE.

[19] OMG is an important consortium and a standardization body in the field of software engineering. For example, UML is an OMG standard (OMG, 2003).

goal of MDA modeling is to shift the designer's focus from PSM towards PIM and CIM and use automated tools to transform PIM to PSM.

MDA metamodeling architecture, illustrated in Figure 4-11, is a layered architectural and development framework for building MDA-based software systems. Typically, developers use UML to represent their domain models (M1 layer). These domain models represent things from the real world: people, things, thoughts, concepts, databases, objects, programs, and other concrete entities (M0 layer).

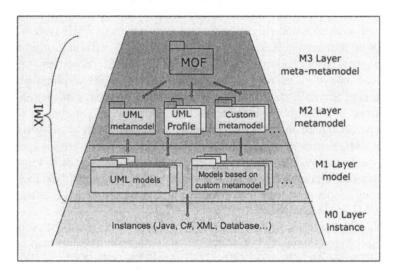

Figure 4-11. Four-layer MDA modeling framework[20]

However, MDA also provides means for defining modeling languages themselves (such as UML and UML profiles). They are defined in the form of metamodels (M2 layer). Specifying metamodels of modeling languages is done using *Meta-Object Facility* (*MOF*) (OMG, 2002a). MOF is also an OMG standard like UML, and is the meta-metamodel (M3 layer). It defines an abstract language and framework for specifying, constructing and managing technology-neutral metamodels. Any modeling language, such as UML (or even MOF itself!) can be defined in MOF. Custom metamodels, specified using MOF as a meta-metamodel, can define mappings to UML and UML profiles. This enables the use of widespread UML tools to manipulate the metamodels. Finally, the mechanism for exchanging the models with other applications, agents, and tools is *XML Metadata*

---

[20] Figure reprinted (with minor adjustments), with permission, from Đurić, D., Devedžić, V., Gašević, D., 2006, Adopting software engineering trends in AI, *IEEE Intelligent Systems* **21** (forthcoming). © 2006 IEEE.

Interchange (*XMI*), which is an open W3C standard (OMG, 2002b). XMI serializes MOF-based metamodels and models into plain text (XML), thus making such data ready to exchange in a standard way and to be read by any platform-specific implementation.

7.2 SWBE perspective on MDA

Adopting the general and rapidly growing MDA trend in designing and developing SWBE systems means, in fact:

- specializing ("instantiating") the four-layer MDA framework to support various EMLs, e-Learning standards and specifications, LO modeling, and other WBE representation formalisms;
- incorporating educational ontologies into the specialized framework;
- providing the mapping from/to the specialized framework and other Semantic Web languages and environments, thus making it an open framework for developing SWBE systems.

These points do not map to one-time activities; they require a process. The initial step in that process is the design and building of software tools and environments to support MDA-based SWBE system development. Such tools must be designed with the following objectives in mind:

- to provide a general modeling and metamodeling infrastructure for analysis, design, and development of SWBE systems;
- to make the infrastructure, the corresponding tools, and the resulting metamodels Semantic Web-ready;
- to be able to instantiate/specialize the general framework, i.e. to define more specific SWBE frameworks (starting from the general one) to support developments in specific subfields of SWBE, such as authoring systems, interactive learning systems supporting different learning theories, assessment systems, LMSs, and the like.

Conceptual model of such tools and environments is shown in Figure 4-12. An experimental integrated environment of that kind (albeit much wider in scope) is described in (Ðurić et al., 2006). The central part of the environment is a *model base*, represented as a *metadata repository*. It can include models of different kinds of SWBE systems, as well as models of any other domains of interest in a specific project. Technically, access to these models can be provided through publicly available Java/XML technologies, such as Java Metadata Interchange (JMI) compliant APIs[21]. Another important part of the environment is an integrated *workbench* with a rich GUI for specifying and manipulating the models. Typically, SWBE system developers and authors access and/or specify metamodels through this workbench.

---

[21] These are beyond the scope of this book; see (Ðurić et al., 2006) for details.

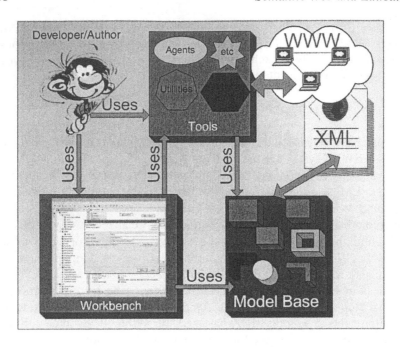

Figure 4-12. Conceptual model of MDA-based software environments for development of
SWBE systems[22]

In addition, SWBE developers may need to use a number of other
knowledge representation, reasoning, communication, and learning tools in
their systems. Moreover, they may want to do parts of their system modeling
with software tools they are used to, such as common UML-based CASE
tools. When the project is already underway, designers might like to switch
to a new tool as well. In all such cases, easy and seamless integration of
different formats, tools, and techniques within the same project is highly
desirable. That is exactly what MDA-based development environments are
used for - they let developers specify the XML-based metamodel of a
desired representational format, language, or paradigm, put the metamodel in
the repository, and make possible for tools and applications to use it along
with the other metamodels for integration purposes. Since any modeling
language (both general-purpose such as UML and education-specific such as
an EML) can be defined in MOF, it is comparatively easy within the MDA
framework to integrate authoring technologies and mainstream software

---

[22] Figure reprinted (with minor adjustments), with permission, from Đurić, D., Devedžić, V.,
Gašević, D., 2006, Adopting software engineering trends in AI, *IEEE Intelligent Systems*
21 (forthcoming). © 2006 IEEE.

technologies that SWBE system developers are familiar with, and expand them with new functionalities.

8. SUMMARY

There are several kinds of SWBE applications, all of them fitting by their architecture into a common architectural reference model. The model distinguishes between three groups of components/modules/activities in a SWBE system - development, publishing, and delivery of learning objects. The architectural reference model is orthogonal to the general model of educational severs.

Learning objects are of primary importance in any SWBE system. There is great variation in LO size, structure, and design across SWBE systems and repositories. LOs are annotated with metadata, most often according to the IEEE LTSC LOM standard, and stored in LO repositories in a highly organized and structured way.

There is a rich heritage coming from architectural design of traditional Web-based ITSs that can be reused (at least to an extent) in SWBE system architectures. Also, P2P computing architectures are proven to be successful in fulfilling many practical requirements of networking LORs, educational servers, LMSs, and other subsystems and components of SWBE systems.

Integration of Semantic Web technologies and AEHSs enables building systems with largely increased modularity and flexibility, especially in terms of combining multiple AEHSs and specifying different application models explicitly. For successful and often complex processing in application scenarios that include ontology-based reasoning and knowledge sharing between different educational severs, it is helpful to introduce an ontology processor in the system architecture. Architectural design of newly developed SWBE systems should consider borrowing from current, increasingly popular frameworks coming from the broad field of software engineering, such as MDA.

Chapter 5

LEARNING TECHNOLOGY
STANDARDIZATION EFFORTS

Standardization in the area of educational technologies is important for several reasons (Anido et al., 2001), (Friesen and McGreal, 2002):
- a set of high-level principles, notions, codes, and rules must be established to serve a regulatory function with respect to different learning resources, systems, and applications;
- educational resources such as learning objects and more complex units of learning are defined, structured, and presented using different formats; in order to enable their reusability across different e-Learning systems, at least some of their features must be represented in a standardized form;
- specific functional modules embedded in the architecture of a particular learning system cannot be reused by a different system in a straightforward way;
- inter-institutional course sharing and quality control should be based on unified frameworks.

In addition, interoperability among different SWBE applications requires an appropriate solution for the problem of disparate and heterogeneous metadata descriptions or schemas across domains (Stojanović et al., 2001). It is important to have ontologies that explicitly and formally describe the semantics of different metadata schemes.

1. THE BASICS

The starting point towards an appropriate understanding of the importance of standardization processes, activities, and initiatives is a clarification of the terminology used in this area. The next step is to obtain an insight into organizational aspects of standardization, i.e. into different standardization bodies and their efforts, products, and impact.

1.1   Definitions

In the context of learning technology standardization efforts, this book uses the following interpretations of the terms *standard*, *specification*, *application profile*, and *reference model*, adapted from (Friesen and McGreal, 2002) and (Mohan and Greer, 2003):

- *standards* are definitions or formats that have been approved by a recognized standards organization; alternatively, such definitions and/or formats can be accepted as *de facto standards* by the learning technology community and industry without a formal approval from a recognized standardization body;
- *specifications* are less evolved than standards and attempt to capture a rough consensus in the e-Learning community; it can take a long time before a widely used specification gets finally approved as a standard, yet specifications are used by the e-Learning community as de facto standards and enable people to get on with the job of system and content development;
- *application profiles* are simplified and interpreted versions of standards and/or specifications; they are typically created by reducing the coverage of standards and specifications to adapt them to the needs of a particular community of users or implementers; elements from more than one specification or standard can be combined into a single profile; however, profiles should not modify the elements, as would have a negative impact on interoperability;
- *reference models* are much like application profiles in terms that they also employ standards and specifications and play an important role in the development of systems; however, they are more focused on architectural aspects; they show how different parts of a system interact with each other and hence provide guidelines for the definition of these parts.

Note that there is no clear cut between application profiles and reference models. Some people in the e-Learning community use the two terms interchangeably. Both application profiles and reference models have a significant influence on standardization efforts, and in turn can be used to build actual systems that conform to a standard (which are then said to be compliant with the model) (Mohan and Greer, 2003).

1.2　　　Relevant standardization bodies

A number of organizations, committees, working groups, and other bodies are involved with standardization efforts and initiatives. Some of them are:

- *IEEE LTSC* (http://ieeeltsc.org/) - The IEEE Learning Technology Standards Committee (LTSC) develops accredited technical standards, recommended practices, and guides for learning technology. The LTSC cooperates formally and informally with other organizations that produce specifications and standards for similar purposes, in terms of actually gathering recommendations and proposals from such institutions and organizations. Standards development in LTSC is done in several working groups; one of them is WG12, that has developed the Learning Object Metadata (LOM) standard, already mentioned in Chapter 4.

- *ISO/IEC JTC1* (http://jtc1sc36.org/) - This is a standardization committee based in the International Organization for Standardization (ISO). IEC stands for ISO's International Electrotechnical Commission, and JTC1 is Joint Technical Committee 1, a joint committee of ISO and IEC. The scope of JTC1 is information technology standardization. Its subcommittees (SCs) work on relatively broad areas of technology standards; specifically, SC36 works on information technology and metadata for learning, education, and trainingSC36 closely cooperates with the IEEE LTSC.

- *DCMI* (http://dublincore.org/) - Dublin Core Metadata Initiative is an organization that develops specialized metadata vocabularies for describing resources on the Internet, thus enabling more intelligent information discovery systems. DCMI also promotes a widespread adoption of interoperable metadata standards, and defines frameworks for the interoperation of metadata sets. Note that DCMI metadata sets do not address exclusively educational applications, but Internet resources in general. However, e-Learning standards, specifications, and interoperability initiatives often refer to at least some of the DCMI metadata elements.

- *IMS Global Learning Consortium* (http://www.imsproject.org/) - IMS is a non-profit organization whose members include hardware and software vendors, educational institutions, multimedia content providers, other consortia, and so on. IMS develops and promotes the adoption of open technical specifications for interoperable learning technology. Several IMS specifications have become de facto standards for delivering learning products and services. IMS Works with other groups, including IEEE LTSC, MERLOT, and others.

- *AICC* (http://www.aicc.org/) - The Aviation Industry CBT (Computer-Based Training) Committee (AICC) is an international association of technology-based training professionals. Its mission is to develop guidelines for development, delivery, and evaluation of CBT and related training technologies. Although their guidelines target primarily CBT in aviation industry, they are fairly general to most types of computer based training and, for this reason, are widely used outside of the aviation training industry. Hence AICC is well recognized among people concerned about reuse and interoperability of online learning AICC also actively coordinates its efforts with other learning technology standards organizations like IMS, ADL, ISO/IEC JTC1 SC36, and IEEE LTSC.
- *ADL* (http://www.adlnet.org/) - Advanced Distributed Learning initiative related to development and implementation of learning technologies was formed to provide access to the highest-quality learning across the US Department of Defense (DoD). ADL's activities include development of standards, tools, and learning content; the objective for their products is to be tailored to learners' individual needs and delivered in a cost-effective way, anytime, and anywhere.
- *ARIADNE Foundation* (http://www.ariadne-eu.org/) - ARIADNE is the acronym for the Alliance of Remote Instructional Authoring and Distribution Networks for Europe. It fosters sharing and reuse of electronic pedagogical material (learning objects) among universities and corporations. The core of the ARIADNE infrastructure is a distributed network of learning object repositories, called the Knowledge Pool System. ARIADNE's important contribution to standardization of educational technologies was made by development of a body of educational standards in the form of the ARIADNE Educational Metadata specification (the "pedagogical header"). This specification later became one of the main ingredients in the creation of the IEEE LTSC LOM standard. ARIADNE has also acted as a co-author of the IMS metadata structure.
- *CEN/ISSS/LT* (http://www.cenorm.be/cenorm/businessdomains/businessdomains/isss/activity/wslt.asp) - CEN is the European Committee for Standardization, and its Information Society Standardization System (ISSS) works on both formal and informal standardization. In other words, ISSS produces both guides to best practices as well as full standards. The ISSS Learning Technologies Workshop encourages effective development and use of relevant and appropriate standards for learning technologies for Europe. Its guiding principle is not to duplicate work done by other organizations; it rather develops specifications, agreements, guidelines, and recommendations for issues not covered by other initiatives. Also, the ISSS Learning Technologies Workshop adapts global standards,

specifications, and reference models in the domain of e-Learning to European requirements. It does so via many national or European initiatives, with the objective of reaching a European-wide consensus on their deliverables.

- *GEM Project* (http://www.thegateway.org/) - GEM (Gateway to Educational Materials) is a consortium effort to provide educators with quick and easy access to numerous educational resources found in different repositories. In fact, GEM tries to integrate various federal, state, university, and other LORs. GEM cooperates with other standardization organizations.

- *OKI Project* (http://www.okiproject.org/) - The Open Knowledge Initiative project, run at MIT, develops specifications that describe how components of an educational software environment communicate with each other and with other enterprise systems. The specifications address issues like behavior of educational technology systems, interoperability, adaptation to new technologies over time, and further specification by communities of practice. An important and pragmatic principle the specifications follow is that components of educational software must be modular enough to allow for independent development and updating, an easy enough to integrate with different educational environments and enterprise applications. The specifications come in the form of Open Service Interface Definitions (OSIDs) that create an abstraction layer (i.e., service-based API) between programmers and educational software infrastructure. OKI team at MIT cooperates with the IMS Global Learning Consortium, ADL initiative, and other standardization organizations.

1.3 Standardization process

Many of the above mentioned standardization organizations, consortia, and other groups include members from both academia and industry. They normally do not produce their specifications and reference models quite independently of each other; they rather collaborate and share efforts. In many cases, they draw from different successful application profiles to improve their specifications.

Also, some groups develop their specifications with the clear goal of improving specifications/standards developed by other groups; for example, IMS consortium has developed its Learning Resource Metadata (LRM) specification (Anderson and Wason, 2000), in order to enhance IEEE LOM standard. Other organizations start from earlier standards and specifications and evolve them into a new standard (e.g., some of the ARIADNE's specifications were the basis for developing the IEEE LOM standard).

Once a draft specification is developed, it is exposed for some time to the community for comments and evaluation before it becomes an official specification. Eventually, to achieve authority, the specifications must be submitted to an organization with the authority to accredit and promulgate them (Horton, 2002). Typically, the first such an organization to submit most standards is the IEEE, and then the highest step to reach is to become ISO standards.

2.   IMPORTANT STANDARDS IN LEARNING TECHNOLOGIES

The word "standards" in the title of this section actually means standards, specifications, application profiles, and reference models. They are presented here with a clear indication of which organization developed and maintains them, and which segment of learning technologies they target.

2.1   Types of standards

There are several types of standards in learning technologies (Friesen and McGreal, 2002; Horton, 2002; McClelland, 2003; Mohan and Greer, 2003); some of them are:

- *metadata standards* are necessary when LO authors provide descriptions of the LOs they create, so that such descriptions can be published along the LOs to facilitate their search and retrieval;
- *packaging standards* regulate assembly of complex units of learning from simple LOs developed by different authors and in different formats (i.e., using different tools); such an assembly can be imported into different delivery systems such as LMSs, educational servers, and LORs;
- *learner information standards* support the exchange of learner information among different WBE systems, LMSs, enterprise e-Learning systems, knowledge management systems, and other systems used in the learning process;
- *communication standards* specify how exactly the learners access educational content stored at educational servers and other delivery platforms in order to use different learning, assessment, collaboration and other services offered;
- *quality standards* are related to the quality of LOs and units of learning, in terms of governing their design and accessibility.

There is a number of standards in different categories listed above. The following subsections survey some of the most important ones from the perspective of SWBE.

2.2 Dublin Core

Dublin Core Metadata Element Set (usually referred to as just Dublin Core, or DC) from DCMI is a standard from the metadata standards category. It is the metadata specification with the broadest scope, intended for cross-domain information resource description, i.e. to facilitate search and retrieval of any kind of Web-based resources (DCMI, 2004; McClelland, 2003). There are no fundamental restrictions to the types of resources to which DC metadata can be assigned - information resource is defined to be "anything that has identity". Hence DC metadata specification does not apply only to learning resources such as LOs.

Table 5-1 shows all 15 elements in the current version of the DC standard.

Looking at the DC elements, it becomes immediately apparent that they are simple and intuitive enough for all Web page authors to use. Marking up Internet resources with DC elements is intended to support resource discovery across multiple disciplines (including publishing, museum information systems, library science, and knowledge management) and within any type of organization (McClelland, 2003). In addition, DCMI provides definitions of the elements in the DC set in 25 different languages.

How is DC standard used in practice?

To answer this question, it is important first to note the following:

- DC metadata can comfortably coexist with the other metadata sets in case a resource (say, a LO) is described by multiple metadata sets;
- Dublin Core is intended to facilitate interoperability between the semantics of metadata specifications (Friesen and McGreal, 2002).
- DC metadata are syntax-independent, and can be encoded in a number of ways - in the <meta> tags in the header of an (X)HTML document, in XML documents, or in RDF/XML markup (McClelland, 2003);
- all DC properties (elements) are optional and repeatable (DCMI, 2004).

If a DC description is used within an (X)HTML document, it is embedded into the <head> section of document, as in Figure 5-1 - a <meta> tag is used for each DC element in the description, containing the name of the DC element as the value of its name attribute and the element's value as the value of its content attribute.

To use a DC description within an RDF document, a namespace is defined and the DC encoding is embedded in an <rdf:Description> element, as in Figure 5-2.

Table 5-1. The elements of the Dublin Core metadata set (adapted from (DCMI, 2004))

Element	Description
Title	A name given to the resource (by which the resource is formally known)
Creator	An entity primarily responsible for making the content of the resource (typically, the name of a person, an organization, or a service)
Subject	A topic of the content of the resource (typically expressed as a list of keywords, key phrases, or classification codes)
Description	An account of the content of the resource (such as an abstract, a table of contents, a reference to a graphical representation of content, or free text)
Publisher	An entity responsible for making the resource available (typically, the name of a person, an organization, or a service)
Contributor	An entity responsible for making contributions to the content of the resource (typically, the name of a person, an organization, or a service)
Date	A date of an event in the lifecycle of the resource (e.g., the date of creation or of availability of the resource)
Type	The nature or genre of the content of the resource (a list of terms describing general categories, functions, or aggregation levels for content)
Format	The physical or digital manifestation of the resource (e.g., media-type or dimensions (like size and duration) of the resource, equipment needed)
Identifier	An unambiguous reference to the resource within a given context (typically a string or number conforming to a formal identification system)
Source	A reference to a resource from which the present resource is derived (typically a string or number conforming to a formal identification system)
Language	A language of the intellectual content of the resource (typically two- and three-letter primary language tags with optional subtags (e.g., *en*, *en-US*))
Relation	A reference to a related resource (typically a string or number conforming to a formal identification system)
Coverage	The extent or scope of the content of the resource (typically, spatial location (e.g., a place name), temporal period (e.g., a date range), or jurisdiction (e.g., a named administrative entity))
Rights	Information about rights held in and over the resource (typically a rights management statement for the resource, such as Intellectual Property Rights, or Copyright)

```
<html>
<head>
...
    <meta name="DC.subject" content="blues"/>
    <meta name="DC.subject" content="jazz"/>
    <meta name="DC.date" content="2005-12-11"/>
...
</head>
<body>
```

Figure 5-1. Embedding Dublin Core description into an (X)HTML document

The Dublin Core metadata set shown in Table 5-1 has been formally endorsed by three accredited standards (DCMI, 2004):

- ISO Standard 15836-2003 (February 2003);
- NISO Standard Z39.85-2001 (September 2001);
- CEN Workshop Agreement CWA 13874 (March 2000, no longer available).

```
<?xml version="1.0"?>
<rdf:RDF xmlns:rdf="http://www.w3.org/1999/02/22-rdf-syntax-ns#"
       xmlns:dc="http://purl.org/dc/elements/1.1/">
  <rdf:Description>
    <dc:creator>Patti Smith</dc:creator>
    <dc:title>Horses</dc:title>
    <dc:subject>rock 'n' roll</dc:subject>
    <dc:language>EN</dc:language>
    ...
  </rdf:Description>
</rdf:RDF>
```

Figure 5-2. Embedding Dublin Core description into an RDF document

Recently, Dublin Core has evolved to allow for including elements other than the original 15 (e.g., Audience), and for more refined specification of individual metadata elements. The so called *Qualified Dublin Core* includes qualifiers to express details about the use of an element, or to identify an encoding scheme or controlled vocabulary as the element's restricted set of values (McClelland, 2003).

Dublin Core is widely used in different metadata encoding schemes in SWBE and elsewhere, typically in combination with other schemes.

2.3   IEEE LOM

IEEE LTSC Learning Object Metadata (LOM) is an approved standard (IEEE LOM, 2002), also from the metadata standards category. It was already briefly introduced in Chapter 4, as the principal metadata standard for LOs. Many other organizations, such as DCMI, ADL, ARIADNE, and IMS, have been involved either directly or indirectly in the development of the specifications on which this standard is based (McGreal, 2004). Also, a variety of application profiles for specific implementations of the LOM standard have been developed, since LOM specifies a number of fields (metadata elements).

Unlike Dublin Core, LOM is specialized for LOs only. It was developed with the idea to define the minimum set of attributes required to fully and adequately describe, manage, locate, and evaluate LOs, bearing in mind the diversity of their granularities, pedagogical characteristics, technology, and media. The resulting metadata set contains 76 elements, grouped in nine categories. As with Dublin Core, all elements are optional; there are no minimum cataloging requirements either (McClelland, 2003).

The nine categories of LOM elements are shown in Table 5-2. The table is a largely simplified and incomplete version of the so called LOMv1.0 Base Schema, and is provided here for an informal insight into the categories, their meanings, and examples of metadata elements in the categories (see (IEEE LOM 2002) for a complete reference). Note also that the Classification category may be used to provide certain types of extensions to the LOMv1.0 Base Schema, as any classification system can be referenced.

Table 5-2. Categories of elements in the LOM standard (adapted from (IEEE LOM, 2002))

Category	Explanation	Example elements
General	General information that describes the LO as a whole	Title, language, coverage, keyword
Lifecycle	Features related to the history and current state of this LO, as well as to those who have affected this LO during its evolution	Version, status, contribute, role, entity, date
Meta-Metadata	Information about the metadata instance itself (rather than the LO that the metadata instance describes)	Catalog, entry, role, entity, metadata schema
Technical	Technical requirements and technical characteristics of the LO	Format, duration, size, location, type
Educational	Educational and pedagogic characteristics of the LO	Interactivity type, context, difficulty
Rights	Intellectual property rights and conditions of use for the LO	Cost, copyright and other restrictions
Relation	Features that define the relationship between the LO and other related LOs	Kind, resource, description
Annotation	Comments on the educational use of the LO and provides information on when and by whom the comments were created	Entity, date, description
Classification	Description of this LO in relation to a particular classification system	Purpose, taxon path, source

Some of the metadata elements in the LOMv1.0 Base Schema take free text for values. Others must take values from predefined vocabularies.

LO metadata instances compliant with the LOM standard can be represented as XML files containing metadata. IEEE LTSC provides an XML Schema binding of the LO metadata data model defined in the LOM standard (LTSC, 2005). The binding specifies XML Schema definitions of all the elements specified by the LOMv1.0 Base Schema. Two examples are shown in Figure 5-3. Currently, the binding has the status of a draft IEEE LTSC standard.

```
<xs:schema targetNamespace="http://ltsc.ieee.org/xsd/LOM"
     xmlns="http://ltsc.ieee.org/xsd/LOM"
     xmlns:xs="http://www.w3.org/2001/XMLSchema"
     elementFormDefault="qualified"
     version="IEEE LTSC LOM XML 1.0">
...
  <!-- 1 General -->
  <xs:group name="general">
    <xs:sequence>
      <xs:element name="general" type="general">
        <xs:unique name="generalUnique">
          <xs:selector xpath="*"/>
          <xs:field xpath="@uniqueElementName"/>
        </xs:unique>
      </xs:element>
    </xs:sequence>
  </xs:group>

  ...
  <!-- 1.1 Identifier -->
  <xs:group name="identifier">
    <xs:sequence>
      <xs:element name="identifier" type="identifier">
        <xs:unique name="identifierUnique">
          <xs:selector xpath="*"/>
          <xs:field xpath="@uniqueElementName"/>
        </xs:unique>
      </xs:element>
    </xs:sequence>
  </xs:group>
...
</xs:schema>
```

Figure 5-3. XML Schema binding for the LOM standard elements *general* and *identifier*

```
<lom ...>
  <general>
    <identifier>
      <catalog>URI</catalog>
      <entry>http://www.stanford.edu/</entry>
    </identifier>
    ...
  </general>
  ...
  <relation>
    <resource>
      <identifier>
        <catalog>URI</catalog>
        <entry>http://www.mit.edu/</entry>
      </identifier>
    </resource>
  </relation>
  ...
</lom>
```

Figure 5-4. An example XML encoding of LOM-based metadata

LOM XML instance is a collection of metadata for a LO that conforms to IEEE LOM standard; it is represented in XML, and adheres to the requirements and constraints of the XML Schema binding defined in the draft standard (LTSC, 2005). An example of a LOM XML instance is shown in Figure 5-4.

Alternatively, metadata elements defined in the LOM standard can be used in RDF files according to the appropriate RDF binding (see section 3).

There are some similarities between Dublin Core and LOM elements, so people have already developed mechanisms for converting data between Dublin Core and LOM. For example, mappings between Dublin Core and LOM are publicly available (e.g., see (GoC, 2004)). However, LOM is much more extensive than Dublin Core, and data can be lost in the translation. The problem is even greater if additional metadata are used by different repositories to describe LOs, if different controlled vocabularies are applied, or if the mapping between such vocabularies is not well defined (McClelland, 2003). In fact, many LORs only partially support Dublin Core, LOM, or another metadata standard or specification, simultaneously introducing their own additional metadata elements and vocabularies in addition to the subset of the standard elements supported.

In reality, organizations and repositories use application profiles based on IEEE LTSC LOM, Dublin Core, and other standards. The profiles typically include standard elements related to the type of LO, its title and author, owner, terms of distribution, and format. Some application profiles also include pedagogical attributes that are not necessarily defined in standards, such as the teaching or interaction style, grade level, mastery level, and prerequisites. A peculiarity of application profiles is that due to various requirements and needs to support different aspects of LOs they may grow to contain impractically large sets of elements. Some organizations, such as the Government of Canada, deal with this problem by differentiating between mandatory and recommended metadata elements in the application profile (GoC, 2004).

The IMS LRM specification (Anderson and Wason, 2000), mentioned in section 1.3, introduces minor changes to the IEEE LOM standard.

2.4   IMS Content Packaging

IMS Global Learning Consortium has developed its Content Packaging specification to define a set of structures that can be used to exchange learning content (IMS CP, 2004). It is a typical example of a packaging standard. It also specifies a standardized XML Schema binding for the structures. The binding enables different authoring tools, LMSs, and WBE environments conforming to the IMS Content Packaging specification to interoperate in exchanging instructional materials.

Figure 5-5 shows the *IMS Content Packaging Information Model,* a packaging scheme that represents the IMS' LO content model. Its principles are as follows:

Figure 5-5. IMS Content Packaging Information Model (after (IMS CP, 2004))

- A LO is represented by an *IMS Package.* It can be thought of as a logical directory, which includes: an XML file, called the *manifest file,* that describes the learning resources constituting the learning content of the LO; any other XML documents that *the manifest file* directly references (such as an XSD file); a set of resource/content files (the actual media elements, text files, graphics, and other resources; these files may be organized in sub-directories). The manifest file is always named *imsmanifest.xml.*
- The structure of the IMS Package is the same for all LOs, regardless of their granularity. In other words, a LO represented by an IMS Package can be a simple LO, an aggregated one, or a unit of learning such as a course or a module. It can also be a part of a course that can stand by itself outside of the context of a course. The point is reusability - authors can describe their content in any way they want it to be reused by applications. Due to the structure of the manifest file, the LO can be reused as is, can be aggregated with other LOs, or can be disaggregated into a set of reusable parts.
- The manifest file, represented by a single top-level <manifest> element, has several sections. They describe the LO resources themselves and how they are (or can be) used within that LO. Each section is represented by a dedicated XML element, but some sections are optional. This structure of the manifest file reflects the general principle that the organization of resources (i.e., files with learning content) within an IMS

Package is independent of their use. An example manifest file is shown in Figure 5-6, and its details are described below.

```
<?xml version="1.0"?>
<manifest identifier="MANIFEST1"
        xmlns="http://www.imsglobal.org/xsd/ims_cp_rootv1p1"
        xmlns:imsmd = "http://www.imsglobal.org/xsd/imsmd_v1p2">
  <metadata>
    <schema>IMS Content</schema>
    <schemaversion>1.1</schemaversion>
    <imsmd:lom>
      <imsmd:general>
        <imsmd:title>
          <imsmd:langstring xml:lang="en_US">Semantic Web</imsmd:langstring>
        </imsmd:title>
      </imsmd:general>
    </imsmd:lom>
  </metadata>
  <organizations default="TOC">
    <organization identifier="TOC">
      <title>The lesson contents</title>
      <item identIfier="ITEM1" identifierref="RESOURCE1">
        <title>Lesson</title>
        <item identifier="ITEM2" identifierref="RESOURCE2">
          <title>Introduction</title>
        </item>
        <item identifier="ITEM3" identifierref="RESOURCE3">
          <title>Content</title>
        </item>
        <item identifier="ITEM4" identifierref="RESOURCE4">
          <title>Summary</title>
        </item>
        <item identifier="ITEM5" identifierref="RESOURCE5">
          <title>References</title>
        </item>
      </item>
    </organization>
  </organizations>
  <resources xml:base="http://repository.imsglobal.org/foo/bar/">
    <resource identifier="RESOURCE1" type="webcontent" href="lesson.htm"/>
    <resource identifier="RESOURCE2" type="webcontent" href="introuction.htm"/>
    <resource identifier="RESOURCE3" type="webcontent" href="content.htm"/>
    <resource identifier="RESOURCE4" type="webcontent" href="summary.htm"/>
    <resource identifier="RESOURCE5" type="webcontent" href="references.htm"/>
  </resources>
</manifest>
```

Figure 5-6. A manifest file (adapted from IMS CP, 2004))

- The optional *metadata* section of the manifest file describes the manifest as a whole. It typically includes LOM-based metadata elements, such as title, description, keywords, and so on, but may also include other elements. The use of appropriate XML namespaces enables differentiating among elements coming from different metadata sets. The metadata section is represented by a `<metadata>` element; note, however, that `<metadata>` elements can appear within other sections nested in the top-level `<manifest>` element.

- The required *organizations* section, represented by a single `<organizations>` element, declares zero, one, or more different presentation views of the LO content. For example, a presentation view of a course may be its outline. Each such a presentation view (called an *organization* and represented by an `<organization>` element) represents a logical structure of the LO content, and may be different from the internal file structure of the IMS Package. A presentation view reflects a possible organization of resources (included in the corresponding IMS Package) for aggregation or disaggregation. Each resource or set of resources supporting a given presentation view is referred to within the `<organization>` element for *that* view; it may be referred to in another way within *another* `<organization>` element. An `<organization>` element may include its own `<metadata>` element; for example, it may be suitable to represent a course outline by its own metadata.

- The required *resources* section, represented by a single `<resources>` element, includes references to all of the resource files needed for a complete interpretation of the `<organizations>` element. A reference to a resource includes the path to the corresponding file through any internal folders or subdirectories comprising the internal file structure. A reference to a resource may be internal (a reference to a file stored within the IMS Package) or external (a URL of an external file). Resources may also contain a `<metadata>` element for each content item referenced.

- The optional *submanifests* section specifies zero or more submanifests nested in the top-level manifest. Each submanifest is represented by its own `<manifest>` element. Submanifests specify how the LO content may be reliably aggregated or disaggregated into other IMS Packages. In case of an aggregated LO, the top-level manifest always describes the IMS Package as a whole, and any nested submanifests describe the content at the level to which the submanifest is scoped, such as a course, a lesson, a simple LO, or other.

- For easy delivery of LOs, IMS Content Packaging standard defines the concept of a *Package Interchange File (PIF)*. A PIF is typically a ".zip" or a ".jar" archive that includes a top-level manifest file (*imsmanifest.xml*) and all other files as identified by the manifest (externally referenced resource files may be excluded from the PIF).

The current version of the IMS Content Packaging specification does not address the important issue of extensibility of the data model shown in Figure 5-5. LOs are supposed to be (re)used for a variety of instructional purposes and delivered through a variety of LMSs, LORs, and computer platforms, hence there is an obvious need for considering the data model extensibility aspects. Also, a future version of the specification will have to take into account how other complementary learning technology standards (such as different learner information standards, communication standards, and quality standards) can be integrated with the data model.

2.5   IMS LD

IMS Learning Design specification is not strictly a packaging standard; it rather integrates content packaging with EMLs, thus providing a standardized framework for instructional design of units of learning. To an extent, IMS LD also includes learner information in the specification.

IMS LD accommodates a wide range of pedagogical approaches and facilitates the development of new pedagogical approaches. It supports the description of individualized learning designs, as well as of collaborative ones. In fact, IMS LD specifies a meta-language with a single relatively small vocabulary that can be used to express what each of the different pedagogical approaches asks of the actors involved in the learning/teaching process (IMS LD, 2003). IMS LD also allows for integration of different pedagogical approaches into a single learning design, since different approaches may be needed to accommodate different types of learners.

A theoretical foundation for IMS LD and for such a wide coverage of this specification, achieved with a relatively small vocabulary, resulted from prior studies of EMLs by Koper (2001) and Koper and Manderveld (2004). The major findings of these studies can be summarized as follows:

- regardless of any specific pedagogical approach that may be deployed, every learning design is essentially about a *method* prescribing various *activities* for *learners* and supporting *staff* (e.g., teachers[23]) in the learning/teaching process in a certain order;
- learner and staff are typical *roles* in the process;
- to perform an activity, a learner or a teacher usually needs an access to a LO or to an educational service; a collection of these is referred to as an *environment*;
- an activity performed by a user taking a role (learner or staff) may create a certain *outcome*, which can be detected as an event during the learning process; for example, after answering the test questions (activity), the learner submits the report (outcome);
- learner *properties* are needed to support individualized learning design; for example, a particular learner's progress is such a property and it may be stored in a dossier;

---

[23] IMS LD does not specify any specialization of the staff role explicitly.

- a certain learning scenario may require introducing some learning design *conditions* that constrain the scenario's evolution; for example, "If the learner's preferred style is X, suppress activity Y";
- an outcome of an activity may trigger new activities; for instance, the student asks a question, and the teacher is triggered to answer it; this mechanism is called *notification.*

Roughly, the concepts from the first four of the above bullet points and the associated workflows represent what IMS LD calls *learning design level A.* Adding the concepts from the next two bullet points (properties and conditions) to learning design level A extends it to *learning design level B.* Adding notifications to level B extends it to *learning design level C.*

Learning design level C is the most complex and the most complete. It is the basis of the conceptual model underlying IMS LD. Figure 5-7 illustrates a part of this model (i.e., a part of the IMS LD concept hierarchy).

```
learning-design
    title
    learning-objectives
    prerequisites
    components
        roles
            learner*
            staff*
        activities
            learning-activity*
                environment-ref*
                activity-description
            support-activity*
                environment-ref*
                activity-description
            activity-structure*
                environment-ref*
        environments
            environment*
                title
                learning objects*
                services*
                environment-ref*
                metadata
    method
        play*
            act*
                role-part*
                    role-ref
                    activity-ref
    metadata
```

Figure 5-7. Hierarchy of major elements of learning design according to IMS LD (adapted from (IMS LD, 2003); an asterisk * means that an element may occur more than once)

```
<?xml version="1.0" encoding="UTF-8"?>
<!-- edited with XML Spy v4.4 U (http://www.xmlspy.com) by Peter Sloep and Hans Hummel -->
<learning-design identifier="LD-boeing-simplified" url="URI" level="A">
   <title>Boeing Fuel Valve Removal simplified</title>
   <learning-objectives>
      <item identifierref="" identifier="LOB-learning-objectives"/>
   </learning-objectives>
   <prerequisites>
      <item identifierref="" identifier="PREQ-prerequisites"/>
   </prerequisites>
   <components>
      <roles>
         <learner identifier="R-learner"/>
      </roles>
      <activities>
         ...
         <learning-activity identifier="LA-lesson-hazards">
            <activity-description>
               <item identifierref="" identifier="I-lesson-hazards"/>
            </activity-description>
         </learning-activity>
         <learning-activity identifier="LA-lesson-components">
            <activity-description>
               <item identifierref="" identifier="I-lesson-components"/>
            </activity-description>
         </learning-activity>
         ...
         <activity-structure identifier="AS-fuel-valve-lessons" number-to-select="2" structure-type="selection">
            <title/>
            <learning-activity-ref ref="LA-lesson-hazards"/>
            <learning-activity-ref ref="LA-lesson-components"/>
         </activity-structure>
         ...
         ...
      </activities>
   </components>
   <method>
      <play identifier="PLAY-Boeing-simplified" isvisible="true">
         <act identifier="ACT-individualized-learning">
            <role-part identifier="RP-individualized-learning">
               <role-ref ref="R-learner"/>
               <activity-structure-ref ref="AS-boeing-simplified"/>
            </role-part>
            <complete-act>
               <when-role-part-completed ref="RP-individualized-learning"/>
            </complete-act>
         </act>
         <complete-play>
            <when-last-act-completed/>
         </complete-play>
      </play>
   </method>
</learning-design>
```

Figure 5-8. Excerpts from an IMS LD XML instance document (adapted from (IMS LD, 2003))

According to the model shown in Figure 5-7, learning design aggregates a collection of *components, learning objectives and prerequisites*, and a *method*. A component can be a role, a property, a property group (which is an aggregation of one or more properties), an activity, an activity-structure (which is an aggregation of one or more activities), an environment, or an outcome. Each component, as well as each objective/prerequisite, typically aggregates different *resources*. A resource can be a *Web content*, an *IMS LD content*, a *person*, a *service facility*, or a *dossier*.

In chapter 7, Figure 7-10 illustrates the relations between the most important IMS LD concepts in another way, using UML notation.

IMS LD is supported by an appropriate XML binding. Figure 5-8 illustrates some of the XML elements from that binding.

Method is a concept that requires special attention. A method aggregates zero or more conditions, zero or more notifications, and also one or more *plays*. A play represents a teaching/learning process and is modeled after the metaphor of theater play. A play has a sequence of *acts* (see Figure 5-7), and in each act has one or more *role-parts* that associate a role with an activity. The activity, in turn, associates a role with an environment by describing what that role is to do in the act and what LOs and services it will use to do it. The assigned activity is like the script for the part that the role plays in the act. There may be more than one role-part within an act; in such a case, the role-parts (i.e., assigned activities) are run in parallel.

In practice, learning design description of a LO is usually integrated with the description of its content (although the corresponding resource files may be distributed). To this end, a learning design is typically (though not necessarily) embedded in the Organizations section of the manifest file of an IMS Content Package, Figure 5-9.

```
manifest
   metadata
   organizations
      learning-design
   resources
   manifests (submanifests of included packages)
```

Figure 5-9. Embedding learning design in an IMS Content Package (after (IMS LD, 2003))

2.6   IMS QTI

The IMS Question & Test Interoperability (QTI) specification belongs to the group of communication standards. It specifies a data model for representing question and test data and their corresponding results reports (IMS QTI, 2005). The main objective of IMS QTI is to enable the exchange of assessment items and the corresponding results data between authoring tools, LORs, different learning systems, and assessment delivery systems.

IMS QTI uses the terms *test* and *assessment* interchangeably, as synonyms. It also assumes that each test is a collection of assessment items used to determine the level of mastery that a learner has on a particular subject. An *assessment item* is the smallest exchangeable assessment object, such as a question. However, an assessment item includes not only the *item body* itself (text, graphics, media objects, and interactions that describe the item's content and information about how it is structured), but also the accompanying *instructions* to be presented, *item variables*, a description of the *response processing* to be applied to the learner's response(s), as well as possible *feedback* that may be presented (including hints and solutions). An assessment item may be used within a number of *item sessions*, each such a session delineating roughly a single set of related interactions between a learner and the item (such as attempts to answer a question). An item session is characterized by its duration, context, a set of item variables to be assigned or updated during the session, completion status (permitted values are *completed, incomplete, not_attempted* and *unknown*), and the like.

IMS QTI data model is described abstractly, using UML (Figure 5-10 provides but a single example). An appropriate XML binding is provided for interchange of assessment items and results between systems. IMS QTI specification is extensible; a set of well-defined extension points can be used to wrap specialized or proprietary data so that they can be used in applications in much the same way as items that can be represented directly.

Figure 5-10 shows a high-level view of assessment according to IMS QTI. Note that the standard makes a clear difference between the roles of a *tutor* (someone involved in managing, directing or supporting the learning process for a learner), a *scorer* (responsible for assessing the learner's responses during assessment delivery), and a *proctor* (a person charged with overseeing the delivery of an assessment), although in practice it may happen for the same person to take more than one of these roles.

IMS QTI defines response processing as the process by which the values of *response variables* (as set by the learner's responses provided during his/her interaction with an assessment item) are judged (scored) and the values of *outcome variables* are assigned. The process involves the application of a set of *response rules*, the testing of *response conditions*, and the evaluation of expressions involving the item variables. In order to facilitate implementation of response processing in different assessment delivery engines, IMS QTI also provides a set of *response processing templates*, specified in XML form, supporting standard response processors such as *match correct* (matching the value of a response variable to its correct value) and *map response* (map the value of a response variable onto a value for the outcome).

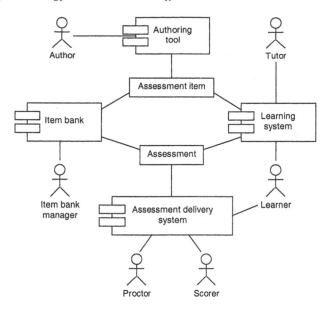

Figure 5-10. The use of assessments and assessment items (adapted from (IMS QTI, 2005))

Figure 5-11 illustrates the look of assessment items when IMS QTI XML binding is used as the encoding scheme. The example shown highlights the prompt of a multiple-choice question that the assessment item encodes. Note the reference to the *map_response* response processing template in the end of the assessment item.

IMS specifications allow for an easy integration of assessment-related content of a LO with other parts of the LO's IMS Content Package (see again the IMS Content Packaging Information Model shown in Figure 5-5). The way it is done in practice is partially illustrated in Figures 5-12 and 5-13. Essentially, the manifest of an IMS Package must contain a resource describing each assessment item, which in turn has to be described in an XML file conformant with the IMS QTI specification. The *type* attribute of the corresponding <resource> element must be *imsqti_item_xmlv2p0* (highlighted in Figure 5-13), and the element must include a reference to the item's XML file and references to each of the item's auxiliary files. In cases when specific metadata need to be included with an assessment item, they are included in the dedicated <qtiMetadata> section of the corresponding <resource> element.

```
<?xml version="1.0" encoding="UTF-8" ?>
<assessmentItem xmlns="http://www.imsglobal.org/xsd/imsqti_v2p0"
      xmlns:xsi="http://www.w3.org/2001/XMLSchema-instance"
      xsi:schemaLocation="http://www.imsglobal.org/xsd/imsqti_v2p0 imsqti_v2p0.xsd"
      identifier="choiceMultiple"
      title="Composition of Water" adaptive="false" timeDependent="false">
   <responseDeclaration identifier="RESPONSE" cardinality="multiple" baseType="identifier">
      <correctResponse>
         <value>H</value>
         <value>O</value>
      </correctResponse>
      ...
   </responseDeclaration>
   <outcomeDeclaration identifier="SCORE" cardinality="single" baseType="integer" />
   <itemBody>
      <choiceInteraction responseIdentifier="MR01" shuffle="true" maxChoices="0">
         <prompt>Which of the following elements are used to form water?</prompt>
         <simpleChoice identifier="H" fixed="false">Hydrogen</simpleChoice>
         <simpleChoice identifier="He" fixed="false">Helium</simpleChoice>
         ...
         <simpleChoice identifier="O" fixed="false">Oxygen</simpleChoice>
      </choiceInteraction>
   </itemBody>
   <responseProcessing template=
            "http://www.imsglobal.org/question/qti_v2p0/rptemplates/map_response" />
</assessmentItem>
```

Figure 5-11. An example assessment item (adapted from (IMS QTI, 2005))

```
manifest
   metadata
   organizations
      learning-design
   resources
      assessment content
      manifests (submanifests of included packages)
```

Figure 5-12. Embedding assessment content in an IMS Content Package (after (IMS QTI, 2005))

```
<imscp:resource identifier="Question_3" type="imsqti_item_xmlv2p0" href="choice_03.xml">
   <imscp:file href="choice_03.xml"/>
   <imscp:file href="sign3.png"/>
</imscp:resource>
```

Figure 5-13. Encoding of an assessment-related resource

Assessment is tightly coupled with learning design. The results of a test may influence the learning process[24], and it must be reflected in the learning

---

[24] This is often referred to as formative assessment.

design. For example, in adaptive learning systems learners experiencing difficulties with some LOs may be directed to other LOs or suggested additional learning activities. To accommodate this need for integration of learning design and assessment, IMS QTI recommends the technique of aligning IMS LD property names and IMS QTI variable names. For instance, an IMS LD property may be declared in the <learning-design> section of the manifest file and then used in a condition to select between alternative learning activities, based on some assessment results. On the other hand, an IMS QTI variable may be declared in an appropriate <outcome> section of an assessment item to represent the assessment score (outcome). If the property identifier and the variable name are lexically identical, they are treated as a shared variable in run-time software environments which involve IMS LD and IMS QTI-based processes. As a consequence, when an IMS QTI processor sets the value of the score variable, it is automatically available to the IMS LD processor for examination of the corresponding condition and possible re-direction of the learning activities. In much the same way, other *adaptive items* can be developed as assessment items that adapt either their appearance, or their scoring (response processing), or both in response to each of the learner's attempts.

It is interesting to note that in spite of the fact that IMS QTI specification deals with assessment data and activities, it actually spans all three major parts of the architectural reference model for SWBE shown in Figure 4-1 (development, publishing and delivery). It specifies a well documented content format for storing assessment items independent of the authoring tool used to create them. With regard to publishing, IMS QTI supports deployment of assessment items and collections of items (called *item banks*) from diverse sources across a wide range of learning and assessment delivery systems. Assessment delivery is further supported by providing the systems with the ability to report test results in a consistent manner.

2.7   IMS LIP

IMS Learner Information Package belongs, obviously, to the learner information standards group. It enables recording and managing the learner's characteristics related to recording and managing his/her learning-related history, objectives, goals, progress, accomplishments, and levels of mastery of the subject domain (IMS LIP, 2001). Furthermore, it supports the exchange of learner information among *learner information systems*[25] of

---

[25] The term that IMS commonly uses to denote e-Learning systems, LMSs, student information systems, knowledge management systems, and other systems storing,

different functionalities. IMS LIP also deals with engaging a learner in a learning experience and with discovering learning opportunities for learners.

IMS LIP assumes that information about a learner in a learner information system may be distributed - parts of learner information may be stored on different servers. Also, the same learner information may be shared by different learner information systems.

The learner information in IMS LIP is separated into eleven main categories, Table 5-3. An appropriate data structure is defined for each category. It is up to the application designers to decide which categories to package and store in their applications.

For the data structure supporting a specific category, the specification defines fields into which the data about the learner can be placed (such as the learner's name, his/her learning objective, preference for a particular type of technology, and so on), and the type of data that may be put into these fields (IMS LIP, 2001).

Suitable metadata can be specified for each field, such as time-related information, identification and indexing information, as well as privacy and data protection information.

Furthermore, all eleven core data structures (identification, goal, ..., relationship) may include a recursive lower-level sub-structure of learner information. Each such a recursive sub-structure may include any of the eleven categories at a lower level of information. The "atomic" sub-structure is the lowest level for which an appropriate content type exists. Also, each of the eleven core structures may occur as many times as necessary within the learner information structure. For example, each activity related to the learner's formal and informal education, training, and work experience will be represented by a separate entry in the learner information.

In addition to the above categories of information and the supporting data structures, IMS LIP also specifies data structures to describe access rights related to learner information stored within a learner information system (i.e., who can see what), as well as the messaging protocol used to implement learner information interchanges among learner information systems and other applications.

Note also that IMS LIP defines learner information from a very broad perspective - learner information includes a collection of information about an individual learner, a group of learners, or a producer of learning content (creators, providers, or vendors).

As with the other standards, an XML binding is included in the IMS LIP specification to support learner information encoding, packaging, and exchange. Figure 5-14 illustrates how some of the binding elements can be

---

providing, and otherwise using learner-related information relevant in the learning process.

used to represent information from the Activity category shown in Table 5-3. The <contenttype> sections contain relevant identification and indexing metadata about the encoded activity, the <typename> section specifies the activity type, and the <learningactivityref> section indicates that the content of the record is based on the external reference to the learning activity.

Table 5-3. Categories of learner information in IMS LIP (adapted from (IMS LIP 2001))

Category	Explanation	Examples
Identification	Biographic and demographic data relevant to learning	Name, address, contact information
Goal	Learning, career and other objectives and aspirations	Personal objectives and aspirations
Qualifications, Certifications and Licenses (QCL)	It is assumed that these are granted by recognized authorities	Title, level/grade, responsible organization
Activity	Any learning-related activity in any state of completion (could be self-reported; includes formal and informal education, training, work experience, and military or civic service)	Activity reference, related product, evaluation, assigned units
Transcript	A record that is used to provide an institutionally-based summary of academic achievement (the structure of this record can take many forms)	Type of transcript, external reference
Interest	Information describing hobbies and recreational activities	Interest type, related product
Competency	Skills, knowledge, and abilities acquired in the cognitive, affective, and/or psychomotor domains	Competency description, external reference
Affiliation	Membership of professional organizations, etc.	Membership type, learner's role in the organization
Accessibility	General accessibility to the learner information as defined through language capabilities, disabilities, eligibilities and learning preferences including cognitive preferences (e.g. issues of learning style), physical preferences (e.g. a preference for large print), and technological preferences (e.g. a preference for a particular computer platform)	Language, preference, disability, eligibility
Security key	The set of passwords and security keys assigned to the learner for transactions with learner information systems and services	Password, encryption key
Relationship	The set of relationships between the data from the other categories (all of these relationships are captured in a single structure)	Type of relationship, source and destination components

```
<learnerinformation>
  <comment>An example of LIP Activity information.</comment>
  <contentype>
    <referential>
      <sourcedid>
        <source>IMS_LIP_V1p0_Example</source>
        <id>2001</id>
      </sourcedid>
    </referential>
  </contentype>
  <activity>
    <typename>
      <tysource sourcetype="imsdefault"/>
      <tyvalue>Education</tyvalue>
    </typename>
    <contentype>
      <referential>
        <indexid>activity_2</indexid>
      </referential>
    </contentype>
    . . .
    <learningactivityref>
      <text>HND in Electronics</text>
    </learningactivityref>
  </activity>
</learnerinformation>
```

Figure 5-14. An example of IMS LIP encoding in XML (adapted from (IMS LIP, 2001))

It is also of interest for exchange of learner information between learner information systems and applications to integrate learner information from multiple sources. IMS recommends using IMS Content Packaging principles to make the integrated learner information in such cases.

2.8 IEEE PAPI Learner

Another frequently used learner information standard is the IEEE Public and Private Information (PAPI) for Learners (PAPI Learner) standard (PAPI Learner, 2001). It specifies the semantics and syntax of learner information and defines and/or references elements for recording and viewing descriptive information about learners from different perspectives (learner, teacher, parent, school, employer, etc.).

PAPI Learner specifies six types of learner information, as shown in Table 5-4. The sets of information elements in each of the six categories are extensible - implementations may extend or combine them to satisfy specific application needs. Some of the elements specified by PAPI Learner are mandatory; others are optional or appear conditionally in a specific learner information.

PAPI Learner accommodates both the implementations that separate the six information types and those that store them together. In practice, PAPI Learner-based implementations typically maintain different types of learner information in separate repositories, in order to satisfy security, administration, regulatory, and system performance needs. In such cases, learner information stored in separate data repositories can be linked via, e.g., the learner's unique identifier. For example, such an identifier may be used to link his/her personal information from, say, students' databases, and his/her performance information from another learner information system.

Table 5-4. Types of information in IEEE PAPI Learner (adapted from (PAPI Learner, 2001))

Type	Explanation	Examples
Personal (Contact)	Primarily related to administration, and not to the measurement and recording of learner performance. Typically private and secure.	Name, postal address, telephone number
Relations	The learner's relationship to other users of learning technology systems, such as teachers, proctors, and other learners.	Classmates, teammates, mentors
Security	The learner's security credentials.	Public keys, private keys, passwords
Preference	The learner's preferences that may improve human-computer interactions.	Useful and unusable I/O devices, learning styles, physical limitations
Performance	The learner's history, current work, or future objectives; created and used by learning technology components to provide improved or optimized learning experiences.	Grades, interim reports, log books
Portfolio	The learner's works or references to them, intended for illustration and justification of his/her abilities and achievements.	Accomplishments, works

Just like other standards, PAPI Learner also defines an XML binding for all elements specified in its six information types. Figure 5-15 shows an example of PAPI Learner XML encoding conformant to that binding. The example represents the Relations information for a learner. His/her relations are stored in a repository and can be uniquely identified through the <relations_identifier> section. The <learner_hid> section specifies an external identifier that is used to correlate PAPI learner information across repositories. Each relationship in his/her relationship list is defined in a separate <relationship> section that typically provides information such as a unique identifier for each other user participating in the relationship, and the type of the learner's relationship to them (classmate, in this example).

```
<!-- XML data instance ("..." is replaced by outer tags) -->
<...>
    <my_relations_identifier_list>
        <relations_identifier>
            <identifier_type>pointer</identifier_type>
            <identifier_value>0x12345678</identifier_value>
        </relations_identifier>
    </my_relations_identifer_list>
    <my_relations_hid_list>
        <learner_hid>
            <identifier_type>IEEE_1484.13</identifier_type>
            <identifier_value>44556677</identifier_value>
        </learner_hid>
    </my_relations_hid_list>
    <relationship_list>
        <relationship>
            <others_identifier_list>
                <others_identifier>
                    <identifier_type>IEEE_1484.13</identifier_type>
                    <identifier_value>44556688</identifier_value>
                </others_Identifier>
            </others_identifier_list>
            . . .
            <relationship_to_them>
                classmate
            </relationship_to_them>
        <relationship>
            . . .
</...>
```

Figure 5-15. A PAPI Learner XML encoding (adapted from (PAPI Learner, 2001))

PAPI Learner also specifies how its elements can be mapped onto another IEEE learning technology standard, the *P1484.1 Standard for Learning Technology - Learning Technology Systems Architecture (LTSA)*. LTSA is a high-level, pedagogically neutral, content-neutral, culturally neutral, and platform/technology-neutral architecture for learning technology systems based on abstract components, Figure 5-16. It covers a wide range of learning technology systems, including education and training, computer-based training, computer assisted instruction, intelligent tutoring, etc. Ovals in Figure 5-16 represent processing elements, boxes represent repositories, solid arrows show data flows, and dashed arrows reflect control flows. Most of the figure's meaning is intuitively clear; *Learner entity* stands for both individual learners and learning groups, and *Locators* are things like lesson plans, URLs, and the like. Table 5-5 indicates the mapping between LTSA and PAPI Learner information.

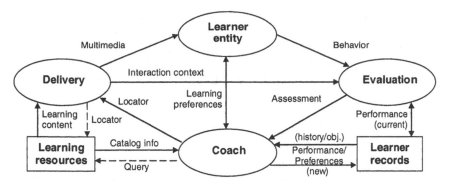

Figure 5-16. LTSA conceptual model (after (LTSA, 2001))

Table 5-5. Mapping from LTSA components to PAPI Learner information

LTSA component	Related PAPI Learner information
Learning preferences	Contact, relations, security, preference
Performance (stored in Learner records)	Performance, portfolio
Assessment	Performance, portfolio
Learner records	All
Coach	All
Evaluation	Performance, preference

Note that LTSA Evaluation component primarily creates LTSA performance information and LTSA assessment information, but the LTSA Evaluation component might also retrieve LTSA performance information from the LTSA learner records (PAPI Learner, 2001). PAPI Learner performance information is primarily intended for consumption by automated systems. PAPI Learner portfolio information is primarily intended for consumption by humans.

2.9   ADL SCORM

ADL Sharable Courseware Object Reference Model (SCORM) combines and interprets a number of interrelated technical specifications and guidelines taken from *other* organizations (AICC, ARIADNE, IMS, and IEEE) to create a unified content and communication reference model for consistent implementations that can be used across the e-Learning community (Friesen and McGreal, 2002). Hence SCORM is actually a collection of standards and specifications adapted from multiple sources to provide a comprehensive suite of e-Learning capabilities that enable interoperability, accessibility, and reusability of Web-based learning content (ADL SCORM, 2004).

By integrating a number of specifications into a comprehensive framework, SCORM specifies the behavior and aggregation of modular, interactive learning components. In fact, SCORM provides a unified framework for developers, content providers, and instructional designers for developing reusable and interchangeable LOs.

Table 5-6 shows the three major parts ("books") of SCORM and the specifications and standards bundled in them. In addition, Table 5-7 introduces the most relevant part of the SCORM terminology - the SCORM Content Model components. Starting from these two tables, the SCORM reference model can be roughly described as follows (ADL SCORM, 2004):

- SCOs are content objects (i.e., subjectively small LOs) which use the RTE to communicate with an LMS[26]. This communication is based on the IEEE ECMAScript Application Programming Interface for Content to Runtime Services Communication draft standard (IEEE API, 2003).
- Manifests that describe SCOs also contain SN information, which affects how content is assembled in a manifest. The SN information is encoded in the <organization> sections to denote the rules that an LMS must follow in order to present a specific learning experience.

Table 5-6. The organization of SCORM

SCORM book	Explanation	Related models and specifications
Content Aggregation Model (CAM)	Assembling, labeling and packaging of learning content	IEEE LOM AICC Content Structure IMS Content Packaging IMS Simple Sequencing Information and Behavior Model
Run-Time Environment (RTE)	Interoperability between shareable content objects (SCOs) and LMSs (content launching, API for content communication with LMSs, and data model for content-to-LMS communication, including tracking, data transfer and error handling)	IEEE API 1484.11.2 IEEE Data Model 1484.11.1
Sequencing and Navigation (SN)	Content sequencing and navigation (dynamic presentation of learning content based on learner needs)	IMS Simple Sequencing Information and Behavior Model

- Sequencing only applies to activities. The sequencing of activities encoded in the <organization> sections is external to the learning

---

[26] Note that the way the ADL SCORM documentation often uses the term "LMS" is not very strict. It rather corresponds to the term "learner information system" used in IMS LIP (see section 2.7).

resources associated with those activities. It is the responsibility of an LMS to interpret the sequencing of activities and launch the SCOs associated with the activities in response.

Table 5-7. Some of the most relevant SCORM concepts (after (ADL SCORM, 2004))

Term	Explanation
Assets	Electronic representation of text, images, sound, assessment objects, etc.; corresponds to resource files in IMS Content Packaging
Shareable Content Object (SCO)	A collection of one or more assets that represent a single launchable learning resource that utilizes the SCORM RTE to communicate with an LMS; corresponds to a LO of the lowest-level granularity that can be tracked by an LMS using the SCORM RTE data model
Content organization	A map that represents the intended use of the content through structured units of instruction (activities)
Metadata	Asset, SCO, activity, content organization, and content aggregation metadata that enable content reuse

- Branching and flow of learning activities can be described in terms of a tree-like structure, optionally augmented with an authored sequencing strategy. Furthermore, it can depend on the learner's interactions with content objects of different granularities (adaptivity). These processes are based on the IMS Simple Sequencing specification (see section 2.10 for more details). For example, the learner may start his/her interaction with a course object at a high level, then traverse the tree structure down to a lesson object, and further down to even smaller content objects; then he/she may return to the lesson level. SCORM assumes that such a structure is managed by the LMS for each learner.
- Different <organization> sections may also describe presentation and navigation instructions for end users of LMSs, as in Figure 5-17.

```
<organization>
  <item identifier="ITEM1" identifierref="RESOURCE1" isvisible="true">
    <title>Content 1</title>
    <adlnav:presentation>
      <adlnav:navigationInterface>
        <adlnav:hideLMSUI>next</adlnav:hideLMSUI>
        <adlnav:hideLMSUI>previous</adlnav:hideLMSUI>
      </adlnav:navigationInterface>
    </adlnav:presentation>
  </item>
</organization>
```

Figure 5-17. An example of SCORM encoding for presentation and navigation (adapted from (ADL SCORM, 2004))

- SCORM defines several application profiles that describe: how to integrate the IEEE LOM within the SCORM environment; how to package assets and SCOs to provide a common medium for exchange (but without having to provide any organization, learning context, or curricular taxonomy); how to bundle learning resources and a desired content structure to create complete lessons, courses, and modules; and so on.

- The RTE part of SCORM specifies a standard set of data model elements used to define the information being tracked for a SCO, such as the SCO's completion status or a score from an assessment such as a quiz or a test. It is the responsibility of the LMS to maintain the state of SCO's data model elements across learner sessions.

- After an LMS launches a content object (i.e., a SCO) in response to the learner's request through a Web browser, the state of communication between the LMS and the content object (e.g., initialized, terminated, in an error condition, and the like) is continuously reported to the LMS. This reporting, as well as data storage and retrieval (e.g., score, time limits, etc.) between the LMS and the SCO, is implemented through the IEEE ECMAScript API.

In summary, SCORM is a reference model that integrates several different specifications and guidelines into a coherent suite. The specifications/guidelines belong partially to the group of packaging standards (the CAM part), and partially also to the group of communication standards (the RTE and SN parts). SCORM supports adaptive instruction based on learner objectives, preferences, performance and other factors (like instructional techniques), and enables dynamic presentation of learning content based on the learner's needs.

2.10   Other standards

In addition to the standards covered in the previous sections, there are a number of other standards, specifications, application profiles, reference models, architectural frameworks, recommendations, guidelines, and other initiatives in the area of learning technology. In order to enhance understanding of the big picture, this subsection briefly covers but a few other efforts.

Open Knowledge Initiative (OKI). The core deliverable of OKI is an open and extensible architectural specification for development of learning management and educational applications (OKI, 2002). The specification particularly targets the needs of the higher education community. The primary feature of the specification is a set of API definitions, called OSIDs (Open Service Interface Definitions). The OSIDs are intended to support learning tool developers in integrating their tools and applications with existing institutional infrastructure, such as campus systems.

In fact, the OKI architectural specification takes a 4-layer approach, with the existing educational infrastructure at the bottom layer. The next layer up is the set of Common Services and associated OSIDs that convert the institution-specific infrastructure into a common services platform that can be used by the educational services (IMS AF, 2003), (OKI, 2002). These include authentication, authorization, hierarchy, scheduling, filing, user messaging, dictionary (support for multiple languages and culture-specific conventions), and the like. Educational Services at the third level rely on the Common Services and are available to the institution's educational applications (situated at the topmost layer) in the provision of the e-Learning framework. OSIDs supporting Educational Services are related to repository, assessment, grading, and course management. OKI services and the associated OSIDs help developers concentrate on the pedagogical issues at hand, without having to re-invent basic functionality (things included in the Common Services), or concern themselves with the details of particular underlying implementations. Simultaneously, OKI services allow for easier intra-institution work sharing.

Note that the OKI specifications and architecture have been recognized by the IMS consortium as an important contribution to the IMS Abstract Framework (IMS AF, 2003), a device that enables the IMS to describe the context within which it develops its e-Learning technology specifications.

Schools Interoperability Framework (SIF). The SIF initiative and the related SIF Implementation Specification (SIF, 2004) target interoperability between software applications from different vendors, focusing on their deployment at schools (especially the K-12 education industry). The point is to promote interoperability without requiring each vendor to learn and support the idiosyncrasies of other vendor's applications. SIF is an open industrial initiative - many software companies in the education industry and educational institutions have joined the initiative.

The SIF Implementation Specification defines the requirements of architecture, communication, software components, and interfaces between them in order to achieve interoperability between applications, making no assumption about how they are implemented and the supporting hardware/software they use. In other words, a SIF implementation must enable different applications to exchange data efficiently, reliably, and securely regardless of what platforms are hosting the applications (IMS AF, 2003). The specification is supported by an appropriate XML Schema binding.

A SIF implementation is a distributed networking system, deployed in a *SIF zone*, which roughly maps to a single building, school, a small group of schools, a district, etc. The network includes a central server called *Zone*

Integration Server (ZIS), and one or more *integration agents*. Each application in a SIF zone gets integrated with the other applications through the ZIS and its own integration agent. The applications do not exchange data and messages directly, but through their agents and the ZIS - the ZIS handles all security information and routes all messages. This, of course, implies a number of further and very strict technical requirements related to performance, scalability, messaging, and event handling. SIF supports all of them.

The applications integrated in a SIF zone are not necessarily only educational ones. For example, a zone may integrate a library system, a WBE system, different student information services, a grade book, but also a food services system, a voice telephony system, a financial management system, and a human resources system. The only requirements for all these systems are to adhere to the SIF Implementation Specification and to provide their integration agents.

SIF cooperates with IMS, looking at the IMS Content Packaging and QTI specifications to support K-12 assessment/quizzes. IMS, on the other hand, is looking at the SIF grade book.

IMS Simple Sequencing. Much of the ADL SCORM Sequencing and Navigation processes described in the previous section rely on the IMS Simple Sequencing specification (IMS SS, 2003). The specification defines how a learning system can sequence discrete learning activities in a consistent way.

IMS Simple Sequencing assumes that an instructional designer or content developer declares the relative order in which elements of content are to be presented to the learner and the conditions under which a piece of content should be selected, delivered, or skipped during presentation. The designer/developer does so by incorporating the sequencing information in the <organization> elements of the manifest files, or in items contained within <organization> elements. The sequencing information is related to learning activities and their subactivities, forming *activity trees*. This information incorporates rules that describe the branching or flow of learning activities through the learning content according to the outcomes of the learner's interactions with the content.

Each activity has an associated set of sequencing behaviors. The specification itself includes a limited number of widely used sequencing behaviors (navigation, flow, sequencing, termination, delivery, exit, selection, randomization, and rollup processes). The sequencing behavior process traverses the activity tree and applies the sequencing rules. This results in the identification of the activities and their associated content resources to deliver to the learner. The delivery creates the desired learning experience.

IMS Simple Sequencing recognizes only the role of the learner. It does not define the roles of other actors (such as instructors, mentors, or peers). Although it does not preclude contexts and applications involving other actors, it does not define sequencing capabilities for such learning contexts. Likewise, Simple Sequencing does not address (but does not prevent either) AI-based sequencing, schedule-based sequencing, synchronization between multiple parallel learning activities, and other complex sequencing behaviors.

3. SEMANTIC WEB ISSUES RELATED TO LEARNING TECHNOLOGY STANDARDS

The standards described in the previous sections are popular among the developers of LOs, LORs, WBE applications, and authoring tools, because they impose some guidance, principles, structure, and unification on the development and maintenance processes. They also provide a certain level of LO reusability and interoperability between tools and applications.

However, current standards are generally not tailored for the Semantic Web. Thus further efforts are needed in order to adapt them for use in SWBE applications.

3.1 Additional requirements

Technically, much of the practical implementations and usage of standards is related to LO annotation. For example, the manifest file used in different IMS standards for content description is actually a way to annotate LOs from different perspectives (general-purpose metadata, learning design, learner information, and so on). This fact creates a number of additional requirements for using the standards in SWBE successfully:
- Development of simple methods and tools for LO annotation - LO annotation is typically a time-consuming task that authors tend to avoid. They often neglect the need for putting an extra effort into an appropriate annotation, and are not highly motivated to do it.
- Differentiating between objective and subjective metadata - Some of the LO metadata are clearly objective, such as the LO title, author, and publication date (Duval et al., 2002; Nilsson et al., 2002). Others depend on the author's personal opinion (e.g., keywords, intended use, and difficulty level).
- Combining metadata sets and schemes from multiple sources - Multiple descriptions of the same LO may exist on the Web. None of the existing metadata schemes is perfect and all-encompassing, so application

designers may decide to integrate subsets of metadata from different specifications into a coherent application profile to suit their own needs. An important prerequisite here is the modularity of metadata descriptions.

- Seamless integration of production and annotation - As Tallis et al. discuss (2002), annotation of LOs should be automated as much as possible and the author should be freed from the extra effort of annotating the LO he/she creates. In other words, the author should concentrate to the development (production) of the LO, and annotation should come as a byproduct. To put this need into the context of using e-Learning standards, it is necessary to create authoring tools that capture standardized LO metadata automatically, while the author is creating the LO. Unfortunately, this process is difficult to automate in a general case, because of the subjective nature of some metadata and because of different application needs.

- Advanced and automated annotation - Since manual LO annotation is time consuming and error-prone, it is quite logical to ask: Is it possible to automate that process using some advanced and/or more sophisticated techniques? To this end, efforts are already underway to develop an automatic LO metadata generator in the form of a Web service (Cardinaels et al., 2005), and to apply machine learning, data mining, text mining (Popov et al., 2003), and different heuristics to support automatic LO metadata generation (Jovanović, 2005). Of course, subjective metadata are more difficult to generate automatically than objective ones.

- Introducing formal semantics into existing standards - Current standards are not published with formally described semantics. As a consequence, they do not support reasoning and semantic search based on LO metadata. For example, a keywords-based query to a LOR intended to retrieve LOs about to World War II would certainly miss some related LOs focusing on Sir Winston Churchill, in spite of the fact that the two concepts are obviously interconnected. Likewise, if a LOR does not contain a LO about rubies it may still be of interest for the learner to retrieve LOs related to gems (a more general concept). Moreover, without formal semantics it is not easy to support mapping from a standard/specification to another and related one. For instance, it is not easy to map/convert information from, say, IMS LIP Competency and Transcript categories into IEEE PAPI Learner Portfolio and Performance information and vice versa, although they are related. Without formally represented semantics, current versions of standards do not support LO annotation that would enable dealing with such problems automatically.

- Flexibility and dynamics of associating metadata with LOs - Brooks et al. (2005) argue that many LORs support only a few metadata fields from standards, and that the standards themselves are too restrictive and rigid in the variety of the metadata they capture. The standards do not account for the dynamics of a LO usage and for the evolution of the metadata that describe the LO's changing features over time. Brooks et al. propose using a larger set of well-defined ontologies sufficient for particular purposes instead of a single highly constrained taxonomy of values like those described in the IEEE LOM standard. Associating multiple metadata instances with a given LO over time, in a much less constrained way than when using LOM, allows for agents to pick and choose those instances that fit the needs of individual learners better.

3.2   Advanced bindings

As mentioned throughout section 2, organizations that developed and maintain different standards also provide appropriate XML bindings for the standards. It is done in order to enable authors to create LO metadata instances compliant with the standards, as well as to allow for validation of those instances by different tools and applications.

However, as Nilsson et al. have noted (2002), there are several problems with using XML-based LO metadata instances. They have proposed using RDF bindings instead, and have provided a rationale for their proposal in the form of a detailed comparison of the two kinds of bindings. In brief, the rationale is as follows:

- An XML document is essentially a labeled tree containing text, whereas an RDF document is a graph that can be described by a set of statements in the form of simple O-A-V triplets. Although semantically interconnected within the graph, RDF statements can be also used independently. Thus they are more flexible and better suited for expressing metadata, much of which is subjective in nature. Contrary to that, XML elements cannot be used independently, and an XML metadata document cannot be arbitrarily inserted into another XML metadata document.
- XML bindings provide XML Schema descriptions of the *syntactic structures* of the corresponding metadata instances. XML-based application profiles do the same, allowing XML elements from different schemas to be combined within the same category of metadata instance documents and specifying precisely which schemas are allowed in the profile. Each time a new schema must be supported, a new application profile must be defined as well. By contrast, RDF bindings are based on RDF Schema and provide *vocabularies* and the associated *semantics* for describing certain features of LOs. Different vocabularies can coexist in the same document, provided that the grammar rules for using the corresponding RDF statements are followed as necessary. Thus LO

metadata from different sets can be easily combined using RDF bindings. An application may support (or may be interested in) only metadata from *some* of the vocabularies used in the RDF document; if unknown or uninteresting, the other metadata are simply ignored. This is much less restrictive than XML bindings.

- XML Schemas are used for modeling categories of XML documents, whereas RDF Schemas model knowledge, i.e. the semantics of the terms used. Since different LO metadata instances can exist for the same LO, RDF descriptions of LOs effectively mean interconnection of different objective metadata, subjective opinions, and dynamic descriptions that results in a global knowledge eco-system (Nilsson et al., 2002).

To this end, one notable exception among different standardization organizations is DCMI, which provides an RDF binding for Dublin Core metadata set, instead of defining an XML binding as most of the other organizations do for their standards (Kokkelink, and Schwänzl, 2002). Apart from that, efforts to provide RDF bindings come from other organizations and research groups. The best known example to date is the RDF binding for the IEEE LOM standard, coming from Royal Institute of Technology, Stockholm, Sweden (Nilsson, 2002), referred to from now on as "the LOM RDF binding".

The developers of the LOM RDF binding have started from the fact that the IEEE LOM standard is closely related to several other specifications, such as Dublin Core. Hence they reused existing RDF vocabularies for those related specifications to the greatest extent possible, without losing conformance to the IEEE LOM itself, and in particular to the LOM XML binding provided by IEEE LTSC (LTSC, 2005). A consequence is that parts of the LOM RDF binding can be viewed as extensions of Qualified Dublin Core.

The LOM RDF binding defines appropriate namespaces for each of the nine categories of the IEEE LOM metadata, and reuses namespaces defined for external specifications like Dublin Core. For example, the binding uses the dc: namespace[27] for Dublin Core elements, the lom-gen: namespace for the General category of the IEEE LOM metadata, the lom-life: for the Lifecycle category, and so on. The lom: namespace is used as the root namespace containing common constructs. Starting with these namespaces, the LOM RDF binding essentially defines for each element in the IEEE LOM standard the corresponding RDF property to use. In the binding table, there are also usage guidelines and a usage example for each element, as well as a recommended practice of how to repeat the element in

---

[27] More precisely, dc: is an alias for the Dublin Core namespace defined as http://purl.org/dc/elements/1.1/. Likewise, the other namespaces/aliases manioned in this paragraph have their precise definitions. See (Nilsson, 2002) for details.

conformance with the IEEE LOM Information Model. Table 5-8 shows an example.

Table 5-8. An example binding from the LOM RDF binding (adapted from (Nilsson, 2002))

LOM element	Usage guidelines	Recommended ordering representation	Example

1.5 Keyword	Use `dc:subject` pointing to a textual description.	Use repeated properties for separate keywords.	`<dc:subject>`
			`<rdf:Alt rdf:ID="keyword1">`
			`<rdf:li xml:lang="en">`
			psychology
			`</rdf:li>`
			`<rdf:li xml:lang="sv">`
			psykologi`</rdf:li>`
			`</rdf:Alt>`
			`</dc:subject>`

3.3 Knowledge organization systems

The term *knowledge organization systems* is used by W3C to denote different types of *controlled vocabularies* or *concept schemes*, such as thesauri, classification schemes, subject heading lists, taxonomies, terminologies, glossaries, and so on. Knowledge organization systems are not used exclusively for educational purposes, but are certainly of high importance in teaching and learning processes in any subject domain.

The Semantic Web Interest Group of W3C mediates the development of specifications and standards to support the use of knowledge organization systems within the framework of the Semantic Web. Their work is known under the name *SKOS* (*Simple Knowledge Organization Systems*), and is currently focused on the development of the following specifications (Miles and Brickley, 2005):

- SKOS Core Vocabulary - a set of RDFS classes and RDF properties that can be used to express the content and structure of a concept scheme in a machine-understandable way, as an RDF graph;
- SKOS Core Guide - a guide for using SKOS Core Vocabulary for development and publishing content schemes on the Semantic Web;
- Quick Guide to Publishing a Thesaurus on the Semantic Web - directions for expressing the content and structure of a thesaurus, and metadata about a thesaurus, in RDF;
- SKOS API - a Web service API for interacting with a knowledge organization system data source.

In addition to the above specifications, the SKOS efforts also include the development of an RDF vocabulary for describing mappings between concept schemes (called SKOS Mapping) and an RDF vocabulary containing extensions to SKOS Core Vocabulary Specification useful for specialized applications (called SKOS Extensions).

Table 5-9 shows some of the classes (beginning with an upper-case letter) and properties (beginning with a lower-case letter) defined in the SKOS Core Vocabulary. The prefix (namespace) `skos:` is defined as `xmlns:skos="http://www.w3.org/2004/02/skos/core#"`.

Table 5-9. Some terms from the SKOS Core Vocabulary (after (Miles and Brickley, 2005))

Term	Explanation
skos:Concept	An abstract idea or notion; a unit of thought
skos:ConceptScheme	A set of concepts, optionally including statements about semantic relationships between those concepts (e.g., a thesaurus)
skos:Collection	A meaningful collection of concepts
skos:prefLabel	The preferred lexical label for a resource, in a given language
skos:altLabel	An alternative lexical label for a resource
skos:hiddenLabel	A lexical label for a resource that should be hidden when generating visual displays of the resource, but should still be accessible to free text search operations
skos:broader	A concept that is more general in meaning
skos:narrower	A concept that is more specific in meaning
skos:hasTopConcept	A top level concept in the concept scheme
skos:inScheme	A concept scheme in which the concept is included
skos:isSubjectOf	A resource for which the concept is a subject
skos:related	A concept with which there is an associative semantic relationship

The way these terms are used in practice is illustrated in Figure 5-18. As in any RDF graph, ovals in the figure denote domain concepts, arrows indicate concept properties, and boxes represent the literal values of the corresponding properties (in this case, the concept labels expressed in natural language). Since SKOS Core Vocabulary is intended for representing concept schemes in a machine-understandable way, Jovanović used it (2005) to specify the vocabulary for the ontology of Intelligent Information Systems (IIS). The course on IIS that she teaches includes selected topics from the broad field of IIS, and the Semantic Web is one of them. Each domain concept from the IIS ontology (indicated by the `iis:` namespace prefix) is represented as an instance of the `skos:Concept` class (via the `rdf:type` property). The IIS concept scheme is represented as an instance of the `skos:ConceptScheme` class. Note also the use of alternative labels for the concept `iis:semweb` (middle right in Figure 5-18), and its associations with the related concepts of Ontologies and Semantic Web Tools (`iis:knowrep002` and `iis:appl01`, middle left). The IIS concept scheme includes several top-level concepts in its hierarchy (e.g., the Semantic Web, intelligent agents, etc.). These are included in the concept scheme using the `skos:inScheme` and `skos:hasTopConcept` properties (middle up).

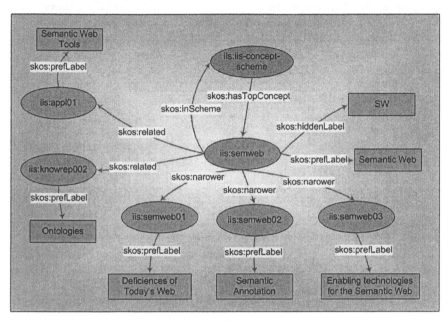

Figure 5-18. A segment of the IIS domain ontology describing concepts of the Semantic Web (after (Jovanović, 2005))

There is an OWL DL-compatible binding of the SKOS Core ontology, developed at the University of Saskatchewan, Canada; it is available from http://ai.usask.ca/mums/schemas/2005/01/27/skos-core-dl.owl.

3.4   Development practices

In practical SWBE developments, it is useful to have standards-compliant authoring and other development tools. They should be capable of importing reusable LOs compliant with the supported standards, and also of generating content (resource) files and the related metadata that comply to one or more standards and/or application profiles. Note, however, that most such tools for SWBE are still under development and are not widely available. On the other hand, some research groups have recognized the need for different supporting tools and utilities that can be used in LO development and possibly integrated into coherent tool suites and development environments. For example, a group from the University of Aachen, Germany, has developed an IEEE LOM Editor, an IMS LIP Editor (see a screenshot in Figure 5-19), a learner model converter from IMS LIP to IEEE PAPI Learner, and an Environment for LIP/PAPI-compliant deployment, transformation and matching of learner models[28]. Efforts are underway to integrate these tools into an adaptive learning platform that will include support for IEEE LOM-compliant automatic annotation of LOs, learner model-based LO retrieval, learner community building, and collaborative work.

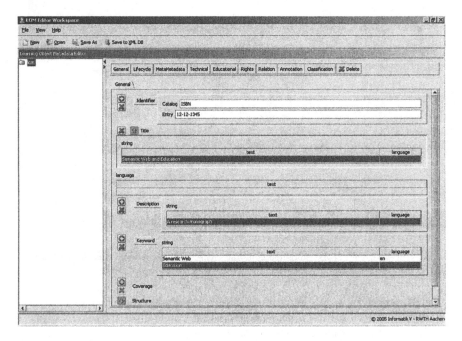

Figure 5-19. A screenshot from the IEEE LOM Editor from the University of Aachen

As already mentioned in section 3.1, there is a need for combining metadata elements from different standards and specifications in practical developments. In such cases, developers typically use small subsets of elements from individual specifications and integrate them into an ontology-based application profile. Chapter 6 presents an example of such a development approach in detail.

It should be also noted that there is no standardized[29] format for marking up *pieces* of content in individual LOs (Mohan and Greer, 2003)[30]. This

---

[28]   The   tools   are   available   from   http://www-i5.informatik.rwth-aachen.de/lehrstuhl/projects/index.html.

[29] Non-standard markup and the appropriate tools do exist. For example, see (Bloehdorn et al., 2005).

severely restricts the reusability of these LOs. There are two major approaches to cope with this problem. The first one is to use domain-specific markup languages, such as MathML (Carlisle et al., 2003), to annotate pieces of LOs related to particular domains. This is not necessarily a Semantic Web approach, and a suitable markup language for a specific domain may not be readily available. Moreover, the learning system that wants to reuse parts of the content of LOs annotated in this way should be able to interpret the meaning of the markup in order to correctly render the LO. The second approach is to develop a domain-independent ontology of content structure according to a certain model, and use it for marking up parts of LOs (Jovanović, 2005). This is a truly Semantic Web approach, but the challenge is to use a widely accepted content model for ontology development and to automate the markup process as much as possible.

4. SUMMARY

An insight into different standards and specifications in learning technology is useful in practical development of SWBE systems because of the standards' regulatory function and because of the need for the systems' interoperability and the reusability of the learning material. Learning technology standards are abundant, and can be categorized as metadata standards, packaging standards, learner information standards, communication standards, and quality standards. Most of them cover general-purpose e-Learning needs and processes. However, the use of the Semantic Web technologies in e-Learning puts additional requirements that need to be addressed by standards and specifications. Learning technology standardization organizations did not take this challenge yet. It is W3C who made the first steps in that direction with their SKOS specification. However, the scope of W3C activities and the SKOS itself is much wider than that of SWBE.

---

[30] IMS QTI is a notable exception to this rule, but it covers only assessment (and not other parts of the learning process).

Chapter 6

PERSONALIZATION ISSUES

Personalization is a central issue in SWBE. It is about tailoring and customizing learning experience to individual learners, based on an analysis of the learners' objectives, current status of skills/knowledge, and learning style preferences (Sampson et al., 2002a). SWBE systems monitor individual learners during their learning sessions and intelligently analyze and evaluate their progress. As a result, the system can dynamically select and adapt the content (LOs) to present to the learner to meet his/her personal needs, adjust the presentation style to the learner's pace and goals, and guide him/her through the learning space.

To personalize the learning process for each individual learner, a SWBE system needs to use strategies that can address individual needs and promote individual success. It must also use different technologies in order to change the appearance of LOs according to the learner's needs. Note that personalization process may take many forms as it adapts content, practice, feedback, or navigation to match individual progress and performance (Martinez, 2000). This may easily result in, say, two individuals using the same instruction and being presented with two completely different sets of LOs. For example, consider part of the outline of a course that deals with linear equations (Schewe et al., 2005). If a learner wants to learn just about how to do some practical calculations and complete the learning session with a practical test, the system would firstly present him/her with a LO that briefly explains the basics of solving linear equations. Then it would proceed with a sequence of LOs comprising illustrative examples and exercises. If, on the other hand, another learner wants to learn also about the theory behind these calculations, the system may decide first to require the learner to pass a test about his/her knowledge in basic linear algebra, then to look at the LOs explaining the related theory, and to pass an examination eventually.

A great benefit of learning personalization is the system's ability to make the instruction as easy or as complex as a particular learner wants or needs, no matter how complex the overall instruction may be (Martinez, 2000). In other words, a system supporting personalization of the learning process presents only the information that is really relevant for the learner, in the appropriate manner, and at the appropriate time. Each time the learner interacts with the system, it learns and stores a little more about his/her unique set of needs.

All personalization relies on *learner (student) modeling*, briefly introduced in Chapter 1, sections 3.1 and 5.1.1. Learner modeling comprises a set of activities, processes, knowledge and data structures, and the related tools and technologies for modeling the learner's background knowledge, cognitive traits, learning preferences, learning pace, and the mastery of the topics being taught, in order to dynamically adapt the process of instruction to him/her.

Personalization attracts a lot of interest in SWBE, but there is no single, widely adopted approach that all systems use. Instead, there is a number different research and development directions and practices, all focusing on the common objective of learner-centered design of SWBE.

1.   THE BASICS

Personalization plays a complex role in SWBE, because it must accurately reflect the fact that all learners are different in terms of their knowledge levels, learning progress, intellectual capacities, and so on. Moreover, these learners' characteristics are not static; on the contrary, many of them are continuously changing over time and may have different values across the learning sessions. Thus personalization requires not only specific representational structures and techniques, but also specific authoring tasks and strategies related to representing learner models. Personalization is the major reason for applying different AH principles and techniques in SWBE, as well as one of the major functions of educational Web services. Hence personalization is an important issue in the general model of educational servers, Figure 3-4.

There is a number of different types of personalization, as well as different approaches to achieve personalization with SWBE systems.

1.1   The Role of Personalization

As soon as a learner starts interacting with a learning environment, it should start adapting to the way the learner likes to communicate and organize information, just as people adapt to each other (Pednault, 2000). Personalization should carry out that adaptation by deploying efficient adaptation algorithms and suitable data structures to represent the learner's characteristics and problem-solving states. To this end, personalization assumes that the learning environment gradually builds and uses predictive models of the learner's behavior as he/she interacts with the environment. To do that, the learning environment needs to maintain the entire history of each learner's requests, the LOs that were presented to each learner, the specific features of the learning context, and how the learners then responded. Through deployment of suitable learner modeling approaches, personalization must ensure for reflecting the rich and fluid learners' interaction, but at a level of abstraction that allows the relationships among stimuli and responses to be readily observed in the data collected.

Sampson et al. (2002a) summarize the role of personalization in learning environments as follows:

- personalized learning environments enable one-to-one or many-to-one learning paradigms (one teacher - one learner, and many teachers - one learner), contrary to traditional learning environments that always adopt one-to-many learning paradigm (one teacher, many students);
- personalized learning environments impose no constraints in terms of learning time, location, etc., whereas traditional ones are fairly restricted by the learning setting;
- personalized learning environments recognize the huge variety in the learner's characteristics and preferences in terms of the learning style, media, interests, and the like, and adapt instruction according to them; traditional ones are usually designed for the "average learner";
- personalized learning environments tailor instruction to suit the learner's requirements (self-directed learning); in traditional learning environments, the curriculum, learning units, and the selection and sequencing of learning material are determined by the tutor.

In addition, Keenoy et al. (2004), as well as Liu and Greer (2004), stress the role of personalization in the learner's interaction with LORs through a learning environment. The LOs that a learning environment supporting personalization returns upon a learner's request will depend on the learner's characteristics. The LOR itself may return, say, n LOs satisfying the query. However, in the resulting set of LOs shown to the learner may be only $m < n$ LOs (the remaining ones will be excluded as unsuitable for that particular learner). Furthermore, the ranking of the returned LOs for two different learners may be different for the same query (the "best" ones for one learner are not necessarily the "best" for the other learner). Also, the presentation of the search results may be personalized (e.g., showing a simple list of returned LOs to one learner, and showing alternative trails through the returned set of LOs to another learner).

1.2   Types of personalization

Personalization is an ill-defined term. Different people may assume very different things under that term. Unfortunately, so do designers of learning environments, hence there is often some confusion about how personalized is a personalized learning environment.

Martinez (2000) suggests considering five different types of personalization, at five different levels of increasing abstraction and sophistication:

*   Name-recognized personalization - for example, showing the learner's name along with the LOs displayed or along with the problems he/she solves and the results accomplished. This strategy is simple and easy to implement, yet valuable since many people feel like being acknowledged as individuals when they see their names on the screen.
*   Self-described personalization - using questionnaires, pre-tests, surveys, registration forms, and the like to have the learners describe their preferences and common attributes, as well as to identify their backgrounds and previous experiences. These create the initial learner models to start with in the instruction to follow.
*   Segmented personalization - grouping learners into smaller, identifiable and manageable groups, based on their common attributes (e.g., class, department, job title), demographics, and surveys. Parts of the instruction are then tailored to the groups, and are applied in the same way to all members of a segmented group.
*   Cognitive-based personalization - tailoring and delivering content and instruction to specific types of learners, defined according to information about their cognitive processes, strategies, capabilities, and preferences. These may include, e.g., a learner's preference for audio over text-based delivery, or linear sequencing over grouping of hyperlinks, as well as recognition of the learner's working memory capacity and capability for inductive reasoning. Cognitive-based personalization is more complex to implement than the previous types, as it requires collecting data, monitoring the learner's activity, comparing it to other learners' behavior, and predicting what the learner would like to do or see next. However, it is usually a very powerful and rewarding type of personalization, since the instruction relying on it proves to be more natural and more efficient.

- Whole-person personalization - combining cognitive-based personalization with support for the complex set of deep-seated psychological sources impacting differences in learning and performance. This type of personalization makes intelligent inferences about the learner throughout the learning experience, updating the learner model dynamically from the whole-person perspective. This is becoming increasingly popular, in spite of its complexity and the needs for approximations. Kim and Schniederjans (2004) note that much of the recent research has been directed at establishing relationships between individual personality characteristics and learning performance. They argue that the following five general personality characteristics (often referred to as the "big five" personality characteristics) are closely related to learning performance: stability, openness, conscientiousness, agreeableness[31], and extraversion. See section 1.3.10 for more details.

1.3   Approaches to personalization

Personalization is typically achieved by applying some form of *information filtering* to the learning material, activities, and processes, according to the learner's context, preferences, goals, etc. (Henze, 2005a), (Keenoy et al., 2004). The filter can be *adaptive* (i.e., learned and adjusted automatically by the system during the learning sessions), and/or *adaptable* (configured and adjusted by the learner). Adaptive and adaptable approaches can be mixed within the same SWBE system.

Technically, the system tracks the learner's interactions, information requests, and problem-solving attempts, and either *responses* to the learner's activity in a personalized manner, or takes a pro-active role and *recommends* information to the learner (LOs, learning steps and activities, references, and the like), or both. In the case of the learner's information request, the system translates it into a query, possibly refines and re-formats it to comply with the native format of an external LOR or an educational Web service, and sends it to the destination. When the requested information is retrieved, the system may rate and rank it according to different criteria (cost, quality, rendering device, and other constraints) before presenting it to the learner. There is a room for information filtering and for creating the learner's awareness of the personalization process in each of these steps. In the case of recommending information to the learner, the system performs information filtering in the background continuously. It decides itself on the moments when to take initiative and present the user some information. The decisions are made taking into account the learner's preferences and goals, the learning

---

[31] The term denotes one's tendency to be courteous, helpful, trusting, good-natured, cooperative, tolerant, and forgiving (Kim and Schniederjans, 2004).

context, previously and currently browsed pages and LOs, the system's awareness of similar resources, and the system's observations about other learners in similar contexts.

The subsections that follow briefly review different approaches to personalization. The first three of them feature not only SWBE systems, but also more traditional ITSs, AEHSs, and other WBE systems. They are included here for the sake of completeness. The approaches covered in subsections 1.3.5 thru 1.3.7 are usually related to SWBE systems. The remaining ones are emerging receiving an increasing interest among the SWBE researchers and practitioners, although all of them draw upon earlier efforts of ITS researchers and educational psychologists.

1.3.1   Personalization with ITSs

ITSs respond to each individual student's learning style by delivering customized instruction based on the Student (Learner) Model, Figure 1-4, which stores information specific to the student (learner). Typically, the system updates the Student Model to reflect how well the student is performing on the material being taught (Sampson et al., 2002a). Some ITSs also record the student's misconceptions.

All of this information is used by the Pedagogical Module to diagnose (infer) the student's learning state and guide the instruction process accordingly. The diagnosis relies on the data from the student's interaction and observed behavior, on his/her knowledge state, his/her personality, motivation, cognitive traits, previous knowledge, and previous understanding of and experience with the ITS itself.

1.3.2   Personalization with Web-based ITSs

Traditional Web-based ITSs model the student in much the same way as ordinary ITSs, hence the personalization with them is much like the personalization with ordinary ITSs. A personalization issue specific to some Web-based ITSs is the student model reliability, which may depend on the system's architectural style (i.e., whether the system stores the student model on the server or on the client side, as discussed in Chapter 4, section 3).

Another issue with Web-based ITSs is the so called *cold start problem* - how to initialize the values of the student model when the student registers with the system, before his/her first learning session? What is his/her level of previous knowledge of the subject domain? What are his/her learning objectives and goals, and the preferred learning style? Web-based ITSs typically apply some of the self-described and/or segmented personalization approaches mentioned above to initialize the student model. However, it is not an ideal solution for the cold start problem as pre-tests, questionnaires, stereotypes, and the like may be imprecise and inaccurate, may take long time (and hence frustrate the student), and may result in a drop of the student's motivation.

1.3.3 Personalization with AEHSs

In AEHSs, the educational material is represented in a hyperspace form, as a network of hypermedia documents connected by different hyperlinks (Henze, 2005a). Adaptation takes forms like re-structuring this hyperspace, modifying the links between the nodes of the hyperspace, modifying the content of each node in the hyperspace, etc. (Sampson et al., 2002a). Chapter 1, section 5.2, introduces content adaptation and link adaptation as the two general categories of adaptation, provides an overview of the supporting techniques frequently used in practical implementations, and discusses the levels of adaptation in AEHSs.

The result of adaptation is a *personalized hyperspace*, constructed dynamically as a subspace of the original hyperspace, according to the learner's needs (Henze, 2005a). The vertices of the personalized hyperspace represent selected content or parts of content from the original hyperspace; the hyperlinks mostly come from the original ones (with possible annotation and grouping), but new ones may be created as well for personalization purposes. Recall also from Chapter 3, section 1.4, that personalization of AEHSs requires a specific set of authoring activities related to the learner models and adaptation strategies and techniques (Aroyo and Dicheva, 2004a). For example, metadata should be used to describe individual LOs (*keywords*, *roles*, *media formats*, etc.) and relations between them (*is_prerequisite*, *requires*, *is_alternative_explanation*, *deepens*, *gives_details*, etc.) in order for the Adaptive Engine to dynamically adapt the hyperspace according to the Student Model (Figure 1-5).

1.3.4 Personalization with pedagogical agents

Pedagogical agents perform a lot of tasks on behalf of the learners, but as section 5 of Chapter 3 clarifies they do most of their work acting behind the scenes of the learners' activities because they belong to SWBE infrastructure. A learner's personal agent is there to access his/her personal, administrative, and other data in the learner model when needed, to communicate it to the other agents and services that need such information, and to arrange for learning content and activities for the learner without his/her direct intervention (see also the example presented in Chapter 3, section 6.1). It is through these arrangements that pedagogical agents help personalize the learning process, because everything a learner's personal agent does depends on the learner model.

An important SWBE function of pedagogical agents is that of relating personalization to ontologies. Keleberda et al. (2004) exemplify how it can be done. The learner's personal agent is in charge of arranging for initial creation of the learner model according to the learner model ontology and the domain ontology. Also, when the learner makes a request for a LO, pedagogical agents consult not only his/her learner model, but also a set of other relevant ontologies (domain ontology, learning resource ontology, etc.) in order to correctly translate the query into the native format of the external LOR or another resource and return the results in a personalized way.

1.3.5   Ontology-based personalization

Continuing the discussion from the previous subsection, it becomes obvious that a *learner model ontology* is at the core of ontology-based personalization. Since ontology-based learner modeling is the central topic of this chapter, Sections 2 and 3 provide several examples of how learner model ontology can be designed and applied in practical SWBE environments.

In addition, there are numerous other opportunities for personalization that use ontologies in combination with other information. For example, a learner's browsing history can be used as a basis for personalization (Peñarrubia et al., 2004). The system can then take a pro-active role and recommend the learner other pages and LOs, covering similar content. As the learner continues working with the environment, his/her browsing history gets dynamically updated and so automatically does the suggested list of similar and related content. The implementation of that idea by Peñarrubia and his colleagues uses a separate frame on the screen to display the related links. However, the point is that the list of related links does not contain only additional resources that are syntactically similar to those registered in the learner's browsing history (keyword-based similarity), but also semantically related ones. The latter are retrieved using the terms and relations (generalization, specialization, equivalence, and so forth) from the domain ontology, as well as synonyms and other words related to the topics of the learner's interest as found by consulting the WordNet lexical ontology (WordNet, 2005).

1.3.6   Semantic Web services and personalization

The deployment of Semantic Web services also opens nice opportunities for personalization. Note that in the context of Semantic Web services personalization can be considered at two different levels (Henze, 2005a): services offering personalization, and personalization of services themselves.

Whenever a SWBE system offers a personalization-related functionality, it is a good idea to represent this functionality as a separate Semantic Web service. Such services can then be implemented within an educational server and exposed that way. For example, many educational Web services depicted in Figure 3-4 can offer personalization at least to some extent (e.g., assessment, collaboration, etc.).

The other level of personalization with Semantic Web services (personalization of services themselves) relies on the idea that a learner may want to use his/her own specific style in learning several different topics and in taking several different courses. Such a learner should be able to select some reusable individual learning support to guide him/her across different courses and learning experiences. To this end, the learner may select from educational Web services exposed on different educational servers and create his/her own personalized instance set of services. The same instance set can then be used in the learner's other learning experiences, to reason about distributed LOs, to implement personalized search, to maintain the learner's privacy in the same way, and the like.

Personalization functionality is closely related to adaptivity, so Semantic Web services can be used effectively to achieve the learning process adaptivity (Henze and Herrlich, 2004).

1.3.7 Web mining-based personalization

Web mining is the process of discovering potentially useful and previously unknown information and knowledge from Web data (Cooley et al., 1997). It encompasses tasks such as automatic resource discovery, automatic extraction and pre-processing of desired data from Web documents, discovery of common patterns across different Web sites, and validation and/or interpretation of discovered patterns (Chakrabarti et al., 1999).

In the context of SWBE, *Web content mining* means collecting information about globally distributed but semantically related LOs based on educational ontologies. *Web structure mining* refers to a SWBE system's activities related to continuous mining of the Web for ranking the most authoritative Web pages, LOs, and services on a given topic, and/or for (re)organizing local hubs of links to such external pages and services. The hubs are ontologically supported and reflect not only the structure of related links, but also the semantic hierarchy of related concepts and their instances. A prerequisite for successful Web structure mining is an appropriate annotation of educational pages, objects, and services. *Web usage mining* is related to intelligent analysis of a SWBE system log files in order to discover typical patterns of how the learners browse, access, and invoke LOs, Web pages, and educational services.

Web mining is still a rather expensive technology to implement, but once it is implemented its benefits for personalization are great. Through Web content mining, a learner can dynamically and constantly (i.e., across multiple learning sessions) receive updates on interesting and semantically related LOs and pages fitting his/her learner model, which itself is continuously changing. Through Web structure mining, the learner can be supplied with a personalized list of authoritative pages of interest. Finally, Web usage mining can help personalize the learner's learning experience by adaptively identifying and displaying activities of interest as needed, creating shortcuts, and providing guidance based on theidentified usage patterns. The good news is that all these benefits come with only a minimum of initial learner profiling, hence the cold start problem is mitigated.

1.3.8   Extending and adapting standards to capture personalization

Standards/specifications like IMS LIP and IEEE PAPI Learner provide a good basis for describing information about learners. However, the information that can be encoded using such specifications is mostly static (see Tables 5-3 and 5-4) and does not reflect the frequently changing parts of the learner model, such as the learner's mastery of a certain topic, his/her learning pace, the changes in his learning interests over time, and the like. Moreover, content packaging standards like IMS CP and ADL SCORM CAM provide no precise guidance on how to describe LOs for personalization support.

Current proposals and research in this direction suggest extensions and adaptations of packaging standards to support different learners' needs. For example, one of the results of the Knowledge-On-Demand (KOD) project was a proposal to use the `<organizations>` section of the manifest file, Figure 5-5, to insert personalization-related information about a LO (Sampson et al., 2002b). Thus a specific `<organization>` may be used to describe in XML which parts (resource files) of the content package should be selected for different learner profiles. An e-Learning environment importing the package on a learner's demand and interpreting its `<organizations>` section can then decide what specific parts of the package to show to the learner and what to withdraw.

Working in the same vein, Abdullah and Davis have proposed (2005) a learning system architecture to provide ADL SCORM with an independent "service" that supplies the learner with dynamic personalized links to alternative resources. For example, learners may want to access alternative materials on the same topic that suit their preferred learning styles. Authoring a special-purpose concept map (essentially, an ontology) of the related topics, the author can insert information on learning styles and concept relations. Through an adaptive user interface, the set of all returned alternative LOs that correspond to a learner's query to a SCORM-based LOR gets filtered according to the pre-authored concept map. Only those alternative LOs that fit with the learner's preferred learning style will be displayed in addition to the "main" LO.

Power et al. (2005) have taken another direction. They used an AH authoring system called MOT to tag the learning materials for their students with information allowing the students to read those materials at the level of detail they choose themselves, and to locate particular passages easily. They call this kind of personalization *goal-oriented personalization* - the students have their own learning goals and often want to skip some passages in favor of detailed reading of other material. The material pre-authored this way with MOT gets then converted into SCORM packages using a special tool. As a result, the material can be delivered via a conventional SCORM-compliant LMS and yet provide notable personalization effects.

A drawback of all of the above approaches is an extra authoring effort, which many authors may dislike.

1.3.9   Formal methods

Just as with formal approaches in any other field, using formal methods to describe information relevant to personalization leads to a stable representation and opportunity to formally manipulate the data structures used to achieve personalization. The already mentioned method of Keleberda et al. (2004) is just that - it defines formal, agent-implemented mappings from the learner-supplied data and the domain ontology to the learner profile, and from the learner profile and a set of ontologies to the query for learning resources. The returned set of resources is automatically personalized, since the query is formulated according to the learner model.

Schewe et al. (2005) formalize the fact that LOs corresponding to a curriculum (course) can be thought of as the nodes in a graph representing the course outline, and the links between the LOs as the graph edges. Also, they formally represent the set of learner's characteristics as a *learner space*, thus enabling different learner types/profiles to be represented as points in the learner space. A set of actions (also formally defined) describe possible transitions within the course outline, reflecting the learner's preferences for different activities. The learner's preferences are described in the learner space, and *preference rules* link the learner space with the course outline. Personalization is formally expressed using the formalism called *Kleene algebras with tests*, which enables one to formulate a set of axioms and equations for describing each learner type and the associated individual learning goals.

1.3.10   Support for whole-person personalization

The principles of whole-person personalization, briefly introduced in section 1.2, come from research in instructional psychology. A good example of such research is the *learning orientations theory* (Martinez, 2000) that stresses the effects of emotions and intentions on learning performance. It also puts emphasis on different other psychological factors (like co-native, affective, social, and cognitive factors), as they notably influence learning. Furthermore, the theory provides design guidelines for supportive learning environments that adapt to how people learn best. Most importantly, learning orientations theory offers strategies for designing, developing, and using LOs for personalized learning.

The findings of a recent study of the "big five" factors are quite clear (Kim and Schniederjans, 2004): statistically, agreeableness, stability, and openness are quite significantly correlated with grade performance of e-Learners, while extraversion and conscientiousness exhibit just moderate impact on learning performance. The challenge is then to design personalized learning environments to tailor instruction in terms of enforcing the more important factors.

So far, Web-based learning environments have largely ignored these holistic approaches to personalization of the learning process, because it is not easy to implement support for eliciting and tracking all the complex psychological factors in practical e-Learning settings. However, recent research efforts revive interest for such approaches starting from suitable simplifications and approximations that reduce complexity without sacrificing the whole-person perspective.

2.   LEARNER MODELING

In a learning environment/system, each learner model is a representation of both objective and subjective information about the learner's interactions, as well as a representation of the learner's performance and learning history. The environment/system uses that information in order to maximize the opportunity to predict the learner's behavior, and thereby adapt to his/her individual needs (Pednault, 2000).

Objective information includes details that roughly correspond to name-recognized, self-described, and segmented types of personalization (see section 1.2). In addition, details related to the learner's background knowledge, initial learning goals and interests, preferences for certain media and certain categories of information and learning resources, the possible contexts of interaction with the learning environment, the actions he/she can take in each context, and the actions the environment can take in response to the learner's interaction are also taken as objective information. Much of the objective information is supplied directly by the learner, typically by editing the learner profile during the registration with the system (or later), or through different questionnaires, pre-tests, surveys, and forms. Note that objective information can be essential for certain approaches to personalization, such as Web mining-based personalization and the use of Semantic Web services.

Subjective information roughly corresponds to the learner's cognitive and whole-person factors and the related types of personalization. Storing and regularly updating this kind of information in the learner model enables the learning system to predict the learner's response to different LOs, suggested learning activities, assignments, and so on. Note that the term "subjective" information can be slightly misleading, because parts of that information can be inferred by the system (although the learners are usually allowed to alter this information themselves).

Learner's performance data in the learner model are related to his/her level of knowledge of the subject domain, his/her misconceptions, progress, and the overall performance in the subject domain. Much of these data can be represented quantitatively, although their number may be quite large (especially in overlay models). It is typically the system that measures the learner's performance and updates these data.

Learning history includes information about the courses and topics the learner has already studied with the system, the related LOs the learner has interacted with, the assessments he/she underwent, etc. A learner's learning history is often called a *teaching history* (looking from the system's side). As with the learner's performance data, it is the system that keeps track of the learning/teaching history.

Some data in the learner model (typically the learner's performance and the learning history) are updated frequently, i.e. each time the learner runs a session with the system. Others are updated less frequently or very rarely.

Technically, a learner model is a data structure (or object) that can be visualized as in Figure 6-1 or modeled in, say, UML to facilitate design and implementation of the related software tools. Architecturally, WBE systems typically maintain a database of learner models to serve multiple learners. The database can be stored on the server or on the client side (see Chapter 4, section 3 for pros and cons of these architectural decisions).

The quality of a learner model is a complex issue. Usually, the more data in the model, the more opportunities for personalization, and the higher the model's accuracy. However, as the complexity of the learner model grows, updating and maintenance problems often multiply. Hence there is a huge variation in the details represented in learner models in different systems. To this end, a heuristics frequently used in practice is to evaluate the quality of the learner model in terms of how well the data represented in it support the learning objectives.

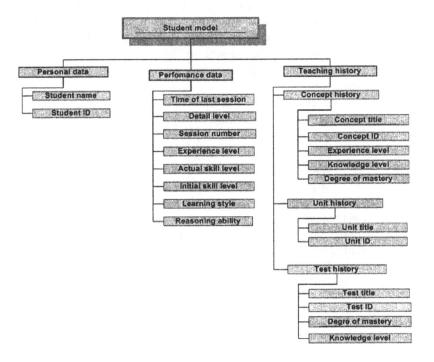

Figure 6-1. Graphical representation of the learner (student) model in the DEPTHS system (after (Jeremić et al., 2005))

2.1   Learner model specifications and markup languages

Learner model specifications such as IMS LIP and IEEE PAPI Learner provide a good starting point for designing learner models since they provide means to specify much of the objective and subjective learner information in a standardized way. But, as discussed in section 1.3.8, specifications do not support all learner information that might be needed in a specific learning environment. Moreover, those two most frequently used specifications are not readily compatible with each other. That fact restricts the interoperability of learner modeling systems relying on different standards. The recently developed LM-DTM tool (Chatti et al., 2005) partially mitigates this problem by providing conversion between the IMS LIP and IEEE PAPI Learner core features.

Learner modeling should also be considered in the more general context of *user modeling*, which refers to construction of models of mental activities and behaviors of users of any (though typically Web-based) system. User models are often used to make predictions about a system's usability or as a basis for interactive help systems. To this end, note that there exists the *General User Modeling Ontology* (*GUMO*) and the associated *UserML* markup language (Heckmann et al., 2005; Heckmann, and Krueger, 2003). Figure 6-2 depicts some of the topics defined in GUMO, and it becomes immediately apparent that GUMO takes the whole-person user modeling perspective. Furthermore, UserML is an RDF-based user model exchange language that enables different systems to represent and exchange their user models. User models represented in UserML can be shared between adaptive systems via both stationary and mobile devices, as well as ubiquitous networks. Additionally, they can be stored in databases and queried via the associated *UserQL* query language, merged, and used for inferencing with both GUMO and other ontologies. The GUMO ontology also defines an exceptionally useful `gumo:expiry` attribute for user modelers to qualitatively specify how long approximately the value of a certain data element in the user model is expected to be valid (which is important for querying the user models).

GUMO
    User model auxiliary
    Basic user dimensions
        Contact information
        Demographics
        Ability and proficiency
        Personality
        Characteristics
        Emotional state
        Physiological state
        Mental state
        Motion
        Role
        Nutrition
        Facial expression
    Domain-dependent data
    Context information
    Low-level sensory data
    Datatypes and ranges

Figure 6-2. Some of the top-level concepts in the GUMO ontology

There is a recent effort in the same line to develop *MLUM*, a *Markup Language for User Modeling* orthogonal to UserML (Chepegin et al., 2005).

2.2   Generic learner modeling

Just as the authors of GUMO, other researchers also argue in favor of generic user/learner models. Tchienehom (2005) goes even one step further in generalization, suggesting that user/learner models can be seen as specializations of the more generic concept of *profile*. A profile can be a learner profile, but also an information profile. Tchienehom has proposed a generic model of any profile, from which instances can be derived to represent, e.g., learners, LOs, and the like. The rationale is simple - all profiles describe some resources (be it learners, LOs, or another information), and are supposed to be reusable elements. Different applications should be able to access these reusable elements and to understand their semantics. Specific taxonomies (ontologies) can be defined to describe semantics of different profile instances, and rules can be specified for deducing pairs of profile instances that have compatible semantics and hence can be matched. For example, one can define the preferred language(s) and publication date as elements of the learner profile, and rules to match this information with the corresponding data in the LO profile.

Generic User Model Component (GUC) is another similar effort from the user modeling community (Van der Sluijs and Houben, 2005) that can be specialized for learner modeling as well. GUC builds on the idea of providing user (learner) model storage facilities for applications and supporting the exchange of user (learner) data between different applications. The motivation is that users typically interact with several different applications, all working with their own user profiles; it is then desirable for applications to be able to "join forces" in representing and exchanging user data. To do that, GUC requires special storage (database) for user modeling schemas used by different applications. A special ontology-based schema mapping module is deployed to map and/or merge different schemas as necessary, in order for different applications to exchange data about their users.

A common deficiency of all generic approaches is the necessary loss of information in model/schema conversion due to the problem of imperfect match of different schemas, as already discussed in Chapter 5, section 3.1.

2.3   Ontology-driven learner modeling

The ideas from the generic learner modeling and GUMO/UserML, as well as those from architectural modeling of adaptive learning systems (see Chapter 4, section 5) boil down to the need for:

- a *learner model ontology* to describe the knowledge of learners' characteristics and competencies in a SWBE system;
- several *other ontologies* (like domain, adaptation, and application ontologies) to drive architectural, design, and communication decisions in building such a system.

There is also an increasing number of SWBE systems that integrate ontology-based learner modeling with Semantic Web services for accessing the learner models and providing personalization of the learning process (Chepegin et al., 2004; De Bra et al., 2004b; Henze and Herrlich, 2004; Kay and Lum, 2005; Razmerita et al., 2003).

As an example, consider the learner modeling approach shown in Figure 6-3, derived from (Razmerita et al., 2003). It illustrates the idea of using different ontologies for learner modeling, and also fits in the learner modeling part of the educational server model (Figure 3-4).

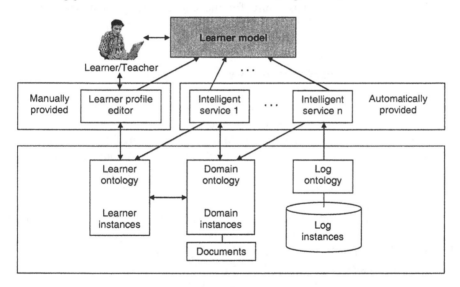

Figure 6-3. Ontology- and service-driven learner modeling (adapted from (Razmerita et al., 2003))

The learner supplies values of more-or-less static data in his/her learner model manually, guided by a learner profile editor. In some cases, the teacher may also update some data in a learner model; these reflect the teacher's observation about the learner and correspond to parts of the subjective information and learner's performance information. In the original work of Razmerita et al. (2003), the learner profile editor relies on a part of the learner model ontology based on the IMS LIP specification.

The other part of the learner model ontology reflects the learner's behavior, i.e. his/her learning activities and contributions. Intelligent Web services use that part along with the domain ontology, log ontology, and data from the activity log to automatically update the dynamic parts of the learner model. For example, the learner's *level_of_activity* (defined in the learner ontology) may be set to a value like *very active, active, passive,* or *inactive.* Likewise, the services may set the *level_of_knowledge_sharing* field in the learner model to *unaware, aware, interested, trial,* or *adopter.* All these characteristics are set and updated for specific parts of the domain knowledge, as defined in the domain ontology. Thus the learner model may indicate that the student taking a course on the Semantic Web is *very active* and *interested* in knowledge sharing about the topic of *semantic markup,* but is *passive* and just *aware* when it comes to the topic of *ontology editors.* Of course, the learner's activities and contributions change over time. The intelligent services will make sure for the changes to be updated in the learner model automatically, and will provide adaptation and personalization of the learner's further activities.

2.4   Learner model ontology

The content of learner model ontology largely depends on the application. More precisely, the learner model ontology should define what objective, subjective, learning performance, and learning history data the SWBE application is supposed to store, track, and update about each learner. One way or another, learner model ontology also typically refers to the concepts from the subject domain (see Figure 6-3). The following two examples provide some illustrations.

The learner model ontology used in the intelligent LMS called Multitutor[32] (Šimić et al., 2006) is shown graphically in Figure 6-4 in UML. It has a rather simple domain-independent part, yet suitable for the purpose. The *Learner* class describes the learner's objective information. When a learner registers with Multitutor to take a course, he/she is required to fill a questionnaire in order for Multitutor to elicit the initial values for the learner model. Much of these are domain-dependent. The *ProjectedSkills* part of the learner model ontology links the domain-independent parts with the domain ontology[33]. As a result, the learner model includes the initial overlay data through the *ProjectedSkills* part and is categorized into a stereotype defined in the *LearnerStereotype* part of the ontology. Over time, the application always updates the *ProjectedSkills* part of the learner model to reflect the

---

[32] Multitutor is covered in more details in Chapter 8.
[33] Not shown in Figure 6-4; a learner can take multiple courses through Multitutor, and each course has its own domain ontology.

current estimate of the learner's knowledge. The actual values are obtained as *MeasuredSkills*, and each of them is described by a set of *Scores*. During the learner's interaction, the application monitors his/her navigation and the times spent on studying each particular concept. These data are used together with the learner's scores to adaptively personalize the learning content to be shown the learner next.

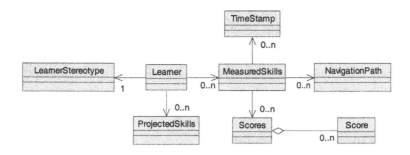

Figure 6-4. Learner model ontology of Multitutor (after (Šimić et al., 2006))

Kay and Lum have constructed semi-automatically the learner model ontology related to a course in user interface design and programming (Kay and Lum, 2004). Initially, the domain ontology was generated automatically starting from an online glossary of terms. The automatically constructed ontology contained over 1100 terms; it needed an additional manual adaptation, but the overall effort was much less than that required to manually develop a domain ontology from scratch. In the end, about 200 terms from the ontology were used as metadata of the LOs for the course, as well as the attributes in the overlay learner model. In fact, the ontology enables to make inferences about the learner's knowledge of the domain topics represented as the terms defined in the ontology.

As in many other cases, this learner model ontology cannot be used directly, because the raw data collected from the learner's interaction do not correspond directly to the terms defined in the ontology. The raw data in this case are the data acquired by tracking the learner's interaction with the LOs, such as the times spent with different slides, the duration of actually playing an audio corresponding to a certain slide (as compared to the total duration of the audio), the lecture notes the learner is required to take in conjunction with the slides, and so on. Lab marks and other assessment data are also included. All these raw data must be converted to the values of the learner model attributes that correspond to the terms defined in the ontology. For some attributes, the conversion is made using different heuristics and numerical methods. For example, a heuristics might be based on comparing the time a learner spent listening the audio explaining a domain term to the total duration of that audio (in a simple case, if the two match it can be considered that the student has a reasonable grasp of the term). For other attributes, the values are established by reasoning about the ontological terms. For example, it is possible to infer the level of the learner's knowledge about *predictive usability* (i.e., the value of the corresponding attribute), starting from the values for *heuristic evaluation* and *cognitive walkthrough* (the three terms are defined in the domain ontology; the latter two are directly related to the higher-level concept of *predictive usability*).

In fact, this illustrates how the initial, automatically generated ontology is used to *structure* the learner models and provide them with a common vocabulary also used in the other parts of the system, in particular metadata. It also illustrates how the refined learner model ontology provides an immediate mechanism for doing inference.

2.5   Open learner models

In *open learner modeling* (also called *scrutable learner modeling*), a learner can see and explore his/her learner model and the processes underlying it (Kay and Lum, 2004). In other words, the learner is aware of what the system "thinks" of his/her knowledge, progress, and needs, can reflect on it, and can control his/her learning. To an extent, the learner may modify some attributes of his/her learner model in order to make adjustments in further personalization of the learning process. Likewise, it may be useful for the learner to understand what inferences can be made from certain elements in his/her learner model. For example, if parts of the learner model can be made public, the learner may want to configure and restrict the levels of inference that a system can make about him/her and expose the results.

Using ontologies as the basis for defining parameters of the learner model is essential for explaining all aspects of the learner models and the underlying processes to the learners. In the case of the learner model ontology of Kay and Lum discussed in the previous subsection, this means explaining the ontology and its construction to the learner. Explaining that particular ontology is relatively straightforward, since it was originally constructed from an online dictionary - its source was actually created to explain the meanings of a wide range of concepts to people. Moreover, the hierarchy of the terms included in the ontology is relatively easy to visualize in order to enhance the explanations by bringing about the structure of the ontology. Thus, in spite of a relatively small amount of information that is readily available at the interface, the open learner model can grow rather large yet easily comprehensible by the learner. This can be critical, especially in the early phases of the learning process.

OWL-OLM is an OWL-based open learner model used for personalization and adaptation in the OntoAIMS adaptive Web-based learning environment (Denaux et al., 2005a), (Denaux et al., 2005b). OntoAIMS integrates interactive learner modeling (OWL-OLM) and learning content to recommend learning resources on the SemanticWeb.

OWL-OLM enables one to handle both the dynamics of the learner's performance and the cold start problem. When a learner logs in for the first time, a dialog agent using an existing domain ontology runs a graphics-and-text-based dialog with the learner in order to elicit his/her conceptualization of the domain. From the dialog, the agent infers the learner's understanding and mismatches related to the dialog topics (selected from the domain ontology). The inference process also includes reasoning about more general and more specific concepts and topics from the ontology, thus making possible to generate initial values for the learner model in an interactive and intelligent way. Both the domain ontology and the initial values of the learner model are represented in OWL.

2.6 Learner model servers and brokers

There is a growing interest for the reuse of the learner model across applications (Brooks et al., 2004; Brusilovsky, 2004; Chepegin et al., 2004; Dolog and Schafer, 2005; Kay et al., 2003; Van der Sluijs and Houben, 2005). The learners may interact with several different applications, they may also take courses in similar domains (e.g., learning two or more programming languages), and their learning styles and other preferences are often the same. For all these reasons, it is highly desirable to avoid spending considerable time and effort to build up a detailed learner model each time from scratch. A *learner model server* can be used instead to support the exchange of learner models between different applications.

On a learner model server, learner models can be stored in a database and accessed from external applications using standardized network protocols and/or pedagogical agents. For example, in the *CUMULATE* learner model server (Brusilovsky, 2004) the database has two parts. The low-level part contains time-stamped events that describe activities (i.e., low-level interactions with LOs from different LORs and applications) that each learner has performed (e.g., "page is read", "audio is played", "question is answered", "example is analyzed"), as well as the outcomes of these activities. The high-level part is derived from the low-level activities and is represented in the form of object-attribute-value triplets and attribute-value pairs. These, in turn, represent shareable parameters that are typical for classic learner models (e.g., the levels of the learner's knowledge of each domain concept, his/her motivation, and so on). This high-level part can then be queried by different agents and applications using a standard querying protocol. In CUMULATE, each learner model parameter in the high-level part is derived from low-level events and updated by a pedagogical agent. Thus there are agents for deriving the learner's knowledge levels related to different domain concepts, his/her focus, etc. The agents may reside on the server, but may also be external (e.g., controlled by external applications).

If a learner model server is integrated with an educational server (Figure 3-4) that also performs other functions than learner modeling, educational Web services may be used to:

- support the native communication protocols of different applications and pedagogical agents that need to interact with the learner models;
- mediate queries and updates to the learner model database by interpreting them and converting their formats at runtime as necessary (which may require a lot of ontological engineering efforts, due to the fact that different learner models in general comply to different ontologies[34]; see Chapter 7 for a detailed coverage of ontological engineering);
- provide different views of the learner models, including/excluding parts of the information from the learner models as configured by the applications and/or the learners themselves;
- ensure the learners' privacy (the learners should be in control over the data from the learner models that may be exposed in public or exchanged among different applications; for example, a learner may not want to approve the exposal of his/her test results)
- support the openness of the learner models by enabling the learners to inspect the models and the processes for personalization (different learner models in the database may originally use different representation and reasoning mechanisms that arc not designed for the learner to examine them easily.

As a simple example of communication between an application and a learner model server, consider the following request sent by the AHA! Adaptive Engine (De Bra et al., 2004b) to the UserModelService (Heckmann and Krueger, 2003) developed to support UserML and answer questions coming from applications (Chepegin et al., 2004):

```
http://www.u2m.org/service.php?subject=Alex&auxiliary=
knowledge&predicate=aha.tutorial&range=aha.statement
```

---

[34] Representing different learner models in the database using the same language (such as UserML) helps solve these problems only at the syntactic level.

It is a UserQL/URI representing the question: "Tell me all about Alex's knowledge on the topic 'aha.tutorial' of which the range of values should be 'aha.statement'." The UserModelService will interpret the query, retrieve the requested information from the Alex's learner model, format it in UserML, and return it to AHA! for applying its adaptation strategy according to the returned information.

Brooks et al. have proposed (2004) to use the framework they call *Massive User Modeling System* (*MUMS*) that further disintegrates the classical notion of a learner model as a data structured hard-wired with an application:

- different software components, WBE systems, and applications may be interested in forming coherent models of learners while they work with different domain applications (and also on an archival basis);
- to support that need, a learner model server may be used for collecting and disseminating learner information to the interested software components to derive the learner models from the information.

The MUMS approach is to collect and manipulate low-level learner modeling "events" by several entities (agents) before they get transformed into high-level learner models. It also introduces the idea of *learner model brokering* (at the "event" level), Figure 6-5.

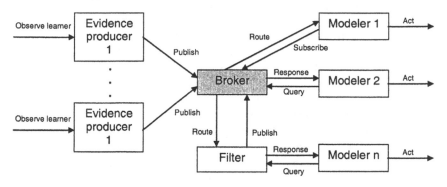

Figure 6-5. A simplified view of the MUMS framework (adapted from (Brooks et al., 2004))

Each "event" is generated by an *evidence producer* and is represented on the server as an *opinion* - a temporally grounded codification of a fact (contextualized statement) about a learner. An opinion can range from a low-level direct observation of the learner's interaction with a learning environment, to beliefs about the learner's knowledge, desires, and intentions. A *filter* is an intelligent entity (agent) that can take a low-level opinion and create a higher-level one, often using different domain-specific rules. Filters can be chained to provide any amount of value-added reasoning that is desired. A *modeler* entity reasons over a subset of opinions it is interested at (and these may come from different producers and filters) to form one or more learner models. An example of a modeler is the AHA! Adaptive Engine that interacts with the learner to provide adaptation. A *broker* receives opinions from producers and filters, and disseminates them to interested modelers and filters. A modeler may query the broker for some opinion, or may subscribe with it for receiving opinions generated by specific producers.

Evidence producers, modelers, brokers, and filters may be implemented as Semantic Web services to encourage interoperability, extensibility, and scalability at both the semantic and the syntactic levels. For example, the broker entity is logically centralized but can be implemented as a set of distributed services to enhance modularization and scalability.

***The MUMS framework implicitly enforces the idea of *learner model fragmentation* (through opinions), also stipulated by the recently proposed *Broker-based Discovery Service for User Models (BD-SUM)*, an architecture for user modeling in a multi-application context (Chepegin et al., 2005). BD-SUM uses the MLUM language mentioned in section 2.1 to represent and query user models. However, BD-SUM also addresses the semantic level of user modeling by deploying user modeling and domain ontologies to represent the meanings of different user models. As in the GUC approach (section 2.2), any application interested in the BD-SUM services is required to provide an ontological description of its internal user model, domain, and possibly other application models, as well as to register with the BD-SUM's User Model Broker (UM Broker). External queries to UM Broker are semantically interpreted according to the ontologies and, in response, the relevant user model fragments are returned to the requester, along with the links to the relevant registered ontologies.

A major consequence of learner model fragmentation and of using learner model servers and brokers is the possibility for different and independent learning systems to *collaboratively build and use learner models* (profiles). As a simple example, consider a learner who has a university degree in social sciences, and then wants to take another online course from an e-Learning provider. The other course may be in, say, demography. Assume also that the learner can access different online course providers and offerings through a specific WBE application. The application may store personal fragments about the learner, as well as his/her preferences and relations (in terms of the IEEE PAPI Learner categories, Table 5-4). The university server can supply fragments about the learner's earlier performance at the university, such as the exams, grades, and projects he/she has completed. The e-Learning provider can supply (as well as update) the fragments related to the learner's performance in the demography course, his/her learning history data, the exercises attempted, etc. Typically, some of the information stored by different providers will overlap; for example, all three servers/applications in this scenario may store the learner's personal data (albeit in possibly different formats and using different identification schemes). Provided that all three servers/applications support open learner modeling and different views over the learner information, the learner may be presented with an integrated, customizable, and non-redundant view of his/her learner information supplied by different providers.

Generally, an individual system can access the learner models and/or their fragments from other systems at a central server (e.g., through a Web service that communicates with a learning model broker), and perhaps contribute to them. Alternatively, it can do so by communicating with peer systems in a P2P network. Individual systems might also create and maintain their own learner models. In either case, it is quite possible that the information about one or more learners is scattered across different systems and learner models (Dolog and Schafer, 2005).

In that context, an individual system is likely to face the need for the important activity of *importing external (fragments of) learner models* from a central server or from a peer system. Example scenarios for this need are
• two learner model servers want to merge their data;
• a system supporting open learner modeling provides some sort of browsing for learner data
• updating the learner data periodically from/at another server for persistence and/or replication purposes.

All such scenarios require the form and the content of learner model fragments data to be thoroughly examined before importing them. The learner model ontology of the importing system should be analyzed in this process to extract information about the kinds of learner model fragments that exist, and that can be expected to be imported as structured objects. Likewise, the ontology can tell what properties these objects can have, and what kind of values these properties can hold. Thus the import process can perform ontology-supported learner model fragment and fragment property checks, in terms of examining the fragment structure, the types of the fragment's properties, the format of property values, and so on. The objects (or just some of their properties) that fail to pass the checks do not conform to the learner model ontology of the importing system and must be discarded. Dolog and Schafer (2005) analyze a number of other checks and actions that also need to be performed during the import process (learner identification check, namespace check and conversion, object structure check, check for overlapping objects, and deletion of redundant data).

2.7   Learner modeling and LO metadata

Critics of the IEEE LOM standard recognize that it is by far the most widely used standard for specifying LO metadata, but also list a number of its deficiencies. These include (Brooks et al., 2005):

- few of the 76 elements are used in practical LO metadata instances, and many are never used at all;
- the elements used often refer to custom or local vocabularies, a practice that effectively eliminates semantic interoperability;
- automatic metadata generation is not easy;
- current practical tools have poor support for the full IEEE LOM standard;
- poor data typing, leading to potentially ambiguous situations (e.g., for the Lifecycle category elements; see Table 5-2).

In addition, most LORs allow for only a single LO metadata instance to be associated with each of the stored LOs. This severely limits the quality of LO descriptions that LORs can offer and restricts the LO query and retrieval.

To overcome these limitations, McCalla has suggested (2004) an alternative approach to creating metadata to describe LOs. His approach, called the *ecological approach*, is based on the idea that LO metadata should not be prescribed; instead, they should stem from information about real use of LOs, by real learners, information that gradually accumulates over time, and is interpreted only in the context of end use. In other words, it is the *purpose* that determines what information to use and how it is to be used.

The suggested implementation of this idea is simple - after a learner has interacted with a LO, the LO is associated with an instance of the learner model. Then another learner (or even the same learner) interacts with the same LO, and the process repeats. Over time, each LO thus slowly accumulates different learner model instances. The instances contain much of the objective, subjective, learning performance, and learning history information as described in the beginning of section 2. Together, the instances collectively represent a record of the experiences of all learners that have interacted with that LO. Data mining methods can be applied over that record to possibly identify patterns of learners' interaction (e.g., "Learners with such-and-such cognitive traits passed this test well", or "Learners interacted with this LO intensively during their exam period"). The identified patterns can be related to an ontology of educational outcomes to create metadata that describe the LO in terms of its usage and the learners' educational goals. As the LOs accumulate more and more learner model instances, the resulting patterns crystallize more clearly and it becomes easier to apply algorithms emulating natural selection to differentiate between really useful LOs and those that are not useful (hence the name, "ecological approach").

In order to get a feeling of how the ecological approach can be used in practice, consider the system of Tang and McCalla (2005) that recommends research papers (LOs) to graduate students (learners) wanting to learn a new research area. The domain in which the system has been applied was software engineering, and the students who used it were mature students with various backgrounds. The learner model ontology contained parameters to define the learner' interests in various subfields of software engineering (e.g., requirements analysis, user interface design, and so forth), his/her background knowledge (in programming, statistics, networks and the Internet, etc.), current job (programmer, academic/teaching, management, and the like), and expectations in taking the course (like agile programming, Web engineering, and so on). After eliciting the values of the learner model instances and associating them with a group of research papers the students were required to read and evaluate, each collection of instances pertaining to a specific research paper was analyzed for patterns. It turned out that the resulting patterns (suitably visualized for easier interactive interpretation) suggested that the useful metadata to annotate each research paper might be:

- the means and standard deviations of the paper's overall ratings (must be updated periodically; determines the general quality of a paper);
- the papers both positively and negatively correlated with the given paper;
- the correlation of the factors that affect learners' overall ratings of the given paper;
- significant correlations of the overall ratings with each feature of the learner model.

Needless to say, these are largely different from IEEE LOM elements.

An obvious deficiency of the ecological approach is that the resulting metadata will have a "local flavor" of the subject domain, learner model ontology, and the local ontology of educational outcomes. It is then necessary to deploy intelligent agents to reason over these metadata and convert them to a more standardized form for export. Unfortunately, as with generic learner modeling, this conversion should not be expected to run smoothly and without data losses.

In practical implementations of the ecological approach so far, elements of the learner model to be associated with a LO were elicited through a simple pre-test that the learner is required to complete before he/she is allowed access to the LO. The pre-test is related to the topic(s) covered by the LO, as defined in the domain ontology. Since many learners get frustrated by pre-tests, an alternative is to rely on a learner's declaration of self knowledge ("I believe I understand this topic *that* much" (on a Likert scale)). The values of such declarations for each topic would then be mapped to the terms in the educational outcome ontology being used.

2.8   RDF binding and API for learner model exchange

There are numerous ways to specify a learner model ontology, even for those parts that are domain independent. On the other hand, it is always a good idea to have a representation of learner models based on standards. The use of standards reduces variability in domain-independent parts of the learner models and thus increases interoperability (Dolog and Nejdl, 2003).

With a rationale much the same as that in favor of RDF binding for LO metadata (see Chapter 5, section 3.2), the RDF model can be used for learner description as well. In order to comply with standards, an RDF Schema that defines a vocabulary to be used in RDF descriptions of learner information should start from learner information standards like IMS LIP and IEEE PAPI Learner. Extensions can be provided as necessary to satisfy the requirements of a specific project or to improve flexibility. There is no restriction on the use of different schemas together in one RDF file or RDF model, hence multiple schemas can be defined to tailor the RDF description to suit the project's needs. The following example illustrates that approach.

As a result of the *Learner* project (Dolog, 2003), an RDF binding has been developed for a learner model that combines parts of the IEEE PAPI Learner, IMS LIP, IMS RDCEO (i.e., IMS Reusable Definition of Competency or Educational Objective (IMS RDCEO, 2002)), and IMS QTI specifications, and also provides some project-specific extensions. The binding is provided as a set of RDF Schemas defining the fragments of the learner model as shown in Table 6-1. The meanings of individual fragments are obvious. The entire binding is fairly general to cover a number of different projects and applications. Figures 6-6 and 6-7 illustrate the binding details and how it can be used in an RDF file to encode learner information.

Table 6-1. The parts of an RDF binding for a learner model (after (Dolog, 2003))

Fragment	Defined according to
Learner	- (integrates the fragment schemas below)
Performance and portfolio	IEEE PAPI Learner
Goals and preferences	IMS LIP
Competencies	IMS RDCEO
Questions & tests, assessment	IMS QTI
Result reporting for questions & tests	IMS QTI
Concept	IMS LIP
Privacy	IMS LIP, IEEE PAPI Learner
Personal information and other extensions	- (project-specific)

Learner model fragmentation and the RDF binding discussed above were also the starting point for Dolog and Schafer (2005) to develop a Java API and Web services for learner model exchange between multiple sources. The API defines a class and properties for each class from the RDF binding.

```
<?xml version='1.0' encoding='ISO-8859-1'?>
<!DOCTYPE rdf:RDF [
        <!ENTITY rdf 'http://www.w3.org/1999/02/22-rdf-syntax-ns#'>
        <!ENTITY a 'http://protege.stanford.edu/system#'>
        <!ENTITY privacy 'http://www.learninglab.de/~dolog/learnerrdfbindings/privacy.rdfs#'>
        ...
        <!ENTITY papi_rdfs 'http://www.learninglab.de/~dolog/learnerrdfbindings/papi.rdfs#'>]>
<rdf:RDF xmlns:rdf="&rdf;"
        xmlns:a="&a;"
        xmlns:privacy="&privacy;"
        ...
        xmlns:papi_rdfs="&papi_rdfs;"
        xmlns:rdfs="&rdfs;">
...
<rdf:Property rdf:about="&papi_rdfs;performance_coding"
              a:maxCardinality="1"
              rdfs:label="performance_coding">
    <rdfs:comment>
              Attribute which is used for performance coding used to measure
              a learner performance.
    </rdfs:comment>
    <rdfs:domain rdf:resource="&papi_rdfs;Performance"/>
    <rdfs:range rdf:resource="&rdfs;Literal"/>
</rdf:Property>
...
<rdf:Property rdf:about="&papi_rdfs;performance_privacy"
              a:maxCardinality="1"
              rdfs:comment="References a privacy information valid for the instance"
              rdfs:label="performance_privacy">
    <rdfs:domain rdf:resource="&papi_rdfs;Performance"/>
    <rdfs:range rdf:resource="&privacy;PrivacyInfo"/>
</rdf:Property>
...
</rdf:RDF>
```

Figure 6-6. An excerpt from RDF binding for performance and portfolio fragment (adapted from (Dolog, 2003))

The API and the services enable:
- accessing learner model fragments from programs, using the Java API (retrieving, inserting, and updating the learner model fragments stored in the structures defined by the classes and properties specified by the API);
- exporting and importing learner model fragments, using the Java API and the Web services that act as a learner model server;
- accessing learner models created in RDF through a query infrastructure for RDF repositories like Edutella.

```
<rdf:Description rdf:ID="r_1">
...
        <papi:performance_coding
                xmlns:papi="http://learninglab.de/papi#">
        number
        </papi:performance_coding>
...
</rdf:Description>
<rdf:Description rdf:ID="r_2">
...
        <ims:language_preference
                xmlns:ims="http://learninglab.de/ims#">
        english
        </ims:language_preference>
...
</rdf:Description>
```

Figure 6-7. Mixing different vocabularies (*ims:* and *papi:*) in describing a learner's performance and language preferences (adapted from (Dolog and Nejdl, 2003))

2.9   Web mining for learner models

Recently, an interesting question related to personalization of the learning process started to attract the attention of SWBE researchers: can some fragments of learner models be constructed automatically starting from the data stored in usage log servers of WBE systems and applying Web usage mining techniques to these data? Kay and Lum (2005) recognize the role of usage data for learner modeling, but do not explicitly mention *learner access behavior modeling* in their review of the roles that ontologies can play in learner modeling. Contrary to them, Zhou et al. (2005) elaborate that role of ontologies in detail. Creating automatically an ontology of learner access behavior by applying Web usage mining techniques is an important contribution to the specification of the learner model dynamics, and can lead to exciting opportunities for personalization.

Figure 6-8 illustrates the idea of a *learner access ontology* as a means of sharing learner access behavior models. The learner's activities with the system are tracked and recorded in a log file as usage data. By transforming these data into an ontology, the system can enable deducing usage knowledge from the ontology (Zhou et al., 2005). Pedagogical agents and Web services can then use the ontology to provide personalized recommendation and search.

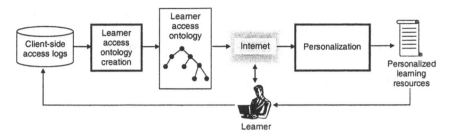

Figure 6-8. The process of creating and using learner access ontology (adapted from (Zhou et al., 2005))

The process of creating a learner access ontology is discussed in detail in Chapter 12, but here is an idea of how it can be done. Each learner may access different SWBE systems, educational servers, LORs, etc., at different times of day. Also, all of his/her activities can be categorized, e.g., in terms of educational needs such as *reading, exercise, assessment, collaboration*, etc., and for each recorded activity its category can be easily extracted from the log file. The log file can be mined for possible discovery of access patterns like "It is *highly likely*[35] that the learner accesses an online dictionary when learning a new topic". Several such patterns may be discovered for a learner, and can be inter-related. There are techniques for converting them into personalization rules. Applying personalization rules in this case may result in showing the learner some links to online dictionaries whenever he/she starts learning a new topic in future sessions with the system.

Another interesting Web mining approach to automatic generation of some learner information from the Web is presented in (Mori et al., 2005). The idea here is to analyze Web pages containing information about a certain learner (starting from his/her name and using a conventional search engine) trying to find terms that frequently co-occur with the learner's name. Furthermore, since there may be different pages that present information about the same learner but in different contexts (e.g., one page may contain information about him/her as a student of a certain university, whereas another one may describe him/her as a successful entertainer), additional terms may be possible to extract to describe the learner's different contexts. Discovering terms that describe a learner and/or his/her context may be extremely useful for automatically populating fragments of his/her learning model represented according to an explicit learner model ontology. For example, discovered terms may be suitable for initializing details of the

---

[35] This fuzzy term obviously suggests some degree of uncertainty for the pattern, which is typical in data/Web mining.

learner model related to the learner's interests (like those in the IMS LIP Interest category), accomplishments (IEEE PAPI Learner Portfolio, IMS LIP Transcript), and social interactions (e.g., IEEE PAPI Learner Relations).

2.10   Open issues and best practices

Building a good learner model for a SWBE system is a difficult task. In addition to the already mentioned design and technical problems related to the accuracy vs. complexity issue, the cold start problem, development of learner model ontology, imperfection of current learner information standards, and integration of different learner model fragments, there are several other open issues that are usually handled on a case-to-case basis (Denaux et al., 2005b; Dolog, 2003; Jovanović, 2005):

- What exactly are the features of a learner that should be used in a specific learner model?
- What types of security and privacy should be considered when designing a learner model?
- How to deal with different aspects of a learner model?
- How exactly to exchange (fragments of) learner models between systems in open learning environments?
- How to identify learner model fragments stored on different servers?
- How to define stereotypes to grasp the differences in the backgrounds of individual learners more realistically?
- Should stereotypes be used at all, given the fact that there is no way for LO and course authors to take into account all specific learning goals of each individual learner and all concepts a learner may rely on when trying to understand the content the system presents?
- How to clearly identify the learning goals of individual learners, given their diversity?
- How to bring closer the goals of the authors and the goals of the learners?
- How open should be an open learner model, i.e. should the learners be allowed to view/modify all their data or just selected ones? To this end, how capable and experienced should they be to let them evaluate their own knowledge? Can all of them clearly formulate their learning goals? Are they aware of their learning styles and other preferences?

Since Semantic Web learner modeling is a young research direction, experiences are not abundant to make possible to answer these questions easily. Still, it is already possible to identify some best practices (so far) and make some recommendations accordingly (Aroyo and Dicheva, 2004a; Winter et al., 2005):

- It is a good idea to take the ontological part of learner modeling as an interplay of three groups of ontologies: those that capture the learner's characteristics, those that encapsulate the domain concepts and relations, and those related to the particular courses and learning resources. In a simple case, the three groups of ontologies shrink to a single learner model ontology, a single domain ontology, and a single course ontology (which models the concrete subset of the domain taught in a particular course). More complex cases require more than one ontology in each group. As a consequence, the learner model ontology may be actually decomposed into a set of inter-related ontologies.

- Loosely coupling the three different types of ontologies is an essential design issue if a goal is to accommodate changes (in course subject matter, learning material, and learner types). Such changes are quite common in courses covering rapidly developing domains, as well as in offering courses more than once.
- It is especially important to decouple the abstract domain ontology of an area of study from those representing the particular topics and learning resources associated with a course. There are several reasons for that. First, recall from Chapter 3, section 1.4, that the authoring activities should be clearly separated in those related to domain authoring and those that focus on resource authoring. Ontological support for these two kinds of activities is much more effective if the two kinds of ontologies are decoupled. Second, a domain ontology is usually relatively static and can be reused across multiple courses. For example, there may be two or more different courses teaching different topics from the same domain, or they may be designed for different depths or levels of difficulties. In such a situation, it is highly likely that the domain ontology will remain the same, while the course and resource ontologies will be different. Third, most developers nowadays opt for using OWL DL for ontology development. Modeling domain concepts and relationships with the OWL DL *subClassOf* property and using the OWL DL *instanceOf* property to connect the concrete course topics to the classes in the domain model is straightforward.
- Using the SKOS family of ontologies is very useful in describing the relationship between topics in a course, because SKOS was specifically developed to describe taxonomies and classification schemes (see Chapter 5, section 3.3).
- Ontologies representing learner behavior and competencies may start from specifications like IMS LIP and IEEE PAPI Learner, but due to their imperfection and lack of some important aspects (e.g., learner marks and grading) they are often insufficient. Additional ontologies are necessary to describe different kinds of knowledge gained in a learning experience (e.g. conceptual knowledge, procedural knowledge, etc.), as well as different kinds and levels of cognitive competencies demonstrated (e.g. remembering, understanding, applying, etc.). These

additional ontologies are especially useful for making statements about the learner's competencies with respect to specific topics in course ontologies.

- The learner's competencies can be specified, assessed and updated according to IMS QTI standard. A specific ontology may be developed to connect his/her answers to the statements about his/her competencies.

- Learner model fragmentation suggests developing a separate ontology for each specific fragment (e.g., such as those listed in Table 6-1). Note that it might be important to anticipate extensions in the design (e.g., by keeping it open for new fragments) to capture any further and/or future information intrinsic to the student.

- Architectures of adaptive learning systems (see Chapter 4, section 5, especially Figure 4-8) suggest developing yet another learner model fragment ontology - application ontology. It can be used to describe the tasks the learner can perform and the interactions he/she can have with the e-Learning application (using, e.g., the Role-Goals-Tasks model (Motta et al., 2003; De Bra et al., 2004b)) and the instructional design decisions.

- Currently, the most widely used ontology development tool is Protégé, and the most widely used ontology representation language is OWL DL. An important feature of Protégé is the possibility for developers to use logical inference engines within the development environment to check the semantic and inferential correctness of ontologies as they develop them.

3.   A CASE STUDY

In order to illustrate personalization and learner modeling in detail by a practical example, this section describes *TANGRAM*, an integrated learning environment for the domain of Intelligent Information Systems (IIS) (Jovanović, 2005; Jovanović et al., 2006a; Jovanović et al., 2006b). Using an ontology-based approach, TANGRAM enables automatic decomposition of LOs into reusable content units and dynamic reassembly of such units into personalized learning content according to the learner's domain knowledge, preferences, and learning styles.

3.1   Learning object decomposition

Why decomposing LOs into smaller pieces? Aren't LOs intended for reuse as they are, in different courses and other units of study?

Current research efforts are almost exclusively oriented towards reusability of LOs in their entirety. Annotating LOs using standards-compliant metadata (e.g., IEEE LOM and Dublin Core) enables search and retrieval of existing LOs stored in LORs. Accordingly, metadata are seen as the primary means for fostering LOs reusability. However, very often a content author needs to reuse just some specific parts of a LO, rather than the entire LO - for example, just a couple of slides from a slide presentation, or an image or a table from a text document. Faced with such a need, a content author typically turns to copy-and-paste approach. However, this approach is inappropriate for a number of reasons: it is tedious, time-consuming, not scalable in terms of maintenance, etc. (Verbert et al., 2005). Automating reuse of individual components of LOs can improve the current practice by reducing the effort that content authors put in preparation of learning materials.

In general, a LO includes a number of components (content units), Figure 6-9. The components can differ in types and in levels of granularity. The concepts of a *content structure ontology* can be used to formally define different kinds of content units (e.g., slide, paragraph, list), whereas using its properties one can formally describe aggregation relationships between content units of different granularity and/or type (e.g., ordering, has part, is part of, etc).

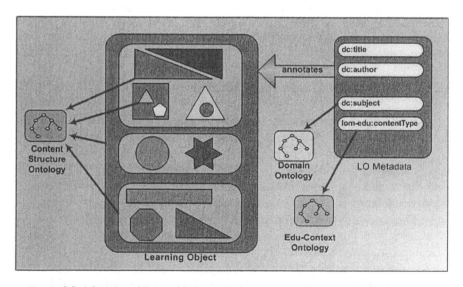

Figure 6-9. A learning object and its associated ontologies (after (Jovanović et al., 2006a)

LOs are typically annotated using a standards-compliant set of metadata. *Domain ontology* concepts can be used as values of the metadata elements describing the content of a LO. For example, concepts of TANGRAM's IIS domain ontology (partially described in Chapter 5, section 3.3, and in Figure 5-18) are assigned to the *dc:subject* element of the standards-compliant metadata schema for annotating LOs that TANGRAM works with. In addition, the concepts from an *ontology of educational context* (Edu-Context Ontology in Figure 6-9) can be used to mark up LOs with their pedagogical/instructional roles (e.g. definition, illustration). TANGRAM also assumes that metadata are attached to each component of a LO, thus making individual components searchable (this detail is left out from Figure 6-9 in order to avoid excessive cluttering).

One benefit of this annotation scheme is that it enables advanced search of LORs - it becomes possible to search for content of a certain type, as defined in the context ontology (e.g., "definition"), for content dealing with a certain topic (from the domain ontology, e.g. "Semantic Web"), and for content of a certain granularity (as defined in the content structure ontology, e.g. "slide"). Another benefit is the possibility to (semi-)automatically compose the retrieved content units into a new LO, compliant to the specific instructional approach of a content author.

This annotation scheme is also relevant in terms of learning content personalization. Explicitly defined structure of a LO facilitates adaptation of the LO, as it enables direct access to each of its components and their tailoring to the preferences, objectives, competencies and/or other specific features of a learner that are relevant for the learning process. If components of a LO can be accessed directly, new and personalized learning content can be created dynamically, on-the-fly.

3.2   TANGRAM and its ontologies

TANGRAM is implemented as a SWBE application built on top of a repository of educational content (a LOR) and intended to be useful to both content authors and university-level students interested in the domain of IIS. It aims at automating the process of building new content out of existing components and shaping up that content differently to satisfy specific needs of individual learners.

TANGRAM provides personalized learning experience by:
- adapting the content to each individual student according to his/her learner (student) model;
- enabling quick access to a particular type of content[36] about a topic of interest from the domain ontology (e.g., access to "examples" of RDF documents, or to "definitions" of the Semantic Web).

---

[36] Defined in accordance with the ontology of educational context.

From the content author's perspective, it is important to upload new LOs in the LOR with the idea of being able to reuse its components later. To this end, the uploaded LO and its components must be described in the LOR with high-quality metadata. However, the markup process should not require much effort from the author. Also, it must be easy for an author to retrieve LOs and/or their components from the LOR in order to reuse them for composing new LOs.

The annotation of a LO as a whole, as well as of its components, is based on a subset of the IEEE LOM standard, actually only those elements that were found necessary to provide the intended functionalities of the system.

Figure 6-10 depicts TANGRAM's architecture and the ontologies it uses. The *ALOCoM content structure ontology* (*ALOCoMCS*) is a content structure ontology based on the *Abstract Learning Object Content Model* (*ALOCoM*) (Verbert et al., 2004). It defines concepts (e.g., slide, slide body, slide title, table) and relationships (like ordering, has part, is part of, etc.) that enable formal definition of the structure of a LO. The *ALOCoM content type ontology* (*ALOCoMCT*) ontology is an ontology of educational context focused on potential instructional/pedagogical roles of content units of varying granularity levels (e.g., abstract, introduction, process, exercise, reference, and so forth). Both ontologies share the same root concepts, defined in the ALOCoM model: *content fragments*, *content objects*, and LOs. Content fragments are content units in their most basic form, like text, audio and video. These elements can be regarded as raw digital resources that cannot be further decomposed. A content object is an aggregation of content fragments and/or other content objects. Navigational elements enable sequencing of content fragments in a content object. LOs aggregate content objects around a learning objective.

The *learning paths ontology* is aimed at specifying some aspects of the instructional design in TANGRAM. Briefly, it defines learning trajectories through the topics defined in the domain ontology. It is further discussed in Chapter 7. The *user model ontology* serves the purpose of formally describing both the content authors and the learners. Thus it is an extension of the concept of learner model ontology discussed in section 2.4. It is covered in detail in the next section.

The *Content Management Module* (Figure 6-10) is responsible for uploading LOs and manipulating the TANGRAM's repository of LOs. It handles decomposition of an uploaded LO into content units of lower granularity according to the ALOCoMCS ontology, automatic annotation[37] of content units according to the ALOCoMCT ontology, storage of LOs in a

---

[37] See (Jovanović et al., 2006b) for a detailed account on how the annotation process is performed, for the heuristics used, and for examples.

format compliant to the applied ALOCoMCS ontology, and search and retrieval of content units from the LOR.

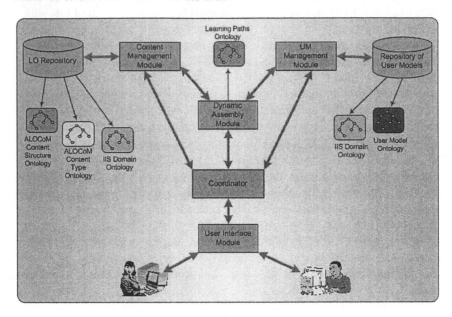

Figure 6-10. The architecture of TANGRAM (after (Jovanović et al., 2006a))

The *Dynamic Assembly Module* is in charge of dynamic (on-the-fly) generation of personalized learning content for a specific learner. This module knows how to combine available content units (obtained from the Content Management Module) to form a coherent learning content that suits a particular learner best. Of course, it does so using the learner information acquired from the UM Management Module.

The names of the other modules in Figure 6-10 clearly indicate their functions.

3.3   Personalization with TANGRAM

To be able to use the system, an author has to register first. The registration is mandatory in order for TANGRAM to acquire the basic set of data about the author. Availability of such data facilitates generation of suggested values for metadata elements in the process of LO annotation.

Just like a content author, a learner also must register with the system during the first session. Through the registration procedure the system acquires information about the learner sufficient to create an initial version of his/her profile (learner model). The system uses this profile to keep track of his/her preferences, learning style, and the levels of mastery of concepts from the IIS domain. With these data, the system can create personalized learning content.

3.3.1   User model ontology

TANGRAM's user model ontology focuses exclusively on the user information that proved to be essential for TANGRAM's functionalities. It is based on elements from IEEE PAPI Learner and IMS LIP specifications. It reuses some parts of the user model ontology developed for the ELENA project (Dolog and Nejdl, 2003) - the learners' performance (based on IEEE PAPI Learner), and their preferences (as specified in the IMS LIP). It also introduces new constructs for representing the users' data that the official specifications do not declare and the existing ontologies either do not include at all, or do not represent in a manner compliant to the needs of TANGRAM.

The ontology is shown in Figure 6-11[38]. The *um:User* class formally describes the concept of a TANGRAM user. Each user, i.e. instance of this class, is related to a set of his/her personal data via the *um:hasPersonalInfo* property. Personal data are formally represented with the *um:PersonalInfo* class and its datatype properties *um:username* and *um:password* that keep the values of secure login data, as well as the *um:name* property representing the user's name. Each user can be a member of one or more organizations (*um:Organization*). Specifically, the user can be a member of a university (*um:University*), a research centre (*um:ResearchCentre*) and/or a research group (*um:ResearchGroup*).

In addition, for each user the system needs data about his/her role/position in the formal organization he/she belongs to. Thus the property *um:hasRole* relates an instance of the *um:User* class to an appropriate instance of the *um:UserRole* class. The latter class formalizes the concept of the role/position a user typically has in an educational environment and is specified as an enumeration (via *owl:oneOf* construct) of the following instances: *um:Teacher, um:TeachingAssistant, um:Researcher, um:Student*. Of course, this enumeration can be extended to encompass additional roles if needed.

Furthermore, each user can have certain preferences (*um:hasPreference*) regarding the language (*ims:LanguagePreference*) and/or domain topics (*ims:ConceptPreference*). Representation of the users' preferences is taken from the user model ontology developed for the ELENA project and is fully compliant with the IMS LIP specification (hence the *ims* prefix). The class

---

[38] Classes and properties that do not have namespace prefix in Figure 6-11 belong to the um:http://tangram/user-model/complete.owl namespace.

ims:Preference, formally representing the user's preference, can have *ims:hasImportanceOver* property that defines the priority of a preference (i.e. its rank in terms of importance) for a specific user. TANGRAM's user model ontology also introduces the *um:AuthorPreference* class as a subclass of *ims:Preference* in order to represent the users' preferred authors of the learning content. The property *um:refersToAuthor* associates this specific type of a user's preference with his/her favorite author of learning content (one or more of them).

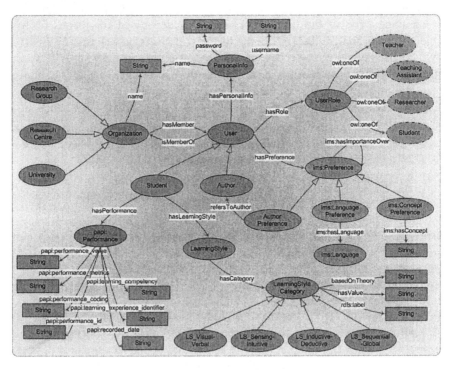

Figure 6-11. Graphical representation of TANGRAM's User Model Ontology (after (Jovanović et al., 2006a))

The remaining classes and properties of the TANGRAM user model ontology are aimed exclusively at formal representation of the learners' data. Each learner/student (*um:Student*) is assigned a set of performance-related data (via *um:hasPerformance* property) represented in the form of the *papi:Performance* class and the following set of properties[39]:

---

[39] The prefix *papi:* is used to denote that the *Performance* class and its properties are defined according to the PAPI Learner Specification.

- the *papi:learning_competency* property refers to a concept of the domain ontology that formally describes the subject matter of the acquired knowledge in the best way (i.e., it contains the URI of that concept);
- the *papi:learning_experience_identifier* property identifies a content unit that was a part of the material already used for learning; in TANGRAM, each instance of the *papi:Performance* class has a number of properties of this type - one for each content unit used to assemble the learning content for the student;
- the *papi:performance_coding* and *papi:performance_metrics* properties define respectively the coding system and the metrics used to evaluate the learner's performance level (i.e., the level of the acquired knowledge);
- the *papi:performance_value* property stores information about the real value/level of the acquired knowledge measured in terms of the specified metrics and coding system;
- the *papi:recorded_date* property is aimed at representing the date and time when the performance was recorded, i.e. when the learning process took place.

In addition, for each student the system maintains data about his/her learning style. The representation of learning styles in the user model ontology is based on the model of learning styles introduced by Felder and Silverman (1988). This model recognizes five categories of learning styles: 1) Visual-Verbal, 2) Sensing-Intuitive, 3) Sequential-Global, 4) Inductive-Deductive, and 5) Active-Reflective. The learning style of a student is formally represented by the *um:LearningStyle* class in the user model ontology. This class is associated (via the *um:hasCategory* property) with the *um:LearningStyleCategory* class that formally stands for one specific aspect (category) of the learning style. Specifically, TANGRAM implements the learning categories defined in the Felder and Silverman model and introduces one subclass of the *um:LearningStyleCategory* class to represent each of those categories (e.g. *um:LS_Visual-Verbal*)[40]. To make the ontology more general and easily extensible, the *um:LearningStyleCategory* class is assigned the *um:basedOnTheory* property enabling the introduction of learning style categories defined by other authors. The class *um:LearningStyleCategory* is also attached the *um:hasValue* property aimed at representing the position of a specific learner on the continuum defined by the opposite poles of a learning style category. The range of this property is restricted to values between -1 and 1 (inclusively). The boundary values (-1 and 1) represent the two extreme poles of each learning style category. For example, assigning the value of -1 to the *um:hasValue* property of the

---

[40] We did not consider Active-Reflective learning style category, as it emphasizes social aspects of a learning process that TANGRAM currently does not support.

um:LS_Visual-Verbal class means that the learner is highly visual. Likewise, the value of 1 for *um:hasValue* identifies a highly verbal learner.

The learner model is initialized during the registration procedure. Each student is required to fill a simplified version of the Felder and Silverman questionnaire for determining his/her learning style[41]. The acquired data enables the system to create personalized learning content for the student. As for initial evaluation of the student's knowledge about the IIS domain, the system relies on the student's self-assessment. The student is asked to estimate his/her level of knowledge of the main sub-domains of the IIS domain (e.g., intelligent agents, Semantic Web). In particular, the student is shown a Likert scale with the following set of options: "Never heard of the topic", "Have a basic idea", "Familiar with", "Know well" and "Demand advanced topics", and has to select an option that best reflects his/her knowledge. Internally, TANGRAM converts the student's selection for each subdomain into its numerical counterpart (0, 0.2, 0.4, 0.6 or 0.8, respectively). These numerical values are later compared to the difficulty values assigned to the domain concepts during the instructional design, to let the system determine the student's initial position in the IIS domain space and provide him/her with proper guidance and support.

3.3.2   Dynamic assembly of personalized learning content

A learning session starts after the user (registered and authenticated as a student) selects a sub-domain of IIS to learn about. The system consults its Learning Paths ontology and the student (learner) model in order to infer the student's level of knowledge about the selected sub-domain, as well as his/her knowledge of the domain concepts essential for successful comprehension of the chosen sub-domain (specified as prerequisite concepts in the Learning Paths ontology). The information resulting from this analysis is used to provide adaptive guidance and direct the student towards the most appropriate topics for him/her at that moment. To do that, TANGRAM uses link annotation and link hiding techniques, Figure 6-12 (the screenshot shown comes from a session in which a student is learning about XML technologies). Specifically, hierarchical organization of concepts of the selected sub-domain is visualized as an annotated tree of links (shown in the upper left corner of Figure 6-12). The link annotations used are as follows:

* blue bullet preceding a link to a domain concept denotes that the student knows the topic that the link points to;
* red bullet is used to annotate a domain topic that the student is still not ready for as he/she is ignorant of the prerequisite topics.

---

[41] The questionnaire is known as the "Index of Learning Styles", and is available at http://www.engr.ncsu.edu/learningstyles/ilsweb.html.

- green bullet denotes a recommended domain concept, i.e. a concept that the student has not learned yet, but has knowledge about all prerequisite topics;

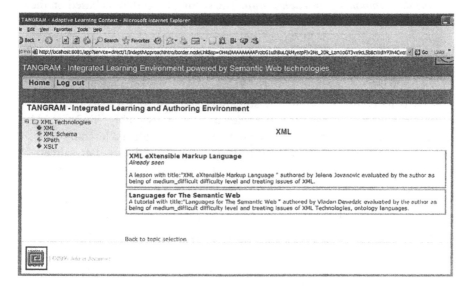

Figure 6-12. TANGRAM: screenshot of a page presenting a ranked list of generated assemblies (i.e., their descriptions; after (Jovanović et al., 2006a))

Link hiding technique is used to prevent the student from accessing topics that are too advanced for him/her. In other words, links annotated with red bullets are set inactive.

After the student selects one concept from the topics tree, the system initiates the process of dynamic assembly of learning content on the selected topic. The process is based on the following algorithm:

1. *Query the LOR for content units covering the selected domain topic.* The query is based on the *dc:subject* metadata element of the content units from the repository. If there are no content units on the selected topic in the repository, the further steps of the algorithm depend on the student's learning style, i.e. on its Sequential-Global dimension, to be more precise[42]. If the student belongs to the category of global learners, the algorithm proceeds normally. Otherwise, the system informs the student that the learning content on the selected topic is currently unavailable and suggests other suitable topics.

---

[42] Global learners prefer holistic approach and learn best when provided with a broader context of the topic of interest; sequential learners tend to be confused/disoriented if the topics are not presented in a linear fashion (Felder and Silverman, 1988).

2. *Classify the retrieved content units into groups according to the "same parent LO" criterion.* In other words, content units originating from the same LO are put in the same group.

3. *Sort the components in each group.* The sorting procedure is based on the original order of content units from the group, i.e. on the value of the *alocomcs:ordering* property of the parent LO. The term *assembly* refers to a group of content units sorted in this manner.

4. *Rank assemblies according to their compliance with the student (learner) model.* Each assembly is assigned a *relevancy value* between 0 and 1 that reflects its compliance with the student (learner) model, i.e. its relevancy for the student. To calculate the relevancy of an assembly, TANGRAM queries the student model for the data about the student's learning style, his/her preferred author, as well as his/her learning history data (already seen content units). The greater the relevancy value, the higher the importance of the assembly for the student.

5. *Present the student the sorted list of assembly descriptions and let him/her decide which one to take* (Figure 6-12). An assembly description is actually the value of the *dc:description* metadata element attached to the LO that the content of the assembly originates from. The idea is not for TANGRAM to make a choice for the student. Instead, the system provides guidance to the student (using link annotation and hiding techniques), and eventually lets him/her decide on the assembly to learn from.

6. *Show the student the learning content from the selected assembly.* As soon as the student selects an assembly from the list, the system presents its content using its generic form for presentation of dynamically assembled learning content.

7. *Update the student (learner) model.* Specifically, the system creates an instance of the *papi:Performance* class in the student model and assigns values to its properties (see Section 3.3.1 for details). For example, the *papi:performance_value* property is assigned a value that reflects the level of mastery of the domain topic. If it was a topic recommended by the system, the property is assigned the maximum value (1). However, if the assembly covered an advanced topic, due to the lack of more appropriate learning content, this property is set to 0.35. This approach was inspired by the work of De Bra et al. (2004a) and is based on the assumption that due to the lack of the necessary prerequisite knowledge the student was not able to fully understand the presented content.

4.   SUMMARY

Personalization plays an essential role in SWBE systems and applications. All learners are different, and a SWBE system needs to adapt the presentation of the learning material, the services it provides, and all the interaction it supports to each particular learner. When the system adapts its functionalities to each learner, it actually closely reflects the learners diversity in terms of their knowledge levels, learning progress, needs, objectives, learning styles, preferred media, intellectual capacities, and so on. Likewise, personalized systems fully support the dynamics of the learning process, since the learners' progress, knowledge, focus, motivation, and many other factors continuously change during the learning process. Personalization not only responds to the learners' diversity as quite a natural phenomenon - it actually supports it by providing different learning experiences to different learners.

Personalization is enabled by learner modeling. Learner model ontology formally describes various learner characteristics. Numerous learner modeling approaches in SWBE systems combine learner modeling ontologies with domain, context, and other ontologies to ensure for personalized learning experience and capture the interdependencies of different factors of the learning process.

Learner modeling is a specialization of the more general concept of user modeling. In SWBE applications, users are not only learners; authoring and teaching processes can be personalized as well. All users interact with the system, and all of the interaction provides useful information to capture. The challenge is to capture it as automatically as possible, with minimum efforts from the user.

Chapter 7

ONTOLOGICAL ENGINEERING FOR
SEMANTIC WEB-BASED EDUCATION

Chapter 2, section 2.2, introduces ontological engineering from a general point of view, stipulating the need for an appropriate ontology development methodology and accompanying tools. A methodology is needed to enforce a more disciplined approach to the set of activities spanning the entire lifecycle of an ontology - from conceptualization and design, to implementation, testing, evaluation, deployment, and maintenance.

Ontological engineering is a complex process. In addition to the use of tools and a methodology, it covers a whole range of other topics and issues, such as (Devedžić, 2002; Mizoguchi, 1998):

- the basics (philosophical and metaphysical issues and knowledge representation formalisms);
- knowledge sharing and reuse;
- knowledge management'
- business process modeling'
- commonsense knowledge;
- systematization of domain knowledge;
- Internet information retrieval;
- standardization;
- evaluation;
- and many more.

It also gives developers a design rationale of the knowledge base they build, helps them define the essential concepts of the domain of interest, and enables them to accumulate the knowledge about it.

How should ontological engineering be perceived from the SWBE perspective? What are the practical implications of it for SWBE researchers and developers? The case study presented in Chapter 6, section 3, as well as the best practices discussed in section 2.10 of the same chapter, provide a part of the answer to this question. In fact, they illustrate the process of ontological engineering of SWBE systems by explaining the design of the TANGRAM environment and by suggesting some more general engineering guidelines for building SWBE systems. On the other hand, they should rather be taken as mere starting points. There is much more to ontological engineering of SWBE, as this chapter explains.

1.   THE COVERAGE

The O4E portal (O4E, 2005), presented in Chapter 3, section 7, provides a good insight into the complexity of ontological engineering for SWBE systems and applications. Three out of four major lattices in the portal's underlying ontology, Figure 7-1 - *Theoretical issues in ontological engineering*, *Ontology development*, and *Technological perspective* - one way or another cover ontological engineering of SWBE (although it seams that only the first one does so). If one focuses more narrowly only on the process of *Building ontologies for education*, i.e. on ontology as an object (the result of an activity), then ontological engineering can be thought of as the set of activities shown in the right-hand half of Figure 7-1. Note, however, that whenever comes to *Using ontologies in education*, a good understanding of the technological perspective and how those ontologies are engineered becomes necessary. Even the fourth major lattice of activities shown in Figure 7-1, *Application perspective*, has a lot of ontological engineering flavor (albeit just implicitly).

Theoretical issues in ontological engineering. These are focused on theoretical and/or practical issues of ontological engineering that are specific to SWBE (upper-right part of Figure 7-1). Note that much of these issues can be seen as "instantiations" of similar but more generic issues, processes, and activities of ontological engineering in general (see again Chapter 2, section 2.2).

Ontology development. Practical aspects of ontology development (lower-right part of Figure 7-1) cover different issues of ontology creation and extraction, as well as the related tools, technologies, standards, and pedagogical issues. Much of the examples and approaches discussed in Chapters 2 thru 6 implicitly belong here.

Technological perspective. Educational ontologies are often used to facilitate and/or support the development and use of (parts of) SWBE systems (upper-left part of Figure 7-1). In this case, they are not a product but a technology; in this role, they help provide semantic interoperability of SWBE systems and their components, comply with standards, and structure the system development. For example, learner model ontologies discussed in Chapter 6, when seen as parts of SWBE systems, facilitate learner model conceptualization, fragmentation, exchange, integration, and reuse.

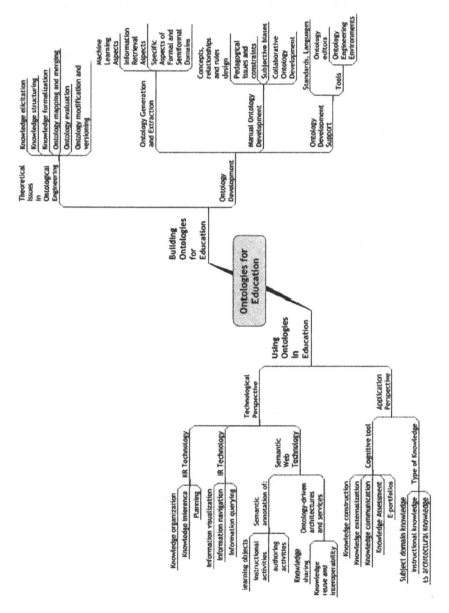

Figure 7-1. Classification of the field of ontologies for education (after (Dicheva et al., 2005))

Application perspective. This lattice (lower-left part of Figure 7-1) indicates that ontologies are considered in SWBE not only as a knowledge base component and/or a technology, but also as a *cognitive tool* (Dicheva et al., 2005). This means that ontologies are used in SWBE applications for modeling and representing different educational issues, such as learner information or instructional design. Recall also from (Fikes, 1998) and Chapter 2, section 2.1.4, that ontologies should serve as a good publication medium and a source of reference for learners, instructors, and authors, providing them with a shared conceptualization of the domain.

2.   RATIONALE FOR ONTOLOGICAL ENGINEERING OF E-LEARNING

A thorough ontological engineering of e-Learning systems makes these systems Semantic Web-ready. It also makes them interoperable with various LORs, educational servers, educational Web services, other SWBE applications, and other Semantic Web technologies. All this brings benefits to the end users - learners, teachers, and authors.

There is, however, an important drawback here - ontological engineering is hard work. It is anything but easy to develop a good-quality ontology that many interested parties would like to use and share. In spite of a lot of supporting technology available, both the development process and the evaluation of ontologies still require a lot of effort from domain experts and engineers alike.

Given this fact, a practical question that comes to mind is: does ontological engineering pay off? In other words, since there are many successful e-Learning applications that have never undergone any ontological engineering process, and since it is difficult to conduct one, why not keep the established development and usage practices of more traditional e-Learning systems?

The answer is simple: there are severe limitations traditionally-built systems, and they can be overcome at the cost of extra effort required to engineer the system ontologically (in addition to engineering it from the system development, instructional, and other perspectives). In support of this stance, there are three kinds of issues to consider (Devedžić, 2004a; Mizoguchi and Bourdeau, 2000): conceptual, technological, and tools-related.

2.1 Conceptual issues

Without ontologies, there is no way for different e-Learning systems to automatically *share and/or reuse course material,* because most such systems use different formats, languages, vocabularies, teaching strategies, assessment procedures, and learner models. Hence there is generally no way for two different e-Learning applications to interoperate even if their teaching and learning contents belong to the same domain. Ontologies enable sharing domain and pedagogical knowledge among applications, thus ensuring interoperability and accurate machine interpretation of course materials.

Furthermore, ontologies provide means for *structuring course material* around some firm, relatively stable, and widely accepted knowledge that many e-Learning applications could use a common point of reference. Moreover, ontological engineering efforts do not necessarily mean developing all ontologies from scratch. In recent years, the situation with ontologies has largely improved - several research groups have published different educational ontologies that can be used in other projects as well, at least as starting points.

As discussed in Chapters 3 and 6, ontologies are also essential for *annotating LOs and educational Web services* for easier access, discovery, invocation, and composition. Ontological engineering helps define metadata for the markup process and create machine-understandable and machine-interpretable descriptions of learning resources. Ontological engineering also helps combine domain, pedagogical, and application-specific knowledge to structure learner models. These, in turn, enable personalization and adaptivity.

Ontologies *underlie and support higher-level interaction* between learners and systems. Browsing of educational material and searching for it, consulting references, taking on-line tests and quizzes, online learner-performance tracking, and collaborative Web-based learning without ontologies require too much manual activities and impose repetitive and routine tasks. Ontologies reduce manual effort and enable delegating much of low-level interaction to supporting technologies like pedagogical agents and Semantic Web services.

2.2 Technological issues

Without ontological engineering, the resulting e-Learning system puts the main burden of locating, accessing, extracting, and interpreting LOs and information they contain on the learner. Even if the external LOs and LORs are ontologically annotated and interconnected, it is of little use if the newly developed system does not provide support for it.

Ontological engineering usually assumes using languages like OWL, RDF(S), etc. to represent ontologies and markup, and makes use of widely-accepted graphical tools to ease the development. As most of the existing and publicly available educational ontologies are developed and represented in these languages as well, reusing, adjusting, and combining them with application-specific ones is alleviated. Other compelling reasons for adopting these technologies are:

- they come from W3C standardization efforts;
- they are accompanied by free tools, such as parsers and format validators;
- they are in line with the Semantic Web layer cake vision (see Figure 2-6).

2.3   Tools-related issues

Mizoguchi and Bourdeau have noticed (2000) many limitations of current authoring tools in general, all of which pertain to tools for building e-Learning systems as well. Some of them are:

- authoring tools like TopClass, WebCT, Authorware, LearningSpace, CourseInfo, Cyberprof, Mallard, CM Online, and the like, are not "theory-aware", which means that they have neither explicit, built-in declarative representations of various domain theories, instructional design theories, and learning theories, nor links to such representations - it is the developer, not the tools, that knows the theories;
- there is a deep conceptual gap between authoring systems and authors;
- authoring tools are neither intelligent nor particularly user-friendly;
- authoring tools themselves provide poor support for sharing and reuse of knowledge and components developed for other educational systems.

Elaborating on the above statements, consider the process of creating a LO by current authoring tools. It is difficult for authors who are not experts in authoring for e-Learning to perform such a task - the knowledge of the domain and some proficiency with computers are not enough. The tools do not support the authoring process in terms of providing guidelines and constraints that should be satisfied. The guidelines might look as concept hierarchies based on a number of underlying ontologies that can drive the creation of coherent resources to be integrated in the LO being created. From the author's perspective, such class hierarchies should describe the domain itself, as well as various theories of learning and instructional design process. Of course, nobody expects an authoring tool to be able to support itself all possible domains and theories, but to support easy access to Web resources (created possibly by other authors) that contain the class hierarchies mentioned, and use them as points of reference (Devedžić and Pocajt, 2003).

Ontologically engineered authoring tools support (in a user-friendly way) development of teaching and learning contents that can then be presented, modified, and interlinked *consistently*. For example, some of the LOs produced by such authoring tools may take the form of Web pages that contain annotation with pointers to appropriate ontologies. A page showing contents related to various kinds of birds may contain several images and clippings from a library that comes with the authoring tool. In an ontology-aware authoring tool, library items can be preannotated with terms from and pointers to various ontologies; in this example, these ontologies are related to birds. Such a tool, in fact, supports automatic annotation of resulting Web pages - when an author creates and saves a page about birds using items from the library, the page gets automatically annotated with terms from and pointers to the appropriate ontologies. The resulting Web page is thus made machine-interpretable (in addition to being annotated with standard metadata such as IEEE LOM). Moreover, the entire course material can be created this way and made truly distributed (different pages and other kinds of LOs dispersed over different servers), yet all of the course material will be semantically interconnected through the network of ontologies, and reusable.

3. METHODOLOGICAL ASPECTS

Introducing ontological engineering into e-Learning design requires methodological considerations. Ontological engineering is there to ensure that all essential issues of the domain, the learner information, the pedagogy involved, and the supporting technology will be supported by based on a coherent and stable set of models that also facilitates the system interoperability. Simultaneously, it should be conducted in such a way to take into account the specifics of e-Learning as a distinct field.

3.1 Modeling and metamodeling

Ontological engineering is a *modeling* discipline. In the context of e-Learning, its purpose is to specify high-level models of knowledge underlying concepts, processes, and phenomena of interest to learning. Just like any other model, an educational ontology does not represent everything about the learning issue of interest; thus it is always incomplete. It leaves out some less important aspects of the learning issue and concentrates on those of higher importance. For example, in the TANGRAM environment (Chapter 6, section 3) the domain is intelligent information systems if an important issue of interest in terms of ontological engineering is user modeling. The user model ontology looks as in Figure 6-11 and assumes that typical learners are university-level students of information systems. Hence it does not include information like, e.g., IMS LIP Transcript (Table 5-3) and IEEE PAPI Learner Security, which would probably be necessary in case of a training environment in a military domain.

As a modeling discipline, ontological engineering frequently uses methods of hierarchical modeling (at least at the conceptualization level). Very often, concept hierarchies (i.e., taxonomies) of an ontology are represented in layers, and some kind of graphs are used to visually enhance the representation (Devedžić, 2002). In an ontology graph, concepts are connected either by labeled, or by unlabeled links. The former case represents ontologies as semantic networks. For example, the user model ontology of TANGRAM is essentially a semantic network of relevant concepts. In the latter case, the main issues are usually concept hierarchies and aggregation levels. For example, an ontology of learning units may represent concepts like *study program*, *course*, *lesson*, and their parts at different levels of the conceptual hierarchy. If the graph can be reduced to a tree, than each subtree can itself be interpreted as an ontology.

When one analyzes the concepts in an ontology at the knowledge level, they exhibit different degrees of domain-dependency. Hence ontological engineers often represent ontologies in several layers, ranging from domain-independent (core) to task-specific and domain-specific. Thus ontologies contain knowledge of appropriate hierarchical and/or layered models of the relevant world.

Activities of conceptualizing and specifying ontologies have a strong *metamodeling* flavor as well. Recall from Chapter 4, section 7 that a metamodel is a conceptual model (a language) of a modeling technique. In fact, metamodels enable improving the rigor of different but similar models. Ontologies do the same for different but similar knowledge models. Without ontologies, different knowledge bases representing knowledge of the same domain are generally incompatible even if they use similar knowledge models (as, for example, in the case of learner models developed exclusively after IEEE PAPI Learner, and those based on IMS LIP only). Generally, an educational ontology is a metamodel that describes how to build models of educational resources, processes, activities, and services, as well as the actors taking parts in the processes and activities - learners, teachers, authors, administrators, and pedagogical agents. The concepts defined in an educational ontology and the relations among them - the terms from the metamodel - are always (re)used as building blocks when modeling parts of an SWBE system. Thus it helps if the authoring tools used to specify educational content, instructional strategies, and learner models have some built-in knowledge - a metamodel, or an ontology - of the content and other models the authors develop. The metamodeling function of the ontology makes the authoring tools intelligent.

Adopting this metamodeling view on ontological engineering methodology never means sacrificing the usefulness of any specific model. For example, TANGRAM defines the ALOCoMCS ontology of content structure. It contains specification of generic terms (such as *content fragments* and *content objects*) that apply to any kind of learning content. These terms never constrain the vocabulary of the ontology (metamodel) used to describe the LOs pertaining to the domain of intelligent information systems, the IIS domain ontology (Figure 6-10). On the contrary, the ALOCoMCS ontology enriches the LO modeling vocabulary by providing the skeleton for the corresponding model of the domain knowledge.

3.2 e-Learning-specific ontological engineering

General-purpose ontology development methodologies discussed in Chapter 2, section 2.2.2, apply to ontological engineering of e-Learning as well. However, there are also efforts to define an e-Learning-specific ontological engineering methodology as well. For example, elaborating on ideas of Lytras et al. (2003) and taking their holistic approach (in order to integrate several conceptual and technological aspects), ontological engineering of an e-Learning system includes the following four phases:

- *Specifications of LOs, learning processes, and learning scenarios.* Essentially, this phase conceptualizes descriptions of LOs to be used in e-Learning systems, and defines appropriate ontologies to represent (fragments of) learner information. These ontologies specify the learners' needs, knowledge, motivation elements, problem solving capacity, team synergy, packaging features, and other learner-centric value ingredients. In addition, each LO is typically featured by several learning processes that can be applied to the LO (e.g., reading, problem solving, question answering, simulation, etc.) A combination of several such processes defines a learning scenario, i.e. a mode of interaction between the learners and the LO. An ontology of instructional design should be provided to support defining these processes and scenarios. This is further elaborated in section 7.
- *Specification of content development.* This roughly corresponds to defining an authoring process (task) ontology (elaborated in sections 8.3 and 9). It includes selection and evaluation of different resources to be included in a content package. Additionally, it assumes enriching the selected contents to provide an added value for the learning process, for example by authoring of adaptation and personalization in the way discussed in Chapter 3, section 1.5.

- *Detailed specification.* This is the phase in which different task ontologies are specified in detail. At the LO creation level, it means: a) formally establishing the "Acquire - Organize - Enable reuse - Transfer - Use - Relate value" cycle for resources to be used to compose LOs (creating a repository of such reusable resources eventually), and b) using the ontologies defined in the previous phases to formalize the metadata description of LOs to include details on how to use each specific LO, how to learn from it, how to adapt it to the learner's needs, how to search for it, and how to relate it to other LOs. At the LO usage level, it means: a) specifying the learning processes to be used in different learning scenarios (such as Presentation, Analysis, Synthesis, Evaluation, Reasoning, Explanation, Collaboration, etc.), and b) specifying how to dynamically match the LOs to the learning processes during the learning sessions.
- *Specification of technology.* This phase requires considering things at the e-Learning system level. It means specifying the technology to support the integration of different ontologies, LORs, and processes (e.g., educational servers, different educational Web services, ontology processors, learner information fragment integrators, etc.). It is possible to overlap this phase with the previous one. Apparently, this phase has little to do with ontological engineering; note, however, that technological considerations may result in the need to modify different ontologies, processes, and specifications from the previous phases.

It is essential to follow the learning technology standards and specifications throughout all these phases.

4.   ACHIEVING INTEROPERABILITY

One of the major goals of ontological engineering of a SWBE system is to make it interoperable with other similar systems, educational servers, LORs, and possibly other external resources and applications. Such interoperability is necessary in the context of WBE, since it is impossible for learners, teachers, and instructors to search and inspect all information relevant to a topic of interest. SWBE must enable intelligent, task-centered information support for solving problems and performing learning tasks (Aroyo and Dicheva, 2004a). Whatever the particular learning environment a learner/teacher/author uses, it should be able to evolve over time to enrich the set of educational functions it can support. This is only possible if such systems can interoperate, collaborate, and exchange each other's content and reuse each other's functionalities, thus increasing their effectiveness.

The first ontological engineering step to make in this direction is to develop a domain ontology (or ontologies) to define the concepts, relations, and vocabulary to be used when authoring content (LOs) for learners. Authoring LOs often includes reusing various resource files and other LOs from external LORs. If this process is to be (domain) ontology-based, LOs and the resources they include should be "attached" to the domain ontology concepts they describe, clarify, or use. Using standards and domain-ontology terms as a part of metadata to describe LOs makes the content reusable, interchangeable, and interoperable.

The next step is ontological engineering of the learner model, to enable adaptivity and personalization of the learning experience across applications. It is covered in detail in Chapter 6. Recall that learner models are best thought of as fragmented, because learners typically interact with several systems and applications, each potentially storing different learner information. The fragments get integrated and/or interchanged among applications through a central learner model server or through a P2P network, both requiring a great deal of interoperability (Dolog and Schafer, 2005) Also, parts of the learner model ontology often include terms from the domain ontology to represent the learner's domain knowledge.

Yet another necessary step is ontological engineering of instructional (learning) design, in order to specify course/learning tasks in terms of subject domain concepts, instructional relationships between those concepts (such as *prerequisite*, *uses*, etc.), and the necessary learning activities accompanying each relevant LO. Although authors typically store learning design descriptions with the corresponding LOs, for interoperability reasons it is necessary for applications to share a common "understanding" - i.e., an ontology - of learning design elements when exchanging and reusing the LOs. The IMS LD specification provides a good starting point for development of such an ontology.

A straightforward way to support interoperability of different educational functionalities of a SWBE system is to represent them as educational Web services (Henze and Herrlich, 2004). They can be seen as wrappers over continuously changing domain ontologies, LOs, LORs, and learner model information that enable exchange and brokerage of the encapsulated content using a common standardized communication syntax (Stutt and Motta, 2004). To this end, it is worth considering development of a communication ontology that defines the vocabulary for describing the content and purpose of the messages exchanged by educational Web services (Aroyo and Dicheva, 2004a). Note that this kind of messaging does not assume only supporting standardized transport mechanisms and common interaction protocols of Web services. On the contrary, it is also important for educational Web services to understand the meaning of the messages they exchange, in terms of the granularity of information exchange, the types of queries they can ask each other, the form of answers expected, the possible need for ontology mapping in order to interpret the content of the message, and the user model awareness.

5.   ONTOLOGY VISUALIZATION

As soon as an ontology grows beyond a certain number of concepts and their relations, it becomes difficult for a human to understand it. The situation becomes even more complicated if more than one ontology contributes to metamodeling of a certain domain or process. In SWBE applications, such situations are highly likely to occur; for example, different ontologies are used to specify intelligent Web services responsible for learner modeling in Figure 6-3. On the other hand, good understanding of ontological relations between different entities involved in the learning process is essential for SWBE system developers, as well as for learners and authors.

Ontology visualization techniques can be used to aid this understanding. They facilitate ontological engineering of SWBE systems by enhancing human expert's understanding of the complex structures and relations present in ontology development (Sabou, 2005a).

Current ontology visualization techniques have roots in research on visual languages for knowledge representation.

5.1   Visual languages for knowledge representation [43,44]

The use of visual languages for knowledge acquisition and representation in an intelligent system is compelling for many reasons (Kremer, 1998). The most obvious one is that the actual domain may require representation in a way that is not possible with purely textual or symbolic languages. Even if another formal language is available and suitable for knowledge representation in later phases, it may not be appropriate in the preliminary phase of knowledge acquisition. The reason is that the appropriate formal structure of knowledge may not be apparent early, although it may be possible to express it in the other language. Domain experts may have

---

[43] This subsection introduces the field of visual languages in order to set the stage for the rest of section 5, and for readers who want to get the big picture. It is included for the sake completeness. Readers already familiar with the basics of visual languages, as well as those interested in ontology visualization specifics only, may want to skip this subsection.

[44] Much of the material presented in this subsection originally appeared in another Springer monograph, *Model Driven Architecture and Ontology Development* (Gašević et al., 2006), co-authored by Vladan Devedžić.

difficulties in communication and articulation of the domain knowledge in terms of formal knowledge structures; hence knowledge engineers may want to use visual representations for easier communication with the experts and for relaxation of formal discipline.

Visual languages for knowledge representation may be based on various kinds of graphs, forms (query by example), purely spatial relationships (iconic sentences), matrices (spreadsheets), and simple text layout (outlining tools). Most of them facilitate knowledge representation by at least partially eliminating the need to use the rigorous syntax of various symbolic and text-based languages. However, under the surface they often transform the represented knowledge into another language (such as first-order logic).

Note that many graphical user interfaces of knowledge acquisition and representation tools serve the purpose of collecting and transforming user input into the knowledge base. However, calling a GUI a visual language may raise objections, especially in the context of visual languages for knowledge representations. In many cases, the GUI is there just to hide the details of the underlying representation language. On the other hand, that role of GUI proves to be very useful in knowledge engineering. For example, JessGUI is a forms-based GUI that transforms knowledge engineer's input into the syntax of Jess tool for building expert systems (Friedman-Hill, 2003), thus making possible for a knowledge engineer to avoid learning the Jess language (Jovanović et al., 2004).

In a more narrow sense of the term, visual languages rely on two- or three-dimensional graphics and always involve pictures of some sort, typically nodes and connecting arcs (Kremer, 1998); text is involved as well, but for labeling and annotation purposes. But more importantly, in order to interpret visual languages reliably, it is necessary to specify their syntax and semantics formally. As for all other formal languages, such a specification involves precise definition of:

- terminal and nonterminal symbols;
- productions (derivation rules), i.e. grammar;
- unambiguous semantics.

Specifying a visual language that way must reflect its primary intent - to render knowledge in a form amenable to computational support, i.e. to straightforward, unambiguous interpretation by a computer program.

Well-known examples of visual languages for knowledge representation include KRS (Gaines, 1991), which is the visual counterpart of the CLASSIC frame language, and Conceptual Graphs (Sowa, 2000). Conceptual Graphs are more elaborate, more complex, more accurate, more expressive, more detailed, and more fine-grained of the two. Although originally intended to represent natural language expressions in a graphical form, they can actually represent many more forms of knowledge, including first-order logic. It is of particular importance that Conceptual Graphs also have their "linear form", i.e. pure text representation that evolved for ease of use by computer programs. For the sake of completeness, that feature of Conceptual Graphs should be noted here as an analog to other graphic-text representation pairs, such as the one existing in RDF, or the one provided by UML tools that enable serialization of UML models to XML representation using XMI.

5.2   Concept maps[45]

Myers (1990) has provided a comprehensive taxonomy of all visual languages, including those for knowledge representation. It includes several categories of visual languages for knowledge representation and shows that all of them are subsumed by the general notion of *concept maps*, i.e. *semantic networks*. For example, visual languages such as Petri nets and flowcharts can be also interpreted as concept maps.

Concept maps (semantic networks) are already implicitly introduced in Chapter 2. For example, Figure 2-2 is a simple concept map. Likewise, the RDF graph in Figure 2-7 is another concept map. Concept maps are visual tools for organizing and representing knowledge (Novak, 1991; 2002). They include *concepts*, usually enclosed in circles or boxes of some type, and *relationships* between concepts (or *propositions*), indicated by a connecting line between two concepts. Words on the line specify the relationship between the two concepts. *Concept map languages* provide graphical elements used to represent concept maps formally - typed *nodes* to represent concepts, typed *arcs* to represent relationships, as well as their labels. Other visual indicators may be used to distinguish between the nodes and arcs of different types (e.g., different shape, color, line type). In fact, concept maps implement a simple graph theory. Frequent extensions include the implementation of *partitions* or *contexts*, usually in the form of a box drawn around a subgraph.

Concept maps are object-oriented, human-centered, and easy to comprehend and use. The way they enable structuring a body of knowledge is much more salient than other forms of knowledge representation such as pure text and logic (Kremer, 1998). They can be used both at an informal level, such as for "brainstorming", as well as at a very formal level, such as representing knowledge in the knowledge base of an intelligent system.

The common point in all categories of visual languages for knowledge representation is that they can be described in terms of relational grammars. As a consequence, all visual languages for knowledge representation used in

---

[45] The first five paragraphs of this subsection are reprinted (with minor changes) from another Springer monograph, *Model Driven Architecture and Ontology Development* (Gašević et al., 2006), co-authored by Vladan Devedžić.

practice fall into the category of concept maps, or have concept map languages which implement them.

In the context of ontological engineering of SWBE systems, concept maps are suitable for eliciting and visualizing initial domain, learner, and other ontologies. Moreover, they can be used to represent ontologies at later stages as well, since they are easy to understand, extend, and manipulate. Of course, elaborated and good concept maps evolve through several extensions and revisions, but as Novak emphasizes (2002), revision of concept maps is a normal and important part of the concept mapping process.

An interesting application of concept maps for SWBE is the *Verified Concept Mapper* tool for capturing and visualizing a learner's conceptualization of the ontology for a domain (Cimolino and Kay, 2002), Figure 7-2. The learner is shown a set of most relevant concepts in the subject domain and a set of possible relevant relationships among the concepts. Using the concepts, the relationships, and a toolbar of graphical symbols, the learner can draw a concept map to express his/her understanding of the domain.

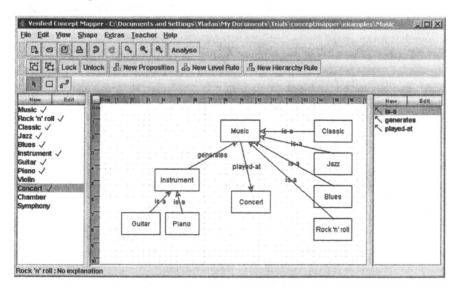

Figure 7-2. A screenshot from Verified Concept Mapper

In general, the learner will put some concepts into correct relationships, but there may be errors as well. Verified Concept Mapper can analyze the errors using the domain ontology (prepared by the teacher). Such concept maps are then used to construct detailed learner models. It is the teacher who can set up the task (the sets of concepts and relationships, as well as a partial map) to get each learner started.

Concept maps are helpful in ontological engineering because they are cognitively demanding, enforce reflection, and implicitly help elicit conceptual hierarchies. Note that the concepts in a concept map are typically represented in a hierarchical fashion with the most inclusive, most general concepts at the top of the map and the more specific, less general concepts arranged hierarchically below (Novak, 2002). Therefore, it is best to construct concept maps with the idea of clarifying or understanding the organization of some knowledge - that way, the ontology emerges by itself. Also, it is a good idea to start with just a few concepts the ontology developer is well familiar with, and let the ontology gradually evolve over time. Visualizing new concepts and their relations in the ontology reflects the way the developer's domain understanding grows and stabilizes.

Note that, ideally, concept hierarchies resemble trees. General-purpose ontology development tools like Protégé visualize ontologies in tree-like structures, because their visualization schemes rely mostly on *is-a* and *has-part* relationships. However, it is difficult to reduce a practical domain to a tree (Dicheva and Dichev, 2005). On the contrary, domains are full of *cross-links* - relationships between concepts in different domains of the concept map. Cross-links help ontology developers to see how some subdomains of knowledge represented on the map are related to each other (Novak, 2002). In the course of ontology development, the moments when cross-links get inserted in the concept map often represent creative leaps and increased understanding on the part of the developer.

Final features that may be added to concept maps are concept instances - specific examples of events or objects that help to clarify the meaning of a given concept.

There are many available general-purpose and easy-to-use concept mapping tools to aid ontology visualization. Gaines and Shaw (1995) and hubs like the one summarized by Lanzing (1997) provide the links.

5.3   Topic maps

Topic maps are an abstraction similar to concept maps in that they also model concepts - *topics* - and their relationships - *topic associations*. However, they are clearly related to (but also clearly separated from) various kinds of electronic information resources supporting topical findings, such as documents, graphics, images, audio/video clips, databases, and so on (Dichev et al., 2004). For example, one can describe the domain of *music* with topics such as *classical music, jazz, blues, rock 'n' roll*, etc., *instrument, harmony, melody*, and so on, as well as by specifying different associations between these topics. That far, it is much like the concept map shown in Figure 7-2. Still, each of these topics can be assigned text, media files, and other resources that describe and illustrate it. The topics and the associations can be manipulated in different ways (add, delete, modify, move, rearrange, etc.) at a meta-layer, regardless of the physical resources. *Occurrences* instantiate topics to one or more resources. Typically, an occurrence is a URI or a document.

Topic maps are becoming increasingly popular in the SWBE community for ontology representation and visualization. For example, two important practical tools are developed as results of the TM4L project (Topic Maps for e-Learning (TM4L, 2005) - TM4L Editor and TM4L Viewer. TM4L Editor, Figure 7-3, is an authoring environment that supports development, maintenance, and use of ontology-aware LORs/courseware. The left-hand side of the screen shows a topic hierarchy corresponding to a certain view (see the next paragraph for more explanation) of the topic map being edited. The right-hand part describes the topic selected on the left-hand side topic tree - its parent topic(s), the resources that instantiate the topic, and its alternative names. TM4L Viewer, Figure 7-4, is a tool for visualization and browsing of educational topic maps. Both tools are based on an open-source topic map engine implemented in Java, called TM4J (TM4J, 2005).

Topic maps enable multiple, concurrent *views* of sets of information objects; an unlimited number of topic maps may be overlaid on a given set of information resources. A *scope* captures the context (the view) within which a name or an occurrence is assigned to a topic, and within which associations among some topics hold. A view can be used to filter/adapt information to be presented to specific users. Views enable topic-centered structuring of unstructured information resources in terms of providing the effect of merging unstructured information around precisely defined network of topics. For example, TM4L Editor supports a *whole-part* view, a *class-subclass* view, and a *class-instance* view. They are used to provide alternative insights into the learning content structure. Likewise, TM4L Viewer enables multiple topic-focused views - *graph* view, *tree* view, and *text* view. Clicking on a topic automatically invokes a visually appealing animation that rearranges the graph to bring the topic and all of its associations and occurrences (LOs) into focus. In fact, topic maps automatically support easy and visually enhanced navigation through information space, indexing, cross-referencing, and filtering of LORs, and topic-oriented user interfaces. The overlay mechanism of topic maps facilitates using multiple views to impose arbitrary, user-centered structures on the content without altering its original form (which is an important way of LO reuse).

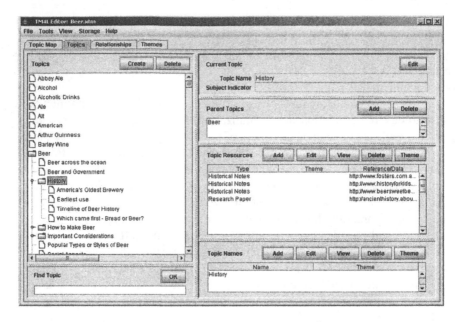

Figure 7-3. A screenshot from TM4L Editor

Topic maps and visualization tools like TM4L Editor and TM4L Viewer offer an insightful ontological overview of the learning collection structure to both the learners and the authors and provide the most important information at the earliest point. They also accommodate the learners' and the authors' different needs, goals, browsing behaviors, and query strategies. Typically, the authors know the domain and what they are looking for, have a rich domain vocabulary, but can make use of topic maps to find quickly the information they need and to structure new information. Contrary to them, the learners' knowledge is usually just vague and their mastery of the domain vocabulary is not high. They often need to switch back and forth between browsing the topic map content and querying it (Dicheva and Dichev, 2005). Hence topic maps provide them support for contextual search, exploratory browsing, making relevant decisions based on multiple views, comparing different perspectives, quickly getting more information, and restricting the amount of displayed information (focusing on selected topics of interest).

An important fact about topic maps is that they are an ISO standard (ISO/IEC, 1999). Starting from the standard, an independent standardization organization called TopicMaps.org has defined an abstract model and XML grammar (schema) for interchanging Web-based topic maps (TopicMaps.Org, 2001).

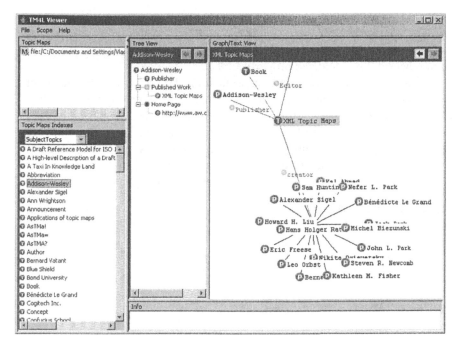

Figure 7-4. A screenshot from TM4L Viewer

Others have noticed similarities between topic maps and the RDF family of languages, including OWL. Garshol (2005) analyzes the relationships between the two technologies and looks at how to convert information between the two technologies, how to convert schema information, and how to do queries across both information representations. However, Dichev et al. (2004) warn about an important difference between topic maps and RDF - while topic maps are tailored for knowledge representation and analysis from the perspective of humans, in terms of facilitating search, navigation, filtering, and customization of Web resources, RDF is machine-oriented, with roots in formal logic and graphs.

5.4 Cluster Maps

Ontology development tools like Protégé include graphical ontology editors based on schema visualization techniques, but these focus primarily on the structure of the ontology, i.e., on visualizing hierarchical relations between entities (concepts and terms). However, in ontological engineering it is often crucial to know other kinds of relations that may exist between entities of different types. This kind of information enormously improves one's understanding of a domain of interest and directly indicates how to create important ontologies. Likewise, the number of instances of a certain concept, the list of LOs that cover it, as well as semantic relations between different concepts other than just *is-a* and *has-part*, also become more comprehensible if visualized properly.

Using that kind of visualization is facilitated to an extent by different views and overlay mechanism of topic maps. Another technique, called *Cluster Map* (Fluit et al., 2005), is implemented in the Aduna AutoFocus tool to visualize instances of classes according to their class membership. An example is shown in Figure 7-5. As such, it provides a powerful tool to analyze, compare, and query instantiated ontologies, and to classify a set of instances according to the concepts of a given ontology (Sabou, 2005a).

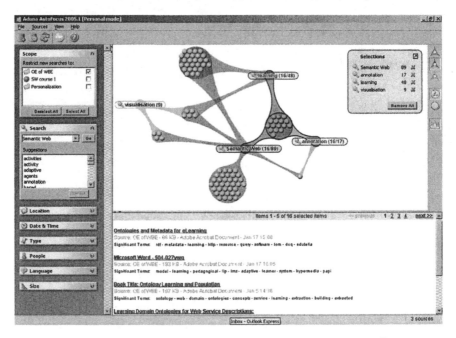

Figure 7-5. A screenshot from Aduna AutoFocus visualization tool[46]

Figure 7-5 visualizes how a set of documents is classified according to the topics discussed in those documents. The topics correspond to classes that are represented as rounded rectangles (stating their names and cardinalities), and each small sphere represents a class instance. Instances of the same class are grouped in clusters (similar to Venn diagrams), but classes usually overlap over some instances (i.e., the same document discusses more than one topic of interest). Each instance is visualized only

---

[46] Reprinted with permission from Aduna, The Netherlands. © 2006 Aduna.

once as belonging to each of its corresponding classes. The fact that two or more classes visually overlap over a set of instances often denotes that the corresponding topics are semantically related.

5.5 Visualizing role concepts and hierarchies

Yet another example of how visualization helps in ontological engineering is the *Hozo* ontology editor (Sunagawa et al., 2004), Figure 7-6. Hozo enables visual differentiation between *basic concepts* (filled labeled rectangles in Figure 7-6) and *role concepts* (transparent labeled rectangles) that denote a role that an object plays in a *context*.

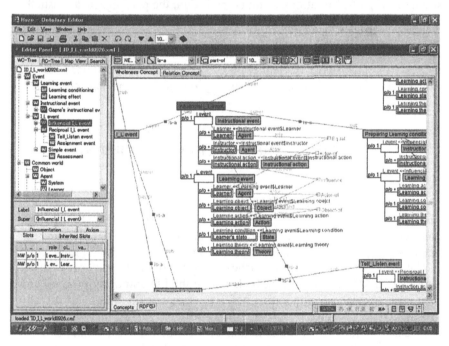

Figure 7-6. A screenshot from Hozo (after (Sunagawa et al., 2004))

For example, in the context of *SWBE environment*, a basic concept (class) such as *person* can be associated with role concepts like *learner*, *author*, and *administrator*. An instance of a basic concept that plays a certain role is the *role holder*. There is a *class constraint* on each role concept, meaning that a role holder for that role must be an instance of a certain basic concept/class. For example, each *teacher* (a role concept) must be an instance of *person* (class constraint). In Figure 7-6, Hozo displays class constraints next to the corresponding role concepts. A role concept and its associated class constraint are typically represented as a leaf of a part-of hierarchy of a basic concept, as in the tree shown in the center of Figure 7-6. In addition, role concepts can have their own hierarchies, much like properties in RDFS and OWL ontologies can be organized in hierarchies using the *rdfs:subPropertyOf* construct.

The possibility to clearly differentiate between basic concepts and role concepts is of high importance in ontological engineering. It helps develop a theoretically-sound ontology that defines concepts and their properties relatively independently. It is also fully in line with the software engineering principle of object-oriented design that stresses the semantic difference between aggregation and composition of object classes in terms of the "strength" of part-of relations. With composition, the part objects are usually expected to live and die with the whole (Fowler and Scott, 1999) - if a *person* dies, his/her *hands* die too. It is different with aggregation - if a *teacher* quits his/her job, only one of its roles as a *person* terminates. Hozo enables visualizing such differences clearly, understand the domain of the ontology better, and make the resulting ontology more closely reflect ontological theories.

6.   SEMANTIC ANNOTATION OF LEARNING MATERIAL

In order to be accessible from SWBE applications, LOs stored in LORs must be annotated with rich, standardized, and widely used metadata. Moreover, machine interpretation of LO content is feasible only if *semantic annotation* of the content is provided using terms from external ontologies.

There are two general approaches to semantic LO annotation: using annotation facilities of authoring tools during the LO authoring process, and using general-purpose annotation tools to semantically mark up already existing LOs.

In addition to semantic annotation of LOs themselves, *semantic links* between different LOs, related Web pages, and other learning resources can be annotated as well.

6.1   Authoring tools perspective

Developers of authoring tools must provide means for creating LOs with ontological information. On the other hand, it should be expected that most users of such tools (the authors) are not experts in ontological engineering. As discussed in Chapter 2, section 5, authoring tools must be designed to enable enriching LOs with ontological annotations as a byproduct of the authoring process. In other words, authoring tools should support non-experts in ontological engineering to semantically annotate their LOs through normal computer use.

A minor number of authors, of course, *will* have to develop suitable domain ontologies and pedagogical ontologies first (Mizoguchi and Bourdeau, 2000), as the basis for the annotation process.

To enable at least a partial annotation of LOs without much extra effort from the authors, there are three suitable functionalities that authoring tool developers can support:

- *Semantic annotation of library contents.* This refers to marking the contents from the libraries that come with the tools with pointers to external ontologies (Devedžić, V., 2004a). For example, an author of LOs in the domain of geometry may want to insert a drawing of a square into a LO he/she is creating. If the drawing comes from the tool's library of geometrical shapes and has associated pointers to the related ontologies in the domain of geometry, saving the LO to a LOR will automatically create a markup enabling, say, pedagogical agents to understand the context of (that part of) the LO.

- *Creating ontologies for semantic annotation from within the authoring tool.* Zarraonandía et al. suggested (2004) that tool developers could implement facility that allows an author to create generic taxonomies (ontologies) as deep and complex as needed. These taxonomies can be visualized and managed using different interactive techniques, just as with any ontology editor. The generated taxonomy can be stored as a separate OWL document and referred to from a LO content package (the manifest file). During the LO authoring, the terms from the ontology should be easily available to the author to semantically markup the LO.

- *Using/Importing external ontologies for semantic annotation.* In this case, the terms from external, predefined domain ontologies are used to specify the content topics. Also, references to the ontologies enable reasoning with sub- and super-topics (Brase and Nejdl, 2004; Zarraonandía et al., 2004). An important assumption here is, of course, that suitable external ontologies already exist and are available; otherwise, they need to be developed and published first. Ideally, such external ontologies should already be parts of internationally accepted classification systems. For example, Brase and Nejdl used terms from the ACM Computer Classification System (ACM CCS, 1998)[47] to annotate their LOs for university-level courses in the domains of AI and software engineering. The same authors note that broad-coverage classifications like ACM CCS are excellent for the annotation of complete units of

---

[47] The corresponding ontology, developed starting from the text-based form of ACM CCS, is available at http://www.kbs.uni-hannover.de/Uli/ACM_CCS.rdf.

learning. To annotate smaller units and single learning resources, there are two other possibilities: extending the overall classification scheme manually by introducing subhierarchies of terms to refine some coarse-grain topic(s) (in fact, defining one or more subtrees in the global classification scheme), or looking for another classification system. Brase and Nejdl have experimented with both possibilities; they have refined the ACM CCS topic of Artificial Intelligence to include more details, and have also used the Software Engineering Body of Knowledge (SWEBOK) classification system (SWEBOK, 1998) to annotate software engineering LOs. Note that, from the ontological engineering perspective, using two different classification schemes for the same domain to annotate the same LO usually requires good mapping to be provided between the two schemes, which may be a demanding task.

From the pragmatic point of view, it is clear that semantic annotation should be merged somehow with the other metadata, typically IEEE LOM. This is an issue that should be also taken into account when designing authoring tools. Since most applications and tools usually define suitable LOM application profiles to tailor their markup process, a practical solution is to include the IEEE LOM Classification category (see Table 5-2) in the tool profile and use it for extending the profile elements with terms from an external classification scheme/ontology/taxonomy. The alias of the namespace typically used for metadata from the IEEE LOM Classification category is *lom_cls*. As Brase and Nejdl (2004), Nilsson (2002), and Zarraonandía et al. (2004) recommend, the external ontology to be used to classify (semantically annotate) LOs should be represented as an instance of *lom_cls:Taxonomy*. It must be formatted in an RDF file, where the topics and subtopics are separated using the *lom_cls:Taxon* and *lom_cls:rootTaxon* elements, as in Figure 7-7. A simplified corresponding example of semantic annotation of a LO with such an ontology is shown in Figure 7-8. Note the reference to the term ("Agent") from the ontology (Figure 7-7) using *dc:subject*.

Since LORs typically store only metadata for LOs but not the content, authoring tools can actually support LO composition through LO metadata assembly/packaging. The authoring process in this case comprises using material from different resources and ontologies available throughout the Internet to assemble a simple LO, a learning unit, or a complete course (Brase and Nejdl, 2004). However, the "physical" result is a set of metadata (including semantic annotation) stored in a LOR.

```
<lom_cls:Taxonomy>
      <lom_cls:rootTaxon>
            <iisOnt:myIIS rdf:about="http://iis.fon.bg.ac.yu/iis-ont.rdf#IIS">
            <rdf:value>Intelligent information systems</rdf:value>
            <lom_cls:taxon>
                  <iisOnt:myIIS rdf:about="http://iis.fon.bg.ac.yu/iis-ont.rdf#Agent">
                  <rdf:value>Agent</rdf:value>
                  <lom_cls:taxon>
                     <iisOnt:myIIS rdf:about="http://iis.fon.bg.ac.yu/iis-ont.rdf#MobileAgent">
                     <rdf:value>Mobile Agent</rdf:value>
                  </lom_cls:taxon>
                  . . .
            </lom_cls:taxon>
            . . .
      </lom_cls:rootTtaxon>
</lom_cls:Taxonomy>
```

Figure 7-7. A hypothetical example of using the IEEE LOM Classification category metadata elements to extend the metadata vocabulary for semantic annotation

```
<rdf:Description rdf:about="http://iis.fon.bg.ac.yu/handouts/Agents.pdf">
      <dc:subject rdf:resource="http://iis.fon.bg.ac.yu/iis-ont.rdf#Agent"/>
</rdf:Description>
```

Figure 7-8. A hypothetical example of semantic annotation of a LO using the reference to an external ontology in the *dc:subject* metadata field

During the authoring process, learning resources scattered all over the Web can be accessed if the copyright is granted. If the copyright was restricted for certain resources, the resources can be listed in the LO, but it should be annotated as restricted using *dc:rights*.

Finally, usefull additional semantic annotation of LOs can be obtained using learner models and assessment data (Zarraonandía et al., 2004). This is possible if authoring tools are integrated with LMSs and learner model servers, so that the learners' performance data is readily available to the authors. To an extent, LO annotation with learners' performance data can be automated as well. Such annotation can serve as useful suggestion for improving the LOs (e.g. refinement of the LOs' objectives and/or prerequisites, inclusion of new examples, splitting or merging contents, etc.), thus making them more appropriate for different learning and authoring contexts.

6.2 Annotation tools perspective

If general-purpose annotation tools are used to semantically mark up already existing LOs, human annotators are faced with specific requirements that the e-Learning context brings to the annotation process. Azouaou et al. (2004) categorize such requirements as follows:

*   *usefulness* of annotation for the teaching/learning context - to be useful, annotation should take into account the subject domain, the teaching/learning objectives, activities, and the users of the annotation (humans or software agents);
*   *communication* of learners and teachers through annotation - the annotations should comply with e-Learning standards, promote sharing of the 'captured' semantics of the teaching/learning context, and be both accessible and comprehensible to other interested users and applications;
*   *usability* of annotation - manual annotation should not disturb teaching/learning activities, and the annotators should be put in their usual teaching/learning context while annotating.

Azouaou et al. have analyzed a number of current general-purpose annotation tools[48] with respect to the above categories of requirements, and have come up with some interesting results that ontological engineers should be aware of:

*   some general-purpose annotation tools already support e-Learning standards, mainly IEEE LOM, in terms of generating useful agent-oriented markup;
*   many aspects of usefulness of annotation for the teaching/learning context (see above) are generally not supported by such tools, but still can be reached with them;
*   manual semantic annotation facilities that these tools provide (mainly based on manipulating some visual elements of the user interface) do disturb teaching/learning activities, thus they are not perfect from the usability perspective;
*   only some general-purpose annotation tools enable (only to an extent) automatic and semi-automatic semantic annotation.

The list of categories of e-Learning-specific requirements for semantic annotation discussed above is not complete. For example, it does not include the requirement to combine domain and different educational ontologies. Likewise, annotation support for adaptive learning requires further investigation.

6.3   Semantic links perspective

Much of the LO annotation will contain some URIs, i.e. *syntactic links* to different resources, Web pages, and the like. Also, many learning resources

---

[48] Many of them, such as Annotea, SMORE, GATE, and KIM Semantic Annotation Platform, are available from The Semantic Web portal, http://annotation.semanticweb.org/tools/.

of all kinds are available on the Web through the appropriate links on different Web pages.

Web links have their own semantics, just like Web pages and resources do. For example, a link from a Web page a learner is browsing may take him/her to a useful reference, a citation, an example, an alternative view of the same topic, and so on. Even more importantly, *semantic links* may exist between different LOs and learning resources without being syntactically represented at all, neither as Web links nor in LO metadata sets. For instance, a LO may be covering the concept of intelligent agents, and another one may discuss Semantic Web services. There is a good deal of similarity/analogy between the two concepts, although the two LOs will typically appear as unrelated. From that perspective, some obvious questions are:

- Can the semantics of different link types be used to augment the usage and representation of learning material, enhance the learner's interaction, and improve the learning efficiency?
- Can the fact that two LOs or other learning resources are semantically related be used to create an additional, typed and independent piece of information, useful for the learning process?

The approaches to semantic annotation of learning resources discussed in the previous subsections focus on using ontologies to map the concepts and topics discussed/used/encompassed by LOs to terms defined in different ontologies. A complementary approach is to mark up links, both syntactic and semantic, rather than LOs. This *semantic annotation of links* starts from a *link ontology* that defines different *link types*. Both syntactic and semantic links can be instances of the same link type.

Different link types are known in hypermedia research from long ago. For example, in the so called *Trigg's taxonomy of links* (Trigg, 1983) there are two broad categories of links:

- *Normal links.* These include subcategories like *citation, background, methodology, data, generalization/specification, abstraction/example, argument, explanation, update*, and so on. Many of these subcategories are further subdivided in smaller-size groups. For example, argument links can be of *induction, deduction, analogy*, and *intuition* types.
- *Commentary links.* Subcategories include *comments, problem posing, supportive, critics, style*, etc.

Taking such different categories of links into account, one can explicitly define their meanings in a link ontology. It is a way to avoid the usual highly restricted approach in which links are constrained to a few predefined interpretations (such as priority and relatedness). The ontology terms can then be used to annotate semantic and syntactic links.

Link ontology-based annotation of syntactic links is closely related to the link annotation techniques used in adaptive hypermedia and introduced in

Chapter 1, section 5.2.1. Just as in AH, ontologically annotated links can appear on the screen in different colors, fonts, font sizes, and so on, to visually indicate semantic differences between the pages/resources they lead to. However, unlike AH, semantic link annotation starts from an independent link ontology.

Annotation of semantic links between different LOs and learning resources of different granularities requires more elaboration (see below). Note that semantic links may or may not be represented as visible/clickable links on Web pages, yet they may significantly contribute to the learning sessions and the learner's goals.

The idea of semantic link annotation for e-Learning represents a major conceptual shift from the current situation, in which most approaches to and standards for interoperability and reusability of learning resources are organized around the concept of LO only. Contrary to these established practices, Sicilia et al. have introduced (2002) the concept of *learning link* and proposed it to be a "first-class citizen" in educational technology reference models. In other words, a learning link represents the semantic link between two LOs or learning resources, and conceptually belongs to the same level as the LOs/resources themselves. The rest of this section is a summary of the learning link concept and the related ideas of Sicilia et al.

A link ontology based on, say, Trigg's taxonomy can provide semantically rich representation of learning links and promote link reuse, independently of the contents they associate. For instance, if A is a LO such that its content provides a generalization of the topics covered in the LO B, one may say that A and B are related by a *generalization* link (A *generalizes* B). The same kind of learning link may connect another two LOs as well (C *generalizes* D), carrying the same semantics independently of the content details of the specific LOs. Moreover, a link ontology enables intelligent reasoning about links, which can largely contribute to the system's adaptivity. For example, suppose that terms defined in a link ontology are used as link type designators. Further, assume that the system implements different heuristics for adaptively recommending LOs suitable for the learner's goals and current knowledge level. One of such heuristics may be to recommend a LO discussing a topic with high degree of analogy with respect to the topic the learner is interested in. The system can then search known learning links for one or more links of *analogy* type that relate(s) the currently used LO to another one. Inferring from the link ontology that *analogy* link is a kind of *argument* link, the system might even extend the applied heuristics. For instance, it may recommend a LO related to the current LO by an *induction* link, which is also a kind of *argument* link. Effectively, an explicit and ontology-based representation of semantic learning links leads to richer and unified models of linking. They can be exploited to provide improved visualization of a learner's interactions with learning resources, as well as to design adaptive behaviors.

Technically, learning links can be represented as *sharable link objects* (*SLOs*), by analogy with SCORM's SCOs (see Table 5-7). Such SLOs are reusable and context-independent, and of the same status as SCOs in that they can be tracked by an LMS. Likewise, SCORM content package manifest files refer to SLOs in much the same way they refer to any other resources (SCOs and assets). However, unlike SCOs, SLOs are capable of launching other SCOs. Also, more than one SLO may be active at the same time. A SLO in a SCORM manifest file represents semantic links between other assets or SCOs (sources and targets), in addition to syntactic links that may be embedded in different resources. According to SCORM best practices, the SLOs included in a content package should be described in a separate metadata file. The file uses terms from the link ontology to describe the link types, as in the annotation shown in Figure 7-9.

```
<metametadata>
        <metadatascheme>ADL SCORM 1.2</metadatascheme>
        <language>en-US</language>
        <metadatascheme> http://www.dei.inf.uc3m.es/Trigg/ </metadatascheme>
</metametadata>
<classification>
        <taxonpath>
                <source><langstring> http://www.dei.inf.uc3m.es/Trigg/ </langstring></source>
                <taxon> <entry>AnalogyLink</entry> </taxon>
        </taxonpath>
</classification>
```

Figure 7-9. Embedding references to the corresponding link ontology in a SLO metadata file (after (Sicilia et al., 2002))

An important feature of learning links is their imprecision, since semantic links are generally vague. A learning link like *A explains B* can be graded (as to "How good is the explanation that *A* provides for *B*?"). In annotations, the grades are typically numerical, in the range [0..1]. However, learning link vagueness is best described using fuzzy linguistic terms for different link types (like "good" and "excellent" for *explanation* links, "rather high" and "very low" for *analogy* links, and so on). All such terms can be represented by different fuzzy sets, and the corresponding membership functions can be used to calculate numerical grades for such *fuzzy links*. The calculation, in turn, can involve learner model parameters, which enables the computation of partial matching between the learning link and the specific learner ("How *relevant* is that *explanation* (or *comment*, *example*, etc.) for *me*?").

In SWBE applications, learning links can greatly enhance the implementation of adaptive behaviors. For example, the application can use a rule like the following one to change the size of the font of the link:

If   L.type is *ArgumentLink* and LM
Then   set L.font-size to *large* and L.font-familiy to *Arial*

The second clause in the premise (LM) denotes taking the learner model into account and generates a fuzzy value like "very important" or "relevant".

7.   ONTOLOGICAL ENGINEERING OF INSTRUCTIONAL DESIGN

Instructional design was briefly introduced in Chapter 1, section 5.1.2, and was also discussed in the context of IMS Learning Design specification in Chapter 5, section 2.5. As Koper notes (2001), the terms *instructional design*, *learning design*, and *educational modeling* are often used interchangeably. In the context of IMS specifications, instructional design is always called learning design.

Grasping the essentials of ontological engineering of instructional design easily requires a thorough understanding of some of the instructional design characteristics, the role of instructional design theories, and the current needs and representations related to instructional design. The first three subsections discuss topics that help develop such an understanding. The rest of this section is focused on ontological engineering of instructional design itself.

7.1   Key characteristics of instructional design

According to IMS LD (2003), a learning design is a description of a method that enables learners to attain certain learning objectives in the context of a certain learning environment. To attain the objectives, the learners must perform certain learning activities in a certain order. A learning design implements the pedagogical principles the designer selects, and must take into account specific domain and context variables. It is essentially a systematic and reflective *process* of applying principles of learning and instruction to develop instructional materials, activities, information resources, and evaluation (Paulsen, 2003).

From the ontological engineering perspective, instructional (learning) design includes the following important characteristics:
- It must be a *systematic process*. It comprises the philosophy, methodology, and a specific approach used for delivering instruction. It requires an assessment of the needs, design decisions related to different levels of interaction, and adoption of strategies and methodologies of

development, evaluation, implementation, and maintenance of learning materials and programs.

- It must *interweave with the process of design and development of instructional materials*. This means that LO and course authoring should produce well-structured instructional materials, based on clearly defined learning objectives, related teaching strategies, systematic feedback, and evaluation. Furthermore, design and development of instructional materials (of both high and low granularity) should include a specification of learning activities needed to meet the learning needs, at all levels of complexity. Although this specification can start at any point in the authoring process, core learning activities can typically be anticipated and included in early phases. As the authoring process proceeds, the initial specifications can and should be refined - authoring of learning design is not a linear process, and many early decisions get revised over time.

- It must be *based on learning and instructional theories*. Instructional specifications should use learning and instructional theories to ensure the quality of instruction. Note that this has two aspects. First, theory about instructional strategies and the process for developing and implementing those strategies should be applied during the development of learning material. Second, tryouts and evaluations of all instruction and learner activities are necessary in order to modify and adjust the design to meet the requirements of the concrete learning environment.

- It must *clearly and explicitly specify the methods and activities needed to attain the learning goal*. For example, the activities in the learning design may include a presentation of introductory topics related to the study domain, a number of sessions of practice possibly including online experiments, collaboration in a virtual classroom, data collection, preparations of reports, and evaluation of the learning process through examination tests (Lama et al., 2005). Also, speaking in terms of IMS LD, if the acts of different plays have the same activities then the differences in their sequencing must be specified unambiguously.

All of the above characteristics of instructional design are in line with general principles of ontological engineering discussed in sections 2 thru 4. However, providing ontological support for instructional design is quite a complex issue.

7.2 Instructional design theories and learning objects

Instructional design theories describe methods of instruction and the situations in which those methods should be used Reigeluth (1999). The methods can be broken into simpler component methods, and are probabilistic. Instructional design theories also define instructional strategies and criteria for their application.

Although such theories naturally must play a large role in authoring, development, and application of LOs and SWBE in general, critical examinations show that much of the current practices underrate the role of instructional design theories in composing LOs and personalizing instruction delivery. For example, the very idea of LO reusability and automatic and dynamic composition of personalized learning experience implies taking individual LOs and combining them in a way that makes instructional sense. However, it is not guaranteed if only LO metadata specifications like IEEE LOM are used. The "LEGO block metaphor" underlying the plug-and-play philosophy of LO composition assumes that any LEGO block can be combined with any other LEGO block, in any manner we choose, and even children can put them together because they are so simple. Unfortunately, LOs are not LEGO blocks - what results from an arbitrary combination of LOs may not be instructionally useful (Wiley, 2000).

There are several ways to mitigate this problem. One of them is to use another, more suitable metaphor that takes into account restrictions implied by instructional design theories. Another one is to embed instruction-theoretic learning design into content packaging of LOs. Note that this approach does not exclude the first one; on the contrary, recall from Chapter 5, section 2.5, that the IMS LD specification is modeled after the metaphor of theater play, and that such learning design can be included in the <organizations> section of a manifest file. Yet another approach is to adopt a taxonomy of LOs, include the LO characterization related to that taxonomy as ontological information in the LO metadata, and use this characterization in instructional design.

7.2.1   New metaphors

Wiley suggests (2000) using the atom metaphor as much more suitable than the LEGO block metaphor. An atom is a small "thing" that can be combined and recombined with other atoms to form larger "things." This seems to capture the major meaning conveyed by the LEGO metaphor as well. However, the atom metaphor restricts the LO composition by implying that not every atom is combinable with every other atom and that atoms can only be assembled in certain structures prescribed by their own internal structure. Also, one needs to undergo some training (i.e., knowledge of instructional design theories) in order to be able to assemble atoms (LOs). Thus the atom metaphor enables combining LOs into instructionally useful and to some degree *inherent* structures, something like "learning crystals". These, in turn, reflect the fact that instruction is more than information (Merrill, 1999).

7.2.2   Learning object taxonomies

There is still no general, widely accepted, broadly applicable taxonomy of LOs, compatible with multiple instructional design theories. There are only some classifications of instructional processes, entities, and activities pertaining to individual theories (e.g., see (Merrill, 1999) and (Reigeluth, 1999)). The lack of such a widely accepted taxonomy significantly hinders the use of existing instructional design theories in ontological engineering of LOs and restricts their reuse from the instructional perspective.

Kopper has proposed (2001) a taxonomy that he calls "the types of LOs in the context of a unit of study". Unfortunately, his taxonomy is not completely suitable for ontological engineering of instructional design and LOs because it does not include clear boundaries between the LOs and the activities needed to use them. For example, the taxonomy includes concepts like *unit of study*, *knowledge object*, *section object*, *tool object*, *index object*, and *questionnaire object*, but also *activity*, *role learner*, *role staff*, *environment*, and *play*; the latter concepts are clearly related to instructional and learning activities, rather than to LOs. IMS LD specification has made an important leap forward by collecting from Kopper's taxonomy only the concepts related to instructional design. Still, what remained is not widely accepted as the taxonomy of LOs alone, completely appropriate for ontological engineering.

Wiley's taxonomy differentiates between five LO types (Wiley, 2000):

- *fundamental* - an individual learning resource uncombined with any other, such as a JPEG image of an airplane;
- *combined-closed* - a small number of digital resources combined at design time by the LO creator, such as a video clip of an airplane on a fly that combines still images and an audio track; generally, constituent LOs are not individually accessible for reuse from the combined-closed LO itself, and include only simple and limited internal logic (e.g., the ability to perform answer sheet-referenced item scoring);
- *combined-open* - a larger number of learning resources combined by a computer on the fly when a request for the object is made, e.g. a Web page combining the above mentioned JPEG, video clip, and some text; constituent LOs of a combined-open LO are directly accessible for reuse from the combined-open LO, which represents a complete instructional unit of its own;
- *generative-presentation* - logic and structure for combining or generating and combining lower-level LOs; a typical example of a LO of this kind is a Java applet capable of graphically generating a set of logically connected learning units to present an airplane identification problem to a learner; they are highly reusable in contexts similar to that for which they were designed, but not in different contexts;

- *generative-instructional* - logic and structure for combining lower-level LOs and evaluating the learners' interactions with those combinations; a larger-scale instructional unit which both instructs (e.g., "remember and perform a series of steps") and provides practice for any type of procedure (e.g., the process of identification of different phases of an aircraft flight).

Although by no means exhaustive, this taxonomy clearly differentiates between possible types of LOs available *for use in instructional design*. The types, especially the higher-level ones, explicitly reference domain-dependent and domain-independent presentation, instruction, and assessment logic, which must come from instructional theories.

Of course, any such a taxonomy alone is not enough for ontological engineering; it is also necessary to provide an appropriate mapping from instructional design theories to the taxonomy and vice versa, as well as guidance of the type "for this type of learning goal, use this type of LO".

7.2.3   Instructional engineering and content packaging

Instructional engineering is a discipline that integrates instructional design, software engineering, and cognitive science processes and principles in order to produce good specifications of a learning system (Paquette, 2003; Paquette et al., 2005). As such, it has much in common with ontological engineering of instructional design.

The learning design part of the phrase "good specifications of a learning system" pertains to standards-based structuring of instructional design elements and their embedding in LO descriptions such as manifest files. If IMS LD is used to specify the instructional design elements, then the task of producing a good specification of instructional design boils down to creating an appropriate sequence of plays and wrapping it into a method (see Figures 5-7 thru 5-9). For each play, a suitable sequence of acts should be specified, and each act must be precisely defined in terms of a set of activities and the corresponding roles to carry out the activities.

Note, however, that an instructional designer can also produce partial IMS LD documents in the form of content-independent pedagogical structures, or *learning design templates*. These specify the plays, the acts, the roles, and the activities, but not necessarily prerequisites and learning objectives (Paquette et al., 2005). Such learning design templates can be then stored in a repository of pedagogical methods, from which instructional designers can choose and reuse them to specify learning design when creating new LOs and units of learning.

Instructional engineering assumes using an instructional design method and a set of tools to facilitate authoring, storing and delivery of LOs. For example, MISA is an instructional design method with a long refinement and deployment history (Paquette, 2003). It is supported by graphical educational modeling (learning design) tools (MOT and MOT+), a Web-based instructional engineering workbench (ADISA), and a learning content management system (Explor@). Efforts are underway to make the tools fully compliant with IMS LD. In general, the result of applying MISA is the instructional model that can be visualized as a network of nodes - LOs and more complex learning units and events. The key concept in MISA is that of *competency*. It refers to one's knowledge, skills, and performance level expected either for accessing a node in the network (*entry competency*), or to be gained after completing the learning tasks associated with a node (*target competency*). Entry and target competencies are associated with the nodes in the instructional model and are represented as numerical values on a predefined scale. Each learning unit is also described by a graphically represented learning scenario, describing learning and support activities related to the corresponding learning resources. Section 7.5.1 further elaborates instructional engineering with MISA and the accompanying tools.

Instructional engineering methods (such as MISA) complement learning design specifications (such as IMS LD) by focusing on processes and principles of instructional design, rather than on the resulting specification. While IMS LD is related to content packaging, delivery, and runtime implementation issues, instructional engineering methods and tools are similar to software engineering ones - they are concerned with how to get to the learning design specification to be embedded in a content package.

7.3   Needs and representations

An important issue in educational modeling (instructional design) for the Semantic Web is *how to represent, preserve, and share knowledge about effective (prototypical) learning designs in a formal, semantic way* so that it can be interpreted and manipulated by computers as well as humans (Koper, 2001; Koper and Manderveld, 2004). One solution to this problem can be to build and share catalogues of effective *learning and teaching patterns* (i.e., learning design templates) that can be communicated very precisely and can be adapted to other contexts, problems, and content. Representing learning and teaching activities and workflows in such formally described patterns enables pedagogical agents to manage the learning processes and content filtering according to the learning design and adaptivity requirements. Moreover, it opens the way to automatic sharing of learning designs across various courses, modules, and LMSs. Likewise, the instructional design part of SWBE becomes more consistent across different systems and applications.

All kinds of formally represented patterns are great sources for ontology development (Devedžić, 1999). To leverage ontological engineering of instructional design, *ontologies for specific pedagogical approaches* should be developed in the future, starting from different instructional design patterns. They would allow for guiding the authors in creating specific units of learning, according to the principles of a certain pedagogical approach (formally represented in the ontology) (Kopper, 2004). A long-term goal is the possibility of building pedagogical agents that can consult such ontologies and construct some simple units of learning on their own.

Another important contribution to the consistency of instructional design of different SWBE applications is the fact that the representational schema underlying IMS LD is precisely modeled in UML. The model is specified as a series of UML diagrams (such as the one shown in Figure 7-10) that capture the general semantic structure of learning design (plays, acts, activities, etc.). As explained in Chapter 4, section 7, UML models can be converted to XML-based representation using XMI, which is an important step towards mapping to other possible bindings (like RDFS and OWL).

In fact, the UML model shown in Figure 7-10 can be viewed as an instance of a *pedagogical metamodel*, i.e. of a model that models/describes pedagogical (instructional design) models. This metamodel is at the very heart of the ontology of instructional design (see section 7.4) and can be described in words as follows (Koper and Manderveld, 2004):

- a person learns by performing goal-directed activities in an environment (a set of objects and/or human beings that are related in a particular way);
- after learning a certain topic or skill, the person can perform new activities, or perform the same activities better or faster in similar environments, or perform the same activities in different environments;
- a person can be encouraged to perform certain activities if his/her knowledge and skills satisfy the prerequisites, his/her personal circumstances (e.g., motivation) and the performance context are appropriate, and the required environment is made available.

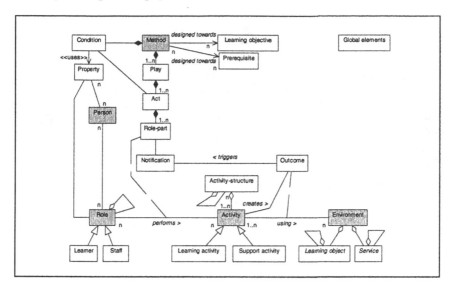

Figure 7-10. A UML diagram of the conceptual model of overall learning design (after (IMS LD, 2003))

The same applies not only to a single learner, but also to a group of learners. Each instructional model instantiating these "axioms" aims at accomplishing learning goals and measuring the results (performance).

In addition to being partially domain-independent and theory-based, instructional design should also be *open to the learners*, in terms of allowing the learners to request the system use particular instructional strategies. However, the system must be capable of deciding on the set of applicable strategies, based on the learner's input (Reigeluth, 1999).

Mizoguchi and Bourdeau proposed (2000) an ontological engineering scheme that can be used as a summary of the above discussion on the needs, representations, and desired features of a SWBE system in terms of instructional design. An elaborated and slightly modified version of that scheme is shown in Figure 7-11. It introduces the notion of an *instructional design knowledge server* (*ID knowledge server*), which is supposed to store the knowledge of instructional design theories and learning sciences. This knowledge should be formally encoded as an *instructional design ontology* (*ID ontology*). Alternatively (or perhaps in addition), there might be a collection of instructional design ontologies, each one covering a specific pedagogical approach or instructional design pattern.

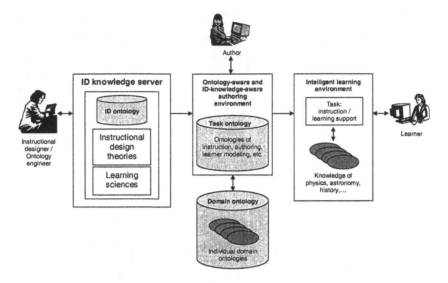

Figure 7-11. Different aspects of ontological engineering related to intelligent instructional systems (adapted from (Mizoguchi and Bourdeau, 2000))

Such an ID knowledge server should support curriculum authoring in terms of enabling systematic and instruction-theoretic learning design specification. Note, however, that not all of the knowledge necessary for instructional design and authoring is theory-based. In any practical learning design, instruction-theoretic knowledge is combined with different heuristics and rules of thumb. Still, ID ontology-aware environments could help find justifications of heuristics. Finally, Bourdeau and Mizoguchi agreed (2002) with Paquette (2003) that instructional design theories should be interpreted from an engineering point of view. The engineering, in turn, must fulfill the requirements of practice. Access to a collection of instructional design ontologies allows an authoring system to respond to the variety of preferences of instructional designers/authors.

The rest of Figure 7-10 should be easy to interpret intuitively, based on the previous sections of this chapter and on the notion of task ontology introduced in Chapter 3, section 6.2. It is also further discussed in section 8.

7.4   Ontology of instructional design

Due to the variety of instructional design theories and heuristics, it is a demanding task to develop a coherent, stable, highly reusable, and relatively complete ontology of instructional design. Thus it is no surprise that the first such an ontology was developed only recently (Lama et al., 2005).

Lama et al. have designed their ontology starting from the IMS LD level A specification. In addition to the ontology that represents the IMS LD concepts and their relations (Figure 7-12), Lama et al. have defined a set of axioms constraining the semantics of the ontological concepts according to the restrictions imposed by the IMS LD specification. *Unit of learning* is modeled as an IMS content package that integrates descriptions of both the learning design and the set of resources related to the learning design. The *Resource* concept hierarchy is defined to support description of various physical resources (Web pages, files, etc.), as well as concepts whose attribute description is domain-dependent (such as learning objectives, prerequisites, activity and feedback descriptions, etc.).

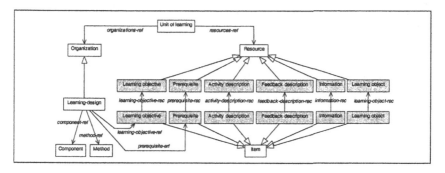

Figure 7-12. An excerpt from the learning (instructional) design ontology, represented in UML (adapted from (Lama et al., 2005))

In addition, the ontology introduces a new concept hierarchy (*Item*) to decouple the references to the resources (*Item* hierarchy) from their modeling (*Resource* hierarchy). The decoupling part is indicated by the grey boxes in Figure 7-12. It was obviously modeled using the well-known software engineering patterns, called Adapter and Proxy (Gamma et al., 1995). The point of decoupling is to let two or more applications (re)use the same learning design regardless of the peculiarities of defining the resources. For example, one application may specify the learning objectives for a course in a pure text-based form (human readable), whereas another one may use *href* attributes of the learning objectives (machine readable). However, *Learning design* refers to the learning objectives through the *Item* hierarchy's *Learning objective* concept, which directly replicates the *Learning objective* of the *Resource* hierarchy and simultaneously hides its specifics. Thus the learning design does not need to be changed, because the links to the resources are indirectly established through the *Item* hierarchy.

The ontology is implemented in OWL. A detail from it is shown in Figure 7-13. Efforts are underway to extend the ontology to include details from IMS LD levels B and C.

```
<!--...-->
<owl:Class rdf:ID="Prerequisite">
  <rdfs:subClassOf>
    <owl:Class rdf:ID="Item" />
  </rdfs:subClassOf>
  <rdfs:comment rdf:datatype="http://www.w3.org/2001/XMLSchema#string">Prerequisites are the
entry-requirements for students, e.g. the pre-knowledge needed. For the item formats see the
description of the element 'learning-objectives'.</rdfs:comment>
  <owl:disjointWith>
    <owl:Class rdf:ID="Activity-Description" />
  </owl:disjointWith>
  <owl:disjointWith>
    <owl:Class rdf:ID="Learning-Objective" />
  </owl:disjointWith>
  <owl:disjointWith>
    <owl:Class rdf:ID="Information" />
  </owl:disjointWith>
  <owl:disjointWith>
    <owl:Class rdf:ID="Feedback-Description" />
  </owl:disjointWith>
</owl:Class>
<!--...-->
```

Figure 7-13. An excerpt from the learning (instructional) design ontology, represented in OWL and showing the definition of the *Prerequisite* concept in the *Item* hierarchy (adapted from (Lama et al., 2005))

7.5   Facilitating instructional design using ontologies

In addition to an ontology of instructional design (such as the one presented in the previous section), an authoring tool, providing support for instructors who develop courses for SWBE, can (and should) rely on other kinds of ontologies as well. These include domain ontologies, ontologies of educational theories, as well as task ontology and its derivatives.

From an engineering point of view, much of the instructional design is about creating appropriate *learning scenarios* supported by different LOs and other resources. Such scenarios often include multiple actors (such as teachers, learners, their peers, and administrators) and resources, and should be designed to reflect typical learning workflows. Different techniques can be used to facilitate development and representation of various learning scenarios.

7.5.1   Learning scenarios and competencies

The MISA instructional design method and its accompanying tools support course designers in constructing the structure of learning activities and a network of learning resources and events (Paquette and Rosca, 2004). These represent the *instructional structure* that is then used as the basis for building and describing multi-actor learning scenarios for each learning unit. The scenarios also include a *competency structure*, corresponding to the domain ontology and represented by entry and target competencies related to the nodes in the instructional structure. The idea of the competency structure is as follows:

- in order to complete a learning goal, the learner should perform one or more learning activities;
- an activity may require a certain level of specific knowledge and skills, i.e. certain competencies;
- at the beginning of an activity, the learner's competencies may be lower than those needed to perform the activity;
- after performing an activity, the learner's competencies are supposed to raise to a level higher than the level of competencies he/she had before performing the activity;
- the resources available to the learner (documents, tools, teachers, trainers, other learners) should make possible for him/her to progress from the (lower) entry competencies to those expected after performing the activity.

Figure 7-14 illustrates a MISA-based learning scenario in the context of an instructional structure and a competency structure. Speaking in terms of IMS LD, assume that *Act 6* of a certain play includes four activities, *Activity 6.1* thru *6.4* as its components ("*C*"). The instructional designer has specified that some activities logically precede ("*P*") some other activities in this learning scenario. If the learning domain is in the area of elementary calculus, say *fractions*, then *Act 6* and its activities may be related to the concept of *fraction multiplication* (which is presumably defined in the domain ontology). For example, at a certain point in the scenario, the learner is supposed to perform *Activity 6.3* (e.g., "complete a test"). It is preceded by *Activity 6.1* ("read the principles") and *Activity 6.2* ("work out an example"). The result of the activity is an output resource (the "test results" in this case). In order to perform the activity, the learner can use two input resources, *Input resource A* and *Input resource B*.

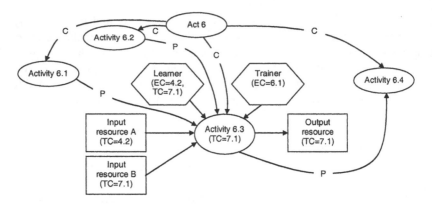

Figure 7-14. An example of a MISA-based learning scenario (adapted from (Paquette and Rosca, 2004))

Activities, resources, and actors are assigned competencies according to a predefined numerical scale (e.g., 0-10). Entry and target competencies of activities and resources are assigned by the instructional designer. To assign these competencies, the designer may want to consult the domain ontology (although in principle he/she can do it on his/her own). The purpose of consulting the domain ontology may be to get a better overview of the relations between various domain concepts. These may reveal relative levels of difficulty that can be attributed to the various domain concepts, related activities, and available resources. The competencies of the learners can be evaluated by the system, by using appropriate parameters of the learner models in each particular case.

The target competency ("*TC*") of *Activity 6.3* in Figure 7-14 is set to 7.1. Then the output resource ("test results") should show a TC greater than or equal to 7.1. The learner's entry competency ("*EC*") for performing *Activity 6.3* is just 4.2, so he/she needs help to perform *Activity 6.3* and reach the desired TC of 7.1. There is also a trainer with *EC* = 6.1, so he/she alone can bring the learner only part the way up. *Input resource A* is of little help either, since its TC=4.2; it can only serve to test the learner's entry competencies in terms of satisfying the necessary prerequisites. *Input resource B* has the TC = 7.1; it may be suitable for the learner, but it is not if its EC is just a little lower than or equal to 7.1. In a more optimistic case, *Input resource B* may be a lesson that aggregates different LOs (different in terms of their ECs/TCs) that can help the learner progress towards his/her learning goal with the help of the trainer. During the interaction with *Input resource B*, the trainer will typically also improve his/her knowledge. At the end the activity, his/her EC may be increased for the next run of the activity.

Note that in such a scenario different actors (learners, teachers, assessors) perform different operations. They use resources and produce resources for other actors or with other actors. The domain ontology is central to referencing learning activities, operations, actors, and resources during the instructional design (creating scenarios and assigning competencies). During both the instructional design and the learning activities, the ontology can be browsed from the graphical tools that support MISA. The terms defined in the ontology may be used to launch search agents to find appropriate persons, information resources, and learning activities useful in different learning scenarios. For example, a search agent may discover the trainer with $EC = 6.1$ in the scenario depicted in Figure 7-14, and create an appropriate link between the trainer and *Activity 6.3* during the instructional design.

7.5.2   Ontology of instructional design theories

Psyché et al. have proposed (2005) to use an *ontology of instructional design theories* that describes these theories and their links to instructional design, in order to make authoring systems theory-aware. The underlying idea is that LO and course authors should have access to instructional design theories in order to enhance the quality of their products and to improve their expertise. It is completely in line with the scheme shown in Figure 7-11, where the ID ontology enables authors to deploy appropriate learning designs and teaching patterns according to the embedded pedagogy developed by instructional designers. In other words, an author should be able to select a relevant learning design strategy (or a learning design template) in order to produce a learning scenario. Thus it is useful for him/her to have access to the theories on which such strategies rely.

The ontology of instructional design theories enables authors to make queries about the most appropriate theories for a specific instructional design, or about design principles, strategies, patterns, and templates related to theories. It also facilitates a structured access to a repository of examples of good learning design scenarios or principles to assist the designers. They can reuse and/or modify the templates and scenario to suit their needs, and then use the ontology to validate (check consistency) of the resulting product against the instructional design principles.

The proposed ontology of instructional design theories is related to an ontology of instructional design (such as that presented in section 7.4) and to the domain ontology. Some of the most important concepts in the ontology of instructional design theories are shown in Figure 7-15. It is important to stress that *Instructional theory* and *ID theory* are modeled as *parts-of* the *Learning theory* concept, but the corresponding *part-of* relations are omitted from Figure 7-15 to avoid clutter. The ontology is implemented in OWL using the Hozo ontology editor (see section 5.5) and mappings (bindings) of its concepts to IMS LD concepts are provided (for instance, *Paradigm* maps to the IMS LD *method*, *Sequencing of instruction* maps to IMS LD *activity structure*, and so on).

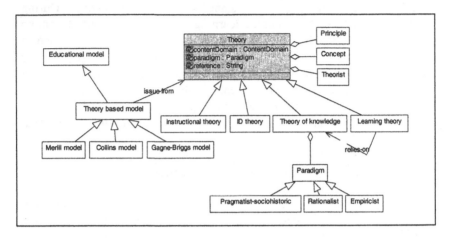

Figure 7-15. An excerpt from the ontology of instructional design theories (after (Psyché et al., 2005))

7.5.3   Instructional design and recommender systems

The reuse and assembly of LOs into useful, learner-centered instructional materials can be supported by careful, ID theory-based search for and selection of LOs. Wiley's atom metaphor introduced in section 7.2.1 can be understood as an instructional design-centric approach in which LOs are not just selected from a general category and wrapped into an online course, but are carefully inspected by *a number of interested individuals* beforehand. As a result, only those LOs that "pass the filters" of the scope, role, audience, level of complexity, adaptability, and most importantly *relevance* for a particular topic, domain, and learning objectives, can be selected for reuse in course development. This generates the idea of selecting LOs on the basis of *recommendations* suggested by the theory-aware systems (in addition to selecting LOs by inspecting the instruction-related metadata previously assigned to them, for example in their respective manifest files).

Recommender systems use explicitly and implicitly collected data on a user's preferences to filter and recommend items that might be interesting and valuable to that user (Ma, 2005). They can be used to support instructors in searching for useful LOs in order to produce instructionally meaningful course design. The motivation to use them is easy to explain:

- as the number of LOs, educational technologies, and supporting tools increases, it becomes more and more difficult for instructors and designers to keep up with all those resources;
- results returned by search engines do not directly capture comments and opinions about a LO from the relevant communities of instructional designers;
- it is difficult to capture aspects surrounding the context of (instructional) *use* of a LO on the basis of standards like IEEE LOM; likewise, standards do cannot suggest how to reuse the LO in different contexts, whereas other instructional designers can.

Contrary to all that, LO recommender systems can return LOs positively evaluated by relevant community members (instructional designers) in much the same way Amazon.com uses collaborative filtering techniques to recommend books by leveraging preferences of users with similar interests.

LO recommender systems are currently just a research effort. Still, it is already clear that their effectiveness mainly depends on the availability of LO instructional metadata defined in accordance with instructional design ontologies. As with other kinds of semantic annotation, the point is to enable ontology-driven authoring of learning design templates and scenarios to be used by instructional designers and to be accessible from authoring tools. Such an authoring process can generate a part of the necessary pedagogical metadata. The other part can be generated dynamically, by applying a variant of the ecological approach discussed in Chapter 6, section 2.7, in the context of learner modeling. Information about real use of different learning design templates and learning scenarios by other instructional designers can accumulate over time. Subsequently, it can be used to dynamically and automatically create metadata to annotate the LOs to be recommended ("This LO has been used a number of times together with the learning design template *X*").

7.5.4 Ontological support for lesson plans

In many cases, the most distinctive unit of an online course is a lesson, both from the organizational and content perspectives. Instructional design of a single lesson is concisely expressed as the *lesson plan*. It is often structured as a sequence of learning and teaching activities, with a set of associated goals, objectives, resources, and prerequisites.

If one takes content- and domain-dependent details out of different lesson plans, the remaining *instructional skeletons* often can be classified in several groups. The skeletons in a single group usually exhibit a great degree of similarity. The groups largely correspond to the already introduced notions of learning design patterns and templates (see sections 7.2.3 and 7.3).

Not all online lessons provide their lesson plans explicitly. In some cases, experienced instructors can infer the lesson plan after examining an online lesson, but it is not always possible. Even if a lesson provides its associated lesson plan explicitly, the format and/or the viewpoint of the lesson plan may be substantially different from those of another lesson developed for the same purpose. In other words, the formats and viewpoints of lesson plans are not unified across teaching and learning environments. These facts drastically reduce the opportunities to reuse available online lessons and lesson plans in different courses.

Practical investigations show that this is a huge problem for teachers and instructors (Kasai et al., 2005). The abundance of online resources for teachers (Web pages, LOs, content files, lesson plans, test sheets, tools, etc.), in many different formats and based on many different technologies, makes it very difficult for them to collect, browse, and filter only the necessary ones. In addition, in many subject domains there is still no consensus about what constitutes a unified set of educationally relevant concepts and practical skills. As a result, different resources often present concepts in a disorganized way that does not convey the concepts and the pedagogical structures (lesson plans) to teachers effectively.

On the other hand, if different lesson plans and instructional skeletons are analyzed from a more generic perspective, it turns out that they have much in common. Thus, suitable ontologies can be developed to represent instructional concepts and structures instantiated in lesson plans.

The basis for such ontologies is an analysis of the problem-solving skills applied, as well as developed, during the learning process. The analysis was conducted and presented by Kasai et al. (2005). It shows that human problem solving process can be appropriately described by the cycle *Problem discovery and planning - Collection of information - Classification, analysis, and judgment of information - Reporting and sending information.* Each of these four phases is featured by a distinct set of problem-solving skills that help perform the expected activities. For example, the first phase is dominated by the *skill to discover a problem* and the *skill to solve a problem.* Likewise, the second phase is featured by the *skill to collect information* and the *skill to investigate.* Some skills, like the *skill to analyze* and the *skill to evaluate*, are required in all four phases.

The *ontology of the fundamental academic ability* of Kasai et al. defines numerous problem-solving skills and their categories. Its terms can be used to tag different lesson plans and instructional skeletons with ontological information. Moreover, the authors of the ontology have also developed tools to extract lesson plans from online lessons and graphically represent them using the terms defined in the ontology. It is justified by the fact that all lessons essentially require and/or help develop a capability to apply certain skills. Lesson plans actually explicate and articulate those skills.

Thus, if instructional skeletons and lesson plans of available online lessons are readily available and expressed both graphically and in terms of the ontology of fundamental academic ability, teachers can browse them and easily judge whether any specific one is appropriate for their instructional objectives without reading all of them in detail.

A major prerequisite for applying this approach effectively is semantic annotation of online lessons and lesson plans using the terms from the ontology.

7.6   An example

This section continues the description of the TANGRAM learning environment for the domain of Intelligent Information Systems (IIS), started in Chapter 6, section 3. The focus of this section is on the instructional design within TANGRAM. It is based on the *learning paths ontology* (*LP ontology*) depicted at the top part of Figure 6-10.

As briefly noted in Chapter 6, the LP ontology defines learning trajectories through the topics defined in the domain ontology (the ontology of IIS, Figure 5-18). It extends the SKOS Core ontology[49] (see Table 5-9) by introducing three new properties: *lp:requiresKnowledgeOf*, *lp:isPrerequisiteFor*, and *lp:hasKnowledgePonder*. The first two define prerequisite relationships between the domain topics, whereas the third one defines the difficulty level of a topic on the scale from 0 to 1.

In fact, the LP ontology relates instances of the domain ontology through an additional set of semantic relationships reflecting a specific instructional approach to teaching/learning IIS. For example, the relations shown in Figure 7-16 represent the instructional view of the author of TANGRAM and the LP ontology. Another instructor/teacher may need to reformulate the order of learning the domain concepts (i.e., the learning paths) explicated in the relations shown in Figure 7-16. He/she would then have to define a new set of learning paths according to his/her own instructional approach. Still, note the pedagogical knowledge (instructional design) represented by the learning paths is fully decoupled from (although related to) the domain knowledge. The point of this decoupling is to enable the reuse of the domain ontology - even if the applied pedagogical approach changes, the domain ontology remains intact (Jovanović et al., 2006a).

The *lp:hasKnowledgePonder* property values in Figure 7-16 are of great importance in terms of learner modeling in TANGRAM. Recall from Chapter 6, section 3.3.1, that TANGRAM represents learners' knowledge of the domain topics as numerical values between 0 and 1. During the learning sessions, these values are compared to the difficulty values assigned to the

---

[49] The ontology in RDF/OWL is available from http://www.w3.org/2004/02/skos/core.

domain concepts by the instructor through the *lp:hasKnowledgePonder* property. The comparison enables TANGRAM to keep track of the learner's levels of mastery of the domain topics and provide personalized instruction accordingly.

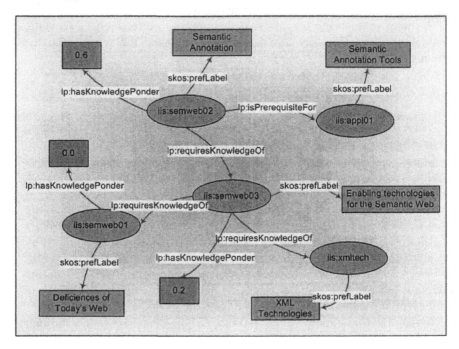

Figure 7-16. A segment of the LP ontology for the domain of IIS (after (Jovanović, 2005))

A drawback of TANGRAM's approach to instructional design is that each modification/extension of the domain ontology needs to be followed by a corresponding modification/extension of the LP ontology. It is necessary in order to define optimal learning paths through the concepts of the extension or to update the instructional design to reflect the modifications of the domain ontology.

8.   TASK ONTOLOGY

So far, the book discussed different kinds of ontologies without indicating a strict classification/typology of ontologies. In Chapter 3, section 6.2, some categories of educational ontologies were identified, but no attempt was made to classify them more accurately. True, such a classification is not a clear-cut issue; nevertheless, even a coarse typology can help develop a more systematic understanding of ontological engineering in general.

The purpose of this section is to describe and illustrate the notion of task ontology in detail, thus making a step towards a categorization of ontologies that should be considered in ontological engineering of SWBE systems.

The origins and the most notable work on task ontology come from the Mizoguchi Lab at Osaka University, Japan (Chen et al., 1998; Ikeda et al., 1997; Mizoguchi and Ikeda, 1996; Mizoguchi et al., 1996). The most elaborated general description of task ontology in the overall context of ontological engineering can be found in (Mizoguchi, 2003; 2004a; 2004b). Task ontology is also in line with the earlier concept of *generic tasks* (Chandrasekaran, 1986) and with the *ontology of tasks and methods* (Chandrasekaran et al., 1998).

8.1   Basic ideas

Roughly speaking, the ontology of any knowledge-based system that performs some task(s) has two major parts (Mizoguchi, 2003):
- *domain ontology*, which characterizes the knowledge of the domain in which the system performs its task(s);
- *task ontology*, which characterizes the computational (problem-solving) architecture of the knowledge-based system.

Here the term *task* denotes a generic problem-solving process like diagnosis, monitoring, scheduling, design, and so on. Task ontology provides a system of relevant concepts and the vocabulary for analyzing and implementing the problem-solving part of a knowledge-based system. In other words, task ontology enables describing the problem-solving structure of an existing task in a consistent and domain-independent way. It does not cover the control structure of performing a task, but the generic knowledge of task components, operations, goals, roles of actors that perform the task, and relations between them.

In the context of a SWBE system, task ontology is an abstract specification of the system's actions in performing its tasks (such as instruction, learning support, training, authoring, and so on). It formalizes different educational tasks and turns them into reusable components for SWBE system design and development. Effectively, it translates the knowledge-level description of educational problem solving processes into symbol-level executable code (e.g., RDF/OWL) and hence helps standardize protocols of communication among different components of SWBE systems and pedagogical agents.

8.1.1   Task ontology of an intelligent learning environment

As an example of task ontology, consider the problem-solving processes supported by an intelligent learning environment. As indicated in Figure 7-11, the principal task supported by such an environment is that of instruction and learning support. It is characterized by an interaction between the learner and the environment. The environment provides different functionalities to help the learner perform various learning activities related to a subject domain. The environment does so according to the learner's capabilities, knowledge, skills, motivation, and so on (the learner's state), and with a certain educational goal. This task is very complex, and its problem-solving processes cluster around several top-level concepts (Ikeda et al., 1997; Mizoguchi and Ikeda, 1996; Mizoguchi et al., 1996):

- *Goals of education.* A general, high-level view of education suggests that it is always related to increasing the learner's capabilities. Hence the goals of education can be first divided into two major categories: *increasing domain-independent capabilities*, and *increasing domain-dependent capabilities*. The former is mainly related to *reasoning capabilities* (such as *creativity* and *thinking*) and *memory-related capabilities* (further divided into *short-term memory capabilities* and *long-term memory capabilities*). The three major subcategories of domain-dependent capabilities are *deep understanding of concepts* (declarative knowledge), *problem-solving capability* (procedural knowledge related to different problem-solving schemas and how to combine them), and *skills*.
- *Learner's state.* Task ontology of an intelligent learning environment is further characterized by the learner's state in terms of the *phase in learning process* he/she is in (which can be related either to learning *concepts* or to learning *problem-solving procedures*), his/her *knowledge state* (either about *numeric representation* or about *symbolic representation* (like representation of *conditions*, *premises*, *bugs*, and so on)), and his/her *mental state* (*motivation*, *concentration*, etc.).
- *Environment's functionality.* This is the most important top-level concept of an intelligent learning environment, and is also extremely complex. For the sake of simplicity, just a few of its high-level subcategories are mentioned here. *Modeling* includes *numeric/symbolic modeling*, *search-space size*, *models*, *operations*, and so forth. *Tutoring* is featured by *tutoring objectives*, *control*, *methods*, and *objects* (*problems*, *explanations*, *hints*, and the like).
- *Learner-environment interaction.* Some features of this concept are *mode of interaction* (*text*, *graphics*, *video*,…), *communication roles* (*teacher*, *learner*, *assessor*, *peer*, etc.), *content types* (*problem*, *question*, *example*,

hypothesis, theorem, and so forth), and *control/sequencing protocol* (*learner-driven, environment-driven, taking turns,* etc.).

- *Knowledge of teaching material.* Roughly, the knowledge of teaching material includes *domain knowledge* (*nodes* like *concepts, facts, rules,* and *principles,* and *links* like *prerequisite, objective, order,* etc.), *search-control knowledge* (*goals, subgoals, preferences,*…) and *strategic knowledge.* These issues and concepts are crucial for selecting the most appropriate teaching approach for a certain subject domain (e.g. some tutoring strategies are not effective for certain kinds of domain knowledge).

Obviously, many of the above concepts and processes can be put in the context of ontologies other than task ontology. Their role in the task ontology is to describe the *problem-solving* context of the task that supports instruction or learning. In other contexts, the same concepts may be seen from different perspectives.

8.1.2   The relation between task ontology and domain ontology

Task ontology can be analyzed at different levels of abstraction, Figure 7-17. The levels are defined according to the degree of the ontologiy's dependency on a specific task and domain.

Core task ontology is a general problem-solving ontology. It does not depend on any specific task or domain. It lays foundation for the other two layers by defining the concepts inherent to all types of problem solving (e.g., *goal, subgoal,* and *activity*).

Task-specific ontology describes (depends on) a certain kind of high-level problem-solving task such as planning, scheduling, and training, but it does not depend on any domain. It provides concepts/system/theory/vocabulary for describing the task model of a certain type of task, regardless of the domain in which the task is performed; for instance, in the field of education, there is a *training task ontology* and an *authoring task ontology* (see the next two subsections). Task-specific vocabulary of such ontologies (such as *training goal, training behavior,* etc.) does not include domain-specific concepts.

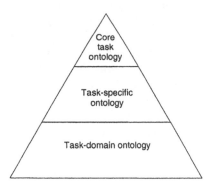

Figure 7-17. The pyramid of task ontology (after (Chen et al., 1998))

Task-domain ontology depends not only on a certain kind of task, but also on a certain domain. Task-domain ontology describes domain models from the task-type perspective. For example, hospital admission training ontology may define concepts like *patient registration, insurance-status checking, referral administration*, and the like.

One can view the core task ontology as a metamodel of task-specific ontologies, and each task-specific ontology is an instance of the core task ontology. Likewise, a task-specific ontology can be seen as a metamodel for defining task-domain ontologies, which are instances of the task-specific ontology.

Core task ontology and task-specific ontologies are useful for describing problem-solving structure inherent to the existing tasks in a domain-independent way. They are derived by analyzing task structures of various real-world problems. The major benefit of defining and using such ontologies in SWBE system design is that they enable developers to specify and build domain ontologies independently of the problem-solving tasks performed in the domain. Core task ontology and task-specific ontologies specify the roles of the domain objects and actors, their activities in the problem-solving process, and their states. Thus all the task-specific concepts are detached from the domain concepts and are subsumed by task-specific roles in the task ontologies. Therefore, task ontology helps develop a use-neutral domain ontology.

8.2   Training task ontology

Much of the early work on task ontology in Mizoguchi Lab was exemplified by the *training task ontology* used in the SmartTrainer authoring tool (Chen et al., 1998; Ikeda et al., 1997; Mizoguchi and Ikeda, 1996; Mizoguchi et al., 1996). According to the pyramid of task ontology, training task ontology is a task-specific ontology.

Training task ontology defines the concepts (italicized in the description that follows) and typical workflows of the training task that enable authors to prepare teaching material efficiently. For example, suppose that a learner uses an interactive learning/training environment to learn the skills of conducting recovery of a technical system (such as a power-plant substation) after an accident. The training procedure in this case is a sequence of *recognition*, *judgment*, and *actions*. It is a typical training task workflow. The initial state describes the situation when the accident happened. There may be several alternative *paths* in the workflow. If an author uses the SmartTrainer tool to prepare the training material, the workflow paths are automatically displayed to him/her on the basis of the training-task ontology. The author can see the actions in each path, and decide on the path to use to specify some *questions* for the learners (as parts of the training material). The questions corresponding to the selected path constitute a *backbone stream* in the problem-solving process. It means that the learner interacting with the system at some point will have to go through that sequence of questions. When answering the questions, he/she may make some mistakes. The author may anticipate the mistakes and develop a teaching strategy to handle each such a mistake. The training task ontology will guide him/her to model the strategy for handling mistakes as a sequence of teaching behaviors which constitute a *rib stream*. Each backbone stream is task-oriented; each rib stream is topic-oriented.

Training task ontology essentially drives the authoring/modeling process at two levels. The first level is used for modeling the task as a sequence of *subtasks*. The second enables modeling a subtask as a sequence of concrete teaching actions (and preparing the corresponding teaching materials), which will be suggested to the learner at an appropriate point during the training session.

In addition to the usual *is-a*, *part-of*, and *property* relations, training task ontology uses another two relations suitable for defining relationships among concepts typical for describing a training task. One of them is the *seq-part-of*, which means that the parts should be in a certain order. The other one is *division-of*, denoting that some contents have to be mutually exclusive.

8.3   Authoring task ontology

Authoring of learning/teaching courseware requires two kinds of task ontologies. One of them is the ontology of instruction and learning support, such as the one discussed in section 8.1.1. It is important for an authoring system to be aware of the task and the purpose it can generate a system for (Mizoguchi, 2004a). The other one is the *authoring task ontology* that provides knowledge and intelligence to the authoring tool itself. It enables the authoring tool to guide the author through the authoring process, and checks the consistency and completeness of the authoring activities (Aroyo and Mizoguchi, 2003). It also offers intelligent assistance to the authors in the form of hints, recommendations, and authoring templates (Aroyo and Dicheva, 2004a; 2004b). The templates are based on recognizing different information patterns (existing within the subject domain content/ontologies), presentation (sequencing) patterns, usage (learning and teaching) patterns, etc.

Authoring task ontology is based on the clear identification of the three groups of authoring activities described in Chapter 3, section 1.4: authoring of educational content, authoring of instructional process, and authoring of adaptation and personalization. Figure 7-18 further illustrates these three kinds of authoring activities and how authoring task ontology supports them. It suggests that the architecture of an ontology-based authoring tool (and process) should include two modules to support the three kinds of activities - *author-assisting module* and *operational module*. The author-assisting module is responsible for immediate interaction with the author and for providing the actual support in the process of application authoring. The operational module implements the set of authoring tasks supported by the tool.

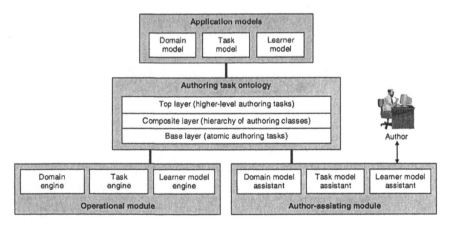

Figure 7-18. Authoring support based on the authoring task ontology (adapted from (Aroyo and Dicheva, 2004a))

The *task model* in Figure 7-18 refers to the learning/instruction task(s) to be supported by the application/courseware. It should make use of an ontology of instructional design. The author-assisting module may enable the author to create such an ontology if necessary, or to use an external one and possibly modify it. A practical implementation of this philosophy may be to use different learning design templates. The same approach goes for the other "assistants" of the author-assisting module as well. The author-assisting module interprets the results of the operational module processing and gives the author hints about how to edit the domain, how to create a course structure, how to link documents to the domain ontology or to course items, etc. (Aroyo and Dicheva, 2004a; 2004b).

The authoring task ontology has three layers. The *base layer* specifies a set of atomic authoring tasks (primitive functions), such as *create(structure)*, *create(object)*, *add(object, structure)*, *delete(object, structure)*, *edit(object, structure)*, *link(object1, object2, structure)*, etc. Here an *object* is an abstraction that encompasses things like domain concepts and relations, task items, and learner model attributes. *Structure* refers to a specific concept-based structure such as a domain model, a learner model, or a task model. Note that atomic tasks are independent of the information structure (learning resources). The *composite layer* defines functional groupings of atomic authoring tasks into a hierarchy of higher-level authoring tasks (classes). These higher-level tasks are inter-related by *sub-task-of* (*part-of*) and *peer-task-of* (*is-a*) relationships. The *top layer* specifies authoring tasks supporting application-specific relationships, such as *precedence* (temporal relationship between two tasks), *prerequisite* (causal relationship), and different task-agent relationships like *is-assigned-to*, *is-achieved-by*, and *is-delegated-to*.

The authoring task ontology actually defines a graph (semantic network) of different authoring tasks and their vocabulary (mostly specified by the atomic authoring tasks). To interpret the graph and possibly find interesting authoring patterns in it, the authoring tool requires query and reasoning capabilities.

9. AUTHORING FRAMEWORKS

Recent developments in SWBE and in ontological engineering, as well as the notion of task ontology, have given rise to the idea of adopting a stable framework for authoring SWBE applications. Starting from fragments of several convergent research efforts (Aroyo and Dicheva, 2004b; Aroyo and Mizoguchi, 2003; Dichev et al., 2004; Dicheva et al., 2005), it is possible to sketch the skeleton of such a framework.

Three key and somewhat "orthogonal" ideas for an ontology-based authoring framework are:

- distinguish between authoring of learning content, authoring of learning design, and authoring of adaptation and personalization;
- divide the authoring activities in three groups, as illustrated in Figure 7-18 - domain authoring, task authoring, and learner model authoring;
- organize the authoring process in three levels: *content level, application level*, and *presentation level* (Aroyo and Dicheva, 2004b); this is illustrated in Figure 7-19.

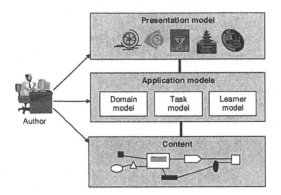

Figure 7-19. Authoring at three different levels

The first two ideas were already discussed (in section 8.3, as well as in Chapter 3, section 1.4). The point of the third idea is to completely separate content and content authoring from the application- and presentation-specific data and authoring. This permits to design multiple applications using the same content. In the case of SWBE applications, the content is typically stored in LORs, on educational servers, and on different peers in P2P architectures. Different applications can access and present the content in their own ways.

Furthermore, organizing the authoring process in the three levels enables conducting the process at each level relatively independently. An important benefit of such an approach is that the complexity of the engineering processes involved in SWBE application development gets reduced to a manageable size.

Authoring at the content level means authoring LOs and the corresponding resources, creation of metadata and appropriate annotation, as well as creation of links (conceptual and functional) between different LOs and resources.

Authoring at the application level includes authoring of domain, task, and learner models, supported by the corresponding ontologies. Domain ontologies provide means for mapping domain models to LOs. Different kinds of task ontologies (like training task ontology and instructional (course) design task ontology) help specify the applications' processes and functionalities. Learner model ontologies define the applications' objective, subjective, performance, and other learner-specific data and relate them to the concepts from the appropriate domain ontologies. In order to support application level authoring, it is useful to define collections of atomic authoring tasks specified at the base layer of the authoring task ontology. The collections correspond to domain authoring, task model authoring, and learner model authoring (see Figure 7-19). These collections provide specification of primitive authoring tasks without referring to the actual content of the application domain, LOs, and their resource files. For example, Figure 7-20 shows a part of the collection of domain authoring tasks.

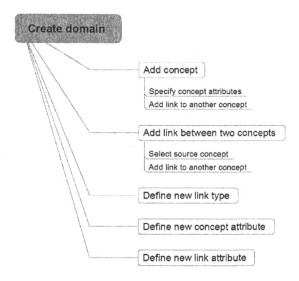

Figure 7-20. An excerpt from the collection of domain authoring tasks (adapted from (Aroyo and Dicheva, 2004b))

Authoring at the presentation level comprises creating a presentation model for information delivery and learner interaction. It makes use of the learner model and other application-related models. Much of the authoring of adaptation and personalization is related to this level. Authoring at this level is also concerned with specifying patterns of browsing, automatic presentation of retrieved data, definition of navigation strategies, etc.

Authoring task ontology should support authoring at all three levels. Figure 7-21 generalizes Figure 7-18 by including content level and presentation level authoring, in addition to application level authoring already indicated in Figure 7-18. The ontology itself may explicitly include the definitions of the aforementioned collections of atomic authoring tasks. Further research efforts are needed to precisely specify the ways and the extent to which the collections should be defined in the ontology.

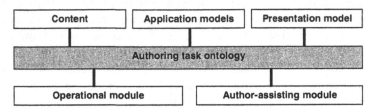

Figure 7-21. Authoring support based on authoring task ontology (adapted from (Aroyo and Dicheva, 2004b))

There are several advantages of applying an authoring framework that clearly separates content, application, and presentation authoring levels (Dichev et al., 2004):

- *Efficient management and maintenance.* Authoring, modifying, indexing, searching, and manipulating content (LOs) can be performed independently. Ontologies help maintain the links between application models and content at the application level.
- *Collaborative authoring.* Different authors can create their products at the three different authoring levels and merge the results. For example, different presentation and application models can be developed to allow for including content "external" to the specific courseware without referencing specific LOs explicitly.
- *Building ontology-aware applications.* Application-level ontologies facilitate development of intuitive and well-structured authoring tools, as well as construction of open-ended learning environments. By means of ontologies, different resources can be organized to support one or more application-level models consistently.
- *Building courseware templates and development patterns.* Instructional design is facilitated by the possibility for authoring tools to support instructional ontology-based authoring templates and development patterns. These enable authors knowledgeable in instructional design to focus on the instructional design itself, adapting it to the course contents.
- *Enhanced navigation and LO retrieval.* Presentation-level authoring is facilitated by advanced Semantic Web technologies such as topic maps. They allow for creating different indexes, cross-references, glossaries, and semantic query tools to act as interfaces to LORs and educational servers.
- *Effective visualization support.* Different visualization techniques can be used to support authoring at different levels. It is as important to

visualize the LOs (along with their metadata) as the structure of the ontologies used to describe them. Multiple views and consistent visualization facilitate authoring across different levels.

10. AUTOMATIC CONSTRUCTION OF LEARNING ONTOLOGIES

Ontological engineering of different aspects of SWBE systems is necessary, but ontologies are often time consuming to construct. Moreover, they must be general enough to support a range of different applications, and easy enough to modify to reflect the dynamics of changes in the domains of interest. Hence finding ways to create ontologies automatically is not only appealing and challenging, but also very practical.

Several approaches to automatic construction of learning-related ontologies have been proposed so far. Chapter 2, section 2.2.1, briefly discusses the approach that uses machine learning techniques (Maedche and Staab, 2001), and Chapter 6, section 2.9, explains how Web mining can be used to automatically construct the ontology of learner access behavior (Zhou et al., 2005). Another two approaches, similar to each other, use online dictionaries and Web service descriptions.

10.1 Constructing ontologies from online dictionaries

Online dictionaries pertaining to specific disciplines of science and technology are fairly reliable resources with broad coverage of the topics of interest. They can be used to construct lightweight ontologies automatically, and then possibly refine them manually. This approach saves a considerable amount of effort and helps minimize errors.

An example of applying this approach is the MECUREO tool, used to automatically create an ontology of computer science (Apted and Kay, 2002; Apted et al., 2004). Its source online dictionary is FOLDOC, The Free On-Line Dictionary Of Computing (FOLDOC, 1993). FOLDOC is quite extensive, as it contains definitions of thousands of computer science terms. In addition, it also covers related disciplines, standards, companies, institutions, products, and projects, and includes many cross- and bibliographical references. Thus it is quite a suitable resource for ontology creation. Moreover, its offline version encloses significant terms (e.g., terms defined elsewhere) in braces, Figure 7-22, which provides markup that can be used in automatic analysis of term definitions and ontology creation. There are other similar kinds of markup in term definitions as well. For example, it is easy to grasp intuitively that a parser designed to extract the markup shown in Figure 7-22 will create a node in the ontology for the main entry (*ontology*), additional nodes for *philosophy* and *artificial intelligence* categories, and more additional nodes for significant terms in braces.

---

ontology
1. **<philosophy>** A systematic account of Existence.
2. **<artificial intelligence>** (From philosophy) An explicit formal specification of how to represent the objects, concepts and other entities that are assumed to exist in some area of interest and the relationships that hold among them.
For **{AI}** systems, what "exists" is that which can be represented. When the **{knowledge}** about a **{domain}** is represented in a **{declarative language}**, the set of objects that can be represented is called the **{universe of discourse}** (e.g. classes, relations, functions or other objects) ...

Figure 7-22. An excerpt from FOLDOC showing the entry for *ontology* (adapted from (Apted and Kay, 2002)); significant terms are shown in boldface for enhanced readability

Also, consistent grammatical conventions used in the dictionary structure can provide additional information about the term relationships. For example, *synonym*, *antonym*, *child*, and *parent* relationships can be extracted if certain keywords are present (e.g., patterns like "a type of X" represent *child* (*is-a*) relationships). *Acronyms* are usually modeled as *synonyms* of their expansions. And so on.

The list of relationships between ontological terms identified this way is rather long (see (Apted and Kay, 2002)). It is quite possible that more than one kind of relationship exists between two terms (concepts), but typically not all of them are equally important for successful querying of such a large ontology. Hence a special heuristic algorithm is used to give each relationship a weight that reflects the strength of the relationship and the amount of work required to "travel" from one concept to the next. For example, using the word *about* in Figure 7-22 in the "{knowledge} about a {domain}" phrase indicates a descriptive relationship between *knowledge* and *domain*. It is computed in this example to have a relatively low weight. The weight is stronger for the relationship between *ontology* and *knowledge*, because *knowledge* is marked up to be a significant term for *ontology*. In general, the ontology construction algorithm first determines that a relationship between two nodes exists and what is its type, and then computes the weight.

10.2   Exploiting Web service descriptions

Web services often have attached different textual resources, such as short descriptions of these services and the documentation of the code of the underlying software (Sabou, 2005b). These descriptions contain valuable information that can be used for building ontologies. Moreover, each such a description uses a specialized form of natural language, largely restricted, dependent on the particular domain or subject matter, and characterized by a specialized vocabulary, semantic relations, and syntactic regularities. For example, a weather report Web service almost always refers to *temperature, highs and lows, winds,* etc., and they are almost always related in a unique way to *heat, frost, sunshine, rain, showers,* etc. The specific nature of these texts makes them suitable for ontology extraction. Likewise, different educational Web services attached to LORs, LMSs, educational servers, and so on can be used to extract learning ontologies. Generally, the extraction process takes the following steps:

- *Identify the corpus.* The term "corpus" denotes the set of specific textual resources that describe the Web services of interest. These can range from *javadoc*-like source code comments to free-form natural language comments in WSDL-based and OWL-S-based service descriptions.
- *Annotate the corpus.* Ontology extraction is greatly leveraged if additional linguistic information about the words and sentences in the corpus is supplied. For example, knowing the possible role of each word in a sentence helps build dependency relations between words in natural language. Typically, in a sentence like "Use learning material for novice students" one can identify head words (e.g., "material"), modifiers ("learning"), and different kinds of words in terms of parts-of-speech analysis (verbs, nouns, prepositions, and the like). Natural language analysis tools (so called part-of-speech taggers) are available that perform such a word/role identification and analysis with high degree of accuracy. The output from these tools can be used to annotate the corpus with additional linguistic information.
- *Apply syntactic patterns.* Based on the syntactic rules of the specific natural language, it is possible to identify and extract domain concepts, functionalities, and relations to be included in the ontology. To do that, one applies different syntactic patterns. For example, domain concepts are usually found as nouns or noun phrases[50] (like "novice student" in the above example). Another syntactic pattern, typical for descriptions of Web service functionalities, is that the functionalities are usually expressed using verbs followed by their objects (which can be in the form of entire noun phrases). For instance, applying that pattern one can identify "Use learning material" as a potential pedagogical functionality in the above example.
- *Build concept hierarchies.* Domain concepts extracted in the previous step can be arranged in hierarchies. Studies have shown that nearly two thirds of the extracted terms expose a high degree of compositionality, i.e. incorporate other meaningful terms as proper substrings (Sabou,

---

[50] In a noun phrase, an adjective or another noun modifies a head noun.

2005b). This compositionality indicates the existence of semantic relations between the terms - if term A is a proper substring of term B, then it is typically more generic than term B. This translates in the ontological *subsumption* (*is-a, kind-of*) relationship (e.g., "material" subsumes "learning material"). A top-level concept such as *DataStructure, Thing*, or *Concept* is used as the root of the overall hierarchy.

- *Build functionality hierarchies*. This is similar to building concept hierarchies. Each generic verb (e.g., "use") can be included as a child of the top-level *Functionality* node in the functionality hierarchy. The related verb-object phrases are then included as children of the corresponding generic verb ("use learning material").

- *Prune the ontology hierarchies*. It is necessary to apply different heuristics to make the concept and functionality hierarchies more accurate and more usable. For example, if a concept or a functionality is included in the respective hierarchy as a direct child of the root node but has no children itself, it is pruned. This is supported by observations and empirical evaluations of ontologies constructed automatically in different domains. The observations and evaluations show that complex terms that generate subhierarchies by decomposition are more likely to be relevant (Sabou, 2005b).

- *Evaluate and enrich the extracted ontology*. This step should involve a domain expert. The expert may leave out some of the extracted terms as irrelevant, create new nodes in the hierarchies and rearrange them to increase accuracy, and otherwise fine-tune the extracted ontology.

An obvious deficiency of constructing an ontology this way is that relevant Web services may still assume ontologies *other than* or *in addition to* the one extracted. Then the ontological engineers need to consider different ontology mapping/integration/merging/alignment techniques to further improve the automatically extracted ontology and increase the overall system interoperability. Yet the process of automatic construction of the ontology at least provides "something to start with". Experts find it much easier to verify and fine-tune an already existing ontology than to build one from scratch.

11.   SUMMARY

Ontological engineering is a central process in developing any SWBE application or system. There is a large set of engineering activities related to the process of building educational ontologies. Likewise, there is a genuine need to understand the structure, context, usability, and technological background for using ontologies in education. A good starting point and an introduction to the complexity of such issues is the O4E portal (O4E, 2005).

General-purpose ontology development methodologies can be used in ontological engineering of e-Learning as well. However, specifications of LOs (their content and metadata), learning processes, and learning scenarios are both crucial and complex enough and hence require specific ontological considerations. The ultimate goals of ontological engineering of a SWBE system are:

- to make the system interoperable with other similar systems, applications, educational servers, LORs, and other external resources;
- to semantically annotate the learning contents and resources and hence make them easily available to the end users, without the need to manually search and inspect all information related to the topics of their interest;
- to enable adaptivity and personalization of the learning experience across applications;
- to support instructional (learning) design, in terms of specifying the necessary learning activities needed to use online courses and the associated resources.

One of the most important steps in ontological engineering of a SWBE system is to clearly and explicitly specify its task ontology, in order to formalize the system's educational tasks. Explicit representation of the system's task ontology provides a stable backbone for system development and enables fostering of standards-based communication among different components of SWBE systems and pedagogical agents. Also, task ontology is a key factor in adopting a stable framework for authoring SWBE applications.

Technological support for ontological engineering is growing. In addition to general-purpose ontology development tools, there are now several tools specific to SWBE that help designers and authors develop their applications and learning material. An important technological contribution to ontological engineering comes in the form of specific techniques that greatly alleviate the process of ontology development and maintenance. These include different ontology visualization techniques and the appropriate tools, as well as recent support for automatic construction of educational ontologies.

Chapter 8

APPLICATIONS AND RESEARCH

This chapter illustrates the use of SWBE principles, architectures, and technology in practical applications. It covers some areas of e-Learning, not discussed in detail in the previous chapters, where the application of SWBE principles and technology brings important benefits and advantages. These include learning management, collaborative learning, and learning communities. The chapter also covers several emerging research issues that currently attract attention of the SWBE community.

1. LEARNING MANAGEMENT AND THE SEMANTIC WEB

Learning management systems (*LMSs*) are software packages designed to help educators create quality online courses and manage learner outcomes (Williams, 2005). An LMS typically includes a robust set of tools, functions, and features for learning (Blackboard, 2002). More precisely, the idea of LMSs is to bring together, in one package, a number of Web-based applications that can be useful teaching tools and make it easy for teachers to use those tools to create and maintain course materials online (DMP, 2004). Thus LMSs can also integrate external applications, tools, content, and services.

1.1 Introduction to learning management systems

There are several related terms, often used as synonyms for LMSs (Williams, 2005). These include *course management systems* (*CMSs*), *virtual learning environments* (*VLEs*) and *learning content management systems* (*LCMSs*). Strictly speaking, differences do exist. For example, LCMSs are systems used to create LOs and metadata (and thus overlap in functionality with authoring tools), whereas LMSs are systems that support e-Learning sessions built from LOs (Van Assche and Massart, 2004). Usually, both LCMSs and LMSs have their own LORs to house LOs and the associated metadata. This chapter uses the term LMSs, unless it is necessary to make a strict difference between LMSs and LCMSs.

LMSs are Web-oriented systems, hosted on both Web and application servers (Šimić et al., 2005; 2006). Typical LMSs are best understood as Web platforms providing a number of different services to different categories of end users (teachers, authors of learning content, learners, administrators). Note, however, that some of the services target more than one category of end users.

For teachers, LMSs provide means for creating LOs, as well as for composing courses out of the newly created LOs and existing LOs available in LORs. These learning units (both LOs and courses) are represented in a standard content packaging format and annotated with standards-compliant metadata. Thus LMSs make learning units ready for reuse - the same learning unit can be incorporated in a number of different online courses. Also, learning design can be associated with courses and other learning units by specifying learning activities and resources to be used. In addition to course content management, teachers can also use LMSs for learning management tasks like course planning, content delivery, virtual classrooms, assessment scheduling and management, learner record management, grading, reporting, and logging various access information.

To authors, LMSs offer a suite of authoring and design tools, editors, and services. Some of these can be external, but are integrated through the LMS into a coherent toolset. In the process of creating learning content using an LMS/LCMS, an author typically either creates a new LO or a course from scratch, or reuses an existing one. He/She can add different activities and resources to the LO/course (e.g., lesson, assignment, quiz, glossary, journal, audio and video, math equations, an entire external LO, chat, choice, forum, etc.). He/She or the teacher can also set up different grading strategies with the LO/course (such as accumulative grading, criterion grading, and rubric grading), possibly using word-based custom grading scales (like "fair", "excellent", etc.) (Williams, 2005). In terms of LO reusability, probably the most important feature is that of including external LOs organized as standards-based content packages (e.g., a SCORM LO).

To learners, LMSs appear as comfortable platforms for accessing different courses and learning material. Such platforms often support some forms of collaborative learning. In most cases, the learners only need a Web browser; the rest appears as integrated through the LMS platform.

To administrators, LMSs provide services like creating new learner accounts, creating and managing groups of learners of different sizes, learner notification and reporting, schedule management, enrolment management, certification management, and financial management.

To all categories of end users, LMSs offer high-level security management and services. Also, LMSs support different learning technology standards.

Once again, the keyword for LMSs is integration. Integration of different learning resources and activities, different actors in the learning process, and different WBE tools, systems, and applications.

Popular LMSs include Blackboard (Blackboard, 2002), WebCT (DMP, 2004), and Moodle (Williams, 2005). Blackboard and WebCT are commercial products, whereas Moodle is an open source software. Blackboard and WebCT have announced plans to merge in 2006.

1.2   Intelligent Learning Management Systems

It follows from the previous section that LMSs provide management, distribution, and sharing of learning contents, student tracking, assignment management, online peer collaboration, and the like. Hence they provide a WBE and virtual classroom equivalence of traditional educational processes. By their nature, LMSs are mainly focused on supporting LO reusability, course authoring, and different administrative tasks (Šimić et al., 2005; 2006).

Intelligent learning management systems (*ILMSs*) combine functionalities and wide coverage of LMSs with Web-based ITSs. Thus ILMSs can be defined as the intersection of LMSs and Web-based ITSs (Yacef, 2003).

1.2.1   The need for intelligence in learning management systems

LMSs are powerful integrated systems that support a number of activities performed by teachers and students during the e-Learning process, but generally offer their users "one size fits all" service (Brusilovsky, 2004). All learners taking an LMS-based course, regardless of their knowledge, goals, and interests, receive access to the same educational material and the same set of tools. To put it differently, LMSs provide interesting learning opportunities and have recognized advantages, but often fail to provide high-level personalization and adaptivity of the learning process. Learners are routinely channeled through a range of e-Learning activities, since LMSs are not designed as individualized learning environments.

Moreover, in certain cases LMSs can frustrate their users. Students often feel lost due to the mass of learning content that lacks personalized guidance; absence of appropriate and timely feedback further aggravates their situation. Teachers complain about time consuming tasks they need to perform when using LMSs, as well as about poor visibility of students' progress and problems.

Worse still, interoperability of traditional LMSs is poor. What is needed is intelligent and seamless integration of different LMSs and educational Web services, tools, and resources.

Web-based ITS technology, in contrast, provides a very domain focused and individualized environment for learning (Šimić et al., 2005; 2006; Yacef, 2003). Web-based ITSs enable a much greater insight into the learners' difficulties and progress and allow for diagnoses and remedial actions. They embed AI techniques and principles to represent the knowledge about the learners, the domains, the teaching strategies, and the communication.

The need to include useful features of Web-based ITSs into LMSs is recognized in the SCORM specification. In SCORM, the term LMS implies a server-based environment in which the intelligence for managing and delivering learning content to students resides (ADL SCORM, 2004). SCORM explicitly specifies that the LMS should track the learner's progress and performance as he/she moves through the learning content. Taking the learner's characteristics into account, the LMS determines what to deliver and when.

1.2.2   Synergy between Web-based ITSs and LMSs

Clearly, by combining the learning management features of LMSs with intelligent capabilities of Web-based ITSs, ILMSs achieve nice synergistic effects, like (Yacef, 2003):
- *Studying individually or in groups, yet putting the teacher in control.* ILMSs let the learners work individually or in groups, under intelligent control, and let the teacher focus on providing effective guidance. Thus the teacher can drive the learning process in a more effective way.
- *Reinforcing the delicate relationship between the teacher and the learners.* ILMSs work like intelligent assistants to the teachers. With ILMSs, teachers get insight into the learner models, the learners' steps and misconceptions, their progress, and learning styles.
- *Providing extra features to LMSs.* Web-based ITSs, both for individual and collaborative learning, are typically considered by educational organizations and institutions as just learning tools. However, embedding them in an LMS brings a subtle but important difference - still having an

important management and administrative platform, but empowered with intelligent features for learning.

- *Providing a reflection tool for teachers.* Since ILMSs track much of the data related to teaching practices, assessments, curricula, grading, learner modeling, and instructional methods, teachers can use ILMSs to assess their own practice over the years. Educational institutions are interested in having their teachers reflect on their own experience and improve their teaching performance.

1.2.3   Architectural issues

Brusilovsky proposed (2004) the *KnowledgeTree architecture* for ILMSs. KnowledgeTree is a high-level architecture that capitalizes on the success of integrated LMSs by providing one-stop comprehensive support for teachers and learners. However, it replaces the monolithic LMS with a community of distributed communicating servers, Figure 8-1, and introduces adaptivity and intelligence by including specialized services. The *Learning portal* plays a role similar to that of an LMS. It provides a centralized single-login point for the enrolled learners. After logging in, the learners get access to all learning tools and LOs provided in the context of their courses. To teachers and authors, the Learning portal provides access to various LORs, and supplies a course authoring interface that facilitates course authoring and maintenance. Thus the Learning portal is the KnowledgeTree component centered on supporting a complete course.

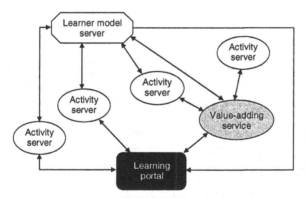

Figure 8-1. The KnowledgeTree architecture (adapted from (Brusilovsky, 2004))

The Learning portal provides access to both the learning content and various learning support services (activities) by means of multiple distributed *activity servers (services)*. The portal can query activity servers for relevant remote activities and launch them either on the learner's request or by itself. Each activity server is much like a LOR, in terms of providing access to various LOs and educational services. However, unlike a LOR an activity server can host highly interactive learning services such as discussion forums or shared annotations.

A *value-adding service* can take a "raw" content or service and add some valuable functionality to it, such as adaptive sequencing, annotation, visualization, or content integration. Like a portal, it can query activity servers and access activities. Value-adding services are course-neutral and can be reused in multiple courses through the Learning portal.

The *Learner model server* enables highly personalized and intelligent instruction delivery. Ideally, it can support a learner for multiple courses. Also, it can serve multiple portals. It collects data about the learners' performance from each portal and each activity server, and returns that information (integrated or fragmented) back to adaptive portals and activity servers when needed. These, in turn, can then deliver personalized and adaptive instruction to each individual learner.

Šimić et al. have proposed (2005; 2006) a categorization of tools to be included in an ILMS (Figure 8-2). The *learning tools* and the *teaching and authoring tools* shown in the figure are self-explanatory. The *administrative tools* support different management tasks. These include classical administration management (such as learner and teacher records), different knowledge management tasks (e.g., LO management and ontology management, see the next section), and important system administration tasks (e.g., security management).

1.2.4   Ontology management

Ontology management, an evolving subdiscipline of ontological engineering, is of particular interest to ILMSs and to SWBE in general. In theory, existing ontologies constructed by third parties could be reused to create a specific course or a LO. The idea is that the course/LO authors can modify, extend, and prune existing ontologies as required, thereby avoiding the considerable effort of starting from scratch. However, to achieve this level of reuse an appropriate infrastructure of tools and methods must be made available. Such tools must allow for search, selection, and general management of the existing ontologies. Collectively, these tools and the activities they enable are called ontology management.

Typical ontology management services that an ILMS should support include:

* *ontology search* - identifying proper ontologies from the plethora of Web resources;

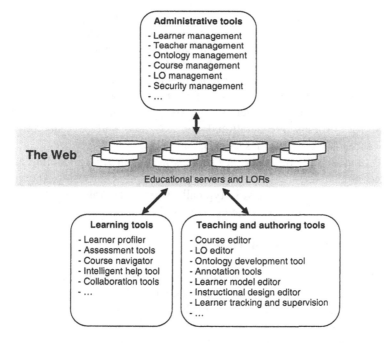

Figure 8-2. An ILMS architecture (adapted from (Šimić et al., 2006))

- *ontology ranking* - ranking of ontologies according to a number of criteria, such as the presence and absence of certain terms, and their position in the ontology;
- *ontology segmentation* or *ontology partitioning* - the ability to select and extract a particular sub-section of an existing ontology for the current needs;
- *ontology visualization* - this is covered in detail in Chapter 7, section 5;
- *other* - services and tasks like ontology evaluation, ontology change management, and ontology versioning.

1.3 Learning content management

The goals of learning content management in SWBE systems and applications are to facilitate personalization and adaptivity of the learning process, and to enable *learning content repurposing*. This term is somewhat more specific than the term "reuse", and denotes the ability to use, without any (significant) changes, the same piece of content for a purpose significantly different than that it was originally intended for when created (Duval and Hodgins, 2003). For example, in order to support a lab exercise for the course *Introduction to Object Oriented Programming* and related to

the topic of *applets*, a teacher may have prepared a Java class called
`SwingApplet.java`. Although originally aimed at introducing students
to the specific features of Java applets, this class can be equally well used for
learning about Swing-based GUI. Furthermore, students may use the same
class not only during learning and practicing, but also during an open-book
assessment. In general, the same piece of content can be used for training,
performance support, or documentation. Also, the same content can be
repurposed for different presentational contexts, and can be rendered as
HTML, Scalable Vector Graphics (SVG), and so on.

   The personalization and adaptivity aspects involve learner modeling and
are covered in Chapter 6. To support learning content repurposing, specific
ontologies are needed. Since LMSs typically support complete courses, an
important ontology to this end is the course ontology.

1.3.1   Learning content repurposing

   Each LO has its content (resource files) and its metadata that annotate the
content. Reusability of a LO can be greatly enhanced if it is annotated using
multiple ontologies and/or classification schemes. The more annotation, the
more semantics attached to the LO. The more different ontologies used to
annotate a LO, the more different views on it when stored in or referenced
from a LOR. The more different views a LO supports, the greater the chance
to repurpose it.

   An author working with a LCMS, Figure 8-3, can create and annotate
both simple LOs and larger units of learning, such as courses. These can be
stored, for example, in a university course database. In case that metadata
and resource files are physically separated, both the authoring tool and the
intelligent learning environment need to access the LOR (metadata) and the
resource files. When authoring complete courses, the author can also use
different learning design templates, either external or from the authoring
tool.

   Speaking in terms of content repurposing, there can be generally different
requirements for using the LOR (i.e. the metadata it stores) and the resource
files from the learner's side. This diversity of requirements results from
different learning and presentation contexts, as well as from differences
among learning environments and tools. To support the variety of
requirements, LOs and courses should be annotated (Figure 8-4) using:

- ontological representation of metadata schemes (MO_1, MO_2, etc.), such
  as the RDF binding of the IEEE LOM standard (Nilsson, 2002),
  discussed in Chapter 5, section 3.2;
- domain ontologies and/or different classification schemes (DO_1, DO_2,
  etc.) to explicitly define the subject matter of the learning content;

- other kinds of ontologies to provide further descriptions of the content (e.g., content structure ontologies (CO_1, CO_2, etc.), such as the one discussed in Chapter 6, section 3.1).

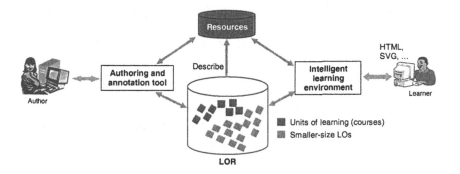

Figure 8-3. Authoring for content repurposing (adapted from (Gašević et al., 2004))

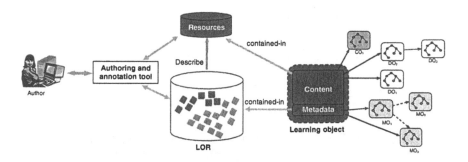

Figure 8-4. Authoring for content repurposing (adapted from (Gašević et al., 2004)

Later on, these annotations can be used to automatically extract LOs (actually their resources) to create new courses or adapt existing ones to different learning contexts. Likewise, learning environments can use adaptive mechanisms to differently present the same LO and/or course to different learners and/or different devices (e.g., desktop and mobile devices).

1.3.2 The course ontology

In addition to using learning design templates, course authors using LCMSs should also enjoy ontological support for explicitly defining the overall course structure. The Multitutor LCMS of Šimić et al. (2005; 2006) uses the course ontology partly depicted in Figure 8-5. It is designed to partially reflect the IMS LD and IMS Content Packaging standards. Also, it models the course authors' natural way of thinking about courses in terms of their structure. The ontology represents the concept of a course as an aggregation of the learning material, the references (further readings and explanations), and the assessment material. The course is structured as a set of *chapters*, each chapter containing one or more *lessons*. Lesson is the basic learning unit. A lesson describes one or more *concepts*. In Multitutor, a concept with its associated *learning content, explanation,* and one or more *test sets* (assessment items) makes a LO. Such a LO can be reused in many lessons and in different courses.

The *LearningContent* class represents the multimedia content of a LO. It is up to the learning design deployed in a specific course, as well as to the adaptivity mechanism of the learning environment, to present different parts of the LO content (stored as usually in various resource files) to different students.

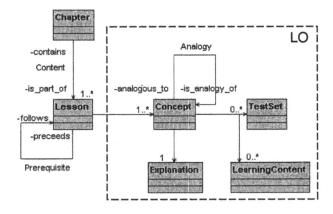

Figure 8-5. The main concepts in the course ontology (adapted from (Šimić et al., 2005; 2006))

The *TestSet* class models a largely restricted version of the IMS QTI specification. It defines a collection of questions and the related answers that the system can use to assess the learners' knowledge about a single concept. Each question has its type and an associated level of difficulty, defined by the course author or the teacher. The answers have associated marks or true/false statements. There can be a number of questions to assess the learners' knowledge at a certain level of difficulty. Typically, the learning environment will ensure that a student gets different questions every time he/she repeats a test.

Concepts can be related by the *Analogy* relation - a concept can serve as an analogy of another concept. Likewise, a lesson can be a prerequisite to another lesson (the *Prerequisite* relation). Analogies are an important part of learning design, so the course ontology assumes that in most cases a concept can be related to an analogous one. If a learner cannot pass the tests about the main concept taught in a lesson, the system may try to explain this concept by a similar one, possibly using a different teaching strategy. Typically, as a part of the learning design, authors use simpler concepts as analogies to the main concept.

2. COLLABORATIVE LEARNING AND THE SEMANTIC WEB

Computer-Supported Collaborative Learning (*CSCL*) is a coordinated, synchronous activity of a group of learners resulting from their continued attempt to construct and maintain a shared conception of a problem (Roschelle and Teasley, 1995). CSCL systems provide a learner with the possibility of interacting with other learners when completing various learning tasks (Devedžić, 2005a; 2006). The purpose of such an interaction is to complete the learning tasks more efficiently, to reduce the effort needed to learn a topic individually, and to widen perspectives on the variety of learning opportunities.

CSCL has received a lot of attention from e-Learning researchers in general, and is an emerging research topic in the area of SWBE as well. However, it is fair to say that a lot of further effort is needed before true, full-fledged SWBE applications in the area of CSCL become common. On the other hand, efforts are already undertaken towards the development of the ontology of collaborative learning.

2.1 A brief introduction to CSCL[51]

CSCL systems offer software replicas of many of the classic classroom resources and activities (Soller, 2001). For example, such systems may provide electronic shared workspaces, on-line presentations, lecture notes, reference material, quizzes, student evaluation scores, and facilities for chat

---

[51] Parts of the material presented in this section originally appeared in another Springer monograph, *Knowledge-Based Virtual Education - User-Centred Paradigms* (C. Ghaoui, M. Jain, V. Bannore, and L.C. Jain, eds., 2005), in a chapter authored by Vladan Devedžić (Devedžić, 2005a). Other parts originally appeared in the Idea Group, Inc., *Encyclopedia of Human Computer Interaction* (Ghaoui, C., ed., 2006), in a chapter authored by Vladan Devedžić (Devedžić, 2006). Used with permission of the publisher.

or online discussions. This closely reflects a typical collaborative learning situation in the classroom, where the learners, participating in learning groups, encourage each other to ask questions, explain and justify their opinions, articulate their reasoning, and elaborate and reflect upon their knowledge, thereby motivating and improving learning.

These observations stipulate both the *social context* and the *social processes* as integral parts of collaborative learning activities. In other words, CSCL is a natural process of *social interaction* and *communication* among the learners in a group while they are learning by solving common problems.

The goals of CSCL are three-fold:

- *personal* - by participating in collaborative learning, the learner attains: elimination of misconceptions; more in-depth understanding of the learning domain; and the development of self-regulation skills (i.e., metacognitive skills that let the learner observe and diagnose his/her thinking process and ability to regulate or control his/her activity);
- *interaction-supportive* - maintaining interaction with the other learners, in order to attain the personal goal associated with the interaction; this leads to learning by self-expression (learning by expressing self-thinking process, such as self-explanation and presentation), and learning by participation (learning by participating as an apprentice in a group of more advanced learners);
- *social* - the goals of the learning group as a whole are setting up the situation for peer tutoring (the situation to teach each other), and setting up the situation for sharing cognitive or metacognitive functions with other learners (enabling the learners to express their thinking/cognitive process to other learners, to get advise from other learners, discuss the problem and the solution with the peers, and the like).

CSCL technology is not a panacea. Learners who use it need guidance and support online, just as students learning in the classroom need support from their instructor. Hence the developers of CSCL tools must ensure that collaborative learning environments support active online participation by remote teachers, as well as a variety of means for the learners to deploy their social interaction skills to collaborate effectively.

In order for each CSCL system to be effective, it must be based on a certain model, such as the one suggested by Soller (2001) that integrates the following four important issues:

- indicators of effective collaborative learning;
- strategies for promoting effective peer interaction;
- technology (tools) to support the strategies;
- a set of criteria for evaluating the system.

CSCL system should recognize and target group interaction problem areas. It should take actions to help the learners collaborate more effectively with their peers, improving individual and group learning.

Since the issue of interaction is central to CSCL, it is useful to introduce the types of interaction the learner typically meets when using such systems (Curtis and Lawson, 2001):

- interaction with resources (such as related LOs);
- interaction with teachers (teachers can participate in CSCL sessions);
- interaction with peers (see the above description of the goals of CSCL);
- interaction with interface (this is the most diverse type of interaction, ranging from limited text-only interactions, to the use of specific software tools for dialogue support (based on dialogue interaction models), to interaction with pedagogical agents (see Figure 3-1)).

It is quite understandable that the learning process is more effective if the user interface is designed to be intuitive, easy-to-use, and supportive in terms of the learners' cognitive processes. With CSCL systems, additional flexibility is required. The learners have to work collaboratively in a *shared workspace* environment, but also use *private workspaces* for their own work. Moreover, since work/learning happens in small groups, the interface should ideally support the group working in one environment, or in synchronous shared environments. It also must support sharing of results, i.e. exchanging settings and data between the groups and group members, as well as demonstrating the group's outcomes or conclusions. A suitable way to do it is by using a shared workspace.

Effective collaboration with peer learners is a successful and powerful learning method, but it has an important prerequisite - the group of learners must be active and well-functioning. Just forming a group and placing the learners in it does not guarantee success. The individual learners' behavior and active participation is important, and so are their roles in the group, their motivation, their interaction, and coordination:

> "While some peer groups seem to interact naturally, others struggle to maintain a balance of participation, leadership, understanding, and encouragement." (Soller, 2001)

From this discussion, it follows that the learning efficiency in collaborative learning on the Web, largely depends on how well the learning group is assembled. Hence the question "How to form a group?" emerges as an important one.

Opportunistic group formation (OGF) is a framework that enables pedagogical agents to initiate, carry out, and manage the process of creating a learning group when necessary and conducting the learner's participation to the group (Supnithi et al., 1999). Pedagogical agents in OGF support individual learning, propose shifting to collaborative learning, and negotiate to form a group of learners with appropriate role assignment, based on the learners' information from individual learning.

In OGF, collaborative learning group is formed dynamically. A learner is supposed to use an intelligent, agent-enabled, Web-based learning environment. When an agent detects a situation for the learner to shift from individual to collaborative learning mode (a "trigger", such as an impasse or a need for review of a learning task completed by the learner), it negotiates with other agents to form a group. Each group member is assigned a reasonable learning goal and a social role. These are consistent with the goal for the whole group.

2.2   Ontology of collaborative learning

The very first thing to say about the *ontology of collaborative learning* is that it is extremely complex. From the pioneering work in this area of Supnithi et al. (1999) till now, the efforts to develop this ontology have resulted in a large, but still incomplete system of concepts and relations that model effective collaborative learning. The major problems related to development of the ontology of collaborative learning originate from the need to (Inaba and Mizoguchi, 2004):

• clarify the behavior and roles of learners in collaborative learning sessions;
• conduct a thorough analysis of the types of interaction among the learners in a collaborative learning group during a learning session;
• specify conditions to be met so that a SWBE system can initiate a collaborative learning session, set up the learning goals for the group members and the group as a whole, and assign appropriate roles to each learner;
• specify a learning group formation framework, such as OGF;
• specify predictable educational benefits for the learners to be achieved by playing the roles.

Supporting collaborative learning on the Semantic Web requires not only the ontology of collaborative learning, but also various other educational ontologies. Two ontologies tightly coupled with the ontology of collaborative learning are the *learning goal ontology* and the *negotiation ontology*.

2.2.1   Theoretical background

Research and development efforts related to the ontology of collaborative learning are based on various learning theories. Some of them are Vygotsky's socio-cultural theory - zone of proximal development (Vygotsky,

1978), constructivism, self-regulated learning, situated cognition, cognitive apprenticeship, cognitive flexibility theory, observational learning, and distributed cognition (see (Andriessen et al., 2003; Collins, 1991; Dillenbourg et al., 1996; Roschelle and Teasley, 1995; and TIP, 2004) for a more comprehensive insight).

These learning theories originate in the cognitive science research on how people work and learn. This research combines the social and cognitive perspectives. Specifically, the *activity theory* (Nardi, 1996) is essential for CSCL in general and for the development of the ontology of collaborative learning in particular. The activity theory is about representing the group activities in situations where the technology plays the role of a mediator. The central concept in the activity theory is that of activity as a unit of analysis. It has a rich internal structure that enables making the context of a situation explicit. For example, it is desirable to explicitly characterize the links between the individual and the social levels, which stress the role of the tools as mediating artifacts (Barros et al., 2002). The concept of activity includes the following important elements: the *subject* and *object* of the activity, the *division of labor* to be followed, the *tools* to be used, the *community* involved and the *social norms* that govern it, and finally, the *outcome* produced by the group.

2.2.2   Overall structure

Starting from learning theories, and especially from the activity theory, collaborative learning scenarios can be described in terms of (Barros et al., 2002; Inaba and Mizoguchi, 2004; Supnithi et al., 1999):
- a group of people with their learning goals;
- the group structure;
- the tools that are available;
- the roles that take into account the learning tasks to be performed;
- the restrictions on the use of the system (all within a particular context and domain).

Figure 8-6 shows a general framework within which the ontology of collaborative learning is being developed. It is closely related to the OGF approach. Note that the ontology of collaborative learning spans all three levels shown in Figure 8-6, not only the middle one. The three levels merely indicate the grouping of concepts in the ontology, as well as areas of its potential links with other educational ontologies. In real collaborative learning scenarios, the concepts from all three levels are interrelated and/or interdependent (Barros et al., 2002).

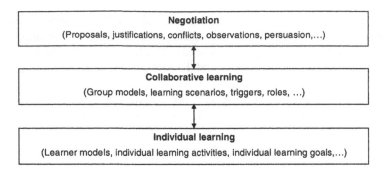

Figure 8-6. The overall framework for the concepts related to collaborative learning

Figure 8-7 depicts some of the top-level concepts in the ontology of collaborative learning, according to Supnithi et al. (1999). Its most important part is the ontology of learning goal, detailed in the next subsection. The concept of a *trigger* comes from OGF and denotes an event or a situation that triggers the CSCL system to initiate a shift from individual to collaborative learning mode for a specific learner. For example, the learner may run into a difficulty of grasping some topic individually (an *impasse*), or may have just completed a learning task that needs a collaborative review (*review*), or it is the corresponding learning design that requires a group of learners to solve a problem collaboratively at that point (*program*). Note also the various *roles* that a learner can take within a *learning group*.

In the extension introduced by Barros et al. (2002), the focus is on the *process* of collaborative learning, Figures 8-8 and 8-9. The concept of the *source of information*, Figure 8-8, is related to different kinds of data and information that CSCL systems can use to analyze various collaborative learning processes. It enables to represent the various states of the learning processes and the activities that the participants have performed individually and as a group. Some of these sources of information are of statistical nature, such as the *number of contributions*. Others can be inferred from statistical data and the system's built-in pedagogical knowledge, such as the *stage in the discussion* among the participants during collaborative problem solving. Both kinds are important in terms of the analysis of the contributions of individual group members to the group's success in solving the problem eventually, as well as in terms of enforcing a balanced participation.

Figure 8-9 shows parts of two concept hierarchies, the *learning goal* and the *learning task*. For the sake of simplicity, only one interdependency between the two hierarchies is indicated - the *task* label (shown in italic face in Figure 8-9a) specifies that the *reflection* ability is related to the *highlight*, *compare*, and *assess* tasks defined as parts of the *task* hierarchy. In other words, if a personal goal of a learner participating in a group is to improve his/her ability to reflect on a domain topic, then the learning tasks that the system should enforce for that particular learner are highlighting, assessment, and frequent comparison of his/her understanding of the topic with that of the peer learners.

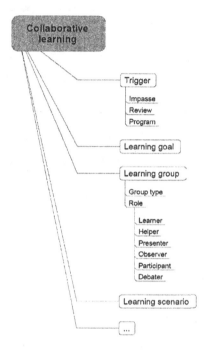

Figure 8-7. The ontology of collaborative learning (excerpt)

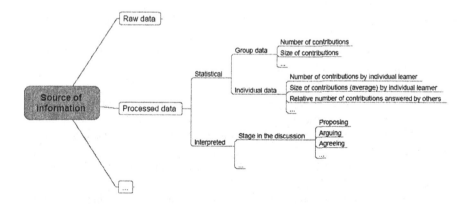

Figure 8-8. Various sources of information for conducting an analysis of the process of collaborative learning

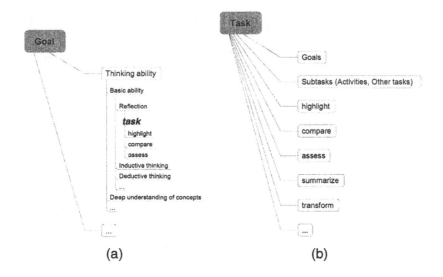

Figure 8-9. Collaborative learning ontology: (a) some concepts related to the *learning goal* (b) some concepts related to different learning tasks

It is important to stress another major problem in the overall organization of the ontology of collaborative learning - the vocabulary. Different learning theories use different terminologies to denote similar or identical concepts. Also, there are cases in which the same term is used in different theories to denote different concepts. For these reasons, various approaches are possible in conceptualizing the ontology of collaborative learning. As an illustration of these observations, consider the extension of the *Logical Framework Approach (LFA)* proposed by Santos et al. (2003). It defines the following four stages of the collaborative learning process:

- *interaction stage* - explaining the LFA methodology to the learners and acquiring useful data from the learners' interactions in order to automatically create the subgroups and select the moderator for each one;
- *individual stage* - each learner works alone to solve a problem put by the system;
- *collaboration stage* - accessing the other learners' solutions to the problem, giving comments, asking questions, and initiating a discussion in a forum, in order for each individual learner to possibly modify his/her own solution;
- *agreement stage* - reaching a consensus on a solution (it is the subgroup moderator that plays the crucial role here).

Furthermore, this extension of the LFA approach also proposes the following three roles for learners, regardless of whether they have been selected to be moderators or not:

- *individual working learner* - a learner who has reached his/her own solution to the problem in the individual stage for the first time, and still has no access to the other learners' solutions;
- *passive collaborating learner* - a learner who has reached his/her own solution, can access the individual solutions of the peers, but cannot modify his/her own solution yet or put a question to the forum;
- *active collaborating learner* - a learner who actively collaborates with the peers by rating their solutions, discussing them, and modifying his/her own solution.

Also, the LFA extension categorizes all students according to yet another criterion - their *reputation*, which is a combination of the values of different quantitative and qualitative indicators of their contributions. The categories have intuitively clear names: *participative learner, insightful learner, useful learner, non-collaborative learner, learner with initiative,* and *communicative learner.*

When the LFA extension is compared to the OGF approach, there are both similarities and differences. Moreover, Inaba and Mizoguchi define an entirely different set of roles for the participants to a collaborative learning session (2004): *anchored instructor, diagnoser, master, apprentice, observer, peer tutee, problem holder, panelist, client, peripheral participant, full participant, audience, peer tutor.* When developing the ontology of collaborative learning, it is necessary to take all of these terminological and other differences into account. Eventually, the developers should extract and represent common features of different issues, concepts, topics, and phenomena of collaborative learning in a unified way.

2.2.3 Learning goal ontology and negotiation ontology

The learning goal ontology represents the concepts related to the learners' goals in CSCL as discussed in section 2.1 - personal, interaction-supportive, and social. More specifically, it defines the following four kinds of goals (Inaba and Mizoguchi, 2004):
- *I-goal* - a personal goal of a learner participating in a CSCL session;
- *Y<=I-goal* - a goal of interaction among the learners in a group (an interaction-supportive goal);
- *W(A)-goal* - a goal of an activity of a learning group (a social goal);
- *W(L)-goal* - a learning goal of a learning group as a whole, or a goal of development of a learning community (also a social goal).

In addition, the learning goal ontology defines two characteristic roles associated with the Y<=I-goal:
- *I-role* - the role to attain a Y<=I-goal; a learner who plays the I-role (I-member) is expected to attain his/her I-goal by attaining the Y<=I-goal ("*I* will interact with you in order to attain *my* I-goal");

- *You-role* - the role of a partner of the I-member in a Y<=I-goal ("I will interact with *you* in order to attain my I-goal");

Table 8-1 exemplifies the four kinds of learning goals. All such examples have justifications in various learning theories. For example, the following assertion is quite obvious from the examples shown for Y<=I-goals: a learner is expected to achieve his/her I-goals through interaction with other learners in order to attain the specific Y<=I-goals shown. It is also clear that that Y<=I-goals can be parts of W(A)-goals. For example, "learning by teaching" can be a part of "a knowledgeable learner teaches something to a learner with poor knowledge". For further details and explanations, see (Inaba and Mizoguchi, 2004) and the resources cited in that paper.

Table 8-1. Examples of different kinds of learning goals

Goal type	Example
I-goal	- acquisition of content-specific knowledge
	- development of cognitive skill
Y<=I-goal	- learning by teaching
	- learning by observation
	- learning by self-expression
W(A)-goal	- a knowledgeable learner teaches something to a learner with poor knowledge
	- a newcomer learns something by his/her own practice
W(L)-goal	- knowledge sharing
	- creating a solution
	- spread of skills

The negotiation ontology is a system of concepts for modeling the negotiation process in collaborative learning. It includes concepts such as opinion exchange, persuasion, compromise, and agreement (Supnithi et al., 1999). It can be used in a SWBE CSCL system to, for example, support forming of a group of learners, and to support reaching a consensus among the participating learners on a group solution of a problem.

Supnithi et al. have proposed the structure of the negotiation ontology as in Figure 8-10. It is intended to support negotiation processes among pedagogical agents in the first place, and is easy to understand it through an example. Assume that an agent needs to *devise* (a kind of a *negotiation process*) a *proposal* (a *negotiation object*) for a collaborative learning activity that its owner (a learner) should perform. Such a situation may occur when the system notices a trigger such as an impasse for that particular learner. In such a case, the agent has to *send* (a *negotiation event*) a *call-for-participation* (a *negotiation message*) to other agents, asking them to communicate with their owners in order to establish a session with the learner who, in this case, has run into an impasse. Then another agent may send this agent a *reply* (another *negotiation message*), and the negotiation process may continue until an agreement is reached.

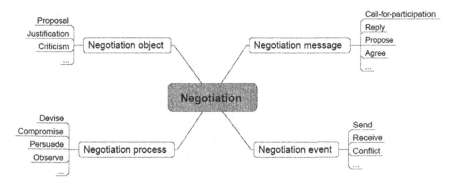

Figure 8-10. The negotiation ontology (excerpt)

2.2.4 Interactions and interaction patterns

Since various learning theories offer somewhat different conceptualizations and explanations of collaborative learning, Inaba et al. (2003a; 2003b) made an important step of establishing a shared understanding of the model of interactions among the participants in a collaborative learning session.

Establishing a shared understanding of a specific domain (interactions in the process of collaborative learning, in this case) is essentially an ontological engineering problem. Interactions among the learners are so much complex and diverse that their appropriate representation and tracking in a CSCL system necessitates a shared vocabulary and a thorough ontological analysis.

To construct a shared vocabulary, Inaba et al. proposed performing an expert analysis of various *utterances characterizing verbal interactions* among the learners in collaborative learning sessions. To analyze the process in terms of ontological engineering, they applied *interaction patterns* supported by various learning theories.

The idea of analyzing verbal interactions among the learners in order to extract a shared vocabulary can be elaborated as follows. Instances of verbal interactions can be collected from learners' sessions with CSCL systems. Based on multiple learning theories and expert suggestions, the collected instances can be subsequently refined into a set of slightly more general, but still rather concrete utterances[52]. This set represents the vocabulary at the concrete level (see the right column in Table 8-2).

Table 8-2. Examples of generic and concrete utterances (adapted from (Inaba et al., 2003b))

Generic	Concrete
Knowledge transfer	Teaching his/her knowledge
	Showing the group's knowledge
	Showing his/her knowledge
	Asking for opinion about his/knowledge
Showing a way to solve a problem	Showing the way in which the group is trying to solve a problem
	Showing his/her way to solve a problem
	Expressing his/her opinion about a problem
	Expressing his/her opinion about a problem the group is trying to solve
	Expressing his/her opinion about another learner's way to solve a problem

On the other hand, to characterize learning sessions in general, a more generic (more abstract) vocabulary is needed. Learning theories and expert opinions help here again - related concrete utterances are grouped under common, more generic utterances[53] (see the left column in Table 8-2). As a consequence, each generic utterance has an associated hierarchal tree (a semantic cluster) of concrete utterances. The generic utterances represent the vocabulary at the abstract level.

Interaction patterns can be extracted by analyzing interaction logs. Log data are first grouped into a set of sequences representing concrete interaction "episodes". Subsequently, log data sequences are labeled with the vocabulary terms representing concrete utterances, and are then converted into sequences of the related abstract/generic utterance terms. The generated sequences are instances of various types of interactions among the learners[54]. Eventually, common and distinct interaction patterns can be recognized and extracted from the transformed sequences. To find good candidates for interaction patterns, one can apply heuristics such as:

• some log data sequences are frequently observed in a session, or in multiple sessions;

• some log data sequences represent the characteristics of the session well;

• most of experts label certain parts of log data sequences using similar concrete utterances.

An example of a pattern extracted this way is shown in Figure 8-11. It is an interaction pattern of cognitive-apprenticeship type of collaborative

---

[52] Inaba et al. (2003b) call them utterance labels.
[53] Inaba et al. (2003b) call them utterance types.
[54] These types of interaction are explained in theories of collaborative learning.

learning (Collins, 1991). The pattern shows the generic utterances (boxes) and transitions between them.

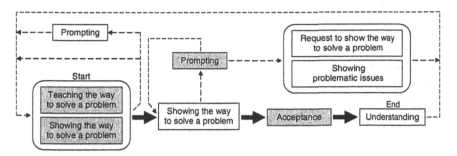

Figure 8-11. An example interaction pattern (adapted from (Inaba et al., 2003b)); gray boxes represent the master's utterances, whereas white boxes represent the apprentice's utterances; solid arrows represent the necessary transitions, and dashed arrows represent desired transitions

Patterns like this one are used to specify the parts of the ontology of collaborative learning related to interactions among the learners during collaborative learning sessions.

2.2.5   Applications

There are several ways to use the ontology of collaborative learning and related ontologies to improve the design of CSCL environments for the Semantic Web. Some of them are already implemented in the CSCL environment called DEGREE (Barros et al., 2002):

- *Workspace design.* Recall that, according to the activity theory, the role of technology in CSCL is that of a mediator for representing various activities of a learning group. The ontology of collaborative learning includes the concept of *mediation tool*. The workspace designer uses an authoring tool that shows him/her the hierarchy of concepts related to various mediation tools. For example, he/she can select (from the ontology) *conversational structure* as a mediation tool, and design the workspace in terms of *proposals, questions, agreements,* and other similar conversational tools for CSCL (represented as sub-concepts of the *conversational structure* concept). Alternatively, the designer may select *visual languages* and structure the workspace in terms of graphical components such as *icons* and *images* to enable more graphically oriented contributions and interactions among the learners when solving a problem collaboratively.
- *Specification of collaborative learning scenarios.* Interaction patterns built into the ontology of collaborative learning are useful sources of

knowledge about learning design for CSCL. Instructional designers can use the ontology in order to specify their preferred designs starting from theory-supported interaction patterns.

- *Analysis and assessment of collaboration.* These activities rely on log data related to the learners' contributions and the problem-solving actions that they have performed during CSCL sessions. By processing these raw data according to various assessment criteria, interesting conclusions can be drawn about the types and quality of collaboration. The ontology of collaborative learning helps organize this assessment process by specifying the set of raw data that can be used in the analysis (see, for example, Figure 8-8).

3.   LEARNING COMMUNITIES AND THE SEMANTIC WEB

Informally, an online *learning community* is a community of online practitioners - learners, teachers, instructors, staff developers, facilitators, and trainers - who could learn from each other. Members of such a community can be from different backgrounds: education, business, industry, etc. They can be individuals or groups.

Learning communities tend to be organized around particular topics of (common) interest, or the practices they are concerned with, or the learning tasks they perform (Stutt and Motta, 2004). Community members fulfill different roles and enter into a variety of relations with each other. Members can belong to more than one community or group.

The members of an online learning community can take various courses, access various LOs and LORs, and use various WBE tools. However, to maintain and further improve their sense of belonging to a specific learning community, the online courseware should be designed in a way that supports equal participation of all members and stimulates active engagement in the activities of the community. In other words, it is essential to provide enough *support* for the community members, both individually and as a group, in terms of their activities, goals, shared visions, and open communication.

One of the key characteristics of an online learning community is the existence of shared learning goals. In essence, the learners in such a community collaborate (e.g. write proposals, ask questions, and exchange solutions, experiences, and opinions) in pursuing their common goals. Thus learning in an online learning community is, in a way, a natural extension of CSCL.

The Semantic Web can support these communities in a variety of ways. The most obvious one is that of providing ontologies that form the underlying knowledge foundation for the community as a whole. The most relevant kinds of ontologies in the context of learning communities are ontologies of learning communities, community structures, member roles, relations, topics, tasks, practices, and so on. Note that learning communities are relatively circumscribed. This fact reduces the problems of formulating and negotiating about the relevant ontologies, and reaching a community consensus eventually. Providing global ontologies from outside of a learning community can greatly increase the risk of failure in accepting them by the community members.

Another way the Semantic Web can support learning communities is related to the Semantic Web services. The Semantic Web already provides full technological support for developing such services. On the other hand, the members of a learning community typically care that their community is further built, maintained, and flourishes (Stutt and Motta, 2004). Thus they can use the Semantic Web service technology to provide a range of services to assist their community. For example, they may be interested in developing intelligent search services for topic-related information. Likewise, members of a learning community typically have greater motivation than other Web users to annotate Web documents of importance to their community with ontologies relevant to the community.

The Semantic Web technology also supports development of a semantic portal that can provide a single point of access to most of the resources of interest for a learning community. Efforts are already underway to develop Semantic Web support for learning and training organizations. As in all other aspects of SWBE, personalization of learning experiences plays an important role within learning communities as well.

3.1   The learners' needs in learning communities

An important objective of each learning process is enabling learners to make sense of the topics, practices, LOs, courses, and other resources, in terms of seeing some *structure* eventually (Laurillard, 2002). In other words, they need to see something (a theory, a concept, a meaning, and the like) emerging as a whole from the elements of learning experiences. Furthermore, they need to see that whole in relation with other ideas and theories. They also have to be able to apply the knowledge they have acquired, in various scholarly, social, economic, job, and political contexts.

Learning communities provide learners a social context for obtaining advice and guidance; critical opinions on their activities and achievements; tips on how to pass examinations; peer-to-peer and learner-to-teacher communication; someone to talk to when problems arise; and help with reading and interpreting multimedia LOs.

In SWBE, these needs of learners and learning communities are addressed as follows (Stutt and Motta, 2004):
•   learning is community-related, rather than generic;
•   learning communities provide contextualized learning, linked to specific separable locations on the Semantic Web;
•   the body of knowledge and learning material relevant for the community is annotated with appropriate ontologies and can be navigated using specific Semantic Web access tools;
•   the learning material is highly structured in terms of pedagogy and learning design;
•   the pedagogical structures and various content types (such as narratives, illustrations, examples, explanations, arguments, and analogies) can be visualized using ontology-supported graphical representations;
•   LOs relevant for the community are interlinked and are also linked to further learning resources;
•   interpretation is facilitated by the contextual knowledge these objects provide.

3.2   The vision of semantic learning webs

Stutt and Motta further elaborate (2004) their ideas on fulfillment of learners' needs by envisioning a number of specialized *semantic learning webs*, related to various learning communities. They argue that the Semantic Web as a global network of knowledge that can be used by personal agents is still out of reach, because the knowledge representation in such a huge network lacks context. Instead, it looks more likely that in a foreseeable future there will be a multiplicity of smaller-size, community-based semantic learning webs. Each semantic learning web will rely on its own community's perpetually changing ontologies, knowledge bases, repositories, and ways of making sense of the world.

In this vision, a learning community is supposed to build its ontologies and LOs on its own (using its preferred and possibly domain-specific tools), annotate the LOs, and publish and deliver them through community-controlled LORs and educational servers. Such ontologically supported community knowledge is called a *knowledge chart*.

Conceptual, taxonomical, and graphical representation of a knowledge chart as a whole is an important new resource for learning. There is a need for an ontology of knowledge chart, in order to represent different types of knowledge included in knowledge charts (such as *debate*, *story*, *analogy*, *claim*, *argument*, and *causal model*). A separate ontology is also needed for each type of knowledge, as well as means of expressing the pedagogic purpose of these charts.

Knowledge neighborhoods are locations on the Web where communities collaborate to create and use representations of their knowledge (knowledge charts). Knowledge neighborhoods are an important means of contextualizing knowledge charts. This is a critical issue, because current LO descriptions and LORs include no ontological information about how LOs should be interpreted in different ways in different contexts. Knowledge neighborhoods provide appropriate community-controlled tools for community members to:

- create and maintain ontologies of interest to the community;
- produce and annotate documents in the way that reflects the common interests of the community members; cooperation and collaboration of community emmbers is essential here;
- perform semantic search and retrieval of documents annotated with terms form community ontologies;
- browse relevant Web pages and documents using semantic browsers; as a user reads a document, such a semantic browser automatically highlights portions of the text which it can assist with, relying on community ontologies and annotations provided;
- portals and Web services to access, publish, and update documents of interest.

Using community-controlled tools to actively access, browse, and process knowledge charts actively is called *knowledge navigation*. Examples of such tools are Semantic Web browsers, such as Magpie (see, Chapter 2, section 2.3).

3.3 Learning portals

From a Web user's perspective, a Web portal is a Web site or service that provides a single point of access to aggregated information of interest to the user. A Web portal usually offers a broad array of resources and services, such as e-mail, forums, search engines, personalization, and on-line shopping.

Web portals are increasingly employed as a means to meet an organization's knowledge management and knowledge access needs. Such *knowledge portals* make available to knowledge workers all the pieces of information they need to access, and all the knowledge applications and resources they need to use (Devedžić, 2005b). Knowledge portals are useful because an organization's knowledge resources may be plentiful, but difficult, costly, and time-consuming to locate. Knowledge portals provide means to capture and share the expertise of more experienced knowledge workers, and integrate it into a single source for learning, performance support, and ongoing knowledge sharing needs of novices.

A *community Web portal* (or just a *community portal*) is an Internet platform for communication and provision of information services to a particular Web community, and possibly to a more general public as well (Staab et al., 2000). Conceptually, a community portal can be seen as a kind of knowledge portal focusing on topics of interest for a specific community.

Learning portals combine features of knowledge portals and community portals by specifically addressing the issue of online learning. A learning community can use a learning portal to build and share its knowledge, in terms of constantly posting and processing information there, and transforming the information into improved practices. A learning portal typically serves as a doorway to an LMS, i.e. it often uses an LMS as its basis. More specifically, a learning portal is the interface that allows learners to locate content, track their progress towards their learning/training goals, and interact with other learners and teachers.

Essential value-added services of learning portals include learning management capabilities, learner assessment and tracking, communities of interest, learning content authoring and upload, and the extension of learning to an organization's value chain (Barron, 2000). From the perspective of higher-education, learning portals also provide access to high-quality courseware.

Learning portals can rely on various learning resources and tools. There is a wide spectrum of possibilities here in terms of focus, variety and availability of resources, the resource formats supported, pricing, access rights, and privacy and copyright management. As an illustration, consider the GEM portal[55], Figure 8-12. Its catalog contains detailed descriptions of over 40,000 educational resources found on various federal, state, university, non-profit, and commercial Internet sites in USA (GEM, 2006). Access to the resources is easy - typically, a user enters a keyword to search for desired resources, but can then refine the search by a number of filters, such as subject, course, and lesson plan. Resources are entered in GEM by collection holders - organizations that have collections of educational materials enter their materials they want to be available from the portal. The portal also provides a freely available set of tools that collection holders can use to prepare descriptions of their educational resources to be included in the GEM portal.

Various learning portals also address other specific issues of interest to individual learners and learning communities, such as:
- learners mobility and access to adaptive content and services from anywhere and anytime;
- personalization of the content, services, and interface;
- support for differences in curricula;

[55] http://www.thegateway.org/

- support for blended mode of education (a mixture of distance and face-to-face education);
- different needs of each learner, their various backgrounds, and the variety of courses they follow;
- creation and hosting of multiple communities, since a learner can simultaneously belong to various communities: institutional, cultural, organizational, sports, etc.;
- facilities to introduce and assign roles to various learners in a community;
- flexible collaborative learning options;
- tools for learners to control the organization of their activities (e.g. timetables), and the conditions under which they are to be performed;
- integration of the portal with the rest of the information infrastructure of an educational institution.

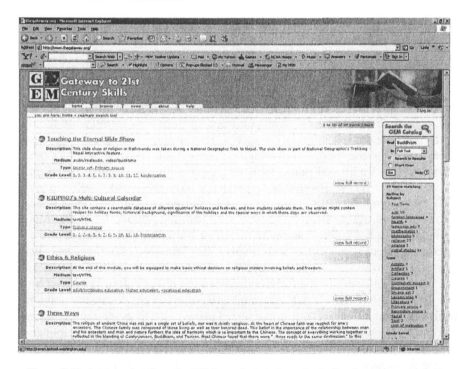

Figure 8-12. A screenshot from the GEM portal - search results (online learning resources) for the term "Buddhism"

By introducing the Semantic Web technology into learning portals, we get *semantic learning portals*. These can reason about the semantics of learning resources; search for relevant LOs and other information more efficiently by exploiting explicit semantic information; and extract, rate and combine information resources in an advanced manner (Brunkhorst and Henze, 2005). Also, semantic learning portals can provide user-adapted, personalized views on the learning resources during the retrieval, selection and presentation processes.

Semantic learning portals provide a learning community with:

- ontologies of interest to the community, so that members can contribute information and news to the portal in a consistent manner;
- advanced search and navigation capabilities, based on the properties and classification of information items and relationships between them (represented in accordance with the portal's ontologies and possibly external ones);
- automatic reasoning about the semantic descriptions of the learning resources available, with respect to the ontologies available from the portal;
- personalization of learning experiences, based on information retrieved from learner models;
- means for members to grasp easily if other users are currently interested in similar information/topic, or whether users with same interests are around;
- facilities for effective collaboration between the community members.

A research challenge for semantic learning portals is to integrate them with tools that exploit information such as relationships between the entities represented in the portal's ontologies. These tools can be much more effective than traditional portal tools that work only with content based on generic text or HTML. Brunkhorst and Henze have presented (2005) such a tool that exemplifies how ontology-based information can be used (albeit their tool need not necessarily be used with learning portals only). The tool includes a Flash Applet, running on the client browser, which can retrieve a document from the portal and display its *browsing distance* and its *professional distance* as radar-screen animations, Figure 8-13. Essentially, the browsing distance is the distance between the pages currently viewed by the users of the portal ("Look how similar is your current document/activity to that of another learner"). It is calculated using an RDF graph representing the current browsing sessions of the portal users, based on the portal domain ontologies. Every resource in the RDF graph, represents a Web page currently viewed by a user of the portal. The browsing distance is then calculated as the shortest path in the graph between the resources representing pages currently viewed by the users of the portal. The algorithm for calculating the professional distance of a document uses a graph representing the authenticated users. For example, learners taking the same course are grouped closer together than those taking different courses.

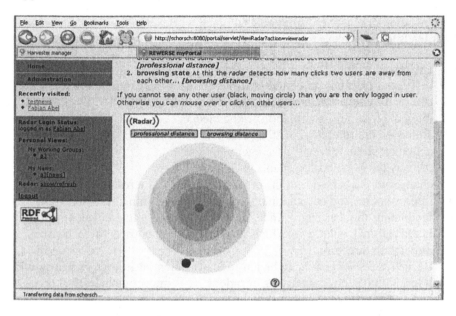

Figure 8-13. Radar-screen representation of a browsing/professional distance of a document
accessible through the REWERSE portal (http://personal-reader.de:8080/portal/)

Of course, in order for the browsing and professional distances to be
meaningful, it is necessary for a semantic learning portal to implement some
kind of user modeling (authentication). This enables the portal to map the
user to an appropriate node in the user ontology, and to relate the pages
visited to the corresponding users.

3.4   Semantic learning organizations

One form of development and organization of learning communities
stems from practical needs of knowledge management in companies and
institutions. Employees in such an organization need to learn and adopt the
organization's knowledge, expressed in the form of various procedures,
rules, work processes, behavior codes, and others means of shared
representation. In some cases, adopting this knowledge may require
considerable effort and/or training (e.g., in nursery and administration),
especially for less experienced employees or novices. However, such an
effort is worth taking since, by enabling its employees to acquire the
necessary knowledge, an organization raises its competency.

Organizational learning is a set of actual learning activities or processes
inside an organization. It is the process by which an organization acquires
the knowledge necessary to survive and compete in its environment. An

organization that actively supports and practices development of knowledge that leads to effective action and fosters sharing of that knowledge among its employees, is called a *learning organization*.

Organizational learning inside a learning organization includes:

- individual learning, as employees interact with the external environment or experiment to create new information or knowledge;
- integration of new information or knowledge;
- collective interpretation of all available information;
- action based on this collective interpretation;
- the way the organization adapts to changes;
- changes in the behavior of the organization itself as a result of learning;
- improvements and adaptation of organizational learning behavior itself;
- facilitating the learning of individuals by supporting the development of organizational culture in which managers are supposed to be coaches, rather than directors.

Recently, researchers have begun to study potential impact of Semantic Web technologies on learning organizations. This impact includes, but is not limited to, the following (Sicilia and Lytras, 2005):

- linking of individual learning plans with the goals of the organization, mediated through ontologies of competency (see Figure 8-12 later in this subsection) that define assessment and evaluation procedures, gathering of evidence, and job roles;
- representing job situations, episodes, and activities in ontologies, in order to enable checking that the learning outcomes are actually put into practice;
- representing individual learning styles as part of the ontologies, so that the selection of learning experiences takes them into account;
- deploying pedagogical agents to mediate LO selection according to the needs of the organization and the knowledge gap to be covered;
- facilitating teamwork through semantic P2P technologies.

In addition, Semantic Web technologies should be applied not only to enhance learning processes, but as a purposeful tool to drive changes in the learning behavior of the organization as a result of changes in the individuals. This creates a vision of what Sicilia and Lytras call a *semantic learning organization*. For example, in a semantic learning organization the notion of employee feedback can be represented in an ontology. This ontology can be used as the basis for feedback gathering and drawing conclusions about the specific climate in work units. These, in turn, can indicate new or modified needs for organizational learning. Likewise, changes in the business environment can be detected through changes in product and services offerings. These can create awareness of the need for new forms of organizational learning. The changes can be detected using business intelligence tools that deploy ontologies to have a coherent view of the environment.

In order for semantic learning organizations to become a reality, it is necessary to develop assessment tools that help figure out the current learning behavior of the organization. Such tools should enable analysis of the volume, effectiveness and efficiency of the current learning processes in the organization, as well as the employees' satisfaction with these processes. However, it is still a research challenge to develop a tool or a set of tools that supports these kinds of analysis.

The first step towards semantic learning organizations is the development of specific ontologies that support this idea. Sicilia has developed the *ontology of competency*, Figure 8-14, that models the notion of competency in the context of job situations and environments. The ontology is based on a number of industrial efforts and standardization activities in the domain of representing and exchanging data about competencies.

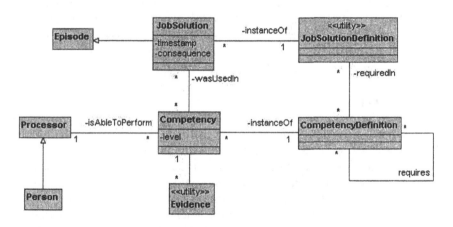

Figure 8-14. Ontology of competency (after (Sicilia, 2006))

Note that this ontology models competencies as characteristics of an abstract *Processor*, thus taking into account not only people, but also software systems that can exhibit some competencies (the *isAbleToPerform* relationship). Typically, a job situation requires a number of competencies, and a competency can be used in multiple job situations (hence multiple cardinality on both ends of the *wasUsedIn* relationship). For both competencies and job situations, the ontology includes their respective "definition" elements. These concepts are aimed at representing stereotypical competencies and job contexts, for example to describe project roles or company positions. Competencies can be "nested" - a competency may depend on previously acquiring one or more other competencies. This is represented with the *requires* relationship of the *CompetencyDefinition* concept. For example, the competency for work in administration may require proficiency with MS Office tools.

4.   PERSONALIZED EDUCATIONAL SERVICES

When a learner wants to interact with a LO through a SWBE environment, the LO has to be displayed (i.e., a LO *reader* has to be used), and hopefully accompanied with personalized, context-aware information. This information may include recommendations about additional readings, exercises, alternative views, the learning objectives, applications where this learning content is relevant, etc.

Educational Web services provide means for implementing such *personal LO readers* - various personalization functionalities can be implemented as services, and orchestrated by a mediator service (Henze, 2005b; Henze and Herrlich, 2004). In addition, another group of services must be applied to take care of visualization and device-adaptation aspects of LO presentation. The learners should be able to select and customize personalization services to suit their needs.

4.1   Architecture

In the Personal Reader project (Henze and Herrlich, 2004), various kinds of Web services are developed and interconnected (in the way shown in Figure 8-15) in order to implement a personal LO reader. The user can select between various personalization and visualization services in order to make a Personal Reader instance that best suits him/her. The services themselves communicate by exchanging RDF documents. All courses, learning resources, and users are supposed to be described in RDF files. For example, each learner model is represented as an RDF file, using properties with self-explanatory names, such as *takesCourse*, *hasVisited*, and *done*. Likewise, courses are described in RDF files that use properties such as *name*, *startPage*, *ontology* (specifies the location of the domain ontology that describes the subject domain concepts and their relations), and *location* (specifies the URL of external RDF file that contain descriptions of the learning resource, i.e., the course). Different descriptions may exist for the same set of learning resources, i.e., different courses can be based on the same learning resources. In that case, an RDF file for each course should be created (containing the course profile), and its URL should be stored as the value of the *location* property. Individual resources are described using the

Dublin Core and IEEE LOM standards, as well as terms from various domain ontologies.

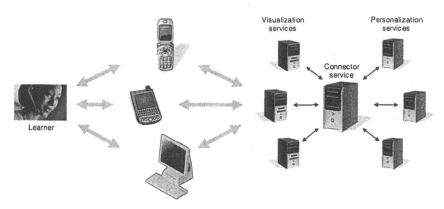

Figure 8-15. Service architecture for personal LO readers (after (Henze and Herrlich, 2004))

The services operate as follows. When a learner clicks on a link, an appropriate RDF request is generated and sent to the visualization service corresponding to the learner's presentation device. This service passes the request to the Connector service, along with additional adaptation information describing the learner's presentation context. The Connector service forwards the request to all personalization services in the learner's Personal Reader instance. Simultaneously, the Connector service searches for the learner's profile, currently visited page, and course description, in order to enable adaptation of the results to the learner. When personalization services return results (in the form of RDF descriptions), the Connector service passes them to the visualization services for adaptation and presentation. All RDF descriptions passed between the various services are understood by the services via the *ontology of adaptive functionality*, specifically developed to support personal LO readers.

Personalization services in Personal Reader instances are similar to the concept of value-adding services depicted in Figure 8-1.

4.2 Authoring and annotation

Authoring is a critical issue here. All learning resources, course descriptions, domain ontologies, and user profiles *must* be annotated according to existing standards and ontologies. Personalization services can then reason about these learning resources, course descriptions, etc. (Henze, 2005b).

Different personalization services consider different aspects in the metadata. For example, a personalization service can calculate recommendations for a LO based on the structure of the learning materials in some course and the user's navigation history. Another service can check for keywords that describe the learning objectives of LOs and calculate recommendations based on relations in the corresponding domain ontology.

Personal Reader instances are created using a specific component of the user interface. The interface enables the user to customize personalization services, add new ones, and specify any of the previously annotated LOs, courses, and learning materials to be used at runtime by the personalization services.

4.3   Examples of personalization services

A typical personalization service is the service for recommending LOs. It can use various heuristics for making recommendations, such as:
- *More specific LO after a more general one.* A LO is recommended if the learner has studied at least one more general (upper-level) LO. The system must consult the learner model in order to make this kind of recommendation. "More general" is determined according to the course ontology.
- *More specific LO after all more general ones.* This is similar to the previous case, but it requires the learner to study *all* more general LOs first.
- *Keyword-based recommendation.* A LO is recommended according to the keywords from a domain ontology that describe its objectives.

Note, however, that using a specific strategy may also depend on the learning context. For example, the keyword-based recommendation may be appropriate if the learner wants to use materials from different courses at the same time. On the other hand, recommendation based on a detailed description of a course structure is usually more accurate than other recommendations within a single course.

Another personalization service also deals with contextual information - a LO presentation can be enriched with the context in which the LO appears in a course (Henze, 2005b). Here the context can be described in terms of the overall learning objectives, the LO topic, and the LO content details. To this end, strategies such as the following two can be used to determine the context:
- *Following the course structure.* The course structure may be specified in a hierarchy of sections, subsections, etc. The hierarchy, if available, can be used to specify the basic context.

- *Ontology-based context specification.* Key concepts of the LO and its details can be determined with respect to the domain ontology. The ontology can be used to check for various *is-a*, *part-of*, and other relationships between the LO concepts.

5.   REPRESENTING LEARNER'S PERSONALITY

Subjective information in learner modeling, as discussed in Chapter 6, section 2, roughly corresponds to the learner's cognitive and whole-person traits, for example his/her working-memory capacity and inductive-reasoning capability. It complements the other (objective) information in the learner model, such as the learner's background knowledge, learning performance, preferred learning style, and learning history (Jeremić et al., 2005).

Many researchers agree that modeling and using learner's individual traits in the learner model is important for SWBE. This importance comes from the need to enable a learning system to predict the learner's response to various LOs, suggested learning activities, and assignments. However, there is little agreement on what subjective information exactly could and should be used, and how to use it.

Pedagogical agents can be deployed to track learners' behaviors that indirectly reflect their cognitive and other personal traits. Moreover, they can perform intelligent reasoning with the data they track, and use the inferences they make to guide the adaptation of the learning process.

5.1   Assessing emotional intelligence and cognitive traits online

In a recently proposed approach (Damjanović et al., 2005), it has been suggested that adaptivity and personalization of a learning experience can be achieved by modeling and using learners' traits such as:
- personality factors (extrovert, introvert);
- cognitive factors (perceptual processing, phonological awareness, ability to maintain focus of attention);
- learning styles (moving, touching, doing, auditory, visual);
- personality types (conventional, social, investigative, artistic, realistic, and enterprising personality).

Many of these characteristics are also studied in the field of *emotional intelligence*. Emotional intelligence (EQ) represents an essential factor of effective communication and adaptability, especially in the field of education. Emotionally and socially intelligent learners can overcome difficulties more easily and can reduce negative behaviors.

These characteristics can be initially extracted by having the learners take specifically designed psychological tests, conducted by a distributed multiagent system acting as a test-sensor system. It is also possible to define learner stereotypes based on the values of these characteristics. In later stages, tracking specific behaviors of the learners can help adjust their characteristics and possibly make the stereotypes more accurate.

In fact, SWBE systems make perfect environments for measuring EQ skills and can suggest new ideas for practicing these skills; over time and through such practice, learners can further develop their EQ skills. To this end, pedagogical agents can be deployed to conduct the activities shown in the loop depicted in Figure 8-16.

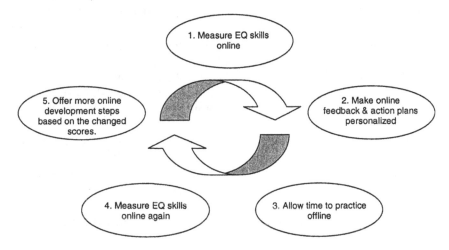

Figure 8-16. Supporting development of EQ skills

The key to making the above loop work is to find out what manifestations of the learner's behavior to track online, and how to convert the collected data to indicators of cognitive traits and EQ skills. Starting from studies in the psychology of computer users and in human-computer interaction, various manifestations can be defined for each specific trait (Jeremić et al., 2005). Each such a manifestation indicates (indirectly) a learner's characteristic. For example, Huai has found (2000) that learners who prefer linear navigation through the course material tend to have higher working-memory capacities. Thus if an agent detects linear navigation pattern in the learner's interaction, it can infer that the learner has a high working-memory capacity. Similar indirect indicators exist for the values of other traits.

Pedagogical agents can combine data from learner interaction logs with appropriate inference rules to detect indicators of the learner's traits. The inference rules can help the agents to make conclusions about the learner's personality. These conclusions, in turn, can partially drive the adaptation and personalization of the learning process. This kind of adaptation and personalization, based on the observations about the learner's cognitive traits and emotional intelligence, nicely complements the one that relies on the learner's performance, style, background, and so on.

As an illustration, assume that a SWBE system is developed for conducting online experiments for training purposes. Assume further that participation in a certain online experiment OE_i requires a learner L_j to have an artistic personality with introverted perception. It follows from psychological research that such a personality type is highly correlated with the concepts such as *inner world*, *ideas*, *images*, *memories*, *reflection*, and *depth*. If it is possible for the system to observe one or more such correlations for a learner (e.g., by indirect manifestations of his/her behavior, or by having him/her fill a questionnaire), then the system can infer his/her personality type using a rule such as:

$\forall OE_i \forall L_j$
observe(OE_i, L_j, inner_world) $\lor$
observe(OE_i, L_j, ideas) $\lor$
observe(OE_i, L_j, images) $\lor$
observe(OE_i, L_j, memories) $\lor$
observe(OE_i, L_j, reflection) $\lor$
observe(OE_i, L_j, depth)
$\Rightarrow$ type(OE_i, L_j, artistic_personality)

5.2   Personality-based adaptivity

It is desirable for the system to perform adaptation of the learning process based on inferences such as the one shown in the above rule, and simultaneously relying on an *ontology of adaptation*. This ontology is similar to the ontology of adaptive functionality used by personal LO readers, mentioned in section 4.2. However, it also includes concepts of learner's personality, such as cognitive and emotional traits.

More specifically, subjective information about a learner in his/her learner model can be represented in accordance with the ontology of adaptation. The part of the ontology that characterizes the learner's personality may include the personality stereotype, various specific personality factors, cognitive factors, EQ factors, and learning styles. Note that the learner type (e.g., schoolchild, college student, and expert) must also be used in adaptation strategies (and hence must be included in the ontology of adaptation), but is not considered a personality characteristic[56]. An example instance of the ontology of adaptation, simplified for the sake of clarity, may look like this:

type: *expert*
personality category: *introverted*
personality stereotype: *artistic personality*
working-memory capacity: *high*
inductive-reasoning capability: *high*
focus of attention: *medium*
learning style: *visual*
...

Using these characteristics, pedagogical agents arranging for adaptive presentation of content to the learner can achieve results better than when using just the learner's performance and historical data. The challenge is to develop and implement a robust adaptation strategy, such as FOSP (Kravcik, 2004)[57], that enables to include personality characteristics easily. However, a prerequisite for using personality characteristics is an appropriate additional annotation of LOs with personality-related terms from the ontology of adaptation.

6.   SUMMARY

As practical applications of the SWBE technology gradually take off, further efforts are needed to speed up the acceptance and widespread use of the SWBE technology. The major challenges are related to the issue of integrating SWBE with the mainstream e-Learning technology, such as LMSs and training applications. To this end, architectures are proposed for intelligent LMSs. Likewise, the need is identified for creating specific tools and methods for ontology management (e.g., modification, extension, and pruning of existing ontologies) since SWBE necessitates ontology-based learning and training applications.

A difficult and complex problem in SWBE is to develop ontological support for collaborative learning. Due to the complexity of interactions between the learners in a group and various objectives of collaboration, it is

---

[56] Likewise, adaptation certainly depends on the device type (for instance, PC and PDA), but it is not considered here in the context of learner's personality.

[57] The FOSP strategy is based on a pattern identified in the adaptation process. The pattern includes four generic operations: Filter (select candidate LOs based on a certain criterion), Order (sort the selected LOs according to the criterion), Select (choose the LO with the highest value), and Present (display the selected LO). See (Kravcik, 2004) for details.

very difficult to develop the ontology of collaborative learning. Other ontologies are needed for collaborative SWBE as well, such as the learning goal ontology and the negotiation ontology. Likewise, further study of the patterns in learners' interactions is necessary if they are to be used as a theoretical basis for the ontology of collaborative learning.

Semantic Web technologies are also a key factor in further development of learning communities. There is a vision that further development of SWBE will take the form of developing a number of small-size, community-based semantic learning webs, rather than building SWBE applications for the Web as a whole. Another specific use of Semantic Web technologies within learning communities is related to semantic learning organizations. These are related to supporting knowledge management and organizational learning in various organizations and institutions.

There is a number of other emerging applications and research issues in SWBE, such as personalized educational services, representation of whole-person factors in learner models, and personality-based adaptivity. A common denominator in all these issues is further improvement of learner-centered design of SWBE.

References

Abdullah, N.A., and Davis, H.C., 2005, A real-time personalization service for SCORM, in: *Proceedings of the Fifth IEEE International Conference on Advanced Learning Technologies (ICALT'05)*, P. Goodyear, D. Sampson, D. Jin-Tan Yang, Kinshuk, T., Okamoto, R., Hartley, and N.-S. Chen, eds., Kaohsiung, Taiwan, pp. 61-63.

ACM CCS, 1998, The ACM Computing Classification System – 1998 Version, Valid in 2006 (January 26, 2006); http://www.acm.org/class/1998/.

ADL SCORM, 2004, Sharable Content Object Reference Model (SCORM) 2004, 2nd Edition Overview (December 27, 2005); http://www.adlnet.org/scorm/history/2004/index.cfm.

Alpert, S.R., Singley, M.K., and Fairweather, P.G., 1999, Deploying intelligent tutors on the Web: an architecture and an example, *International Journal of Artificial Intelligence in Education* **10**:183-197.

Anderson, T., and Wason, T., 2000, IMS Learning Resource Meta-data Information Model, Version 1.1 - Final Specification (December 10, 2005); http://www.imsproject.org/metadata/mdinfov1p1.html.

Anderson, T., and Whitelock, D., 2004, The Educational Semantic Web: visioning and practicing the future of education, *Journal of Interactive Media in Education (JIME)*, 2004(7):1-15.

Andriessen, J., Baker, M., and Suthers, D., eds., 2003, *Arguing to Learn: Confronting Cognitions in Computer-Supported Collaborative Learning Environments*, Kluwer, Dordrecht.

Anido, L., Llamas, M., Fernández, M.J., Caeiro, M., Santos, J. and Rodríguez, J., 2001, A component model for standardized Web-based education, in: *Proceedings of The Tentth International World Wide Web Conference*, Hong Kong (December 08, 2005); http://www10.org/cdrom/papers/106/.

Apted, T., and Kay, J., 2002, Automatic construction of learning ontologies, in: *Proceedings of The ICCE Workshop on Concepts and Ontologies in Web-based Educational Systems*, L. Aroyo and D. Dicheva, eds., Auckland, New Zealand, pp. 57-64.

Apted, T., Kay, J., and Lum, A., 2004, Supporting metadata creation with an ontology built from an extensible dictionary, in: *Proceedings of the Adaptive Hypermedia Conference 2004*, LNCS 3137, W. Nejdl and P. De Bra, eds., Eindhoven, The Netherlands, Springer-Verlag, Berlin/Heidelberg, pp. 4–13.

ARIADNE, 2004, Ariadne Foundation for the European Knowledge Pool (November 18, 2005); http://www.ariadne-eu.org/.

Aroyo, L., and Dicheva, D., 2004a, The new challenges for e-Learning: The Educational Semantic Web, *Educational Technology and Society* 7(4):59-69.

Aroyo, L., and Dicheva, D., 2004b, Authoring support in concept-based Web information systems for educational applications, *International Journal of Continuous Engineering Education and Lifelong Learning* 14(3):297-312.

Aroyo, L. and Mizoguchi, R., 2003, Authoring support framework for intelligent educational systems, in: *Shaping the Future of Learning through Intelligent Technologies* (*Proceedings of the 11th Conference on Artificial Intelligence in Education*, Sydney, Australia), U. Hoppe, F. Verdejo, and J. Kay, eds., pp.362-364.

Azouaou, F., Chen, W., and Desmoulins, C., 2004, Semantic annotation tools for learning material, in: *Proceedings of The International Workshop on Applications of Semantic Web Technologies for E-Learning*, SW-EL@AH04, P. Dolog, M. Wolpers, L. Aroyo, and D. Dicheva, eds., Eindhoven, The Netherlands (January 26, 2006); http://www.win.tue.nl/SW-EL/2004/AH-SWEL-Camera-ready/SWEL04-AH-PDF/%234-Azouaou-Desmoulins-Weiqin-SWEL-AH.pdf.

Barkai, D., 2000, An introduction to peer-to-peer computing, *Intel Developer UPDATE Magazine* (February 2000):1-7.

Barker, P., Cross, P., Fernandez, A., Hardy, S., Jewell, N., Poulter, M., and Powell, A., 2003, RDN/LTSN Resource Type Vocabulary, Version 1.0, Resource Discovery Network (November 14, 2005); http://www.rdn.ac.uk/publications/rdn-ltsn/types/.

Barron, T., 2000, A portrait of learning portals, Learning Circuits - ASTD's Online Magazine for e-Learning, May 2000 (February 20, 2006); http://www.learningcircuits.org/2000/may2000/Barron.htm.

Barros, B., Verdejo, M.F., Read, T., and Mizoguchi, R., 2002, Applications of a collaborative learning ontology, in Proceedings of the Mexican International Conference on Artificial Intelligence (MICAI 2002), Lecture Notes in Artificial Intelligence, Vol.2313, Coello, C.A., Albornoz, A.D., Sucar, L.E., and Battistutti, O.C., eds., Springer-Verlag, pp. 301-310.

Berners-Lee, T., Fischetti, M., and Dertouzos, T.M., 1999, *Weaving the Web: The Original Design and Ultimate Destiny of the World Wide Web by its Inventor*, Harper, San Francisco.

Berners-Lee, T., Hendler, J., and Lassila, O., 2001, The Semantic Web, *Scientific American* **284**:34-43.

Blackboard, 2002, Blackboard Learning System Student Manual, Release 6 (February 20, 2006); http://company.blackboard.com/docs/cp/learning_system/release6/student/index.htm.

Bloehdorn, S., Petridis, K., Saathoff, C., Simou, N., Tzouvaras, V., Avrithis, Y., Hanschuh, S., Kompatsiaris, Y., Staab., S., and Strintzis, M, 2005, Semantic annotation of images and videos for multimedia analysis, in: *Proceedings of The Second European Semantic Web Conference*, *ESWC 2005*, A. Gómez-Pérez, and Euzenat, J., eds., Heraklion, Crete, Greece, pp. 592-607.

Boley, H., Tabet, S., and Wagner, G., 2001, Design rationale of RuleML: a markup language for Semantic Web rules, in: *Proc. SWWS'01, The first Semantic Web Working Symposium*, Cruz, I.F., Decker, S., Euzenat, J., McGuinness, D.L., eds., Stanford University, California, pp. 381-401; http://www.semanticweb.org/SWWS/program/full/paper20.pdf.

Bonk, C., and King, K., 1998, *Electronic Collaborators*, Lawrence Erlbaum, Mahwah, NJ.

Bourdeau, J., and Mizoguchi, R., 2002, Collaborative ontological engineering of instructional design knowledge for an ITS authoring environment, in: *Proceedings of The 6th*

International Conference on Intelligent Tutoring Systems, ITS2002, S. Cerri, G. Gouarderes, and F. Paraguacu, eds., Biarritz, France and San Sebastian, Spain, pp. 399-409.

Brase, J., and Nejdl, W., 2004, Ontologies and metadata for eLearning, in: *Handbook on Ontologies,* Staab, S., and Studer, R., eds., Springer-Verlag, Berlin, pp. 555-573.

Brickley, D., and Guha, R.V., 2004, RDF Vocabulary Description Language 1.0: RDF Schema, W3C Working Draft (October 05, 2005); http://www.w3.org/TR/PR-rdf-schema.

Brooks, C., Winter, M., Greer, J., and McCalla, G., 2004, in: *Intelligent Tutoring Systems 2004, Lecture Notes in Computer Science,* Vol.3220, J.C. Lester, R.M. Vicari, and F. Paraguacu, eds., Springer, Berlin, pp. 635-645.

Brooks, C., McCalla, G., and Winter, M., 2005, Flexible learning object metadata, in: *Proceedings of The International Workshop on Applications of Semantic Web Technologies for E-Learning,* SW-EL05@AIED05, L. Aroyo, and D. Dicheva, eds., (November 22, 2005); http://www.win.tue.nl/SW-EL/2005/swel05-aied05/proceedings/.

Brunkhorst, I., and Henze, N., 2005, User awareness in semantic portals, in: *Proceedings of the Workshop on Personalization on the Semantic Web, PerSWeb'05,* Aroyo, L., Dimitrova, V., and Kay, J., eds., Edinburgh, UK (January 04, 2006); http://www.win.tue.nl/persweb/full-proceedings.pdf.

Brusilovsky, P., 2004, KnowledgeTree: a distributed architecture for adaptive e-learning, in: *Proceedings of The 13th World Wide Web Conference (Alternate Track Papers),* New York, USA, pp. 104-113.

Brusilovsky, P., and Miller, P., 2001, Course delivery systems for the virtual university, in: *Access to Knowledge: New Information Technologies and the Emergence of the Virtual University,* T. Tschang, and T. Della Senta, eds., Elsevier Science, Amsterdam, pp. 167-206.

Brusilovsky, P., 1999, Adaptive and intelligent technologies for Web-based education, *Künstliche Intelligenz* **4**:19-25.

Brusilovsky, P., Schwartz, E., and Weber, G., 1996, ELM-ART: an intelligent tutoring system on the World Wide Web, in: *Proceedings of the Third International Conference on Intelligent Tutoring Systems,* Montreal, Canada, pp. 261-269.

Cardinaels, K., Meire, M., and Duval, E., 2005, Automating metadata generation: the simple indexing interface, in: *Proceeding of the 14th International World Wide Web Conference,* Chiba, Japan (January 02, 2006); http://www2005.org/cdrom/docs/p548.pdf.

Carlisle, D., Ion, P., Miner, R., Poppelier, N., 2003, eds., Mathematical Markup Language (MathML) Version 2.0 (Second Edition) (January 04, 2006); http://www.w3.org/TR/2003/REC-MathML2-20031021/.

Chakrabarti, S., Dom, B., Gibson, D., Kleinberg, J., Kumar, S., Raghavan, P., Rajagopalan, S., and Tomkins, A., 1999, Mining the link structure of the World Wide Web, *IEEE Computer* **32**(8):60-67.

Chandrasekaran, B., 1986, Generic tasks in knowledge-based reasoning: high-level building blocks for expert system design, *IEEE Expert* **1**(3):23-30.

Chandrasekaran, B., Josephson, J.R., and Benjamins, R., 1998, Ontology of tasks and methods (February 05, 2006); http://www.cse.ohio-state.edu/~chandra/Ontology-of-Tasks-Methods.PDF.

Chandrasekaran, B., Josephson, J.R., and Benjamins, V.R., 1999, What are ontologies, and why do we need them?, *IEEE Intelligent Systems* **14**(1):20-26. Special Issue on Ontologies.

Chatti, M.A., Klamma, R., Quix, C., and Kensche, D., 2005, LM-DTM: An environment for XML-based, LIP/PAPI-compliant deployment, transformation and matching of learner models, in: *Proceedings of the Fifth IEEE International Conference on Advanced*

Learning Technologies (ICALT'05), P. Goodyear, D. Sampson, D. Jin-Tan Yang, Kinshuk, T., Okamoto, R., Hartley, and N.-S. Chen, eds., Kaohsiung, Taiwan, pp. 567-569.

Chen, W., 2003, Web services in Web-based education systems, in: *Proceedings of the The IASTED International Conference on Computers and Advanced Technology in Education*, CATE 2003, Rhodes, Greece, pp. 345-349.

Chen, W., Hayashi, Y., Jin, L., Ikeda, M., and Mizoguchi, R., 1998, Ontological issues on an intelligent authoring tool, in: Proceedings of The ECAI'98 Workshop on Model-Based Reasoning for Intelligent Education Environments, Brighton, England (November 21, 2005); http://www.ei.sanken.osaka-u.ac.jp/pub/wendy/wendy-icce98.pdf.

Chepegin, V., Aroyo, L., De Bra, P., and Heckman, D., 2004, User modeling for modular adaptive hypermedia, in: *Proceedings of The AH'2004 Workshop on Applications of Semantic Web Technologies for Educational Adaptive Hypermedia*, P. Dolog, M. Wolpers, L. Aroyo, and D. Dicheva, eds., Eindhoven, The Netherlands (January 10, 2006); http://www.win.tue.nl/SW-EL/2004/AH-SWEL-Camera-ready/SWEL04-AH-PDF/%239-Chepegin-Aroyo-DeBra-Heckman.pdf.

Chepegin, V., Aroyo, L., and De Bra, P., 2005, Broker-based discovery service for user models in a multi-application context, in: *Proceedings of the Fifth IEEE International Conference on Advanced Learning Technologies (ICALT'05)*, P. Goodyear, D. Sampson, D. Jin-Tan Yang, Kinshuk, T., Okamoto, R., Hartley, and N.-S. Chen, eds., Kaohsiung, Taiwan, pp. 956-957.

Cimolino, L., and Kay, J., 2002, Verified concept mapping for eliciting conceptual understanding, in: *Proceedings of The ICCE Workshop on Concepts and Ontologies in Web-based Educational Systems*, L. Aroyo and D. Dicheva, eds., Auckland, New Zealand, pp. 11-16.

Collins, A., 1991, Cognitive apprenticeship and instructional technology, in: *Educational Values and Cognitive Instruction*, Idol, L., and Jones, B.F., eds., Lawrence Erlbaum Associates, Hillsdale, N.J.

Constantino-González, M, Suthers, D., and de los Santos, J.G.E., 2002, Coaching Web-based collaborative learning based on problem solution differences and participation, *International Journal of Artificial Intelligence in Education* **13**:37-63.

Cooley, R., Mobasher, B., and Srivastava, J., 1997, Web Mining: information and pattern discovery on the World Wide Web, in: Proceedings of the 9th IEEE International Conference on Tools with Artificial Intelligence (ICTAI'97) (January 07, 2006); http://maya.cs.depaul.edu/~mobasher/papers/webminer-tai97.pdf.

Corcho, O., Fernández-López, M., and Gómez-Pérez, A., 2003, Methodologies, tools and languages for building ontologies. Where is their meeting point?, *Data and Knowledge Engineering* **46**(1):41-64.

Curtis, D.D., and Lawson, M.J., 2001, Exploring collaborative online learning, *Journal of Asynchronous Learning Networks* **5**(1):21-34.

Damjanović, V., Kravcik, M., and Devedžić, V., 2005, An approach to realization of personalized adaptation by using eQ agent, in: *Proceedings of the Workshop on Personalization on the Semantic Web, PerSWeb'05*, Aroyo, L., Dimitrova, V., and Kay, J., eds., Edinburgh, UK (January 04, 2006); http://www.win.tue.nl/persweb/full-proceedings.pdf.

DAML Ontology Library, 2005, DARPA (October 03, 2005); http://www.daml.org/ontologies/

De Bra, P., 2002, Adaptive educational hypermedia on the Web, *Communications of the ACM* **45**(5):60-61.

De Bra, P., Aroyo, L., and Cristea, A., 2004a, Adaptive Web-based educational hypermedia, in: *Web Dynamics, Adaptive to Change in Content, Size, Topology and Use*, M. Levene, and A. Poulovassilis, eds., Springer Verlag, Berlin, pp. 387-410.

De Bra, P., Aroyo, L., and Chepegin, V., 2004b, The next big thing: adaptive Web-based systems, *Journal of Digital Information* **5**(1) (November 18, 2005); http://jodi.ecs.soton.ac.uk/Articles/v05/i01/DeBra/.

Decker, S., Melnik, S., van Harmelen, F., Fensel, D., Klein, M., Broekstra, J., Erdmann, M., & Horrocks, I., 2000, The Semantic Web: The roles of XML and RDF, *IEEE Internet Computing* 4:63-74.

Denaux, R., Aroyo, L., and Dimitrova, V., 2005a, OWL-OLM: interactive ontology-based elicitation of user models, in: *Proceedings of the Workshop on Personalization on the Semantic Web, PerSWeb'05*, Aroyo, L., Dimitrova, V., and Kay, J., eds., Edinburgh, UK (January 04, 2006); http://www.win.tue.nl/persweb/full-proceedings.pdf.

Denaux, R., Dimitrova, V., and Aroyo, L., 2005b, Integrating open user modeling and learning content management for the Semantic Web, in: *User Modeling 2005, Lecture Notes in Artificial Intelligence*, Vol. 3538, L. Ardissono, P. Brna, and A. Mitrović, eds., Springer-Verlag, Berlin, pp. 9-18.

Denny, M., 2002, Ontology building: a survey of editing tools, XML.com (October 05, 2005); http://www.xml.com/pub/a/2002/11/06/ontologies.html.

Devedžić, V., 1999, Ontologies: Borrowing from software patterns, *ACM intelligence* **10**(3):14-24.

Devedžić, V., 2002, Understanding ontological engineering, *Communications of the ACM* **45**(4ve):136-144.

Devedžić, V., 2003a, Next-generation Web-based education, *International Journal of Continuing Engineering Education and Lifelong Learning* 13(3/4):232-247.

Devedžić, V., 2003b, Key issues in next-generation Web-based education, *IEEE Transactions on Systems, Man, and Cybernetics, Part C – Applications and Reviews* 33(3):339-349.

Devedžić, V., 2004a, Education and The Semantic Web, *International Journal of Artificial Intelligence in Education* 14:39-65.

Devedžić, V., 2004b, Web intelligence and artificial intelligence in education, *Educational Technology & Society* 7(4):29-39.

Devedžić, V., 2005a, Intelligent Web-based computer-supported collaborative learning, in: *Knowledge-Based Virtual Education - User-Centred Paradigms*, C. Ghaoui, M. Jain, V. Bannore, and L.C. Jain, eds., Springer-Verlag, Berlin, pp. 81-110.

Devedžić, V., 2005b, Research community knowledge portals, *International Journal of Knowledge and Learning* 1(1/2):96-112.

Devedžić, V., 2006, Computer-supported collaborative learning, in: *Encyclopedia of Human Computer Interaction*, Ghaoui, C., ed., Idea Group Reference, Hershey, UK, pp. 105-111.

Devedžić, V., and Pocajt, V., 2003, What does current Web-based education lack?, *International Journal of Computers and Applications* 25(1):65-71.

Dichev, C., Dicheva, D., and Aroyo, L., 2004, Topic Maps for Web-based education, *Advanced Technology for Learning* 1(1):1-7.

Dicheva, D., and Dichev, C., 2005, Authoring educational Topic Maps: can we make it easier? in: *Proceedings of the Fifth IEEE International Conference on Advanced Learning Technologies (ICALT'05)*, P. Goodyear, D. Sampson, D. Jin-Tan Yang, Kinshuk, T., Okamoto, R., Hartley, and N.-S. Chen, eds., Kaohsiung, Taiwan, pp. 216-219.

Dicheva, D., Sosnovsky, S., Gavrilova, T., and Brusilovsky, P., 2005, Ontological Web portal for educational ontologies, in: *Proceedings of The International Workshop on Applications of Semantic Web Technologies for E-Learning*, SW-EL05@AIED05 (November 22, 2005); http://www.win.tue.nl/SW-EL/2005/swel05-aied05/proceedings/.

Dillenbourg, P., Baker, M.J., Blaye, A., and O'Malley, C., 1996, The evolution of research on collaborative learning, in: *Learning in Humans and Machines: Towards an Interdisciplinary Learning Science*, P. Reimann and H. Spada, eds., Pergamon, Oxford, pp. 189-211.

DMP, 2004, The Digital Media Project: The DMP's WebCT Guide (February 20, 2006); http://english.osu.edu/programs/dmp/WebCTGuide/default.html.

Dolog, P., 2003, RDF Schema for the Learner Project (January 14, 2006); http://www.l3s.de/~dolog/learnerrdfbindings/.

Dolog, P., and Nejdl, W., 2003, Challenges and benefits of the Semantic Web for user modeling, in: Proceedings of AH2003, Workshop on Adaptive Hypermedia and Adaptive Web-Based Systems, Budapest, Hungary, P. De Bra, and H. Davis, eds., pp. 99-112. (January 14, 2006); http://wwwis.win.tue.nl/ah2003/proceedings/numberedproceedings.pdf.

Dolog, P., and Schafer, M., 2005, Learner modeling on the Semantic Web, in: *Proceedings of the Workshop on Personalization on the Semantic Web, PerSWeb'05*, Aroyo, L., Dimitrova, V., and Kay, J., eds., Edinburgh, UK (January 04, 2006); http://www.win.tue.nl/persweb/full-proceedings.pdf.

Domingue, J., Dzbor, M., and Motta, E., 2004, Semantic layering with Magpie, in: *Handbook on Ontologies*, Staab, S., and Studer, R., eds., Springer-Verlag, Berlin, pp. 533-553.

DCMI, 2004, Dublin Core Metadata Element Set, Version 1.1: Reference Description, (December 11, 2005); http://dublincore.org/documents/dces/.

Duval, E., Hodgins, W., Sutton, S., and Weibel, S.L., 2002, Metadata principles and practicalities *D-Lib Magazine* **8**(4) (December 30, 2005); http://www.dlib.org/dlib/april02/weibel/04weibel.html.

Duval, E., and Hodgins, W., 2003, A LOM research agenda, in: *Proceedings of The Twelfth International World Wide Web Conference*, Budapest, HUNGARY (November 14, 2005); http://www2003.org/cdrom/papers/alternate/P659/p659-duval.html.html.

Đurić, D., Devedžić, V., Gašević, D., 2006, Adopting software engineering trends in AI, *IEEE Intelligent Systems* **21** (forthcoming).

e-Learning Guru, 2005, Glossary (September 9, 2005); e-learningguru.com/gloss.htm.

ECDL, 2004, ECDL - Computer Skills For Life, European Computer Driving Licence Foundation Ltd. (November 19, 2005); http://www.ecdl.com/main/index.php.

EducaNext, 2005, The EducaNext Portal for Learning Resources (November 30, 2005); http://www.educanext.com/ubp.

Erickson, J., and Siau, K., 2003, e-ducation, *Communications of The ACM* **46**(9ve):134-140.

Felder, R., and Silverman, L., 1988, Learning and teaching styles in engineering education, *Journal of Engineering Education* **78**(7):674–681.

Fensel, D., and Musen, M.A., 2001, The Semantic Web: A brain for humankind, *IEEE Intelligent Systems* **16**(2):24-25.

Fensel, D., van Harmelen, F., Horrocks, I., McGuinness, D.L., and Patel-Schneider, P.F., 2001, OIL: An ontology infrastructure for the Semantic Web, *IEEE Intelligent Systems* **16**(2):38-45.

Fernández-López, M., Gómez-Pérez, A., Sierra, J.P., and Sierra, A.P., 1999, Building a chemical ontology using Methontology and the Ontology Design Environment, *IEEE Intelligent Systems* **14**(1):37-46. Special issue on ontologies.

Fikes, R., 1998, Multi-use ontologies, Stanford University (October 03, 2005); http://www.ksl.stanford.edu/people/fikes/cs222/1998/Ontologies/tsld001.htm.

Fluit, C., Sabou, M., and Van Harmelen, F., 2005, Ontology-based information visualisation: towards Semantic Web applications, in: *Visualising the Semantic Web* (2nd ed.), V. Geroimenko, and C. Chen, eds., Springer, Berlin, pp. 149-163.

FOLDOC, 1993, The Free On-Line Dictionary Of Computing (February 11, 2006);http://www.foldoc.org/.

Fowler, M., and Scott, K., 1999, *UML Distilled - A Brief Guide to the Standard Object Modeling Language*, 2nd ed., Addison Wesley, Reading, MA.

Friedman-Hill, E., 2003, *Jess in action*, Manning Publications Co., Greenwich, UK.

Fridman-Noy, N., and McGuinness, D.L., 2001, Ontology Development 101: A Guide to Creating Your First Ontology, Technical Report KSL-01-05, Knowledge Systems Laboratory, Stanford University.

Fridman-Noy, N., Sintek, M., Decker, S., Crubézy, M., Fergerson, R.W., and Musen, M.A., 2001, Creating Semantic Web contents with Protégé-2000, *IEEE Intelligent Systems*, 16(2):60-71.

Friesen, N., and McGreal, R., 2002, International e-Learning specifications, *International Review of Research in Open and Distance Learning* 3(2) (November 27, 2005); http://www.irrodl.org/content/v3.2/tech11.html.

Gaines, B. R., 1991, An interactive visual language for term subsumption languages, in: *Proc. IJCAI-91, International Joint Conference on Artificial Intelligence*, Sydney, Australia, pp. 817-823.

Gaines, B.R., and Shaw, M.L.G., 1995, Concept Maps as Hypermedia Components (January 22, 2006); http://ksi.cpsc.ucalgary.ca/articles/ConceptMaps/.

Gamma, E., Helm, R., Johnson, R., and Vlissides, J., 1995, *Design Patterns: Elements of Reusable Object-Oriented Software*, Addison-Wesley, Reading, MA.

Garshol, L.M., 2005, Living with Topic Maps and RDF (January 24, 2006); http://www.ontopia.net/topicmaps/materials/tmrdf.html.

Gašević, D., Jovanović, J., and Devedžić, V., 2004, Enhancing learning object content on the Semantic Web, in: *Proceedings of The Fourth IEEE International Conference on Advanced Learning Technologies (ICALT'04)*, Joensuu, Finland, pp. 714-716.

Gašević, D., Đurić, D., and Devedžić, V., 2006, *Model Driven Architecture and Ontology Development*, Springer, Berlin.

GEM, 2006, The Gateway to Educational Materials (March 14, 2006); http://www.thegateway.org/.

Genesereth, M.R., and Fikes, R.E., 1992, Knowledge Interchange Format, Version 3.0, Reference Manual (September 16, 2005); http://www-ksl.stanford.edu/knowledge-sharing/papers/kif.ps.

GoC, 2004, Metadata Application Profiles for the E-Learning Domain in the Government of Canada: An Introduction, Government of Canada (December 14, 2005); http://www.tbs-sct.gc.ca/im-gi/mwg-gtm/ems-sml/docs/2004/meta-profil/meta-profil_e.rtf.

Gómez-Pérez, A., and Corcho, O., 2002, Ontology languages for the Semantic Web, *IEEE Intelligent Systems* 17(1):54-60.

Gruber, T.R., 1992, Ontolingua: A Mechanism to Support Portable Ontologies, Technical report, Knowledge Systems Laboratory, Stanford University.

Gruber, T.R., 1993, A translation approach to portable ontology specifications, *Knowledge Acquisition* 5:199-220.

Guarino, N., 1995, Formal ontology, conceptual analysis and knowledge representation, *International Journal of Human-Computer Studies* 43(5/6):625-640. Special issue on The Role of Formal Ontology in the Information Technology.

Handschuh, S., and Staab, S., 2002, Authoring and annotation of Web pages in CREAM, in: *Proceedings of the 11th International World Wide Web Conference (WWW2002)*, Honolulu, Hawaii, pp. 462-473.

Handschuh, S., Staab, S., 2003a, *Annotation for the Semantic Web*, IOS Press, Amsterdam.

Handschuh, S., Staab, S., 2003b, CREAM - Creating metadata for the Semantic Web, *Computer Networks* **42**:579-598.

Handschuh, S., Staab, S., and Volz, R., 2003a, On Deep Annotation, in: *Proc. WWW 2003, The Twelfth International World Wide Web Conference*, Budapest, Hungary (October 21, 2005); http://www2003.org/cdrom/papers/refereed/p273/p273_handschuh.html

Handschuh, S., Volz, R., and Staab, S., 2003b, Annotation for the deep Web, *IEEE Intelligent Systems* **18**(5):42-48.

Heckmann, D., and Krueger, A., 2003, A user modeling markup language (UserML) for ubiquitous computing, in: User Modeling 2003, Lecture Notes in Artificial Intelligence, Vol.2702, P. Brusilovsky, A. Corbett, and F. de Rosis, eds., Springer-Verlag, Berlin, pp. 393-397.

Heckmann, D., Schwartz, T., Brandherm, B., Schmitz, M., and von Wilamowitz-Moellendorff, M., 2005, GUMO - the general user model ontology, in: *User Modeling 2005, Lecture Notes in Artificial Intelligence*, Vol. 3538, L. Ardissono, P. Brna, and A. Mitrović, eds., Springer-Verlag, Berlin, pp. 428-432.

Heflin, J., and Hendler, J., 2001, A portrait of The Semantic Web in action, *IEEE Intelligent Systems* **16**(2):54-59.

Hendler, J., 2001, Agents and the Semantic Web, *IEEE Intelligent Systems* **16**(2):30-37.

Hendler, J., and McGuinness, D., 2000, The DARPA agent markup language, *IEEE Intelligent Systems* **15**(6):72–73.

Henze, N., 2005a, Challenges and Trends for Personalization in the Semantic Web (Invited Talk), PerSWeb'05 Workshop on Personalization on the Semantic Web (January 04, 2006); http://www.win.tue.nl/persweb/presentations/Nicola-Henze-invited-talk.pdf.

Henze, N., 2005b, Personal readers: personalized learning object readers for the Semantic Web, in: *Proceedings of The 12th International Conference on Artificial Intelligence in Education*, C.-K. Looi, G. McCalla, B. Bredeweg, and J. Breuker, eds., Amsterdam, July 18-22, 2005, pp. 274-281.

Henze, N., and Herrlich, M., 2004, The Personal Reader: a framework for enabling personalization services on the Semantic Web, in: *Proceedings of the Twelfth GI-Workshop on Adaptation and User Modeling in Interactive Systems (ABIS 04)*, S. Weibelzahl, and N. Henze, eds., Berlin, Germany, pp. 25-32.

Henze, N., and Nejdl, W., 2003, Logically characterizing adaptive educational hypermedia systems, in: *Proceedings of The International Conference on Adaptive Hypermedia, AH 2003* (held in conjunction with The Twelfth International World Wide Web Conference), Budapest, Hungary, pp. 15-28.

Horrocks, I. and van Harmelen, F., 2002, Reference description of the DAML+OIL ontology markup language (September 19, 2005); http://www.daml.org/2001/03/reference.

Horton, W., 2002, Standards for E-Learning - Consumers' Guide (December 08, 2005); http://www.horton.com/content/handout_files/206_standards.pdf.

Huai, H., 2000, *Cognitive style and memory capacity: effects of concept mapping as a learning method*, PhD Thesis, University of Twente, The Netherlands.

ID Glossary, 2005, *Glossary of Instructional Design Terminology*, Hutchinson Community College (November 03, 2005); http://www.hutchcc.edu/distance/glossary.htm.

IEEE API, 2003, IEEE 1484.11.2 Standard for Learning Technology – ECMAScript Application Programming Interface for Content to Runtime Services Communication (December 27, 2005); http://ltsc.ieee.org/wg11/files/IEEE_P1484-11-2_ballot-d2.pdf.

IEEE LOM, 2002, 1484.12.1 IEEE Standard for Learning Object Metadata, IEEE LTSC (November 15, 2005); http://ltsc.ieee.org/wg12.

Ikeda, M., Seta, K., and Mizoguchi, R., 1997, Task ontology makes it easier to use authoring tools, in: *Proceedings of The Fifteenth International Joint Conference on Artificial Intelligence, IJCAI-97*, IJCAI, and M.E. Pollack, eds., Nagoya, Japan, pp. 342-347.

IMS AF, 2003, IMS Abstract Framework: White Paper, Version 1.0 (December 28, 2005); http://www.imsglobal.org/af/afv1p0/imsafwhitepaperv1p0.html.

IMS CP, 2004, IMS Content Packaging Information Model, Version 1.1.4 Final Specification (December 14, 2005); http://www.imsglobal.org/content/packaging/cpv1p1p4/imscp_infov1p1p4.html.

IMS LD, 2003, IMS Learning Design Information Model, Version 1.0 Final Specification (December 15, 2005); http://www.imsglobal.org/learningdesign/ldv1p0/imsld_infov1p0.html.

IMS LIP, 2001, IMS Learner Information Packaging Information Model Specification , Final Specification, Version 1.0 (December 21, 2005); http://www.imsglobal.org/profiles/lipinfo01.html.

IMS QTI, 2005, IMS Question and Test Interoperability Information Model, Version 2.0 Final Specification (December 20, 2005); http://www.imsglobal.org/question/qti_v2p0/imsqti_infov2p0.html.

IMS RDCEO, 2002, IMS Reusable Definition of Competency or Educational Objective - Information Model, Version 1.0 Final Specification (January 14, 2006); http://www.imsglobal.org/competencies/rdceov1p0/imsrdceo_infov1p0.html.

IMS SS, 2003, IMS Simple Sequencing Information and Behavior Model, Version 1.0 Final Specification (December 28, 2005); http://www.imsglobal.org/simplesequencing/ssv1p0/imsss_infov1p0.html.

Inaba, A., Ikeda, M., and Mizoguchi, R., 2003a, What learning patterns are effective for a learner's growth? - an ontological support for designing collaborative learning, in: *Shaping the Future of Learning through Intelligent Technologies* (*Proceedings of the 11th Conference on Artificial Intelligence in Education*, Sydney, Australia), U. Hoppe, F. Verdejo, and J. Kay, eds., pp. 219-226.

Inaba, A., Ohkubo, R., Ikeda, M., and Mizoguchi, R., 2003b, Modeling learner-to-learner interaction process in collaborative learning - an ontological approach to interaction analysis, in: *Supplementary Proceedings of the International Conference on Computer Support for Collaborative Learning* (*CSCL2003*), Bergen, Norway, pp. 4-6.

Inaba, A., and Mizoguchi, R., 2004, Learners' roles and predictable educational benefits in collaborative learning - an ontological approach to support design and analysis of CSCL, in: *Proceedings of the Seventh International Conference on Intelligent Tutoring Systems* (*ITS2004*), Lester, J.C., Vicari, R.M., and Paraguaçu, F., eds., Maceió-Alagoas, Brazil, pp. 285-294.

ISO/IEC, 1999, ISO/IEC 13250 Topic Maps (January 23, 2006); http://www.y12.doe.gov/sgml/sc34/document/0129.pdf.

Jeremić, Z., Lin, T., Kinshuk, and Devedžić, V., 2005, Synergy of performance-based model and cognitive trait model in DP-ITS, in: *User Modeling 2005, Lecture Notes in Artificial Intelligence*, Vol. 3538, L. Ardissono, P. Brna, and A. Mitrović, eds., Springer-Verlag, Berlin, pp. 407-411.

Johnson, W.L., Rickel, J., and Lester, J.C., 2000, Animated pedagogical agents: face-to-face interaction in interactive learning environments, *International Journal of Artificial Intelligence in Education* **11**:47-78.

Jovanović, J., 2005, *Dynamic Generation of Educational Contents on the Semantic Web*, MSc Thesis, University of Belgrade, Serbia and Montenegro.

Jovanović, J., Gašević, D., and Devedžić, V., 2004, A GUI for Jess, *Expert Systems With Applications* **26**(4):625-637.

Jovanović, J., Gašević, D., and Devedžić, V., 2006a, Dynamic assembly of personalized learning content on the Semantic Web, in: *Proceedings of The Third European Semantic Web Conference, ESWC 2006*, Budva, Montenegro (forthcoming).

Jovanović, J., Gašević, D., and Devedžić, V., 2006b, Ontology-based automatic annotation of learning content, *International Journal of Semantic Web and Information Systems* (forthcoming).

JXTA, 2005, Sun Microsystems (December 2, 2005); http://www.jxta.org/.

Kalfoglou, Y., 2001, Exploring ontologies, in: *Handbook of Software Engineering and Knowledge Engineering Vol.1 - Fundamentals*, Chang, S.K., ed., World Scientific Publishing Co., Singapore, p. 863-887.

Kant, K., Iyer , R., and Tewari, V., 2002, A framework for classifying peer-to-peer technologies, *2nd IEEE/ACM International Symposium on Cluster Computing and the Grid (CCGRID'02)*, pp. 368-375.

Kaplan-Leiserson, E., 2000, E-Learning Glossary, Learning Circuits (October 28, 2005); http://www.learningcircuits.org/glossary.html.

Kasai, T., Yamaguchi, H., Nagano, K., and Mizoguchi, R., 2005, Goal transition model and its application for supporting teachers based on ontologies, in: *Proceedings of The 12th International Conference on Artificial Intelligence in Education*, C.-K. Looi, G. McCalla, B. Bredeweg, and J. Breuker, eds., Amsterdam, July 18-22, 2005, pp. 330-337.

Karampiperis, P., and Sampson, D., 2004, Using ontologies for adaptive navigation support in educational hypermedia systems, in: *Proceedings of The AH'2004 Workshop on Applications of Semantic Web Technologies for Educational Adaptive Hypermedia*, P. Dolog, M. Wolpers, L. Aroyo, and D. Dicheva, eds., Eindhoven, The Netherlands (December 03, 2005); http://www.win.tue.nl/SW-EL/2004/AH-SWEL-Camera-ready/SWEL04-AH-PDF/%235-Karampiperis-Sampson-SWEL-AH.pdf.

Kay, J., Kummerfeld, B., and Lauder, P., 2003, Personis: a server for user models, in: *Adaptive Hypermedia 2002, Lecture Notes in Computer Science Vol.2347*, P. De Bra, P. Brusilovsky, and R. Conejo, eds., Springer-Verlag, Berlin, Heidelberg, pp. 203–212.

Kay, J., and Lum, A., 2004, Ontologies for scrutable student modelling in adaptive e-Learning, in: *Proceedings of The AH'2004 Workshop on Applications of Semantic Web Technologies for Educational Adaptive Hypermedia*, P. Dolog, M. Wolpers, L. Aroyo, and D. Dicheva, eds., Eindhoven, The Netherlands (January 10, 2006); http://www.win.tue.nl/SW-EL/2004/AH-SWEL-Camera-ready/SWEL04-AH-PDF/%2310-Kay-Lum-SWEL-AH.pdf

Kay, J., and Lum, A., 2005, Ontology-based user modeling for the Semantic Web, in: *Proceedings of the Workshop on Personalization on the Semantic Web, PerSWeb'05*, Aroyo, L., Dimitrova, V., and Kay, J., eds., Edinburgh, UK (January 04, 2006); http://www.win.tue.nl/persweb/full-proceedings.pdf.

Keegan, D., 1995, *Distance Education Technology for the New Millennium: Compressed Video Teaching*, Institute for Research into Distance Education, Hagen, Germany.

Keenoy, K., Levene, M., and Peterson, D., 2004, Personalisation and trails in self e-Learning networks, SeLeNe Working Package 4 Deliverable 4.2 (December 05, 2005); http://www.dcs.bbk.ac.uk/selene/reports/Del4.2-2.1.pdf.

Keleberda, I., Lesna, N., Makovetskiy, S., and Terziyan, V., 2004, Personalized distance learning based on multiagent ontological system, in: *Proceedings of The Fourth IEEE International Conference on Advanced Learning Technologies (ICALT'04)*, Joensuu, Finland, pp. 777-779.

Kim, E.B., and Schniederjans, M.J., 2004, The role of personality in Web-based distance education courses, *Communications of The ACM* **47**(3):95-98.

Klein, M., 2001, Tutorial: The Semantic Web - XML, RDF, and relatives, *IEEE Intelligent Systems* **16**(2):26-28.

Kokkelink, S., and Schwänzl, R., 2002, Expressing Qualified Dublin Core in RDF/XML, DCMI (January 02, 2006); http://dublincore.org/documents/dcq-rdf-xml/index.shtml.

Koper, E.J.R., 2001, Modeling Units of Study from a Pedagogical Perspective - The Pedagogical Meta-Model Behind EML, Open University of The Netherlands (November 24, 2005);http://eml.ou.nl/introduction/docs/ped-metamodel.pdf.

Koper, R., 2004, Use of the Semantic Web to solve some basic problems in education: increase flexible, distributed lifelong learning, decrease teachers' workload, *Journal of Interactive Media in Education* (*JIME*), 2004(6), Special Issue on the Educational Semantic Web (January 30, 2006); http://www-jime.open.ac.uk/2004/6.

Koper, E.J.R., and Manderveld, J.M., 2004, Educational modelling language: modelling reusable, interoperable, rich and personalised units of learning, *British Journal of Educational Technology* **35**(5):537-552.

Kravcik, M., 2004, Specification of adaptation strategy by FOSP method, in: *Proceedings of the AH 2004 Workshop on Authoring Adaptive and Adaptable Educational Hypermedia*, A. Cristea, and F. Garzotto, eds., Eindhoven, The Netherlands (March 18, 2006); http://wwwis.win.tue.nl/~acristea/AH04/papers/AAAEH-proceedings_1-11newest.pdf.

Kremer, B., 1998, Visual languages for knowledge representation, in: *Proc. KAW'98, Eleventh Workshop on Knowledge Acquisition, Modeling and Management*, Banff, Canada (September 20, 2005); http://ksi.cpsc.ucalgary.ca/KAW/KAW98/kremer/.

Lama, M., Sánchez, E., Amarim, R.R., and Vila, X.A., 2005, Semantic description of the IMS learning design specification, in: *Proceedings of The International Workshop on Applications of Semantic Web Technologies for E-Learning*, SW-EL05@AIED05, L. Aroyo, and D. Dicheva, eds. (January 30, 2006); http://www.win.tue.nl/SW-EL/2005/swel05-aied05/proceedings/6-Lama-final-full.pdf.

Lanzing, J., 1997, The Concept Mapping Homepage (January 22, 2006); http://users.edte.utwente.nl/lanzing/cm_home.htm.

Larman, C., 2001, *Applying UML and Patterns - An Introduction to Object-Oriented Analysis and Design*, 2nd ed., Prentice-Hall, Upper Saddle River, NJ.

Lassila, O., 1998, Web metadata: a matter of semantics, *IEEE Internet Computing* **2**(4):30-37.

Laurillard, D., 2002, *Rethinking University Teaching: A Conversational Framework for the Effective Use of Learning Technologies*, 2nd ed., Routledge Farmer, London.

LearnAlberta, 2005, Alberta Government (November 30, 2005); http://www.learnalberta.ca.

Liu, J., and Greer, J., 2004, Individualized selection of learning object, in: *Proceedings of The Workshop of Applications of Semantic Web Technologies for Web-based ITS* (*SW-EL'04: Semantic Web for E-Learning*), L. Aroyo, and D. Dicheva, eds., Maceió-Alagoas, Brazil (January 06, 2006); http://www.win.tue.nl/SW-EL/2004/ITS-SWEL-Camera-ready/SWEL04-ITS-PDF/%234-Liu-Greer-ITS04.pdf.

LORNET, 2005, Portals and Services for Knowledge Management and Learning on the Semantic Web, LORNET (November 30, 2005); http://www.lornet.org/eng/index.htm.

LTSA, 2001, IEEE P1484.1/D9, Draft Standard for Learning Technology - Learning Technology Systems Architecture (LTSA) (December 26, 2005); http://ltsc.ieee.org/wg1/files/IEEE_1484_01_D09_LTSA.pdf.

LTSC, 2005, IEEE P1484.12.3, Draft 8 - Draft Standard for Learning Technology Extensible Markup Language (XML) Schema Definition Language Binding for Learning Object Metadata (November 28, 2005); http://ieeeltsc.org/wg12LOM/1484.12.3/Public/IEEE_1484_12_03_d8.pdf.

Lytras, M., Tsilira, A., and Themistocleous, M.G., 2003, Towards the semantic e-Learning: an ontological oriented discussion of the new research agenda in e-Learning, in: *Proceedings of the Ninth Americas Conference on Information Systems (AMCIS 2003)*, pp. 2985-2997.

Ma, W., 2005, Learning object recommender systems, in: *Proceedings of the IASTED International Conference on Education and Technology*, Calgary, Canada, pp. 113-118.

MacGregor, R., 1991, Inside the LOOM clasifier, *SIGART bulletin* 2(3):70–76.

Maedche, A., and Staab, S., 2001, Ontology learning for the Semantic Web, *IEEE Intelligent Systems* 16(2):72-79.

Manola, F., and Miller, E., eds., 2004, RDF Primer, W3C Recommendation (October 04, 2005); http://www.w3.org/TR/REC-rdf-syntax/.

Martin, D., Burstein, M., Hobbs, J., Lassila, O., McDermott, D., McIlraith, S., Narayanan, S., Paolucci, M., Parsia, B., Payne, T., Sirin, E., Srinivasan, N., and Sycara, K., 2004, OWL-S: Semantic Markup for Web Services (October 24, 2005); http://www.daml.org/services/owl-s/1.1/overview/.

Martinez, M., 2000, Designing learning objects to mass customize and personalize learning, in: *The Instructional Use of Learning Objects*, D. A. Wiley, ed. (January 05, 2006); http://reusability.org/read/chapters /martinez.doc.

McCalla, G., 2004, The ecological approach to the design of e-Learning environments: purpose-based capture and use of information about learners, *Journal of Interactive Media in Education, Special Issue on the Educational Semantic Web*, 2004(7):171-193.

McClelland, M., 2003, Metadata standards for educational resources, *IEEE Computer* 36(11):107-109.

McGreal, R., 2004, Learning objects: a practical definition, *International Journal of Instructional Technology and Distance Learning* 1(9) (November 14, 2005); http://www.itdl.org/Journal/Sep_04/article02.htm.

McGuinness, D.L., 2002, Ontologies come of age, in: *Spinning the Semantic Web: Bringing the World Wide Web to Its Full Potential*, Fensel, D., Hendler, J., Lieberman, H., and Wahlster, W., eds. MIT Press, Boston, p. 1-18.

McIlraith, S.A., Son, T.C., and Zeng, H., 2001, Semantic Web services, *IEEE Intelligent Systems* 16(2):46-53.

Melis, E., Andrès, E., Büdenbender, J., Frischauf, A., Goguadze, G., Libbrecht, P., Pollet, M., and Ullrich, C., 2001, ActiveMath: a generic and adaptive Web-based learning environment, *International Journal of Artificial Intelligence in Education* 12:385-407.

Merrill, M.D., 1999, Instructional transaction theory (ITT): instructional design based on knowledge objects, in: *Instructional design theories and models: a new paradigm of instructional theory*, C.M. Reigeluth, ed., Lawrence Erlbaum Associates, Hillsdale, NJ, pp. 397-424.

MERLOT, 2005, Multimedia Educational Resource for Learning and Online Teaching (November 18, 2005); http://www.merlot.org/.

Middleton, S.E., De Roure, D., and Shadbolt, N.R., 2004, Ontology-based recommender systems, in: in: *Handbook on Ontologies*, Staab, S., and Studer, R., eds., Springer-Verlag, Berlin, pp. 477-498.

Miles, A., and Brickley, D., 2005, SKOS Core Guide, W3C Working Draft (December 29, 2005); http://www.w3.org/TR/2005/WD-swbp-skos-core-guide-20051102.

Mitrović, A., and Devedžić, V., 2004, A model of multitutor ontology-based learning environments, *International Journal of Continuing Engineering Education and Lifelong Learning* 14(3):229-245.

Mitrović, A., and Hausler, K., 2000, Porting SQL-Tutor to the Web, in: *Proceedings of the International Workshop on Adaptive and Intelligent Web-based Educational Systems*, Montreal, Canada, pp. 50-60.

Mizoguchi, R., 1998, A step towards ontological engineering, in: Proceedings of The 12th National Conference on AI of JSAI, pp.24-31.

Mizoguchi, R., 2001, Ontological engineering: foundation of the next generation knowledge processing, in: *Web Intelligence: Research and Development. Lecture Notes in Artificial Intelligence (LNAI2198)*, N. Zhong et al., eds., Springer-Verlag, Berlin, pp. 44-57.

Mizoguchi, R., 2003, Tutorial on ontological engineering - Part 1: Introduction to ontological engineering, *New Generation Computing* 21(4):365-384.

Mizoguchi, R., 2004a, Tutorial on ontological engineering – Part 2: Ontology development, tools and languages, *New Generation Computing* 22(1):61-96.

Mizoguchi, R., 2004b, Tutorial on ontological engineering – Part 3: Advanced course of ontological engineering, *New Generation Computing* 22(2):193-220.

Mizoguchi, R., and Ikeda, M., 1996, Towards Ontology Engineering, Technical Report AI-TR-96-1, I.S.I.R., Osaka University, Japan.

Mizoguchi, R., Sinitsa, K., and Ikeda, M., 1996, Task ontology design for intelligent educational/training systems, in: Proceedings of the Workshop on Architectures and Methods for Designing Cost-Effective and Reusable ITSs, Montreal, Canada, pp. 1-20.

Mizoguchi, R., and Bourdeau, J., 2000, Using ontological engineering to overcome common AI-ED problems, *International Journal of Artificial Intelligence in Education* 11:1-12.

Mizoguchi, R., and Kitamura, Y., 2001, Knowledge systematization through ontology engineering - a key technology for successful intelligent systems, Invited paper at PAIS 2001, Seoul, Korea (September 21, 2005); http://www.pais2001.org/english.htm.

Mohan, P., and Brooks, C., 2003, Learning objects on the Semantic Web, in: *Proceedings of International Conference on Advanced Learning Technologies*, V. Devedžić, J.M. Spector, D.G. Sampson, and Kinshuk, eds., Athens, Greece, pp. 195-199.

Mohan, P., and Greer, J., 2003, Reusable learning objects: current status and future directions, in: *Proceedings of ED-MEDIA 2003 World Conference on Educational Multimedia, Hypermedia and Telecommunication*, D. Lassner, and C. McNaught, eds., Honolulu, Hawaii.

Moore, M.G., and Kearsley, G., 1996, *Distance Education: A Systems View*, Wadsworth Publishing Company, Belmont, CA.

Mori, J., Matsuo, Y., and Ishizuka, M., 2005, Finding user semantics on the Web using Word co-occurrence information, in: *Proceedings of the Workshop on Personalization on the Semantic Web, PerSWeb'05*, Aroyo, L., Dimitrova, V., and Kay, J., eds., Edinburgh, UK (January 04, 2006); http://www.win.tue.nl/persweb/full-proceedings.pdf.

Motta, E., Domingue, J., Cabral, L., and Gaspari, M., 2003, IRS-II: a framework and infrastructure for Semantic Web services, in: *Procedings of The Second International Semantic Web Conference*, Florida (November 16, 2005); http://www.cs.unibo.it/~gaspari/www/iswc03.pdf.

Muehlenbrock, M., and Hoppe, U., 2001, A collaboration monitor for shared workspaces, in: *Proceedings of the International Conference on Artificial Intelligence in Education AIED-2001*, J. D. Moore, C. L. Redfield, and W. L. Johnson, eds., San Antonio, TX, pp. 154-165.

Myers, B.A., 1990, Taxonomies of visual programming and program visualization, *Journal of Visual Languages and Computing* 1(1): 97-123.

Nardi, B.A., ed., 1996, *Context and Consciousness. Activity Theory and Human-Computer Interaction*, MIT Press, Cambridge, MA.

Nejdl, W., Wolf, B., Qu, C., Decker, S., Sintek, M., Naeve, A., Nilsson, M., Palmer, M., and Risch, T., 2002, Edutella: a P2P networking infrastructure based on RDF, in: *Proceedings of the 11th International World Wide Web Conference (WWW2002)*, Hawaii, USA, May 2002.

Neven, F., and Duval, E., 2002, Reusable learning objects: a survey of LOM-based repositories, in: *Proceedings of the Tenth ACM International Conference on Multimedia table of contents*, Juan-les-Pins, France, pp. 291-294.

Nilsson, M., ed., 2002, IEEE Learning Object Metadata RDF binding (November 21, 2005); http://kmr.nada.kth.se/el/ims/md-lomrdf.html.

Nilsson, M., Palmer, M., and Naeve, A., 2002, Semantic Web metadata for e-Learning - some architectural guidelines, in: *Proceedings of The Eleventh International World Wide Web Conference*, Honolulu, Hawaii (November 27, 2005); http://www2002.org/CDROM/alternate/744/.

Novak, J.D., 1991, Clarify with concept maps: a tool for students and teachers alike, *The Science Teacher* **58**(7):45-49.

Novak, J.D., 2002, The Theory Underlying Concept Maps and How To Construct Them (January 22, 2006); http://cmap.coginst.uwf.edu/info/.

O4E, 2005, Ontologies for Education (November 22, 2005); http://iiscs.wssu.edu/o4e/.

Obringer, L.A., 2005, How E-learning Works (October 28, 2005); http://computer.howstuffworks.com/elearning4.htm.

Ohlsson, S., 1994, Constraint-based student modeling, in: *Student Modelling: the Key to Individualized Knowledge-based Instruction*, J.E. Greer, G. McCalla, eds., Springer-Verlag Berlin, pp. 167-189.

OKI, 2002, What is the Open Knowledge Initiative? (December 28, 2005); http://web.mit.edu/oki/learn/whtpapers/OKI_white_paper_120902.pdf.

OMG, 2002a, Meta Object Facility (MOF) Specification v1.4, OMG Document formal/02-04-03 (December 10, 2005); http://www.omg.org/cgi-bin/apps/doc?formal/02-04-03.pdf.

OMG, 2002b, XMI Specification, v1.2, OMG Document formal/02-01-01 (December 10, 2005); http://www.omg.org/cgi-bin/doc?formal/2002-01-01.

OMG, 2003, OMG Unified Modeling Language Specification (December 10, 2005); http://www.omg.org/cgi-bin/apps/doc?formal/03-03-01.zip.

OWL Ontology Library, 2005, Stanford University (October 03, 2005); http://protege.stanford.edu/plugins/owl/owl-library/

OWL-S, 2005, DAML (October 22, 2005); http://www.daml.org/services/owl-s/.

Ott, D., and Mayer-Patel, K., 2004, Coordinated multi-streaming for 3D Tele-immersion, in: *Proceedings of the eleventh ACM international conference on Multimedia*, New York, pp. 185-194.

Paquette, G., 2003, *Instructional Engineering for Network-based Learning*, Wiley/Pfeiffer, San Francisco.

Paquette, G., and Rosca, I., 2004, An ontology-based referencing of actors, operations and resources in eLearning systems, in: *Proceedings of The International Workshop on Applications of Semantic Web Technologies for E-Learning, SW-EL@AH04*, P. Dolog, M. Wolpers, L. Aroyo, and D. Dicheva, eds., Eindhoven, The Netherlands (January 31, 2006); http://www.win.tue.nl/SW-EL/2004/AH-SWEL-Camera-ready/SWEL04-AH-PDF/***

Paquette, G., Marino, O., De la Teja, I., Lundgren-Cayrol, K., Léonard, M., and Contamines, J., 2005, Implementation and deployment of the IMS learning design specification, *Canadian Journal of Learning and Technology* **31**(2) (January 30, 2006); http://www.cjlt.ca/content/vol31.2/paquette.html.

PAPI Learner, 2001, IEEE P1484.2.5/D8, 2001-11-25 Draft Standard for Learning Technology - Public and Private Information (PAPI) for Learners (PAPI Learner) (December 25, 2005); http://www.edutool.com/papi/drafts/08/.

Paulsen, M.F., 2003, *Online Education and Learning Management Systems - Global Elearning in a Scandinavian Perspective*, NKI Forlaget, Oslo.

Payne, T., and Lassila, O., 2004, Semantic Web services, *IEEE Intelligent Systems* 19(4):14-15.

Pednault, E.P.D., 2000, Representation is everything, *Communications of The ACM* 43(8):80-83.

Peñarrubia, A., Fernández-Caballero, A., and González, P., 2004, Ontology-based interface adaptivity in Web-based learning systems, in: *Proceedings of The Fourth IEEE International Conference on Advanced Learning Technologies (ICALT'04)*, Joensuu, Finland, pp. 435-439.

Pinkwart, N., 2003, A plug-in architecture for graph-based collaborative modeling systems, in: *Shaping the Future of Learning through Intelligent Technologies (Proceedings of the 11th Conference on Artificial Intelligence in Education*, Sydney, Australia), U. Hoppe, F. Verdejo, and J. Kay, eds., pp. 535-536.

Popov, B., Kiryakov, A., Kirilov, A., Manov, D., Ognyanoff, D., and Goranov, M., 2003, KIM - Semantic annotation platform, in: *Proceedings of the 2nd International Semantic Web Conference, ISWC2003*, D. Fensel, K. Sycara, and J. Mylopoulos, eds., Florida, USA. pp. 834-849.

Power, G., Davis, H.C., Cristea, A.I., Stewart, C., and Ashman, H., 2005, Goal oriented personalisation with SCORM, in: *Proceedings of the Fifth IEEE International Conference on Advanced Learning Technologies (ICALT'05)*, P. Goodyear, D. Sampson, D. Jin-Tan Yang, Kinshuk, T., Okamoto, R., Hartley, and N.-S. Chen, eds., Kaohsiung, Taiwan, pp. 467-471.

Preece, A., and Decker, S., 2002, Intelligent Web services, *IEEE Intelligent Systems* 17(1):15-17.

Protégé, 2005, Stanford University (September 28, 2005);http://protege.stanford.edu/.

Protege Ontologies Library, 2005, Stanford University (October 03, 2005); http://protege.cim3.net/cgi-bin/wiki.pl?ProtegeOntologiesLibrary.

Psyché V., Bourdeau, J., Nkambou, R., and Mizoguchi, R., 2005, Making learning design Standards work with an ontology of educational theories, in: *Proceedings of The 12th International Conference on Artificial Intelligence in Education*, C.-K. Looi, G. McCalla, B. Bredeweg, and J. Breuker, eds., Amsterdam, July 18-22, 2005, pp. 25-32.

Rawlings, A., van Rosmalen, P., Koper, R., Rodríguez-Artacho, M., and Lefrere, P., 2002, Survey of Educational Modelling Languages (EMLs), Version 1 (November 14, 2005); http://www.cenorm.be/cenorm/businessdomains/businessdomains/isss/activity/emlsurveyv 1.pdf.

Razmerita, L., Angehrn, A., and Maedche, A., 2003, Ontology-based user modeling for knowledge management systems. in: *User Modeling 2003, Lecture Notes in Artificial Intelligence 2702*, P. Brusilovsky, et al., eds., pp. 213-217.

Rebai, I., and de la Passardiere, B., 2002, Dynamic generation of an interface for the capture of educational metadata, in: *Proceedings of The Sixth International Conference on Intelligent Tutoring Systems, ITS 2002*, Biarritz, France, and San Sebastian, Spain, pp. 249-258.

Reigeluth, C. M., 1999, The elaboration theory: guidance for scope and sequence decisions, in: *Instructional design theories and models: a new paradigm of instructional theory*, C.M. Reigeluth, ed., Lawrence Erlbaum Associates, Hillsdale, NJ, pp. 5-29.

Retalis, S., and Avgeriou, P., 2002, Modeling Web-based instructional systems, *Journal of Information Technology Education* 1(1):25-41.

Ritter, S., 1997, PAT Online: a model-tracing tutor on the World-Wide Web, in: *Proceedings of the Workshop "Intelligent Educational Systems on the World Wide Web"*, Kobe, Japan, pp. 11-17.

Roschelle, J., and Teasley, S., 1995, The construction of shared knowledge in collaborative problem solving, in: *Computer-Supported Collaborative Learning*, C. O'Malley, ed., Springer-Verlag, Berlin, pp. 69-97.

Rodriguez, W., 2000, Web classroom of the future: integrating course management software in a Java-based environment, *Interactive Multimedia Electronic Journal of Computer-Enhanced Learning* 2(1) (October 31, 2005); http://imej.wfu.edu/articles/2000/1/07/index.asp.

Ryder, M., 2005, *Theoretical Sources*, University of Colorado at Denver, School of Education (November 03, 2005); http://carbon.cudenver.edu/~mryder/itc_data/theory.html.

Sabou, M., 2005a, Visual support for ontology learning: an experience report, in: *Proceedings of the Ninth International Conference on Information Visualisation (IV'05)*, London, UK, pp. 494-499.

Sabou, M., 2005b, Learning Web service ontologies: an automatic extraction method and its evaluation, in: *Ontology Learning and Population*, P.Buitelaar, P. Cimiano, and B. Magnini, eds., IOS Press, Amsterdam, pp. 1-15.

Sampson, D., Karagiannidis, C., and Kinshuk, 2002a, Personalised learning: educational, technological and standarisation perspective, *Interactive Educational Multimedia* 4(Special Issue on Adaptive Educational Multimedia):24-39.

Sampson, D., Karagiannidis, C., Schenone, A., and Cardinali, F., 2002b, Knowledge-on-Demand in e-Learning and e-Working Settings, Educational Technology & Society 5(2) (January 04, 2006); http://ifets.ieee.org/periodical/vol_2_2002/sampson.html.

Santos, O.C., Rodríguez, A., Gaudioso, E., and Boticario, J.G., 2003, Helping the tutor to manage a collaborative task in a Web-based learning environment, in: *Towards Intelligent Learning Management Systems* (AIED 2003 workshop), Calvo, R.A., and Grandbastien, M., eds., pp. 93-101. (March 09, 2006); http://www.weg.ee.usyd.edu.au/ilms/prc_dwnl/ilms_proceed_v2.pdf..

Schewe, K.-D., Thalheim, B., and Tretiakov, A., 2005, Personalised Web-based learning systems, in: *Proceedings of the Fifth IEEE International Conference on Advanced Learning Technologies (ICALT'05)*, P. Goodyear, D. Sampson, D. Jin-Tan Yang, Kinshuk, T., Okamoto, R., Hartley, and N.-S. Chen, eds., Kaohsiung, Taiwan, pp. 655-658.

Schreiber, G., Wielinga, B., de Hoog, R., Akkermans, H., Van de Velde, W., 1994, CommonKADS: a comprehensive methodology for KBS development, *IEEE Expert* 9(6):28-37.

Scott Cost, R., Finin, T., Joshi, A., Peng, Y., Nicholas, C., Soboroff, I., Chen, H., Kagal, L., Perich, F., Zou, Y., and Tolia, S., 2002, ITtalks: a case study in the Semantic Web and DAML+OIL, *IEEE Intelligent Systems* 17(1):40-47.

Sicilia, M.A., 2006, Ontology-based competency management: infrastructures for the knowledge-intensive learning organization, in: *Intelligent Learning Infrastructure for Knowledge Intensive Organizations*, M.D. Lytras, and A. Naeve, eds., Information Science Publishing, London, pp. 302-324.

Sicilia, M.A., García, E., Díaz, P., and Aedo, I., 2002, Learning links: reusable assets with support for vagueness and ontology-based typing, in: *Proceedings of ICCE 2002 Workshop on Concepts and Ontologies in Web-based Educational Systems*, L. Aroyo, and D. Dicheva, eds., Auckland, New Zealand, pp. 37-42.

Sicilia, M.A., and Lytras, M.D., 2005, The semantic learning organization, *The Learning Organization* 12(5):402-410.

SIF, 2004, Schools Interoperability Framework Implementation Specification, Version 1.5r1 (December 28, 2005); http://www.sifinfo.org/upload/docs/SIF%20Implementation%20Specification%201.5r1.zip.

Sirin, E., Parsia, B., and Hendler, J., 2004, Filtering and selecting Semantic Web services with interactive composition techniques, *IEEE Intelligent Systems* 19(4):42-49.

SMETE, 2005, SMETE Digital Library, SMETE Open Federation for teachers and students (November 30, 2005); http://www.smete.org/.

Smith, M.K., Welty, C., McGuinness, D.L., 2004, *OWL Web Ontology Language Guide*, W3C (October 01, 2005); http://www.w3.org/TR/owl-guide/.

Soller, A.L., 2001, Supporting social interaction in an intelligent collaborative learning system, *International Journal of Artificial Intelligence in Education* 12:54-77.

Sowa, J.F., 2000, *Knowledge Representation: Logical, Philosophical, and Computational Foundations*, Brooks Cole Publishing Co., Pacific Grove, CA.

Staab, S., Angele, J., Decker, S., Erdmann, M., Hotho, A., Maedche, A., Schnurr, H.-P., Studer, R., and Sure, Y., 2000, Semantic community Web portals, *International Journal of Computer and Telecommunications Networking* 33(1-6):473-491.

Staab, S., and Studer, R., eds., 2004, *Handbook on Ontologies*, Springer-Verlag, Berlin.

Stojanović, Lj., Staab, S., and Studer, R., 2001, eLearning based on the Semantic Web, in: Proceedings of the WebNet 2001 - World Conference on the WWW and the Internet, Orlando, Florida, USA (December 08, 2005); http://www.aifb.uni-karlsruhe.de/~sst/Research/Publications/WebNet2001eLearningintheSemanticWeb.pdf.

Stutt, A., and Motta, E., 2004, Semantic learning webs, *Journal of Interactive Media in Education (JIME)*, 2004(10):253-285.

Sunagawa, E., Kozaki, K., Kitamura, Y., and Mizoguchi, R., 2004, Organizing Role-concepts in Ontology Development Environment: Hozo, Technical report AI-TR-04-1, Institute of Scientific and Industrial Research, Osaka University, Japan.

Supnithi, T., Inaba, A., Ikeda, M., Toyoda, J., and Mizoguchi, R., 1999, Learning goal ontology supported by learning theories for opportunistic group formation, in: *Proceedings of the International Conference on Artificial Intelligence in Education, AIED-1999*, S.P. Lajoie, and M. Vivet, eds., Le Mans, France, pp. 263-272.

Suraweera, P., and Mitrović, A., 2002, KERMIT: a constraint-based tutor for database modeling, in: *Proceedings of The 6th International Conference on Intelligent Tutoring Systems*, S. Cerri, G. Gouarderes, and F. Paraguacu, eds., Biarritz, France, pp. 377-387.

Swartout, W., and Tate, A., 1999, Ontologies (Guest editors' introduction), *IEEE Intelligent Systems* 14(1):18-19. Special Issue on Ontologies.

SWEBOK, 2006, The Guide to the Software Engineering Body of Knowledge (January 26, 2006); http://www.swebok.org.

Šimić, G., Devedžić, V., 2003, Building an intelligent system using modern Internet technologies, *Expert Systems With Applications* 25(3):231-246.

Šimić, G., Gašević, D., Jeremić, Z., and Devedžić, V., 2005, Intelligent virtual teaching, in: *Knowledge-Based Virtual Education - User-Centred Paradigms*, C. Ghaoui, M. Jain, V. Bannore, and L.C. Jain, eds., Springer-Verlag, Berlin, pp. 171-202.

Šimić, G., Gašević, D., and Devedžić, V., 2006, Classroom for the Semantic Web, in: *Intelligent Learning Infrastructure for Knowledge Intensive Organizations*, M.D. Lytras, and A. Naeve, eds., Information Science Publishing, London, pp. 251-283.

Tallis, M., Goldman, N.M., and Balzer, R.M., 2002, The Briefing Associate: easing authors into the Semantic Web, *IEEE Intelligent Systems* 17(1):26-32.

Tang, T.Y., and McCalla, G., 2005, Paper annotation with learner models, in: *Artificial Intelligence in Education 2005*, C.-K. Looi et al., eds., IOS Press, Amsterdam, pp. 654-661.

Tchienehom, P.L., 2005, Profiles semantics for personalized information access, in: *Proceedings of the Workshop on Personalization on the Semantic Web, PerSWeb'05*,

Aroyo, L., Dimitrova, V., and Kay, J., eds., Edinburgh, UK (January 04, 2006); http://www.win.tue.nl/persweb/full-proceedings.pdf.

TIP, 2004, Explorations in Learning & Instruction: The Theory Into Practice Database (March 09, 2006). http://tip.psychology.org/theories.html.

TM4J, 2005, Topic Maps for Java Project (January 24, 2006); http://sourceforge.net/projects/tm4j.

TM4L, 2005, Topic Maps for e-Learning Project (January 24, 2006); http://compsci.wssu.edu/iis/NSDL/index.html.

TopicMaps.Org, 2001, XML Topic Maps (XTM) 1.0 Specification (January 23, 2006); http://www.topicmaps.org/xtm/1.0/.

Trigg, R., 1983, A Network-Based Approach to Text Handling for the Online Scientific Community (January 27, 2006); http://www.workpractice.com/trigg/thesis-chap4.html.

Valentine, D., 2005, Distance Learning: Promises, Problems, and Possibilities (October 30, 2005); http://www.westga.edu/~distance/ojdla/fall53/valentine53.html.

Van Assche, F., and Massart, D., 2004, Federation and brokerage of learning objects and their metadata, in: *Proceedings of The Fourth IEEE International Conference on Advanced Learning Technologies (ICALT'04)*, Joensuu, Finland, pp. 316-320.

Van der Sluijs, K., and Houben, G.-J., 2005, Towards a generic user model component, in: *Proceedings of the Workshop on Personalization on the Semantic Web, PerSWeb'05*, Aroyo, L., Dimitrova, V., and Kay, J., eds., Edinburgh, UK (January 04, 2006); http://www.win.tue.nl/persweb/full-proceedings.pdf.

Van der Vet, P.E., and Mars, N.J.I., 1998, Bottom-up construction of ontologies, *IEEE Transactions on Knowledge and Date Engineering* **10**(4):513-526.

Verbert, K., Klerkx, J., Meire, M., Najjar, J., and Duval, E., 2004, Towards a global component architecture for learning objects: an ontology-based approach, in: *Proceedings of The OTM 2004 Workshop on Ontologies, Semantics and E-learning*, Agia Napa, Cyprus (January 16, 2006); http://www.starlab.vub.ac.be/events/OTM04WOSE/.

Verbert, K., Jovanović, J., Gašević, D., Duval, E., and Meire, M., 2005, Towards a global component architecture for learning objects: a slide presentation framework, in: *Proceedings of the 17th World Conference on Educational Multimedia, Hypermedia and Telecommunications*, Montreal, Canada, pp. 1429-1436.

Vinoski, S., 2002, Web services interaction models, part 1: current practice, *IEEE Internet Computing* **6**(3):90-92.

Vouk, M.A., Bitzer, D.L., and Klevans, R.L., 1999, Workflow and end-user quality of service issues in Web-based education, *IEEE Transactions on Knowledge and Data Engineering* **11**(4):673-687.

Vygotsky, L., 1978, *Mind in Society: The Development of Higher Psychological Processes.* Harvard University Press, Cambridge, MA.

W3C SPARQL, 2005, *SPARQL Query Language for RDF*, W3C (October 11, 2005); http://www.w3.org/TR/rdf-sparql-query/.

W3C SW Activity, *Semantic Web Activity Statement*, W3C (October 11, 2005); http://www.w3.org/2001/sw/Activity.

Wenger, E., 1987, *Artificial Intelligence and Tutoring Systems: Computational Approaches to the Communication of Knowledge*, Morgan/Kaufmann Publishing Co., Los Altos, CA.

Wiley, D.A., 2000, Connecting learning objects to instructional design theory: a definition, a metaphor, and a taxonomy, in: *The Instructional Use of Learning Objects*, D. A. Wiley, ed. (November 27, 2005); http://reusability.org/read/chapters/wiley.doc.

Williams, B.C., 2005, Moodle for Teachers, Trainers, and Administrators, v.1.4.3 (February 19,   2006);

http://moodle.blackpool.ac.uk/file.php/1/Moodle_resources/Moodle_1.4.3_For_Teachers_ and_Trainers.pdf.

Winter, M., Brooks, C., and Greer, J., 2005, Towards best practices for Semantic Web student modelling, in: *Artificial Intelligence in Education 2005*, C.-K. Looi et al., eds., IOS Press, Amsterdam, pp. 694-701.

WordNet, 2005, Princeton University (October 05, 2005); http://wordnet.princeton.edu/w3wn.html.

Wu, H., Houben, G.J., and De Bra, P., 1998, AHAM: a reference model to support adaptive hypermedia authoring, in: *Proceedings of the "Zesde Interdisciplinaire Conferentie Informatiewetenschap"*, Antwerp, Belgium, pp. 77-88.

Wuwongse, V., Anutariya, C., Akama, K., and Nantajeewarawat, E., 2002, XML declarative description: a language for the Semantic Web, *IEEE Intelligent Systems* 17(1):54-65.

XML, 2004, *Extensible Markup Language (XML) 1.0* (Third Edition), W3C (October 12, 2005); http://www.w3.org/TR/2004/REC-xml-20040204/.

XML Schema, 2005, W3C (October 12, 2005); http://www.w3.org/XML/Schema.

Yacef, K., 2003, Some thoughts on the synergetic effects of combining ITS and LMS technologies for the service of education, in: *Towards Intelligent Learning Management Systems* (AIED 2003 workshop), Calvo, R.A., and Grandbastien, M., eds., pp. 93-101. (February 22, 2006); http://www.weg.ee.usyd.edu.au/ilms/prc_dwnl/ilms_proceed_v2.pdf.

Zarraonandía, T., Dodero, J.M., Díaz, P., and Sarasa, A., 2004, Domain ontologies integration into the learning objects annotation process, in: *Proceedings of The International Workshop on Applications of Semantic Web Technologies for E-Learning, SW-EL@ITS04*, L. Aroyo, and D. Dicheva, eds., L. Aroyo, and D. Dicheva, eds., Maceió-Alagoas, Brazil (January 26, 2006); http://www.win.tue.nl/SW-EL/2004/ITS-SWEL-Camera-ready/SWEL04-ITS-PDF/%235-Zarraonandia-Dodero-Diaz-Sarasa-ITS04.pdf.

Zhou, B., Hui, S.C., and Fong, A.C.M., 2005, Web usage mining for Semantic Web personalization, in: *Proceedings of the Workshop on Personalization on the Semantic Web, PerSWeb'05*, Aroyo, L., Dimitrova, V., and Kay, J., eds., Edinburgh, UK (January 04, 2006); http://www.win.tue.nl/persweb/full-proceedings.pdf.

Index